1989

THEORIES OF ADOLESCENCE

THEORIES OF ADOLESCENCE

FIFTH EDITION

Rolf E. Muuss
Goucher College

RANDOM HOUSE, NEW YORK

Fifth Edition

24689753

Copyright © 1962, 1968, 1975, 1982, 1988 by Random House, Inc.

Library of Congress Cataloging-in-Publication Data

Muuss, Rolf Eduard Helmut, 1924–
  Theories of adolescence.

  Bibliography: p.
  Includes index.
  1. Adolescent psychology. I. Title.
BF724.M8 1988   155.5   87-16546
ISBN 0-394-37517-3

Cover design: Sandra Josephson

Manufactured in the United States of America

Grateful acknowledgment is made for permission to quote from *The Growth of Logical Thinking from Childhood to Adolescence: An Essay on the Construction of Formal Operational Structures,* by Bärbel Inhelder and Jean Piaget. Translated from the French by Anne Parsons and Stanley Milgram. Copyright © 1958 by Basic Books, Inc. Reprinted by permission of the publisher.

ACKNOWLEDGMENTS

THOUGH the first edition of *Theories of Adolescence* was published by Random House a quarter of a century ago, the need for the continuous revisions of the book demonstrates both the importance of theories in understanding psychological phenomena and the ever changing nature of the field. Not only are new theories continuously emerging, but the nature of those theories of development has changed as well. Because few new macro-theories such as Freud's, Erikson's, and Piaget's have recently been proposed, one may be inclined to think that the era of global theories is part of history. However, a closer look reveals that numerous micro-theories have emerged, theories that focus on a more narrowly defined specific dimension of adolescent development, theories often intensively researched. The current edition of *Theories of Adolescence* reflects these developments.

A book of this nature is never the accomplishment of just one person; its creation is nurtured, challenged, and encouraged by many people. The author is especially grateful for valuable suggestions and critical comments on earlier drafts of one or several of the new and revised chapters of the fifth edition from Frona Brown, Joan Burton, Barbara Gould, John Rose, Clarence Schulz, M.D., Eli Velder, and Alma Nugent. A special thanks goes to my Random House editor Mary Falcon and her staff who have inspired and effectively guided not only the fourth, but now also the fifth edition from its inception through its various stages of production.

I always feel deeply indebted to the students in my courses "Adolescent Development" and "Adolescents and the Secondary Schools," who have used earlier editions of my book, questioned its content, challenged my conclusions, and stimulated my thinking.

A special feeling of gratitude goes to Ms. Elizabeth C. Todd, an alumna of Goucher College, through whose generosity the Elizabeth C. Todd Distinguished Professorship was established. As the holder of the Elizabeth C. Todd Distinguished Professorship for the customary five year cycle, I have benefited immensely from its financial support. These benefits are still being felt, even though the endowed chair has been passed on. I am deeply indebted to Goucher College for supporting this revision by granting me a sabbatical leave without which I could not have completed the work as swiftly.

ROLF E. MUUSS
March, 1987

Contents

THEORIES OF ADOLESCENCE

1: THE PHILOSOPHICAL AND HISTORICAL ROOTS OF THEORIES OF ADOLESCENCE

LONG before psychology became a science, there existed philosophical, theological, and educational theories that contributed to an understanding of human nature and development. G. Stanley Hall, as a result of his famous two-volume work *Adolescence* (1916), is considered the father of a scientific "psychology of adolescence." Prior to Hall it was frequently the philosopher-educator who was especially concerned with a theory of human development with its implications for teaching. This was the case with Plato, Aristotle, Comenius, Rousseau, Herbart, Froebel, and Pestalozzi.

One difficulty in identifying prescientific theories of adolescent development is that prior to Hall adolescence was not considered a separate stage of human development and received no special emphasis. The word "adolescence" first appeared in the fifteenth century, indicating that historically adolescence was subordinated to theoretical considerations about the nature of human development. Contemporary theories of adolescence have their historical roots in general theories of development. Some important ideas about human development come from philosophers who are concerned with the question: What is the nature of man? For example, what Locke and Darwin had to say about the nature of man is so profound that it is reflected in the writings of Rousseau and Hall respectively and thus constitutes a philosophical basis for a theory of development.

In classifying theories of development, Ausubel (1958) distinguishes between preformationistic and predeterministic approaches to human development on the one side and tabula rasa approaches on the other side. The preformationistic theory is reflected in the theological proposition of man's instantaneous creation, in the homunculus theory, and in the doctrine of man's basic sinfulness as well as in the more recent theories emphasizing instincts and innate drives. Predeterministic theories postulate universally fixed stages of development, but allow for environmental influences, as is obvious in Rousseau's romanticism, Hall's theory of recapitulation, Freud's stages of psychosexual development, and Gesell's emphasis on maturation. In contrast to this are the tabula rasa approaches that minimize the biological and genetic factors and place heavier emphasis on environmental determinants of human development. As the name implies, this includes Locke's tabula rasa theory, the humanistic approaches, and the modern theories of behaviorism, social learning theory, and cultural determinism.

EARLY GREEK CONCERN WITH HUMAN NATURE

A historical approach to a theory of adolescence must begin with the early Greek ideas about human development. Their influence remained prevalent through the Middle Ages and is still noticeable today. The philosophical idea of dualism, for instance, is essentially Greek. Plato (427–347 B.C.) made a clear distinction between two aspects of human nature: soul and body. He expounded that body and soul are different substances and that although there is some interaction between them, the soul is an entity in itself, capable of leaving the body without losing its identity. It can perceive more clearly and reach higher realities when freed from the body; *soma sema* ("the body is the grave of the soul"), he declared. The body and sensuality are the fetters that hinder the soul in reaching those higher realities. Body is matter and has all the defects of matter. The idea of dualism between mind and body reappeared later in Christian theology and became of primary importance in the philosophical thinking of the seventeenth century, especially under Descartes, Leibnitz, and Spinoza.

Of greater interest from a developmental point of view is the idea of the layer structure of the soul which Plato developed in the dialogue *Phaedo*. According to Plato, the soul has three distinguishable parts, layers, or levels. Thus, probably for the first time in the history of psychology, a threefold division of soul, or mind, is advanced. The lowest layer of the soul is described as man's desires and appetites. Today we might describe this level in terms of drives, instincts, and needs, and its resemblance to Freud's concept of "id" can hardly be denied. According to Plato, this part of the soul is located in the lower part of the body and is primarily concerned with the satisfaction of the physical needs. ". . . [I]t fills us full of love, and lusts, and fears, and fancies of all kinds, and endless foolery, and . . . takes away the power of thinking at all" (Plato, 1921: 450). The second layer of the soul, the spirit, includes courage, conviction, temperance, endurance, and hardihood; aggressiveness and fierceness also originate here. Man has both the first and the second layer in common with the animal world. These two layers belong to the body and die with it. The third layer is divine, supernatural, and immortal; it constitutes the essence of the universe. This is the real soul, which Plato described as reason and which has its temporary seat in the body. Plato's theory concerning the layer structure of the soul is reflected in several central European personality theories, which are developed on the assumption of a layerlike stratification of personality. They perceive development as a process by which the lower layers mature earlier and are superseded by higher layers as the child grows older. Plato had already postulated such a developmental theory. Reason is latent during the first stage when perception is most important. Among contemporary theorists, Piaget maintains that percepts develop into concepts. The second stage of development is characterized by conviction and understanding and brings the second layer of the soul, spirit, into the foreground of psychological development. The third stage, which we might identify with adolescence, but which, according to Plato, is not reached by all people, relates to the development of the third part of the soul, reason and intelligence.

Interspersed in most of Plato's dialogues—but particularly in *Laws* and *The Republic*—are descriptive accounts of children and youth as well as advice concerning the control of their behavior. While this material does not constitute a theory of development as we understand it today, it does give insight into Plato's conception of the nature of development.

During the first three years of life the infant should be free from fear and pain and sorrow. This point of view would be endorsed by many psychologists today. Interestingly enough, in the dialogue *Laws* Cleinias suggests that in addition to freeing the infant from pain we ought to provide pleasure. This is in agreement with Plato's basic goal, which is the possession of happiness. However, the Athenian Stranger objects that this would spoil the child, since during the early years "more than at any other time the character is engrained by habit" (Plato, 1953: 359). Character is formed at such an early age because the experiences and impressions leave a lasting influence. However, Plato did admit that "the characters of young men are subject to many changes in the course of their lives." The argument about the consistency of personality versus its modifiability has continued, and proponents for both of Plato's statements can be found today.

From three to six the child needs sports and social contact with age-mates in order to get rid of his self-will. Plato would punish but not disgrace the child. Social development is taken into consideration at this age, and children ought to come together in a kind of kindergarten arrangement under the supervision of a nurse. However, children should find for themselves the "natural modes of amusement" appropriate to their age.

Plato suggested a division of the sexes at six. "Let boys live with boys and girls . . . with girls." The boy now has to learn horsemanship, the use of bow and arrows, the spear, and the sling. Boys will not be allowed to drink wine until they are eighteen because of their easy excitability, "fire must not be poured upon fire." A related adolescent desire is argument for amusement's sake. In their enthusiasm they will leave no stone unturned, and in their delight over the first taste of wisdom they will annoy everyone with their arguments. Plato believed that the character is formed through habit at a very early age.

Plato developed his educational philosophy in *The Republic*. He perceived education as the development of the soul under the influence of the environment, "and this has two divisions, gymnastic for the body, and music for the soul." Reasoning in the young child is undeveloped, but since the young child is impressionable, Plato suggested establishing "a censorship of the writers of fiction," since "anything that he receives into his mind is likely to become indelible and unalterable: and therefore . . . the talks which the young first hear should be models of virtuous thoughts" (Plato, 1921: 642). Rational and critical thought develop mainly during adolescence. The training that began with music and gymnastics during childhood was continued through adolescence with mathematical and scientific studies. The latter brought out critical thought and dissatisfaction with direct sense knowledge; during this training students would develop methods of finding the truth and of distinguishing truth from opinion. In *Laws* Plato spoke of education as "that training which is given by suitable habits to the first instincts of virtue in children;—when pleasure, and friendship, and pain, and hatred are rightly implanted in souls not yet capable of understanding the nature of them, and who find them, after they have attained reason, to be in harmony with her" (Plato, 1953: 218). The meaning of education in this view is to provide experiences for children prior to the development of reason that are nevertheless in agreement with reason when it does develop during adolescence. Plato already recognized the importance of individual differences; children are born with different abilities and should be guided into those kinds of activities that are in line with their aptitudes.

Plato postulated that the attainment of knowledge might be explained by his doctrine of innate ideas. Though undeveloped, vague, and nebulous, innate ideas are nevertheless present at birth. Learning is a process of remembering these ideas, which once—probably before the soul entered the body—were clear. Sensations help in reawakening these partially lost ideas. The mind-body dualism is of relevance here, since the body contributes sensation while the mind contains the ideas. In this way, Plato's theory of innate ideas opens the discussion about the influence of heredity and environment.

Aristotle (384–322 B.C.), in contrast to Plato, denied the separation of body and soul and returned to the older Greek idea of the unity of the physical and mental worlds. Body and soul, according to him, are related in structure and function. The relationship between body and soul is the same as that between matter and form; body is matter and soul is form. Soul-life, for which Aristotle used the word "entelechy," is the principle by which the body lives. Aristotle accepted Plato's idea concerning the levels of the soul-life; however, he viewed soul structure from a biological, almost evolutionary, point of view. The lowest soul-life form is that of the plant, the life functions of which are supply of nourishment and reproduction. The next higher form of soul-life is also found in animals, its additional functions being sensation, perception, and locomotion. The third soul-life function is distinctly human and sets men apart from the animal world. It includes the ability to think and reason. Consequently, there are three layers of soul-life—the food-supplying, or plant, soul; the perceiving, or animal, soul; and the thinking, or human, soul. Aristotle further divided the thinking, or human, soul into two different parts: the practical soul by which we "deliberate about those things which depend upon us and our purpose to do or not to do" (Aristotle, 1925: 1196) and the theoretical soul, which deals with higher and abstract knowledge such as distinguishing between what is true and what is false.

Aristotle advanced a theory of development concerning the layer structure of the soul that appears to have some resemblance to Darwin's more scientific biological theory of evolution, even though it does not include the idea of evolution of one species from another. Furthermore, Aristotle made an impassable division between the different levels of soul-life. Plato, in describing the stages of development, held that the first (plant) soul level developed before the second (animal) soul level and this, in turn, was a prerequisite for the rational soul level. Aristotle followed this idea of the level structure of the soul and applied it to the development of the child.

> As the body is prior in order of generation to the soul, so the irrational is prior to the rational. The proof is that anger and wishing and desire are implanted in children from their very birth, but reason and understanding are developed as they grow older. Wherefore, the care of the body ought to precede that of the soul, and the training of the appetitive part should follow; none the less our care of it must be for the sake of the reason, and our care of the body for the sake of the soul [Aristotle, 1941c: 1300–1301].

Aristotle divided the developmental period into three distinguishable stages of seven years each. The first seven years he named infancy; the period from seven to the beginning of puberty, boyhood; and from puberty to twenty-one, young manhood. This division of the period of development into three stages was generally accepted during the Middle Ages and recurs in some modern theories of development.

Infants and animals are alike in that both are under the control of their appetites and emotions. "Children and brutes pursue pleasures" (Aristotle, 1941a: 1053). Aristotle emphasized that moral character is the result of choice, "for by choosing what is good or bad we are men of a certain character. . . ." Even though young children are able to act voluntarily, they do not have choice, "for both children and the lower animals share in voluntary action, but not in choice, and acts done on the spur of the moment we describe as voluntary, but not as chosen'' (Aristotle, 1941a: 967–968). This seems to imply that children first go through an animallike stage of development; what distinguishes them from animals is that children have the potential for higher development than animals, "though psychologically speaking a child hardly differs for the time being from an animal" (Aristotle, 1941b: 635). It is the characteristic of adolescence to develop the ability to choose. Only if the youth voluntarily and deliberately chooses will he develop the right kind of habits and thus in the long run build the right kind of character. By making choices adolescents actively participate in their own character formation. Voluntary and deliberate choice thus becomes an important aspect in Aristotle's theory of development, since it is necessary for the attainment of maturity. Among contemporary writers M. Mead and E. Friedenberg claim that prolonged education and dependency have reduced choices to the extent that they interfere with the attainment of maturity.

Although Aristotle did not offer us a systematically stated theory of adolescence, in *Rhetorica* he provided us with a detailed description of the "youthful type of character," part of which resembles descriptive statements that could have been written by G. Stanley Hall. "Young men have strong passions, and tend to gratify them indiscriminately. Of the bodily desires, it is the sexual by which they are most swayed and in which they show absence of self-control" (Aristotle, 1941d: 1403). Sexuality in adolescence is of concern in any contemporary text, whether theoretically, empirically, or clinically oriented. Aristotle, in his description of adolescents, commented on their instability: "They are changeable and fickle in their desires, which are violent while they last, but quickly over: their impulses are keen but not deep-rooted" (Aristotle, 1941d: 1403). Lewin among the contemporary writers deals with the instability of the psychological field of the adolescent, who stands in a psychological no man's land. This makes many sociopsychological situations unclear, indefinite, and ambiguous, and the resulting behavior is "changeable and fickle." "For owing to their love and honour they cannot bear being slighted, and are indignant if they imagine themselves being unfairly treated" (Aristotle, 1941d: 1403–1404). Adolescent complaints about being "unfairly treated" in home, school, and society in general are so common today that they need no further elaboration. The list of quotes from *Rhetorica* in which Aristotle described the characteristics of adolescence could be continued, and other analogies to contemporary theories would not be too difficult to find. Aristotle discussed, among other issues, adolescents' desire for success, their optimism, trust, concern with the future rather than the past, their courage, conformity, idealism, friendship, aggressiveness, and gullibility.

The education of the adolescent in the fourth century B.C. was based on the study of mathematics and included astronomy, geometry, and the theory of music; these subjects taught abstraction but did not require the life experiences and the wisdom that were considered necessary in order to become a philosopher or a physicist.

Under the early impact of Christian theology, Aristotelian thought seemed to get lost; however, it was later combined with Christian ideas by Saint Thomas Aquinas. The Aristotelian-Thomistic philosophy became dominant in the twelfth and thirteenth centuries, and its influence was felt during the Middle Ages—particularly in the form of Scholasticism. Aristotle is also considered as influential in laying the foundation for a more scientific approach to science and psychology.

MEDIEVAL CHRISTIAN VIEW OF HUMAN DEVELOPMENT

The theological view of human nature and development cannot as readily be identified in terms of one man, a specific historical period, or even a particular church. We find the idea of original sin expressed by Tertullian in the second century when he spoke of the depravity of human nature. It was emphasized by John Calvin in the sixteenth century and is prevalent in Catholic Scholasticism, Protestant Calvinism, and American Puritanism.

The theological view of human nature as found in the medieval, early Reformation period encompassed several relevant ideas:

1. Mankind's unique position in the universe, being created in the image of God.
2. Mankind's evil due to Adam's original sin.
3. Mankind's dual nature: a spiritual, immortal soul and a material, mortal body. Salvation and life after death places the immortal soul on a higher level of importance.
4. Knowledge as revealed to mankind from without. It comes from God and is revealed to us through the Bible.
5. The homunculus idea of instantaneous creation. The last point is not so much biblical as medieval.

Most of these ideas can be found in biblical sources, but they were also influenced by Greek philosophy, especially Plato's dualism. We will see later that theories that followed in the seventeenth, eighteenth, and nineteenth centuries, especially those advanced by Locke, Rousseau, and Darwin, can partly be understood as antitheses to these earlier theological ideas.

The idea that God created mankind in his own image and thus gave it a unique position in the universe is expressed in Genesis 1:27–28: "And God created man to his own image: to the image of God he created him: male and female he created them." Furthermore, he gives them the power to rule over all living creatures. Prior to Darwin man was seen as being divinely created and basically different from the animal world.

The second important idea concerning the nature of humanity is the theological doctrine of human depravity. The human being is seen as having innate tendencies toward ungodliness and sinfulness, as fundamentally bad, with the badness becoming stronger during the developmental years if it is not counteracted by stern discipline. The idea of original sin as based on Genesis 3:6–7 relates the sinfulness of each individual to Adam's first sin. And "as sin came into the world through one man and death through sin, and so death spread to all men because all men sinned. . . . Yet death reigned from Adam to Moses, even over those whose sins were not like the transgression of Adam . . ." (Romans 5:12–14).

This pessimistic view of human nature, prevalent in Catholic theology before the Reformation, received a new impetus with Calvin's theology and thus set the intellectual climate for Puritanism. The educational objective in this theory was to bring forth the innate ideas that are God-given—knowledge of his laws and commands. Such a stern disciplinary approach to education was prevalent under the influence of Catholic Scholasticism and Calvinism in Europe and Puritanism in New England. There was little room for individual differences, since the quality of the mind was the same for all individuals and the child who failed to learn was seen as willfully resisting the efforts of the teacher. The role of the teacher was defined by the teacher's authority and a belief that learning could be facilitated by physical punishment. The role of the child was defined by obedience. Calvin in particular expressed a strong faith in the value of education.

The theological view that mankind is the result of instantaneous creation results in preformationist thinking (Ausubel, 1958). During the Dark Ages, it was believed that the child came into the world as a miniature adult. The difference between a child and an adult was considered to be only a quantitative one, not a qualitative one. If one were to accept this point of view, then it follows that there should be no difference in the physiological functions of the child and the adult. Therefore, girls wore long dresses and corsets of adult style, only smaller in size, as is obvious from many medieval paintings. The qualitative difference in body build, body function, and mental abilities was disregarded. Growth was understood to be only a quantitative increase of all physical and mental aspects of human nature, not a qualitative one. This is a regression of thought when contrasted with the logical theories of Plato and Aristotle. The theory of preformationism held that children had the same interests as adults and therefore should be treated correspondingly, which meant that adult requirements were put upon them and were enforced by stern discipline. According to this view, the child did not "develop" but was preformed.

Figure 1 illustrates the homunculus concept; it represents a view of the preformed "little man" in the sperm as conceived by seventeenth-century scientists.

It was seriously believed that a miniature but fully-formed little man (i.e., an homunculus) was embodied in the sperm, and when implanted in the uterus simply grew in bulk, without any differentiation of tissues or organs, until full-term fetal size was attained at the end of nine months [Ausubel, 1958: 23–24].

This idea of homunculism was soon to be challenged by the beginning of modern science and advancements in the field of medicine. It was learned that young children have qualitative and quantitative characteristics of their own and are not miniature adults. One might speculate that the reason for the limited concern of pre-Hallian writers with the basic physiological changes that take place during pubescence—many of these changes are obvious to the keen observer, and their detection does not require medical knowledge or technology—is due to the theoretical position that the child is a miniature adult. In the philosophical realm it was Rousseau who stated that "nature would have children be children before being man. If we wish to prevent this order, we shall produce precocious

FIGURE 1. Drawing of a Small Man (an Homunculus) in a Human Spermatozoon.

Adapted from Hartsoeker, 1694.

fruits which will have neither maturity nor flavor, and will speedily deteriorate; we shall have young doctors and old children" (Rousseau, 1911: 54). Thus a new conception of human nature contributed to a more scientific concept of growth and development.

JOHN AMOS COMENIUS' DEVELOPMENT-CENTERED THEORY OF EDUCATION

The Renaissance may be seen as a revolt against authoritarianism in church, school, and society. The Aristotelian logic, the presupposition of universal ideas, and Scholasticism in general were challenged by Erasmus and Vives. Vives felt that one had "to begin with the individual facts of experience and out of them to come to ideas by the natural logic of the mind" (Boyd, 1965: 179). Learning was no longer seen as a deductive process, but as an inductive process beginning with experiences, and he suggested that an understanding of the learning process came from psychology. Learning, it was believed, was determined by the mind of the learner, and, therefore, education became concerned with individuality in pupils.

Comenius (1592–1670) accepted these ideas of the Renaissance, combined them with Aristotle's classification of development, and advanced a theory of education that was based on psychological assumptions. In his *Great Didactic,* first published in 1657, Comenius suggested a school organization based on a theory of development. Rather than dividing the developmental period into three stages of seven years, as Aristotle did, Comenius proposed four developmental stages of six years each and a different school for each of these four stages.

The suggested school organization was based on assumptions concerning the nature of human development and a specific theory of learning, that of faculty psychology. Interestingly enough, present-day school organization in parts of the United States closely resembles this pattern. Comenius argued that the temporal sequence of the curriculum content should be borrowed from nature; in other words, it should be suitable to the psychological development of the child. "Let our maxim be to follow the lead of nature in all things, to observe how the faculties develop one after the other, and to base our methods on this principle of succession" (Comenius, 1923: 257).

In the first six years of life children learn at home in the mother-school at their mother's knees. They should exercise the external senses and learn to discriminate among the various objects around them. The nature of the development of the faculty of sense perception is such that it precedes all other faculties, and, consequently, sensory experiences and sensory knowledge should be provided first. The significance of early sensorimotor experiences is emphasized in Piaget's theory.

The child from six to twelve attends the vernacular-school and receives a general well-rounded elementary education, which is provided for all children, rich or poor, boy or girl. Included in the curriculum are the correct use of the vernacular language, social habits, and religious training. The program at this level would emphasize training of the "internal senses, the imagination and memory in combination with their cognate organs." Comenius accepted the faculty psychology point of view in respect to memory. "The memory should be exercised in early youth, since practice developes it, and we should therefore take care to practise it as much as possible. Now, in youth, labour is not felt, and thus the memory developes without any trouble and becomes very retentive" (Comenius, 1923: 152).

For the next six years, from twelve to eighteen, which include the adolescent period as we understand it today, education was to be provided in the Latin school. The psychological purpose of the school at this age was to train the faculty of reasoning. The student learned to "understand and pass judgment on the information collected by the senses." Included were judgments about relationships of the things perceived, imagined, and remembered. Understanding here implies utilization of the principle of causality. The curriculum of the school was divided into six years, which results in the following six classes: Grammar, Natural Philosophy, Mathematics, Ethics, Dialectics, and Rhetoric.

The following six years, from eighteen to twenty-four, consist of university education and travel, and during this period the faculty of the will is trained. Considering our present conception of will this appears to be a strange notion and becomes more meaningful only if we consider that the concept of will, as used by Comenius, includes the self-direction of one's life. Corresponding ideas can be found in the theories of Erikson and Piaget.

Comenius strongly advocated that the instructional procedure should fit the level of comprehension of the child in contrast to the Scholastic education, which he attacked. For Comenius, development is not uniform, continuous, and gradual—as the homunculus theory of development implies—but each stage of development has its own characteristics, "teachable moments" as Havighurst would say today. Development was seen as a process in which the intellectual functions gain progressively more control over the other aspects of the soul.

> To attempt to cultivate the will before the intellect (or the intellect before the imagination, or the imagination before the faculty of sense perception) is mere waste of time. But this is what those do who teach boys logic, poetry, rhetoric, and ethics before they are thoroughly acquainted with the objects that surround them. It would be equally sensible to teach boys of two years old to dance, though they can scarcely walk [Comenius, 1923: 257].

The right time for the education of each of the faculties must be chosen correctly, and the sequence must be "borrowed from nature." In Comenius' continuous focus on what children can do, know, and are interested in at each stage of development, we seem to find the historical roots of a child-centered theory of education.

JOHN LOCKE'S EMPIRICISM

The idea of homunculism with its emphasis on preformationism and Plato's theory of innate ideas—a basic Scholastic principle—was most seriously challenged and opposed by John Locke (1632–1704). Locke was influenced by Thomas Hobbes' (1588–1679) idea that the human being, both body and mind, is part of the natural order; he further expanded Hobbes' theoretical position, known today as empiricism, that all of our knowledge is derived from sensation. Hobbes stated in *Leviathan* that "there is no conception in man's mind, which has not at first, totally, or by parts, been begotten upon the organs of sense" (Hobbes, 1651: 7). Locke further developed the theory that there are no innate ideas; ideas that we hold in our consciousness are either obtained through our senses directly or are derived from those ideas that have been obtained through sensations previously. The child's mind at the time of birth is, according to an analogy used by Locke, a tabula rasa, a blank tablet, as the following quote implies:

> Let us then suppose the mind to be, as we say, white paper, void of all characters, without any ideas;—How comes it to be furnished? . . . To this, I answer, in one word, from EXPERIENCE. In that all our knowledge is founded, and from that it ultimately derives itself. Our observation employed, either about external, sensible objects, or about the internal operations of our minds, perceived, and reflected on, by ourselves, is that which supplies our understandings with all the materials of thinking. These two are the fountains of knowledge, from whence all the ideas we have, or can naturally have, do spring [Locke, 1753: 76].

This assumption has had far-reaching influence on social theory and has with amplification become the cornerstone of democracy. Since the mind of each person at birth is a tabula rasa, all ideas and knowledge come from experience. Since present differences and inequalities found in people are due to environment and experiences, all are completely equal at birth. Thus the principle of democracy is in part derived from a philosophical-psychological theory concerning the child's mind at birth. Locke discussed his views concerning democracy in *Treatise of Civil Government* (1768). He blamed environmental conditions, such as poor education and poor social environment, for the human misery in the world and gave hope to those who lived under unfavorable conditions. Thus emerged a theory that is an expression of faith in the perfectibility of the human race.

Locke found rather enthusiastic followers in Helvetius and Condillac in France. They carried his empiricism to its extreme, since for them even the powers of faculties of the mind were the result of sensation. Furthermore, since poor living conditions existed for the French lower and middle classes prior to the Revolution, many people in France were especially susceptible to such ideas. Thus the words *liberté, egalité, fraternité* became the powerful symbols of a new concept of human nature. A new hope emerged, that by changing the environment, human nature could be changed.

Locke's proposition that there are no innate ideas and that the mind is a tabula rasa contrasts sharply with several theories of development already discussed. The more outstanding examples are as follows:

1. The doctrine of human depravity and original sin appeared to be in contradiction to Locke's new concept of the human mind. If our mind is formed by experience only, then it follows that whether a child becomes "good" or "bad" is due to environmental experiences. Locke's psychology stresses nurture rather than nature.

2. The medieval class system of Europe was based on what we would consider today as hereditary assumptions. The nobility was noble by birth, regardless of personal merits and qualities. This notion was challenged by the empiricist assumption that "all men are born equal." If everyone is alike and begins life at the same point, then everyone should have the same rights and opportunities to obtain better social positions. King and subject, rich and poor, begin life at the same point. Therefore, support for social mobility is found in this theory. Locke's early form of environmentalism, even though it is not directly related to behaviorism, social learning theory, and cultural relativism, may be viewed as a historical forerunner to these schools of thought.

3. The doctrine of innate ideas was interpreted during the medieval period to imply that the child is a miniature adult and grows only quantitatively. Locke's tabula rasa concept implied that the child at birth is qualitatively and quantitatively different from the adult. If ideas are not innate, then the newborn child is radically different from the adult in respect to intellectual properties. Locke pointed out that the child's personality is different from that of the adult and thus laid the foundation for a new theory of child development; he also urged the scientific study of human nature. Development occurred in a gradual process from mental passivity in the early years of childhood to increased mental activity in adolescence. The rational faculty emerges toward the end of this developmental process and therefore was seen as characteristic of the period of adolescence.

Locke, even though he advanced many important ideas about human nature, foreshadowed rather than developed a specific theory of human development. It was Rousseau who, influenced by Locke, proposed a new theory of human development.

JEAN JACQUES ROUSSEAU'S ROMANTIC NATURALISM

Rousseau (1712–1778) was greatly influenced by Locke's ideas, but he developed his own theoretical positions concerning human nature. While for Locke reason was the most important aspect of human nature, Rousseau considered human nature as primarily feeling. While Locke was concerned with constitutional government, Rousseau made a great plea for individualism and individual freedom and directed his critical attack against society and social institutions. Although he, too, was concerned with the social well-being of all, he distinguished between the "will of all" (majority will, determined by vote) and the "general will" (that which is really best for every member of society). Rousseau was not truly democratic, for he was afraid that a majority vote could be as bad as any monarchy. Ideally the majority will and the general will would coincide. This, however, was only possible if men were educated and wise.

Rousseau brought about a revolutionary change in thought concerning the nature of human development, with its corresponding educational implications, the main ideas of which he expressed in *Émile* (1780). The traditional approach toward childhood education had been to see the child from the adult point of view. Rousseau claimed that such an approach is not only false, it may even be harmful. He started with the needs and interests of the child and saw development as a natural preplanned process. If one were to free the child from the restrictions, unnatural limitations, and rigid discipline of the adult world, nature would assure a harmonious and healthy development. The child was innately good, but the restrictions of adult society and poor education had corrupted the child. To correct this, he advocated a natural development in a sound and healthy environment, which for him was one that posed few restrictions on the child, especially in the first twelve years. Rousseau was one of the strongest proponents of individualism in education, basing his proposition on a deep faith in the natural goodness of man.

Rousseau advocated a revision of the treatment children received at home and in school as well as changes in the methods of instruction; if development were left to the laws of nature, the outcome would be most desirable. Each of Rousseau's four stages of development had specific psychological characteristics. Consideration of these characteristics resulted in definite educational objectives, the attainment of which helped children grow toward maturity. The educational methods, the content to be taught, and the objectives at each age level were to be determined by the characteristics of the child at that developmental level. Learning was most effective if the child had freedom and could learn and grow according to his own impulses.

Rousseau most strongly opposed the homunculus idea and asserted that it was the plan of nature that children play, live, and behave like children before they become adults. "Childhood has its own way of seeing, thinking, and feeling, and nothing is more foolish than to try to substitute ours for them" (Rousseau, 1911: 54). Rousseau advised teachers and parents, "You ought to be wholly absorbed in the child—observing him, watching him without respite, and without seeming to do so, having a presentiment of his feelings in advance" (Rousseau, 1911: 169). Even though Rousseau himself had only limited and not always successful educational experiences—his five children lived in a foundling asylum—his theory had a tremendous impact on educational practice in the latter part of the eighteenth and most of the nineteenth centuries. Rousseau's ideas are obvious in the works of Pestalozzi, Froebel, Spencer, Horace Mann, and Dewey and are reflected in a child-centered approach to education.

Rousseau, like Aristotle, saw the development of the child occurring in certain stages; however, he identified four stages rather than three and believed that teaching and training should be in harmony with the developmental nature of each of these stages. According to Rousseau, these various stages are breaks in the developmental process, and each can be distinguished by its special characteristics and functions. He spoke of a metamorphosis that takes place when the child changes from one stage to another. Thus, Rousseau introduced a saltatory theory of human development according to which the nature of development is seen as change that is more sudden at certain age levels than at others. He, like G. Stanley Hall, spoke of puberty as a new birth. New functions may emerge rather suddenly and become dominant in the psychological organization. This saltatory aspect of Rousseau's theory can be understood in the light of his own temperamental saltatory experiences.

The first stage, that of infancy, includes the first four to five years of life. The child is dominated by the feeling of pleasure and pain. This period is called the animal stage, because the child is like an animal in regard to its physical needs and undifferentiated feelings. This idea had been expressed earlier in the writings of Aristotle. Education, such as training motor coordination, sense perception, and feeling, is primarily physical. He advocated that the method of nature be followed in everything and proposed the following rule: "Observe nature, and follow the route which she traces for you. She is ever exciting children to activity; she hardens the constitution by trials of every sort; she teaches them at an early hour what suffering and pain are."

The second stage, which Rousseau characterized as the savage stage, includes the years from five to twelve. Dominant during this stage is the faculty of sense. Sensory experiences are provided by play, sport, and games, and the curriculum is centered on the training of the senses. During this stage self-consciousness and memory develop, and human life in the proper sense begins here. The child still lacks reasoning ability and is not yet sufficiently aware of moral considerations. Education during this stage should be free from external, social, and moral control. Formal training in reading and writing are seen as harmful and therefore postponed until the beginning of the third developmental stage. In the first twelve years education

. . . ought to be purely negative. It consists not at all in teaching virtues or truth, but in shielding the heart from vice, and the mind from error. If you could do nothing and allow nothing to be done, if you could bring your pupil sound and robust to the age of twelve years without his being able to distinguish his right hand from his left, from your very first lesson the eyes of his understanding would be open to reason [Rousseau, 1911: 59].

Rousseau's method of "negative education," which assumes that there is an innate developmental plan that cannot be improved upon by environmental factors, finds its corresponding modern psychological concept in "maturation." The defenders of the maturational concept of development frequently advocate, as did Rousseau, a permissive and unrestricted atmosphere for childrearing.

The third stage, the years from twelve to fifteen, is characterized by an awakening of the rational functions, including reason and self-consciousness. Youth at this age possess an enormous amount of physical energy and strength. The excess of energy leads to curiosity, which the school curriculum should utilize by encouraging exploratory behavior and the desire to discover what is true about the world. The only book that should be read is *Robinson Crusoe*. Rousseau saw in Crusoe the great model and ideal for the preadolescent, since his style of life was characterized by exploration of the world and a primitive curiosity, which corresponds to the needs and interests of this developmental stage. The curriculum should be geared to the study of nature, astronomy, science, art, and crafts. Rousseau in agreement with contemporary educational theory emphasizes the learning process rather than the product. "He is not to learn science, he is to find out for himself." This is the age of reason; curiosity and personal utility are the main motives for behavior; social conscience and emotionality are still undeveloped. It is interesting to observe that, in opposition to other developmental theories, the rational aspect of personality develops prior to the emotional. Rousseau's theory was a reaction to the historically earlier philosophy of rationalism, with which he differed.

The fourth period, adolescence proper, from the age of fifteen to twenty, finally culminates in the maturation of the emotional functions and brings about a change from selfishness to self-esteem and social consideration. The adolescent is no longer dominated by self-interest but develops a strong interest in other people and a need for genuine affection. This stage is characterized—late by comparison to knowledge about youth today—by the emergence of the sex drive, which Rousseau considered a second birth. "We have two births, so to speak—one for existing and the other for living; one for the species and the other for the sex" (Rousseau, 1911: 193). Now conscience is acquired, and morals and virtues become possible. This is the period of preparation for marriage, which ideally coincides with the attainment of maturity.

Maturity could be considered as a fifth stage in the process, but it appears to be less clearly defined. The faculty that becomes dominant during this period is will. Comenius also placed the development of the will at the time of late adolescence. The will is the faculty of the soul by which we choose between two alternatives.

These stages of development, according to Rousseau, correspond to certain stages in the development of the human race. Thus it was assumed by this recapitulation theory that the human race had gone through the stages of animallike living, the stage of savagery, the stage of reason, and, finally, through a stage of social and emotional maturity. He used the historical development of the race in order to explain the development of the individual child. This hypothesis was further developed by educators, such as Froebel and Ziller, as well as by G. Stanley Hall and the Child Study Movement of America.

Critics feel that Rousseau overemphasized the individual nature of human growth and development and underemphasized the importance that education, society, and culture have in the developmental process and especially in the formation of the personality. He saw the influence of society and culture as negative forces in personality development; he wanted to remove them to make possible the free natural development of what is good in the child.

CHARLES DARWIN'S THEORY OF BIOLOGICAL EVOLUTION

A new trend of thought concerning the nature of development emerged with the publication of Darwin's *Origin of Species* (1859). Darwin's (1809–1882) idea of evolution—growth and development from the simpler to the more complex forms of organic life—has been one of the most revolutionary and influential ideas in man's thinking about himself and the nature of his development. Every living organism from the simplest structure to the most complex, man himself, is brought together under the order of natural explanation. The psychological implications resulting from this biological concept of development were accepted, elaborated, and applied to adolescence by G. Stanley Hall, thus leading to a science of adolescent development.

Since Darwin's theory is well known, only its basic principles will be stated. Darwin collected substantial, though not complete, evidence for a theory that claimed that the evolution of biological life is continuous, from a single cell organism through numerous higher developmental stages to the complexity of human mind and body. This evolutionary theory assumed variability and adjustability in all organisms as well as the overproduction in the number of offspring of each species. Darwin showed that the overproduction of offspring threatened a species' capacity to survive. The result is a "struggle for existence." In this struggle of the selection of some and elimination of others, a "natural selection process" takes place by which the increase in population is checked. The stronger, healthier, faster, more immune, more intelligent, and physically better-adjusted organisms survive and reproduce, while the weak, sick, and less adaptable species perish. In time this leads to the "survival of the fittest." The qualities that account for the survival of the fittest are inherited by the offspring. Since the conditions for survival frequently differ in various kinds of environments, changes in the organism occur. Thus in the selection process, variations, new kinds, new races, and eventually new organisms come into existence. This process began with the simple one-cell organism, and from the lower forms of organic life more and more complex forms have developed. The last link in this biological evolution is the human being. Since climatic, geological, and general life conditions change, the evolutionary process is a perpetual one.

This theory of evolution is in complete contrast to the theological doctrine of the divine creation of humankind. Through Darwin's theory mankind was placed in the order of nature. Most theological and many philosophical positions previous to Darwin's—for example, that of Aristotle—had postulated an essential dichotomy between man and nature. This absolute distinction between human nature and the nature of the organic world was seriously challenged by Darwin. Humans were now seen as part of the organic world, albeit a more advanced and more intelligent species.

G. STANLEY HALL'S BIOGENETIC PSYCHOLOGY OF ADOLESCENCE

G. Stanley Hall (1844–1924) was the first psychologist to advance a psychology of adolescence in its own right and to use scientific methods in his study of adolescence. It can be said that he bridged the philosophical, speculative approach of the past and the scientific, empirical approach of the present.

Hall expanded Darwin's concept of biological "evolution" into a psychological theory of recapitulation. In this theory he stated that the experiential history of the human species had become part of the genetic structure of each individual. The law of recapitulation asserted that the individual organism, during its development, passes through stages that correspond to those that occurred during the history of mankind. That is, the individual relives the development of the human race from early animallike primitivism, through a period of savagery, to the more recent civilized ways of life that characterize maturity.

Hall assumed that development is brought about by physiological factors. He further assumed that these physiological factors are genetically determined, that internal maturational forces predominantly control and direct development, growth, and behavior; there was little room in this theory for the influence of environmental forces. It follows that development and its behavioral concomitants occur in an inevitable and unchangeable pattern that is universal, regardless of the sociocultural environment. Cultural anthropologists and sociologists have challenged this point and asserted that Hall's position was extreme and untenable. They further refuted the claim that the behavioral predispositions of physiological drives, as expressed in the recapitulation theory, are highly specific. Hall held that socially unacceptable types of behavior—those characteristic of earlier historical phases—must be tolerated by parents and educators, since they are necessary stages in social development. He advocated childrearing practices of leniency and permissiveness. However, he reassured parents and educators that unacceptable behavior would disappear in the following developmental stage without any corrective educational or disciplinary efforts.

A corollary of Hall's theory of recapitulation is his concept of stages of human development; the characteristics of a certain age in the development of the individual correspond to some primitive historical stage in the development of the human race. Hall did not divide human development into three stages, as advocated by Aristotle and many present-day "stage" psychologists. He followed a four-division pattern similar to that proposed by Comenius and Rousseau. Hall's developmental stages are infancy, childhood, youth, and adolescence.

The period of infancy includes the first four years of life. While children are still crawling, they are reenacting the animal stage of the human race when the species was still using four legs. During this period, sensory development is dominant; the child acquires those sensorimotor skills that are necessary for self-preservation.

The period of childhood—the years from four to eight—corresponds to the cultural epoch when hunting and fishing were the main activities of man. This is the time when the child plays hide-and-seek, cowboys and Indians, uses toy weapons, and so on. The building of caves, shacks, tree houses, and hiding places parallels the cave-dwelling culture of early history.

Youth—from eight to twelve—includes the period that today is referred to as "preadolescence." During this stage the child recapitulates the "humdrum life of savagery" of several thousand years ago. This is the period when the child has a favorable predisposition to practice and discipline, when routine training and drill are most appropriate.

Never again will there be such susceptibility to drill and discipline, such plasticity to habituation, or such ready adjustment to new conditions. It is the age of external and mechanical training. Reading, writing, drawing, manual training, musical technic, foreign tongues and their pronunciation, the manipulation of numbers and of geometrical elements, and many kinds of skill have now their golden hour, and if it passes, unimproved, all these can never be acquired later without a heavy handicap or disadvantage or loss [Hall, 1916: xii].

Adolescence is the period from puberty until full adult status has been attained. According to Hall, it ends comparatively late, between the twenty-second and twenty-fifth years. Hall described adolescence as a period of *Sturm und Drang,* "storm and stress." In German literature, the period of *Sturm und Drang* includes, among others, the works of Schiller and the early writings of Goethe. It is a literary movement full of idealism, commitment to a goal, revolution against the old, expression of personal feelings, passion, and suffering. Hall saw an analogy between the objectives of this group of writers at the turn of the eighteenth century and the characteristics of adolescence. In terms of recapitulation theory, adolescence corresponds to a time when the human race was in a turbulent, transitional stage. Hall described adolescence as a new birth, "for the higher and more completely human traits are now born" (Hall, 1916: xiii).

The characteristics of adolescent *Sturm und Drang* are pictured in detail by Hall in the chapter "Feelings and Psychic Evolution" (Hall, 1916). He perceived the emotional life of the adolescent as an oscillation between contradictory tendencies. Energy, exaltation, and supernatural activity are followed by indifference, lethargy, and loathing. Exuberant gaiety, laughter, and euphoria make place for dysphoria, depressive gloom, and melancholy. Egoism, vanity, and conceit are just as characteristic of this period of life as are abasement, humiliation, and bashfulness. One can observe both the remnants of an uninhibited childish selfishness and an increasing idealistic altruism. Goodness and virtue are never so pure, but never again does temptation so forcefully preoccupy thought. Adolescents want solitude and seclusion, while finding themselves entangled in crushes and friendships. Never again does the peer group have such a strong influence. At one time the adolescent may exhibit exquisite sensitivity and tenderness; at another time, callousness and cruelty. Apathy and inertia vacillate with an enthusiastic curiosity, an urge to discover and explore.

There is a yearning for idols and authority that does not exclude a revolutionary radicalism directed against any kind of authority. Hall (1916) implies these antithetical impulses of Promethean enthusiasm and deep sentimental *Weltschmerz* in his use of the concept of *Sturm und Drang*, which for him is so characteristic of the adolescent.

In late adolescence the individual recapitulates the stage of the beginning of modern civilization. This stage corresponds to the end of the developmental process: the adolescent reaches maturity. Hall's genetic psychology did not see the human being as the final product of the developmental process; it allowed for indefinite development.

2: THE PSYCHOANALYTIC THEORY OF ADOLESCENT DEVELOPMENT

INTRODUCTION TO PSYCHOANALYTIC THEORY

Sigmund Freud (1856–1939) developed a comprehensive theory of psychopathology, of personality, and of human development and founded the psychoanalytic school of thought. His theory was revolutionary, since it fundamentally changed the conceptual foundation of psychology and psychiatry of his time; it has remained influential to this day. Psychoanalysis was based on concepts and on insights into the workings of the human mind that had received little systematic attention in pre-Freudian psychology. The new ideas of physics and biology that emphasized energy and dynamics and were prevalent toward the end of the nineteenth century, as well as Darwin's notion of evolution, influenced Freud's thinking and became part of his psychodynamic theory. He believed that all psychological events are tied to energy, drive, and instincts based on biological characteristics.

Freud's theoretical assumption concerning the nature of man has dramatically changed man's conception of himself. Freud is often identified as one of the most important thinkers of the twentieth century, comparable in influence to Copernicus and Darwin. Copernicus changed our geocentric view of the world. Darwin's theory removed the human race from its special position in relationship to God and placed it within the continuum of natural evolution as part of the animal world; humans were seen as no more than just another animal with specific survival mechanisms. Freud, in turn, made explicit that humans were not the rational, logical, and intelligent beings they had been believed to be but were irrational, influenced by hidden, unconscious motives of which they themselves were often not aware. Freud implied that the crucial psychological reality is desire rather than reason.

The significance of Freud's work is not limited to psychology, psychiatry, and psychoanalysis proper; his ideas have also become influential in literature, art, advertisement, philosophy, sociology, medicine, and education. His contributions to our understanding of the mind have penetrated many areas of modern Western culture and thought to such an extent that his ideas have become part of each individual's "implicit psychology" to a much larger extent than is commonly acknowledged. Freud's contribution to our understanding of the nature of the mind contains several identifiable elements and ideas:

1. All behavior is motivated, often by unconscious dynamics.
2. Freud's theory of dreams emphasized the meaningfulness of dreams as manifestations of the unconscious mind.
3. Similarly, Freud ascribes meaning to errors, forgetting, slips of the tongue, and other unintended behavior, believing that they reveal unconscious forces.
4. A major motivating force in human behavior is sexuality, including the idea of infantile sexuality. Freud emphasized the conflictual relationship between sexuality and civilization.
5. Early childrearing experiences, especially in weaning, toilet training, and the role of the family in the handling of sexuality and aggression, are seen as significant factors in development.
6. Freud gave new hope to the treatment of psychopathology and changed social attitudes toward the neurotic and psychotic.

After completion of his medical training, Freud began his medical career in Vienna as a research scientist in neurology, hoping to become a professor rather than a practicing physician. However, because of his limited opportunities for advancement in the university setting and since he needed to support his family, he was forced to practice medicine. As a medical specialist in neurology, he began to see patients with neuropsychological problems. The treatment of nervous disorders was a branch of medicine that was, at that time, primitive, and few treatment modalities existed that could successfully be used in dealing with patients with mental aberrations.

Freud's scientific inclination led him to the discovery and development of new treatment methods. He systematically collected observational and case study data, supplementing it with his own famous self-analysis, to which he devoted the last half hour of each day from 1897 until his death in 1939. Freud's theory evolved only slowly and was a multifaceted theory of various models and explanatory systems of psychopathology, the nature of dreams, human motivation, and the inner workings of the mind. Like the theories of Copernicus, Darwin, and other revolutionary thinkers before him, Freud's formulations were met with bitter resistance and objections from other scientists.

A rather careful review of the empirical research literature attempting to test Freud's theoretical assumptions concludes:

Large masses of experimental information are available for testing psychoanalytic propositions. We have been amused by the fact that while there is the stereotyped conviction widely current that Freud's thinking is not amenable to scientific appraisal, the quantity of research data pertinent to it that has accumulated in the literature grossly exceeds that available for most other personality or developmental theories. We have actually not been able to find a single systematic theory that has been as frequently evaluated as Freud's [Fisher and Greenberg, 1977: 396].

While not all of Freud's concepts receive unequivocal empirical support, many do, and many others receive at least partial support. Apparently, Freud's concepts of the oral and the anal personality, the etiology of homosexuality, several aspects of the Oedipus complex theory, and his theory of the origin of paranoid delusions seem to find substantial support from empirical investigations. Other aspects of Freud's theory, such as the nature of dreaming, the effectiveness of psychoanalytic therapy, the psychology of women, and sex differences are not borne out by empirical studies. In general, there is much more support for Freud's overall theoretical propositions concerning human nature and personality development than for his practical suggestions about conducting psychotherapy (Fisher and Greenberg, 1977).

Space does not allow a discussion of the entire system of psychoanalytic theory. Therefore, in the context of theories of development and especially theories of adolescence, only those models especially relevant to an understanding of personality development and to the discussion that will follow in Chapters 3 and 4 is presented here.

1. The topographical model of the mind consists of three layers: the conscious, the preconscious, and the unconscious. This conceptualization of the tripartite organization of the mind grew out of Freud's book *The Interpretation of Dreams* (1900/1953).
2. Another tripartite model of the mind, which Freud later developed in *The Ego and the Id* (1923a/1961), was based on the structural hypothesis. It comprises the id, the ego, and the superego. These two systems are not only compatible but have been integrated into a more dynamic view of the inner workings of the mind and thus contribute to our understanding of personality development as well as to the dynamics of psychopathology.
3. The psychosexual stages of human development are the oral, anal, phallic, latency, and genital stages. These are of particular significance for our concern with theories of adolescence, since they constitute the cornerstone of Freud's developmental theory.
4. The mechanisms of defense: repression, displacement, identification, rationalization, reaction formation, introjection, projection,

undoing, and denial. These are mechanisms by which the ego, by one means or another, defends against the unacceptable and painful or anxiety-arousing wishes of the id. Anna Freud considered asceticism and intellectualization especially characteristic of pubescence. O. Rank also viewed asceticism as typical for adolescents but contrasts it with its opposite, promiscuity.

Freud's theory of psychosexual development has stimulated considerable research interest and further theoretical development in personality development in general and adolescent development in particular by such psychoanalysts as Hartmann, Horney, Sullivan, Winnicott, Fromm, Reich, Rank, A. Freud, Erikson, and Blos. Freud himself, partly because of his preoccupation with the role of infantile sexuality in normal and abnormal development and partly because of his emphasis on the importance of the first five years of life in human development, climaxing in the Oedipus complex, placed relatively little emphasis on pubescence and adolescence. Many neo-Freudians seem to agree with this neglect of the period of adolescence in Freud's original theory. Among the neo-Freudians, E. Erikson and P. Blos in particular have attempted to rectify this theoretical neglect of adolescence.

CONSCIOUS—PRECONSCIOUS—UNCONSCIOUS

The first tripartite model of the mind emerged from Freud's efforts to explain the psychology of the dream processes. The mind, according to Freud (1900/1953, 1915/1957), consisted of three layers: the conscious, the preconscious, and the unconscious. This early comprehensive theory of personality and development is referred to as the topographical model.

The *conscious* is that layer of the mental apparatus of which the individual is aware. It provides contact with both the external world—through perceptions, motor activity, and feelings—and with the internal personal world of dreams, images, and thoughts. Consciousness itself contains only a very small and limited part of the mental life. The metaphor often used is the iceberg, of which only a very small part floats over the surface while most of it is under the water. (See Figure 2.) Freud emphasized that only a very limited part of our mental activity takes place in the conscious at any one time. However, the conscious also has the function of censorship, admitting or excluding material from awareness.

The much greater part of our mental activity remains more or less inaccessible in the lower regions of the mental structures. One of the major tasks of psychoanalytic treatment is, according to Freud, the uncovering of this hidden material to make unconscious content, motives, and dynamics conscious. Only the patient's conscious understanding of these hidden dynamics makes a realistic and thoughtful adjustment possible, hence

FIGURE 2. Freud's Model of the Mind. A schematic presentation of Freud's theory of the mind in which the structural model and the topographical model are combined.

Adapted from S. Freud (1933/1964) and Kaplan and Baron (1952).

therapy is primarily concerned with making unconscious material conscious.

The *preconscious,* in a certain sense, is part of the unconscious, since the individual is not aware of its content. Yet much of it, particularly in the upper regions of the preconscious, is easily accessible to the conscious, since the content can voluntarily be retrieved by directing one's attention to it. This can be achieved by asking relevant questions or by providing appropriate stimuli. The preconscious constitutes much of the mental warehouse of information and experiences, accessible through memory and, therefore, basically accessible to the conscious on request. Most of the ideas that are not at present in our awareness but that can, through the process of memory, retrieval, and thinking, be brought back into our conscious mind are, according to Freud, in our preconscious.

The preconscious, however, is not a passive storehouse of information but is actively involved in many mental activities. According to Kubie (1958), sudden insights into complex problems or creative thoughts and discoveries do emerge from preconscious processes. Often the solution to a problem does not emerge while one is deliberately working on it but seems to pop into one's mind from the preconscious, without any conscious thinking effort, when one is relaxed or about to go to sleep, and sometimes solutions emerge even when one is not consciously aware of the problem.

The *unconscious* contains experiences and information that cannot readily be brought into awareness by volition, but require special efforts, treatment, hypnosis, or interpretation to be brought back into the conscious. However, for Freud, the unconscious was the dominant force in the mental apparatus, especially in psychopathology. The pathway between the unconscious and the conscious is normally blocked, but the pathway between the preconscious and the conscious is at least partially open. The content of the unconscious (traumatic experiences, unacceptable impulses, and such) are kept in the unconscious by repression; however, they are not dormant but remain dynamic and active. Although the constant process of repression itself is not conscious, it consumes psychological energy. However, repression is unable to suppress the unconscious impulses permanently, hence these impulses and experiences manifest themselves in distorted, nonrecognizable form in dream content, errors, accidents, and neurotic symptoms. Thus, an accident may be understood as an unconscious desire to punish oneself for forbidden thoughts or deeds. The craving for sweets is viewed as an unconscious, symbolic, repressed desire for human love. Dreaming is a process by which the repressed unconscious wish (the latent dream content) finds a distorted conscious manifestation in the dream experiences (the manifest dream content).

Considerable scientific evidence supports Freud's basic assumption that motives, wishes, feelings, and fantasies exist in an individual without the individual being consciously aware of these hidden dynamic forces; furthermore, these hidden forces are known to influence behavior (Fisher and Greenberg, 1977).

Id—Ego—Superego

Later Freud developed in *The Ego and the Id* (1923a/1961) another tripartite model of the mind that is closely related to the topographical model of conscious, preconscious, and unconscious; each component of this id–ego–superego model emerges during different stages of psychosexual development (the developmental model will be discussed later). In the structural model Freud conceptualizes the structure of the mind as consisting of three major systems: the id (biological), the ego (psychological), and the superego (social). In the healthy adult person, these three systems—id, ego, and superego—form an integrated personality pattern, which aids the individual in conducting daily interactions with the environment and allows satisfaction of basic needs and desires within socially prescribed limits. In the neurotic person, these systems are in conflict, necessitating the use of defense mechanisms or maladaptive manifestations and thus reducing the efficiency of that person's everyday functioning.

ⅹ A number of psychoanalysts assert that some of the reemergence of infantile or childish behaviors that may occur in early adolescence is due to regression. Faced on the one hand by the problem of coping with a sudden upsurge in sexual and aggressive drives and the anxiety that they create, and on the other hand by greatly increased social demands, the adolescent may temporarily abandon anxiety-producing and not always successful efforts at more mature responding, and retreat to more "primitive" responses that were successful and rewarding in an earlier, simpler period [Conger, 1977:84].

The id is present at birth and governed by the pleasure principle. The id provides the mind with its psychological energy, impulses, and motivation to act. It represents the biological component of the mental apparatus, including untamed passion. It contains irrational instinctual appetites and impulses, and its purpose is to gratify basic instinctual and bodily needs and reduce the tensions produced by these biological needs. The contents and the processes of the id are primarily but not exclusively unconscious. Tension reduction, which comes about when basic biological needs are gratified, is pleasurable. Hence, the object that reduces bodily tensions becomes attached (or cathected) to the id. Freudians speak extensively of libidinal object finding, and the object can be a thing, the self or part of the self, or another person: oral object choice, anal object choice, parent object choice, Oedipal object choice, homosexual object choice, and heterosexual object choice. In the young infant the drive of the id is not yet restrained by moral or practical considerations but is directly oriented toward drive gratification. The operations of the id are, therefore, referred to as primary processes.

Even later in life, an id-dominated personality asserts little or no control over instinctual wishes and sexual desires. Such a person's behavior is mainly influenced by the immediate gratification of the pleasure-seeking motive and would show little concern either for the demands of reality or for social or ethical values. The acting-out juvenile delinquent as well as the promiscuous sexual behavior of the adolescent seems to be id-dominated.

DEVELOPMENT OF THE EGO

According to Freud the ego develops in part out of the id during the end of the first through the second year of life and is defined by its reality-testing functions. The most important function of the ego is the adaptation of the individual to reality (S. Freud, 1933/1964).

Toilet training contributes greatly to ego development, since it contributes to the delineation of body boundaries or, in a more general sense, to a distinction between the self and the outside world. The ego represents the psychological component of the personality, but the id still remains the dominant element in the partnership between id, ego, and superego. This development of the ego out of the id takes place when the demands of the id are not met and transactions between the organism and the outside world become necessary to discharge tensions. When needs are not satisfied two consequences can occur:

1. The infant remains in a state of tension.
2. The id, having to cope with unresolved tension, is transformed into a new structure, the "I" or the ego, which takes into account the external reality that does not allow the gratification of impulses, and in the process the maturing child learns to cope with the tensions stemming from the needs of the id that are in conflict with the demands of reality.

The ego serves several functions in the mental apparatus. First and foremost, the function of the ego is to compromise between the inner world of subjective experiences, the id, and the demands of the external (objective) world. It obeys the reality principle. The ego has a reality-testing function; that is, it delays, inhibits, restrains, and controls the demands of the id—not permanently, however, but only in order to maximize its gratification at the appropriate time and place, when short-range as well as long-range consequences are being considered, and when the gratification of a desire is actually in the individual's best interest. The ego also considers whether the object is appropriate for the gratification of the needs of the id. The ego takes on several other functions. It prevents the drive discharge when such behavior would not be in the individual's best interest; that is, it helps the individual develop frustration tolerance. It also controls the ideas that enter consciousness. Furthermore, through various defense mechanisms at the disposal of the ego, ideas that are dangerous or arouse anxiety may be prevented from entering the conscious or may be distorted. The ego thus guides the behavior of an individual toward acceptable goals. In that sense all cognition is a function of the ego. Finally, the ego encompasses logical thinking.

The ego represents the external world to the id. It consists of reason, common sense, and reality-testing functions, but serves the purpose of the id from which it borrows its energies. The metaphor used by Freud was that of the horse (id), constituting instinctual drive and energy, and the rider (ego) who controls where and how fast the horse can go.

The ego's relation to the id might be compared with that of a rider to his horse. The horse supplies the locomotive energy, while the rider has the privilege of deciding on the goal and of guiding the powerful animal's movement. But only too often there arises between the ego and the id the not precisely ideal situation of the rider being obliged to guide the horse along the path by which it itself wants to go [Freud, 1933/1964: 77].

On the other hand, there often is no real difference between the goals of the id and the ego, only differences in the way these goals can be attained. The ego tries to avoid the negative consequences that could result from an uninhibited gratification of the id impulses.

DEVELOPMENT OF THE SUPEREGO

Later in human development, during the latency period, the superego develops, primarily as a function of the resolution of the Oedipus complex. Freud (1923b/1949) views the superego as the "heir of the Oedipus complex."

Research findings suggest that the development of the superego is less a direct outgrowth of oedipal tensions and conflicts with the father than Freud suggested. Instead, the mother's and other people's standards play a larger role and are more positively assimilated and gradually integrated in the self-structures than Freud had theorized. The oedipal struggle itself is resolved most effectively, not out of fear of the father (castration anxiety) but out of the nurturant, friendly attitude on the father's part (Fisher and Greenberg, 1977: 405).

The superego represents the social-moral component in the personality. It represents the ideal rather than the real and strives for perfection. The individual's internalized moral code develops out of a process of identification with one's parents and their standards as to what is good or bad, virtuous or sinful. Later, the superego becomes the internal representation not only of parental mores but, in a more generalized sense, of societal rules and cultural restrictions on the expression of instinctual drives. The development of the superego approaches its completion at the beginning of puberty, which means that self-control begins to replace the control through reward and punishment by parents, and anxiety and guilt become the self-administered punishment of the superego. The superego has two components. The *conscience,* which reacts when we transgress moral values and makes us feel guilty, and the *ego-ideal,* which makes us feel proud when we behave according to our ideals. At this point of development, when the tentative balance between id, ego, and superego is just beginning to emerge, the newly awakening sexual tensions of puberty demand id gratification and thus produce serious conflicts in the personality structure.

The superego serves three functions:

1. To inhibit, especially the aggressive and sexual impulses of the id that are not approved by society
2. To persuade the ego to substitute moralistic goals for realistic goals
3. To strive for perfection (Hall, 1954: 47)

Considering the relationship between the topographical model of the conscious, preconscious, and unconscious to the structural model of the id, ego, and superego provides a more dynamic understanding of the mental apparatus. The id corresponds most closely to the unconscious in the topographical model. The ego is not sharply distinguished from the id, but its lower portions flow into the id and the unconscious. Repressed ideas merge into the id but are sharply segregated from the ego by the resistance of repression. The ego cuts across all three layers of the topographical model; it is obviously present in the perceptual system of conscious. "It may be that much of the ego is itself unconscious, only part of it, probably is covered by the term preconscious" (S. Freud, 1923a/1961). The superego is also located in all three layers of the topographical model, and while it is part of the ego, it also decides what part of the id may be allowed into the region of the ego.

It must be emphasized that the model set forth in Figure 2 is obviously only a human construct, developed to explain the inner workings of the mind. It is not material or physiological, and the dividing lines are not as neat and clear-cut as the illustration suggests. What are depicted are functions of awareness, not locations in the brain.

FREUD'S STAGES OF PSYCHOSEXUAL DEVELOPMENT

Psychosexual development, according to Freud, begins in early infancy and passes through a series of predetermined, highly differentiated stages, named according to the body zones or erogenous zones that provide libido satisfaction during a particular developmental period. Freud assumed that these stages are universal, in that each individual, regardless of society and culture, must move through this invariable sequence of psychosexual experiences to reach maturity, almost as if it was part of human nature. Development progresses because the child obtains pleasure from different parts of the body at different times, and therefore, each developmental stage is identified by the psychosexual mode of the body area that dominates in its urge toward pleasure and satisfaction: oral, anal, phallic, and genital; during the latency period the libidinal drive is repressed. An adult personality structure can be classified into the oral, anal, phallic, or genital type.

X This sequential order of normal development can be disrupted by *fixation or regression*. Fixation can occur at any point in development, with the individual remaining at least partially at an immature level of libido gratification and not moving on to more mature levels. Illustrations of oral fixation are alcoholism, excessive smoking, or compulsive eating. Regression takes place when the individual encounters serious frustration in psychosexual development and therefore returns to less mature and safer stages in order to attain libido satisfaction. The typical example is the child's return to thumb-sucking when a younger sibling is born.

The sexually rejected adolescent may regress to masturbation; the girl unsuccessful in dating may regress to playing with dolls. Fixation and regression occur when progress toward more mature levels of sexual development encounters serious frustration from the environment. Fixation can also result from overgratification at a particular stage; thus, spoiling the child may impede progress toward heterosexual maturity.

THE ORAL STAGE

During the first year of life the oral region is the primary source of pleasure. The child gets pleasurable autoerotic stimulation not only from sucking, drinking, and eating but also through oral activity not motivated by hunger, such as thumb-sucking and sucking a pacifier or various other objects placed in the mouth. At this stage the mouth is the dominant erogenous zone. Displeasure is expressed by spitting out. Libidinal energies are directed toward an oral object choice. The love object at this early stage of development is the self. Self-love often precedes object love, since the young infant has no perception of objects in the outside world as separate from the self. Self-love is narcissistic, a concept Freud adopted from Greek mythology. During this stage the ego remains undeveloped, and the energies of the id seek satisfaction with little concern for reality or awareness of possible dangers.

Oral characteristics manifest themselves later in life through overeating or by finding primary satisfaction through drinking, smoking, kissing, or talking. Even the aggressive component of this stage can express itself in making "biting" remarks or in oral sarcasm.

THE ANAL STAGE

During the second year of life, partly as a result of the social demand for toilet training, the primary erogenous zone shifts from the oral to the anal region; libido is now invested in an anal object choice. During this stage the infant must learn to regulate natural impulses and to postpone immediate gratification to meet the demands of the external reality; hence, the ego develops. From anal activity the infant may derive not only pleasure but also a feeling of power over the mother from both "holding back" (prolonging evacuation in order to obtain stronger sensations) and "letting go" (experiencing relief and pleasure from evacuation). The oral and the anal stages are basically autoerotic phases.

Depending on how toilet training is administered, anal attributes may shape the development of personality characteristics. Fixation at the anal stage or regression to this stage may produce anal-erotic conflicts, which manifest themselves in one of the two modalities of the anal stage: retention or expulsion. The retentive component is most obvious in the stingy person who holds on to all kinds of things, especially money. This person is most likely stubborn, overcontrolled, fussy, and excessively concerned with neatness, cleanliness, and orderliness. The expulsive type, in contrast, lets go, both emotionally and physically (emotional outbursts, temper tantrums, and rage). This person is a spendthrift, is rebellious, unclean, messy, and disorderly.

Factor analytic studies have demonstrated that clusters of traits corresponding to the basic qualities of the oral or anal personality, such as parsimony, neatness, and obstinacy, do occur together in children and adults as would be predicted on the basis of Freud's theory (Fisher and Greenberg, 1977: 393, 397). There is a paucity of data, rather than negative evidence, to clearly show that the oral and anal personality traits originate in these crucial early developmental stages. Scattered bits of evidence suggest that such a relationship between early childhood experiences and adult personality patterns does indeed exist.

THE PHALLIC STAGE

Although the oral and the anal stages are basically pregenital stages, children in the phallic stage, from about age three to six, become interested in their own sex organs and feelings; fantasies and preoccupations with sexuality begin to predominate. Touching and manipulating one's sex organs is experienced as pleasurable, and masturbation can be expected at this stage, even though it does not necessarily lead to orgasm. The oral, anal, and phallic stages are narcissistic stages, since all libido satisfaction is derived from stimulation of one's own erogenous zones. However, during the phallic stage the object of the libido begins to change. The self as the love object is replaced by a parent object choice, and the parent object is the opposite-sex parent, leading to the *oedipal situation*. In Greek mythology Oedipus kills his father and marries his mother. Since the reproductive organs of the sexes are different and since the roles each parent plays in the life of the child are different, the events that occur during the phallic stage are also different for the two sexes. However, Freud is much more explicit in explaining the events in the boy, and his account of the male's oedipal situation receives stronger support from empirical investigations than the female's.

During the phallic stage the male child begins to take pride in his penis; he values and idealizes it. With increased sexual desire, his love for his mother becomes erotic, and he begins to view his father as a rival. Wanting exclusive possession of his mother leads to the oedipal conflict. His feelings toward his father are ambivalent. On the one hand he identifies with his father and loves him; on the other hand he sees his father as an obstacle to his incestuous wishes and has aggressive feelings toward him. Since he knows his father is more powerful than he is, he fears that the father may cut off the offending sex organ, something that apparently must have happened to girls, who lack the protruding penis. This insight leads to a fear that Freud identified as *castration anxiety*.

As an outgrowth of castration anxiety the incestuous wishes for the mother are repressed. Three additional factors contribute to the resolution of the Oedipus complex: (1) the realization that social taboos forbid him to possess the mother sexually, (2) disappointment from the mother, and (3) maturation. The child resolves the conflict by identifying with his father, hoping to become like his father, so that he too can eventually possess a wife. Through the resolution of the Oedipus complex the child begins to incorporate parental and later social moral values into his personality structure, thus contributing to the development of the superego during the latency period, which follows.

Fisher and Greenberg (1977: 400) report, based on their extensive review of the research literature concerned with the oedipal concept, that there exists fairly convincing evidence "that men do have differential attitudes about their parents that mirror a history of sexually tinged rivalry with father for mother as a love object. The male does, as Freud proposed, experience castration anxiety, and this anxiety is intensified by exposure to erotic stimuli."

The oedipal processes in the female are reversed, less complicated, less dramatic, begin later, and last longer than in the boy; and Freud is less specific in identifying the underlying dynamics. He has also received less empirical support for these conceptualizations. The girl, like the preoedipal boy, loves her mother. With the increasing awareness of her sex organs she discovers that she lacks something the boy has, feels castrated, and blames her mother for her missing organ. As her relationship with her mother weakens, she turns her love to her father and develops an attitude of both jealousy and sexual attraction, referred to as *penis envy*. Again, confrontation with the impossibility of attaining the desired penis, aided by maturational processes, leads the girl to the resolution of the Electra complex; however, the resolution of the Electra complex proceeds more slowly and continues throughout the latency period into adolescence. Empirical evidence suggests that the female is more likely to resolve her oedipal conflict out of fear of loss of love than the male and is less motivated by castration anxiety. In general, fewer empirical investigations have tested the oedipal theory as it applies to females; some of Freud's assumptions have been challenged, and others remain unsupported.

THE PHALLIC STAGE AS "LITTLE PUBERTY"

The phallic stage is sometimes referred to as "little puberty." Apparently, Freud felt that in terms of evolutionary theory the human race had evolved from a species that reached its reproductive maturity at the age of about five or six. Thus, the "little puberty" is a hypothesized remnant of sexual development in evolutionary terms. Even the body zone identified by the names given to these two stages—"phallic" for "little puberty" and "genital" for "actual puberty"—refer basically to the same body zone. The masculine term "phallic" in the earlier stage reflects the strong male orientation of much of Freud's theory. However, the implications of this evolutionary aspect of Freud's theory allow for interesting comparison. "The phallic stage is then the vestige of the prehuman adolescence. The period between these two adolescences has some stability, while the periods before and after latency are full of rapid change, conflict, and psychological problems stemming from urgent libidinal demands" (Baldwin, 1967: 368).

SEXUAL LATENCY

With the successful resolution of the Oedipus complex, the child enters the relatively calm period of latency; the libido drive is less urgent, and more importantly, no new object choice emerges. It is during latency, as a by-product of the resolution of the Oedipus complex, that the identification with the parents becomes strong, and hence the superego develops. The period itself covers the elementary school years, although there are wide individual variations. During this period the aggressive impulses, the sexual instincts, and the libidinal forces go under cover. The traumatic experience of having been deprived of fulfilling the sexual desires during the oedipal situation restrains the child for several years from seeking an overt affectionate relationship.

Several writers disagree with Freud's assumption of a period of sexual inactivity and sexual latency during this stage. White states:

> His assumption about the quiescence of sexual energies seems to be simply wrong. Anthropological evidence and better observation in our society have combined to cast grave doubt on the hypothesis of a biologically determined sexual latency. For once we can almost say that Freud underestimated the importance of sex [1960: 127].

The latency period, during which the child identifies with parents, is viewed by psychoanalysts as a period when important social and moral values are acquired. Schooling greatly facilitates the learning of general cultural values and the acquiring of fundamental social skills. New roles are tried in games and in play, and the development of motor ability is encouraged. Psychoanalysts are quick to point out that this is the period in the human life cycle when all known societies provide some formal training in essential skills, even though not necessarily the academic schooling of most Western societies.

Toward the end of the latency period, orientation of interests, games, and play activities enter a homosexual phase in which friendship ties to one's own sex grow strong and often involve an exclusion of the opposite sex. During the transition from latency to puberty and with the increase in sexual tension, sexual awareness, and sexual interests, even these same-sex friendship patterns may become erotic in nature. Hence, homosexual activity in the form of genital exhibitionism, genital exploration, and masturbation are not uncommon during this prepubertal or early pubertal phase. Kinsey reports that 50 percent of all male teen-agers participated at one time or another in such forms of homosexual play. Other studies put this figure as high as 70 percent. Freud does see as one of the problems of this period "not missing the opposite sex" (S. Freud, 1925: 87), implying that friendship ties could become too strong, binding boys and girls to their own sex, with the possibility of an inversion of the sex object.

PUBERTY, OR THE GENITAL STAGE

Adolescence proper, brought about by the biological maturation of the reproductive system, is characterized by a rapid increase in sexual tensions demanding gratification. The sexual needs and fantasies become more explicitly concerned with tension release and later with the sexual union of male and female. However, these inclinations are restrained by the social demands for adaptation to the moral values of society and the norms of the community. The seriousness of this situation becomes obvious if one considers that pubescence requires—for the first time since birth—that a basic biological drive, which acquires full strength only as a result of the pubescent growth changes, must be integrated into the personality structure of the young, still developing adolescent. This fact is complicated further by the traditional social-moral-religious standards, which demand that the heterosexual gratification of this drive be postponed until marriage, often as long as ten to fifteen years after the drive acquires its full biological strength. In terms of psychoanalytic conceptualizations, this means that the "id impulses" seek gratification with new urgency but clash with the recently developed and still formative "superego," producing guilt feelings because the superego finds the demands of the id unacceptable. The

A. Libidinal Localization (erotogenic zones)	B. Aim, or Mode of Pleasure-Finding	C. Libidinal Object-Finding		
INFANCY PERIOD				
Pregenital Period	*Infantile Sexuality*	Auto-eroticism	Narcissism	Allo-eroticism
1. Oral Stage				
a. early oral	Sucking, swallowing (incorporating)	at first objectless		Oral object-choice
b. late oral	Biting, devouring (destroying, annihilating)		Primary Narcissism	Oral-sadistic object-choice
2. Anal Stage				
a. early anal	Expelling (rejecting) (destroying) — looking exhibiting handling inflicting pain			Anal and anal-sadistic object-choice
b. late anal	Retaining (controlling) (possessing) — submitting to pain			
Early Genital Period (phallic stage)	Touching, rubbing, exhibiting and looking at genitalia, investigating, comparing, questioning, fantasizing (tender affection)			Parent object-choice Oedipus-phantasies
LATENCY PERIOD				
No new zone	Repression Reaction-formation Sublimation Affectional trends	Further decline of auto-eroticism	Diminished Narcissism	Development of social feelings
ADOLESCENT OR PUBERTAL PERIOD				
Late Genital Period Revival of zone sensitivity of infancy period	Reactivation of modes or aims of infancy period	Revival of auto-eroticism	Fresh wave of Narcissism	Revival of Oedipus object-choice
Later, functioning of vaginal zone	Emergence of adult mode of pleasure-finding			Homo-sexual object-choice Hetero-sexual object-choice

FIGURE 3. Freud's View of Normal Development. The theoretically normal development of children according to Freud's hypotheses of psychosexual development.

Reprinted from *The Structure and Meaning of Psychoanalysis* by Healy, Bronner, and Bowers, by permission of Alfred A. Knopf, Inc. Copyright 1930 by Alfred A. Knopf, Inc.

ego, unable to satisfy both, feels crushed between the two powerful contenders. Thus, the new balance between id, ego, and superego, recently established during the latency period, is suddenly thrown out of balance, producing conflict, turmoil, and a psychological disequilibrium. These conflicts can be internal, a struggle between temptation and conscience, or they can be external, between parents and self. The ego attempts to cope with these conflicts, on the one hand, by denying the demands of the id through such mechanisms as repression or denial or, on the other hand, by quieting the superego through intellectualization, rationalization, asceticism, and regression.

Sexual attraction, once more as in the phallic stage, turns to the opposite-sex parent, and Freud does speak of a revival of the oedipal situation during puberty, accompanied by the reawakening of castration anxiety (Freud, 1925). However, during latency the development of the superego has proceeded to the point at which an internalized "incest barrier" will no longer allow these taboo feelings into consciousness, and hence the ego uses defense mechanisms, especially displacement, to divert the incestuous demands of the libido toward somewhat more acceptable love objects. Freud (1925) commented that during early adolescence, a boy's first serious love object is most likely a mature woman—not unlike his mother—a common theme in French literature and movies. In much the same way the pubescent girl often falls in love with older men (as seen in her crushes and infatuations for teachers, movie stars, and entertainment heroes) before she shows much interest in boys of her own age group. Thus, the first opposite-sex love object of the adolescent is often, symbolically speaking, a mother or father figure, allowing the oedipal wish an acceptable nonincestuous substitute. And even later in adolescence, when the sexual object choice begins to turn to an opposite-sex partner of the same age, the choice is often unconsciously motivated by patterns and traits prevalent in one's own parents. This idea finds expression in the song "I want a girl just like the girl that married dear old dad." Thus, unconscious motives determine the adolescent's attraction to a particular individual when falling in love, allowing the fulfillment of the oedipal wish.

Related to this second oedipal situation is the adolescent task of freeing oneself from emotional dependency on one's parents. The boy's libidinal attachment to his mother must be released, and he must also free himself from the dominance of his father. This process of detachment from the incestuous love object brings the "problem of the generation" into the foreground and gives it its psychoanalytic explanation. This process of emotional detachment results, at least for a time, in rejection, resentment, and hostility toward parents and other authority figures. The conflict between the generations has been described frequently in the literature on adolescence and is a fairly common, everyday experience in many families. A fundamental task of the adolescent, as seen by psychoanalytic theory, is the "attainment of genital primacy and the definitive completion of the process of nonincestuous object finding" (Spiegel, 1951: 380). In other words, only through the emotional detachment from parents is the libidinal attachment to the opposite-sex partner possible.

According to psychoanalytic theory, the origin of a primary homosexual orientation is also related to an unresolved oedipal conflict rather than to the above-described homosexual interest of the late latency/preadolescent period, which may merely be an expression of the constitutional bisexuality of both male and female and generally is a normal developmental phase. However, a primarily homosexual orientation may be created if, during the height of the Oedipus complex, the male forms an intense "erotic attachment" to his mother and is received favorably by his mother, who responds with too much erotically tinted love while the father remains distant, cold, detached, and aloof. Such a family constellation of the seductive mother and the rejecting father enhances the castration anxiety to such an extent that the boy becomes concerned with the loss of his penis. Hence, he cannot tolerate the sight of female genitals because that is a dreadful reminder of what could happen to him. Any heterosexual contact would therefore recreate the guilt and anxieties related to the oedipal feelings toward his mother. In an extensive and comprehensive review of the empirical evidence pertaining to the family pattern of the homosexual, Fisher and Greenberg find partial support for Freud's proposition. "The father of a homosexual is likely to be an unfriendly, threatening person who would presumably be an unusually intense Oedipal competitor" (1977: 247). Similarly, Fisher and Greenberg report, "There is also moderate support for the view that the mother of the homosexual is particularly close, intimate, and restrictive in her relationship with her son. She fits well the stereotype of the seductive mother" (1977: 248). Finally, they also report that "the male homosexual has an elevated concern . . . about getting hurt" (1977: 248), which psychoanalysts would interpret as an indication of "castration anxiety."

MECHANISMS OF DEFENSE

One of Freud's major contributions to an understanding of the dynamics of the mind—widely recognized, even by people who tend to disagree with other assumptions of psychoanalysis—is the identification of defense mechanisms. They help the ego cope with anxiety, frustration, and unacceptable impulses and help relieve tension and inner conflicts. Since anxiety is likely to increase during periods of rapid developmental changes and since adolescence is such a period—old ways of responding no longer seem to work and new patterns of adjusting have not yet been tried—the need for defense mechanisms is heightened during adolescence (Conger,

1977). Individuals develop such mechanisms, especially if they cannot deal with anxiety in a rational fashion, to defend themselves against the demands of the id or against conflicts with reality. Some mechanisms of defense, such as denial, reaction formation, and projection, are considered more primitive, since they reflect more of a loss of touch with reality; others, such as sublimation, undoing, rationalization, displacement, identification, and intellectualization, represent higher (closer to normal) levels of functioning. Everybody seems to utilize some defense mechanisms at one time or another to cope with conflictual situations and to protect the personality from the stresses, anxieties, and frustrations of everyday living. It is only when a particular defense is used exclusively to deal with the tension between inner psychological reality and the demands of the external world that use of defense mechanisms becomes symptomatic of neurotic tendencies and even psychopathology.

> Of course, no individual makes use of all the possible mechanisms of defense; each person merely selects certain of them, but these become fixated in his ego, establishing themselves as regular modes of reaction for that particular character, which are repeated throughout life whenever a situation occurs similar to that which originally evoked them [S. Freud, 1937/1950: 340].

The most common defense mechanism, widely used even by normal people, is *rationalization,* a process in which one advances more or less plausible reasons to justify an act or an opinion, concealing to others and even to one's self the true reason or motive. Sometimes this mechanism is referred to as the "sour-grapes reaction," based on the famous fable in which the fox who cannot reach the luscious grapes claims that he doesn't want them because they are sour.

The adolescent unable to attain a date with a highly desirable girl will tend to rationalize that he is better off without her because she talks too much or is too spoiled or is too popular or is likely to lose her pretty figure at an early age. The high school girl ignored by the student council president may rationalize that the latter does not recognize her because he wears glasses and is probably nearsighted, when the school leader actually does not even know she exists (Lambert et al., 1978).

Rationalization can help us to cope with disappointment in two ways: (1) it provides an acceptable justification for what we did, or what we believe, or what we really wanted but could not attain and (2) it helps soften the anxiety and the disappointment connected with unattainable goals. We often rationalize failure by blaming circumstances rather than ourselves; we thus avoid the feeling of anxiety and guilt that would result if we acknowledged our failures and inadequacies. Rationalization aids the ego by providing an excuse for something unattainable, unpleasant, or unacceptable. And we do use methods of rationalization, especially if criticized or called upon to explain unacceptable or undesirable behavior. Children use it vis-à-vis parents, and students vis-à-vis their teachers. However, frequent use of rationalization makes it impossible to learn from error and avoid mistakes, since such an approach prevents our recognizing the error or mistake or the personal shortcoming as such. By rationalizing, one is denying a personal responsibility for one's shortcomings. The student who fails the exam but blames the test or the teacher rather than himself frees himself from anxiety but also absolves himself from studying harder next time; the student believes that it was not his fault.

Repression to some extent is the purpose of all mechanisms of defense, and repressive components do accompany most of them. Repression deals with impulses from within, while denial relates to events that happen in the outside world. Repression should also be distinguished from suppression. Suppression is a conscious effort not to let ideas or impulses surface to awareness. Repression, in contrast, is an unconscious process of refusing to let into awareness the traumatic event, the stressful incident, or the unacceptable impulse. It was one of Freud's earliest constructs. Repression is less reality-oriented than rationalization since the impulse is cut off from awareness but remains dynamically operative in the unconscious. Most people are unaware of their earlier sexual feelings toward the opposite-sex parent. Socially taboo and highly traumatic early sexual experiences such as incest or rape may be repressed but dynamically operative in the adolescent's attitude toward sexuality. "Thus, for example, a girl who is sexually attracted to her father will simply remove this intolerable incestuous thought from her consciousness. It may come up again in her dreams, but upon awakening, these, too, will be repressed" (Calhoun, 1977: 35). Repression is the metaphorical rug under which we sweep the garbage of our life to hide it, and although the garbage is no longer visible, it is still there.

Displacement is a very important psychoanalytic defense mechanism used to explain how the affect or libidinal energy toward one object is transferred to a substitute object, which, while logically inappropriate, is quite appropriate for unconscious thinking. The original emotions remain the same, but the object to which the emotions are directed changes. An adolescent girl who experiences an intense fear of snakes may be displacing her underlying fear of a male's sexual advances. Displacement seems to be common when the original impulse or object is accompanied by a high degree of guilt or anxiety or when libidinal energy is blocked. For example, the libidinal drive toward masturbation during adolescence may be transferred to a compulsive need to wash one's hands. The connection between the two behaviors appears inappropriate. However, the hand is the body part that executes the masturbatory behavior, and since masturbation is viewed as a "dirty habit," hand washing is an unconscious undoing of masturbation. It cleans what is dirty, it relieves anxiety, and some of the libidinal energy seeking release in masturbation may actually find discharge in the substitute behavior. Even the motions of the hands around the soap may contain some similarity to masturbatory behavior. In a more general sense, the unavailable or unattainable gratification of sexual needs may find displaced expression in oral activities, such as smoking, kissing, applying lipstick, drinking, whistling, singing, talking, chewing gum, and spitting. The adolescent's first serious infatuation with a somewhat older, motherly teacher may be viewed as a displacement of the unacceptable love impulse toward his mother. However, since even the teacher is unavailable and socially unacceptable as a love object, a further displacement directs the love need to a more readily available girl of a similar age; however, she, too, may possess some characteristics of his mother. Thus, in the search for a mother substitute, one displacement may be put on top of an earlier displacement.

Identification is a process by which characteristics and qualities of an external object, frequently another person, are absorbed into one's own personality. Freud prefers the term "identification" over the term "imitation" since identification implies the involvement of deeper, more significant layers of the personality as well as a more permanent change. Imitation, which is part of identification, is superficial copying of behavior. The person with whom a child identifies changes as the child moves through the developmental stages. The successful resolution of the oedipal conflict requires an identification with the same-sex parent, a process that greatly enhances superego formation. However, with the beginning of adolescence, parental identification dramatically declines and identification with movie heroes, entertainment personalities, and famous athletes as well as coaches and teachers is common, a process that aids in achieving independence and establishing a personal identity. A primitive form of identification finds expression in eating something in order to become more like the object eaten. Thus, the hunter may eat the lion's heart in an attempt to become as brave as the lion. In the Christian sacrament the body and blood of Christ are eaten in order to become more Christlike.

In *isolation* or *intellectualization* the actual impulses reach the conscious, but they are isolated from the strong affect that usually accompanies such impulses. Feelings and intellect are separated so that a threatening situation loses its emotional impact. The feelings are repressed and the problem is viewed in abstract intellectual terms. The psychoanalyst refers to the process as decathexis, since the object has lost its cathexis. Cathexis is the concentration of mental energy on a specific idea or object. In other words, affect has become separated from content, as in a person who is insulted but does not feel anger. Isolation of affect means mental activities that usually occur together are separated, a phenomenon not at all uncommon in adolescent sexual development when, for example, sexual-sensual needs are gratified with one person (for example, a prostitute), while the erotic affectional feelings are reserved for the beloved sweetheart. In a religious, scientific sense, isolation would find expression in a dual incompatible belief system by the same person who, for example, as a religious person believes in the biblical story of creation and as a biological scientist believes in the Darwinian theory of evolution. Patients in therapy may develop an elaborate and abstract self-analysis of their problem but have no real feelings about it; instead, they try to convince the therapist of how much insight they already have.

Among the many defense mechanisms that the ego can use, Anna Freud (1948) considers two especially characteristic of the adolescent coping with the onslaught of sexual tensions: *intellectualization* and *asceticism*. Both may be used before pubescence, but they become especially important during this period of sexual disequilibrium. Asceticism is characterized by rigor, self-denial, and mortification of the flesh. It is typically seen as a phase in puberty, where it indicates a fear of sexuality and a simultaneous defense against sexuality. Asceticism in an adolescent results from a generalized mistrust of all instinctual wishes. This mistrust goes far beyond sexuality and includes eating, sleeping, and dressing habits. The increase in intellectual interest and the change from concrete to abstract interests (thinking) are accounted for in terms of these defense mechanisms against the anxiety produced by the libido.

Otto Rank (1945) contrasts promiscuity with asceticism as the two adolescent defense mechanisms that aid in maintaining independence. Having just freed themselves from the emotional dependence on parents, adolescents avoid any kind of strong emotional attachment, including an intimate personal love relationship, since it implies a new kind of mutual dependency. Being promiscuous satisfies sexual urges without the loss of the newly acquired independence, since such sexual gratification takes place without genuine love, personal commitment, and ego involvement. Separating the physical side of sexuality from its emotional component, as the idea of promiscuity implies, is of course a form of intellectualization as defined by Anna Freud. By being ascetic, adolescents retain their independence because they willfully reject any kind of involvement. Periods of asceticism may alternate with periods of instinctual gratification. In both instances the adolescent avoids the real love relationship in which self-restraint, self-subordination, and dependency are necessary to maintain permanent intimacy.

In *reaction formation*—"reversal into the opposite"—the unacceptable impulse is repressed from consciousness but readmitted as its very opposite. Thus, the hostility an unmarried teen-age mother may feel toward her newborn baby is unacceptable and is replaced by too much kindness, resulting in overprotection. Over-compensation often accompanies reaction formation, so that, in this illustration, too much kindness is provided. The expression "killed with kindness" aptly illustrates the tendencies that underlie this kind of defensive kindness. The function of kindness is not really to help other people but to release the anxiety and guilt associated with the true feeling of hostility. Similarly, hate may be transformed into love. The question arises, how can the new defensive emotion of kindness or love be distinguished from true kindness or love? Several characteristics suggest that an emotion may be the product of reaction formation: extreme forms of the defense emotion; some inconsistency, since the negative emotions may break through when one is off-guard; extravagant showiness; and compulsivity. The extreme and intolerant crusades against various vices are often a reaction formation against unconscious impulses toward that very same vice. The individual inclined toward criminal behavior may, through a reaction formation, become a highly effective police detective. Unacceptable homosexual tendencies may manifest themselves as extreme disgust and crusading against homosexuals. The puritanical censor of pornographic films and books may gain secret satisfaction from viewing the suspect material.

Introjection (internalization) has certain similarities to identification, such as the internalizing of outside events or characteristics of other people into the protagonist's personality structure for defensive purposes. However, introjection is more limited in scope. The whole personality is not restructured, only a specific part, as when an individual internalizes society's values as a guide to behavior. An extreme form of introjection is the "identification with the aggressor," seen even in concentration camps among older, surviving inmates who assumed the behavior and the values of the hated Gestapo. Apparently, an attitude of "if you can't defeat your enemies, join them" prevailed.

Projection is the opposite of introjection, in that one attributes or projects to somebody else impulses unacceptable within oneself. In other words, we ascribe to others those feelings that we ourselves have but find unacceptable. Projection is, in certain respects, similar to rationalization. The adolescent boy, for example, claims that none of his peers like him, when actually he likes neither himself nor others. This mechanism of defense serves a dual purpose: (1) we free ourselves of the unacceptable and frustrating feeling (relieve anxiety) and (2) we get rid of some of our tension and frustration by complaining about the nastiness of the individual to whom we have assigned our own unacceptable impulse, and we can pretend that we are the innocent party. A highly irritated adolescent girl, for example, angrily accuses her parents of being inconsiderate and ill-tempered. If asked what the parents did, she might respond, "They irritate me." Or to take another example, if we dislike someone, projection allows us to interpret everything that individual does as an expression of personal dislike for us.

Although almost all mechanisms of defense distort reality in one way or another, *denial* is the most primitive defense because it not only distorts the cognition of reality but denies the existence of some emotionally significant part of reality. We refuse to acknowledge that the source of our distress actually exists. In contrast to repression, denial focuses on external reality; however, it does seem to serve a function quite similar to repression. This defense is not common in very young children, since they have not learned to distinguish between fantasy and reality. It begins to appear in the anal stage and is very common in neurotics and psychotics. In its extreme form, denial means that an existing sector of reality is blotted out. An example is the rejected bride in one of Dickens's novels who kept the wedding table set and her wedding gown on for years after the groom left her waiting at the altar. Another is the boy who plans and talks of graduate school and of becoming a lawyer even though he barely receives passing grades in his academic high school subjects. Still another is the girl who has no boyfriends but sits anxiously near the telephone every Friday evening in the hope that "someone may want to invite me out tonight."

Because the process of denial is unconscious, the person is not lying. The most common form of denial is blocking a past event out of memory; we say "I don't remember," and we actually do not, but everybody else remembers quite well. Less serious use of denial seems to occur when we attempt to avoid unpleasant events in our real environment; we look away from an unpleasant or disgusting sight. We postpone the unpleasant job, day after day, for a tomorrow that never comes.

There is some debate as to whether *sublimation* ought to be considered a defense mechanism, since it is basically a constructive and adjustive process. On the other hand, sublimation is really a specific kind of displacement. In sublimation the libidinal instincts, rather than being displaced in neurotic behavior, are rechanneled into constructive and socially acceptable behavior. According to Freud, the libidinal impulse, even though it is transformed, is actually discharged. In the sense that the unacceptable impulse is discharged, sublimation differs from all other defense mechanisms where the energy is repressed or distorted. The common illustration is the creative artist who sublimates his anal impulse to smear feces all over by painting a beautiful picture on canvas. More to the point, Freud maintained that the gorgeous male and female nudes created by Renaissance painters were really the result of sublimated erotic impulses. Lincoln chopped wood to sublimate his anger. For Freud, the development of civilization was the result of sublimation of instinctual energies. Sublimation takes place if a socially acceptable and closely associated substitute object can be found for a libido force, so that partial satisfaction can take place. This process of seeking and finding a substitute activity is still an unconscious one (except when the football coach demands sexual abstinence from his players two weeks before the big game). Psychoanalytic treatment is intended to direct the patient toward sublimation. The final goal of psychoanalytic treatment is to have the patient accept his desires and wishes, sublimate them in a socially acceptable way, and find a normal way for sexual satisfaction.

Undoing takes the form of atonement, penance, repentance, apology, restitution, and being punished or punishing oneself. When an unacceptable impulse has broken through and manifested itself in actual behavior, through the process of undoing we attempt to counteract the undesirable acts or desires or thoughts and to reduce our anxieties.

Children are taught at an early age that when they engage in socially disapproved behavior they are punished, or they have to make up for it, since it is only through punishment or atonement that the misdeed can be negated and the individual can start over with a clean slate. If this cleansing process does not take place, the anxiety, guilt, and self-debasement will threaten the ego. Hence, the individual, in combination with projection and introjection, tends to "undo" what has been done, just as one erases a misspelled word to start over.

Freud provided an illustration of undoing. "His patient, while walking down a country road, kicks a stone onto the middle of the road. He then reflects that when his beloved's carriage comes down the road it will hit this stone, overturn, and kill her. To undo this potential murder, he now kicks the stone off the road. On reflecting further, he decides this is all very silly, and so he kicks the stone back to the center of the road. He repeats this sequence endlessly" (Corsini, 1977: 31).

The outcome of the use of defense mechanisms is a reduction in drive and anxiety. Defense mechanisms satisfy immediate needs and do reduce frustration, but often their benefit is short-lived. The damaging effects are evident in their long-range consequences and their negative impact on other people. Frequent use of defense mechanisms impedes learning, personal growth, and satisfactory interpersonal relationships in the individual using them, since most defense mechanisms tend to increase the social distance between the individual and others.

EDUCATIONAL IMPLICATIONS

Freud assumed that "frustration of normal sexual satisfaction may lead to the development of neurosis" (S. Freud, 1900/1953). Even at the risk of overgeneralizing, the psychoanalytic argument may be stated as follows: therefore, if parents do not want their child to be neurotic, they must not discipline the child. This statement implies that educators should avoid frustrating adolescents unnecessarily and question the prudish Victorian attitude toward sexuality prevalent at Freud's time. But since "sexuality" for Freud is defined rather broadly—that is, to include everything that relates to and grows out of a person's love life—one might go one step further and assume that parents and educators should keep frustrations to a minimum, especially those frustrations that block the satisfaction of basic human needs. What is needed instead is an atmosphere of leniency, love, affection, approval, and attention in which the child can grow up feeling secure, wanted, and loved.

A similar idea was expressed in Rousseau's natural romanticism and especially in his emphasis on "negative education." More recently psychoanalytic ideas have been influential in the creation of a variety of educational experiments, the best known of which is A. S. Neill's school, Summerhill. Summerhill attempts to remove all restrictions and frustrations from the educational process, including many of the common restrictions on children's sexual curiosity and exploratory sexual behavior. The school is designed to fit the child rather than to make the child fit the school, and Neill hopes that the result is to make Summerhill the happiest school in the world.

But even for the regular classroom teacher in a more conventional setting, some of Freud's ideas can be applied for the benefit of the pupil and the educational process. By applying psychoanalytic thought to classroom management, discipline becomes less authoritarian and therefore less frustrating. Even when the kind of freedom provided in Summerhill may be inappropriate, there can be a genuine concern with the underlying causes and dynamics of disturbing, disruptive, antisocial, acting-out behavior. Even for a teacher with only rudimentary understanding of psychoanalytic principles, misbehavior can no longer be viewed as arbitrary, as simple meanness or a personal affront, but rather it must be seen as a symptom of underlying conflicts and causes (Muuss, 1962). What an individual does or says is not meaningless but has a cause. Just as errors in conceptual development reflect lack of understanding, use of a false method, or incorrect reasoning, so errors in self-control or rudeness serve a psychological purpose. A basic assumption of psychoanalytic theory is that all behavior is meaningful. Dreams, neurotic behavior, even a slip of the tongue, and forgetting and losing things are motivated; if there is no conscious motive, there must be an unconscious one.

Education has been slow in providing a place for the "affective domain" in its structure and curriculum. However, much of the recent efforts to legitimize emotions in the educational process have their roots in the writings of Freud and are made explicit in the writings of some of his followers—Anna Freud (1948), Lawrence Kubie (1960), and Richard Jones (1960).

The child's fifth freedom is the right to know what he feels; but this does not carry with it any right to act out his feelings blindly. This will require a new mores for our schools, one which will enable young people from early years to understand and feel and put into words all the hidden things which go on inside of them . . . [Jones, 1969: vii–viii].

Psychoanalytic theory assumes that talking about and acting out dreams, fears, and aggressive or hostile feelings not only brings them out into the open but cleanses them and reduces their magnitude. In addition, openly sharing emotional problems in a classroom of peers leads to the realization that others have similar, if not the same, fears and feelings. "The freedom of one individual to express what another individual inhibits often results in freeing the latter" (Jones, 1960: 16). Adolescents in their concern about normality in regard to physical development, sexual needs, social sensitivities, and personal problems can benefit from the realization that their concerns and thoughts are not really too different from those of their peers.

The inhibition of sexual energies that most Western societies demand of their youths is the basis of Freud's concept of sublimation. Damming up libidinal energies "must swell the force of the perverse impulses, so that they become more powerful than they would have been had no hindrance to normal sexual satisfaction been present" (S. Freud, 1953: 319). It follows that early infantile sexual activities should not be repressed or pushed into the unconscious, unless normal sexual development be perverted. If libidinal energies are forced to regress to earlier stages of sexual development and denied any normal satisfaction, substitute satisfactions in the form of fetishism, sadism, masochism, narcissism, or other neurotic symptoms may manifest themselves. Yet psychoanalytic theory does not advocate uninhibited gratification of sexual impulses. Freud suggested redirecting sexual energy by means of sublimation. Most Western cultures oppose unrestricted sexual gratification in their young and assume that uninhibited sexuality would create new conflicts. Furthermore, since society's values are already represented in the adolescent's personality structure by means of the superego—which develops during the latency period—the sociosexual conflict is a psychological, internal one, a conflict of the conscience. Freud does not make a specific statement about adolescent sexual gratification. But since during this time the sexual drive and internal and external forces controlling the expression of sexuality are strong, sublimation can be a means of guiding these energies into productive activities, thus contributing constructively to the learning process.

In practicing sublimation an individual finds substitute forms of satisfaction and tension release for unsatisfied libidinal energies. It is assumed that nonsexual aims and socially useful activities absorb some of the sexual energy. Hence many educationally desirable activities may be stimulated by denying sexual gratification. For a long time football players and athletes have been advised prior to major sports events to abstain from sexual activity. Through sublimation "sources of sexuality are discharged and utilized in other spheres, so that a considerable increase of psychic capacity results" (S. Freud, 1925: 95). The connection between sexual energy and productivity in the fields that appeal more to emotion, such as music, art, poetry, and literature, is one of the assumptions of psychoanalytic theory. Freud himself went much further. He developed a theory of culture and civilization in which all human creations—from the learning of language to the composition of symphonies and scientific inventions—are due to sublimation. "Sexual impulses have contributed invaluably to the highest in cultural, artistic, and social achievements of the human mind" (S. Freud, 1953: 27). Since sexual urges appear to be strongest in the late adolescent period—if Kinsey's "outlets" are taken as an indication of the strength of sexual drive—and since internal and external restrictions are also strongest during this period, at least for middle-class American youth, sublimation appears to be one important educational objective in this period. If society can use sublimation to provide a harmonious balance between realistic denial of gratification and fulfillment of basic needs without repression and utilization of sexual energies and thus avoid the two extremes of maladjustment—neurosis and delinquent behavior—the productivity and creativity of the individual could be vastly increased. Sublimation remains a theoretical model, and Freud stated quite frankly that very little is actually known about the physiological and neurological process of sublimation.

Freud believed that applying psychoanalysis to education was most important. But he admitted quite openly that he had no "special understanding of it" (S. Freud, 1933/1964). He did credit his daughter, Anna, with making this aspect of psychoanalysis her life work and thus expanding his theories. Anna Freud's interest in child psychoanalysis and education is expressed in many of her publications, but it is especially clear in a lecture, "The Relation Between Psychoanalysis and Pedagogy" (A. Freud, 1931).

3: ERIKSON'S THEORY OF IDENTITY DEVELOPMENT

ERIKSON'S EIGHT STAGES OF DEVELOPMENT

Erik H. Erikson's (1902–   ) theory reflects in part his psychoanalytic training, but it embraces social aspects of development to a much larger extent than Freud's theory did. With little more than a German high school education, Erikson attended art schools and travelled in Italy, apparently in search of his own identity. (Erikson's later writings popularized the concept of "identity," a concept especially applicable to the period of adolescence.) As a young artist Erikson was offered a teaching position in a private school in Vienna that served the children of Sigmund and Anna Freud's patients. Peter Blos worked as a teacher in the same school, and the friendship of these two men stems from this time. During his tenure as a teacher Erik Erikson was invited to undergo psychoanalysis with Anna Freud, and in the process his interest changed from art and teaching to the study of psychoanalysis. He graduated from the Vienna Psychoanalytic Institute in 1933 as a lay analyst, since he held no medical or academic degrees. Later that year he moved to the United States and became associated with the Harvard Psychological Clinic.

Erikson has published extensively, his best-known and most widely read book being *Childhood and Society,* published in 1950 and revised in 1963. Of particular interest to our understanding of adolescence is his *Identity: Youth and Crisis* (1968). However, the idea of identity formation appears in other book titles, such as *Identity and the Life Cycle* (1959), and is the theme of much of Erikson's writing. Even when he examines historical figures, as in *Young Man Luther* (1958), *Gandhi's Truth* (1969), and Thomas Jefferson, he is concerned with the identity crisis of each of these men as well as with the respective national identity crises at the time of their most notable contributions. Revealing his basic philosophy, he says one cannot separate "the identity crisis in individual life and contemporary crisis in historical development because the two help to define each other and are truly relative to each other" (Erikson, 1968: 23). Erikson has written about his own identity crisis as well as the philosophical and psychoanalytic foundation of the concept in "Autobiographic Notes on the Identity Crisis" (1970).

In his chapter "Eight Stages of Man," Erikson (1950) modifies and expands the Freudian theory of psychosexual development. The modifications come from anthropological findings and a concern with social forces and thus shift from an emphasis on the sexual nature to a new theory of psychosocial development. The core concept in this theory is the acquisition of an ego-identity, and the identity crisis becomes the outstanding characteristic of adolescence. Although the specific quality of a person's identity differs from culture to culture, the accomplishment of this developmental task has a common element in all cultures. In order to acquire a strong and healthy ego-identity, the child must receive consistent and meaningful recognition of his achievements and accomplishments.

Humans develop according to the *epigenetic principle of development,* which is borrowed from embryology and states "that anything that grows has a ground plan, and that out of this ground plan the parts arise, each part having its time of special ascendancy, until all parts have risen to form a functional whole" (Erikson, 1968: 92).

In the epigenetic model (see Figure 4) the basic ground plan of increasing psychosocial differentiation is depicted. The diagonal axis, beginning with "Trust vs. Mistrust," shows the developmental sequence of the well-known eight stages of man. Movement upward along the diagonal axis represents development and shows the successive differentiation of the originally undifferentiated structure, and thus represents increasingly more mature levels of functioning. This diagram demonstrates:

1. That each item of the vital personality is systematically related to all others, and that they all depend on the proper development in the proper sequence of each item; and
2. That each item exists in some form before "its" decisive and critical time normally arrives [Erikson, 1968: 93, 95].

Each of the eight developmental stages is characterized by a conflict that has two opposing possible outcomes. This dual aspect of the social crisis gives each stage its name, rather than the body zones that give pleasure as in the original Freudian theory. If the conflict is worked out in a constructive, satisfactory manner, the positive quality becomes part of the ego and further healthy development is enhanced. However, if the conflict persists or is resolved unsatisfactorily, the negative quality is incorporated into the personality structure. In that case the negative quality will interfere with further development and may manifest itself in psychopathology.

	1	2	3	4	5	6	7	8
VIII								INTEGRITY vs. DESPAIR
VII							GENERATIVITY vs. STAGNATION	
VI						INTIMACY vs. ISOLATION		
V	Temporal Perspective vs. Time Confusion	Self-Certainty vs. Self-Consciousness	Role Experimentation vs. Role Fixation	Apprenticeship vs. Work Paralysis	IDENTITY vs. IDENTITY CONFUSION	Sexual Polarization vs. Bisexual Confusion	Leader- and Followership vs. Authority Confusion	Ideological Commitment vs. Confusion of Values
IV				INDUSTRY vs. INFERIORITY	Task Identification vs. Sense of Futility			
III			INITIATIVE vs. GUILT		Anticipation of Roles vs. Role Inhibition			
II		AUTONOMY vs. SHAME, DOUBT			Will to Be Oneself vs. Self-Doubt			
I	TRUST vs. MISTRUST				Mutual Recognition vs. Autistic Isolation			

FIGURE 4. Erikson's Epigenetic Diagram.

From *Identity: Youth and Crisis*, by Erik H. Erikson, by permission of W. W. Norton & Company, Inc. and Faber and Faber Ltd. Copyright © 1968 by W. W. Norton & Company, Inc.

Each crisis or conflict is never completely solved but appears to be most pronounced at the age at which it is placed. However, as in psychoanalytic theory, these stages occur in a sequential order. Ego-"identity is never 'established' as an 'achievement,' " as something static or unchangeable, but is a "forever to-be-revised sense of reality of the Self within social reality" (Erikson, 1968: 24, 211). Although the identity crisis is most pronounced during adolescence, a redefinition of one's ego-identity is not at all uncommon when the college freshman leaves home and has to learn to fend for himself. Any time a major role change takes place, such as one's first job, marriage, parenthood, divorce, unemployment, serious illness, widowhood, or retirement, identity issues reemerge. The ability to cope with identity issues that result from changes in one's role in life may well depend on the degree of success with which the adolescent identity crisis was mastered.

The vertical sequence in Figure 4, beginning with "Mutual Recognition vs. Autistic Isolation" and ascending until it coincides with "Identity vs. Identity Confusion" in the diagonal sequence, demonstrates how each of the four preceding stages contributes significantly to the development of an ego-identity or identity diffusion during adolescence. Thus "Mutual Recognition," "The Will to Be Oneself," "Anticipation of Roles," and "Task Identification" are secondary outcomes of the earlier stages of psychosocial development that are essential contributing factors to the achievement of a positive identity in adolescence. On the other hand, failure in the earlier stages resulting in "Autistic Isolation," "Self-Doubt," "Role Inhibition," and a "Sense of Futility" may contribute to a personal estrangement or identity confusion in adolescence.

The horizontal sequence in Figure 4 beginning with "Temporal Perspective vs. Time Confusion" depicts the derivatives of earlier relative achievements that now become part and parcel of the struggle for identity. "It is necessary to emphasize [that] the early relative achievements [diagonal] must be . . . renamed in terms of that later stage. Basic Trust, for example, is a good and a most fundamental thing to have, but its psychosocial quality becomes more differentiated as the ego comes into the possession of a more extensive apparatus, even as society challenges and guides such extension" (Erikson, 1959: 140–141).

The symptoms of confusion that make up the negative alternative on the horizontal sequence represent the earlier failures to progress normally and to resolve conflicts; they become therefore part of the identity confusion issue. The experience of time confusion during adolescence, for example, arises out of the undifferentiated mistrust that may have occurred much earlier. Time confusion may develop into an attitude of not trusting time, of interpreting an unnecessary delay, lateness, or forgetfulness related to a meeting-time as deceit.

THE RELATIONSHIP OF ERIKSON'S "STAGES OF MAN" TO THE ADOLESCENT IDENTITY CRISIS

TRUST VERSUS MISTRUST

During infancy—Erikson's first stage in the human life cycle—the major developmental crisis is between becoming a trusting or a mistrusting person. The development of trust includes becoming trustful of others and developing a feeling of one's own trustworthiness. The necessary healthy experience for the development of trust is maternal love and care. Initially, the infant "lives through, and loves with, his mouth" (Erikson, 1968: 97). Being fed regularly does contribute to trust. However, the infant is receptive to maternal love in many ways besides orality. Children learn to trust because mother does come and take care of them regularly. They thus experience living in a predictable, secure world in which basic needs are being satisfied. Later, as motor skills develop and they are given freedom to explore their environment, they also learn to trust themselves and their own body, especially as they begin to control body movements such as grasping, holding, and reaching and later crawling, standing, and walking.

The mistrust of time and the *time confusion* that Erikson sees as "more or less typical for all adolescents at one stage or another" (Erikson, 1968: 182) grow out of unhealthy experiences at this early stage and are related to the regularity of the cycle in which the infant's basic needs are satisfied. Repeated delay or irregularity in essential body satisfactions results in mistrust of time.

The conviction that emerges from this receptive state is "I am what I am given," and it is an incorporative stage. The healthy, positive outcome is the ability to trust others and to trust oneself. Later in the life cycle the capacity to experience faith is a result of the positive experiences at this early stage. The trusting infant has developed the first requisite for later developing confidence, optimism, and finally a feeling of security. The trusting infant recognizes people and smiles at them. *Mutual recognition* and mutual trustworthiness are the earliest and most undifferentiated experiences of what is later to become a sense of identity.

The negative outcome is mistrust of others and mistrust of oneself. Lack of trust in infancy may contribute to the identity confusion in adolescence. Absence of experiences leading to the development of trust in early childhood may impair the "capacity to feel identical" with others during adolescence (Erikson, 1968: 105). *Autistic isolation* in infancy is the earliest contribution to identity diffusion in adolescence (see Figure 4).

AUTONOMY VERSUS SHAME AND DOUBT

The issue at the second stage of life is between becoming an *autonomous*, creative individual and a dependent, inhibited, and *shameful individual* filled with *self-doubt*. The stage falls approximately between the ages of eighteen months and three and one-half years. During this stage children—although still dependent on others in many ways—begin to experience an autonomy of free choice. They now develop motor ability and the intellectual capacity to experience themselves as entities in their own right. They realize that they are different from father and mother. This newly gained sense of autonomy is often used in an exaggerated fashion, which leads to conflicts. The battle for autonomy may show in stubborn refusal, temper tantrums, and the "yes–no" syndrome. An important task is the beginning mastery of self-control; particularly important in this process is the control of body waste products. Toilet training means "holding on and letting go" when the child wishes, representing highly autonomous activities over which nobody has direct control. The child can—and at times does—retain body wastes even though his mother may want him to let go. On the other hand, he can release them even though his mother wishes him to hold back. However, with proper training the child can develop a feeling of mastery for a job well done and a sense of autonomy of choice in a general sense as well as in regard to toilet training.

The conviction that emerges during this stage is "I am what I will be," reflecting the child's new sense of autonomy. The positive attributes that can be gained during this stage are pride, control, self-assurance, autonomy, *self-certainty,* and the *will to be oneself.* The development of a rudimentary form of the *will to be oneself* during the autonomy stage is an essential prerequisite for the development of a mature ego-identity during adolescence. "There are clinical reasons to believe that the adolescent turning away from the whole childhood milieu in many ways repeats this first emancipation" (Erikson, 1968: 114). The autonomy attributes gained during this period contribute to the formation of an identity in adolescence, leading to the conviction: "I am an independent person who can choose freely and who can guide my own development and my own future."

The negative outcome is *shame, self-doubt,* dependency, *self-consciousness,* and meek compliance resulting from too many restrictions, unfair punishment, and the parents' inability to cope with the budding *autonomy* of their young child. The identity crisis of adolescence revives and grows out of an unresolved autonomy issue. Since autonomy is one of the essential ingredients for the development of identity, the battle for autonomy becomes once more an important issue in the adolescent's struggle for independence from the family and in early attempts at self-determination. This involves two problems. Adolescents may become so self-conscious and lacking in autonomy that they are afraid of being seen in an exposed and vulnerable situation. They may question their self-worth and the reliability of the whole experience of their childhood and therefore be unable to achieve an identity. On the other hand, entering adolescence with too much autonomy may contribute to brash and shameless defiance of parents, teachers, and other authorities.

INITIATIVE VERSUS GUILT

The psychosocial conflict in the third stage of life is the development of a sense of *initiative versus a sense of guilt*. A conflict exists between an aggressive intrusion into the world by way of activity, curiosity, and exploration or an immobilization by fear and guilt. The child from about three and one-half to six years of age normally shows a great deal of exuberance, a feeling of power, curiosity, a high level of activity, and surplus energy. In play activities the child moves around much more freely and more aggressively and develops an increasingly larger radius of operations. This is also the stage when language develops rapidly. The child expresses his emerging intellectual initiative by endless questions. Beginning early in this stage he starts with an endless number of "what" questions that later lead to long sequences of "why" questions. These questions are basically learning tools, since new words, concepts, and ideas are acquired in this fashion. In addition, one can observe aggressive manipulation of toys. The child takes things apart to see what is inside, not because of destructive tendencies but out of curiosity. However, if this curiosity is interpreted as destructiveness, the child is made to feel guilty, and as a result initiative may wane. Children will also explore and manipulate their own bodies as well as those of friends, and this exploration does involve curiosity about the sex organs. Social criticism and punishment may foster the development of guilt feelings in regard to sex. The aggressive behavior, including exploration of the bodies of other people, is accompanied by a rudimentary form of cooperation with others in play activities.

The conviction that emerges from this intrusive mode is "I am what I can imagine I will be." The intrusive mode is characterized by a variety of thoughts, fantasies, and behaviors: "(1) the intrusion into space by vigorous locomotion, (2) the intrusion into the unknown by consuming curiosity, (3) the intrusion into other people's ears and minds by the aggressive voice, (4) the intrusion upon or into other bodies by physical attacks, and (5) often most frighteningly, the thought of the phallus intruding the female body" (Erikson, 1968: 116).

If the crisis of this stage is mastered successfully, a sense of initiative emerges that will later in adolescence become the basis for curiosity, ambition, and *experimentation with different roles* just as the child's play activities often reflect an *anticipation of different roles*. The sexual self-image and the differentiation between masculine (making) and feminine (catching) initiative become important prerequisites for the sexual identity crisis during adolescence. The ability to take the initiative contributes to the development of an identity in adolescence since it fosters the anticipation of what one might become and of one's future role in life by "freeing the child's initiative and sense of purpose for adult tasks which promise a fulfillment of one's range of capacities" (Erikson, 1968: 122).

A negative outcome is likely if parents restrain, resist, and punish the newly developing initiative too much, for example, by making the child feel guilty for taking toys apart or exploring his own body. If the child's exploration and initiative encounter severe reprimand and punishment, the result may be a more permanent immobilization by guilt, inhibition by fear, *role inhibition, role fixation,* and too much dependence on adults. Since these attributes interfere with identity formation during adolescence, a negative outcome at this stage would contribute to the development of identity diffusion in adolescence (see Figure 4).

INDUSTRY VERSUS INFERIORITY

The task at the fourth stage is the development of a *sense of industry versus the emergence of feelings of inferiority*. Freud's idea of the Oedipus complex followed by a period of sexual latency is adopted by Erikson. Unable to marry his mother, the boy must learn to become a potential provider, so that he eventually will become a husband who has his own sexual partner. Therefore, this period between school entry and puberty becomes a period of learning and mastering the more basic skills needed in society. Children now acquire much fundamental knowledge and, even more important, they learn to take pride in their work and acquire an attitude to do well in their work. This period is therefore described as *the apprenticeship* of life. In all known cultural groups children receive during this stage some kind of formal training, although not necessarily the kind of schooling provided in Western societies. The child must learn to win approval, recognition, and a feeling of success by producing things and doing his job well. An important aspect of industry is the "positive identification with those who know things and know how to do things" (Erikson, 1968: 125). The free play of the earlier period now becomes subordinated to rules and regulations and more structured activities. The child must learn to follow and respect rules and become committed to the ideas of cooperation in team effort and fair play. Through team activities, games, and cooperative play, the child learns to anticipate the behavior, roles, and feelings of others. This idea of role-taking receives greater emphasis in the social cognition theory of Selman (see Chapter 11).

The conviction that emerges during this apprenticeship is: "I am what

I will learn" or even more production oriented: "I am what I can learn to make work." If the *sense of industry* is established successfully, the child will need and want accomplishments and strive for completion of tasks and for recognition for work well done. He will develop a sense of duty, a feeling for workmanship and work participation, and an attitude of wanting to do well that is based on industriousness and a desire for success. The contribution that this stage makes to identity formation is "the capacity to *learn* how to be, with skill, what one is in the process of becoming" (Erikson, 1968: 180)—that is, an *identification of the task* ahead and a willingness to learn and master it (see Figure 4).

If the child fails in the task to acquire a feeling of success and a desire for recognition for work well done, there will be a lack of industriousness and a feeling of uselessness. Such children may not develop the feeling of enjoyment and pride for good work. On the contrary, they may be plagued by feelings of inadequacy and inferiority and may become convinced that they will never amount to much. As a result there is *work paralysis* and a *sense of futility* that is most likely to contribute to ego diffusion in the next stage.

IDENTITY VERSUS IDENTITY CONFUSION

Adolescence has been characterized by Erikson (1950) as the period in the human life cycle during which the individual must establish a *sense of personal identity* and avoid the dangers of *role diffusion* and *identity confusion.* Identity achievement implies that the individual assesses his strengths and weaknesses and determines how he wants to deal with them. He must answer for himself where he came from, who he is, and what he wants to become. Identity, or a sense of sameness and continuity, must be searched for. Identity is not readily given to the individual by society, nor does it appear as a maturational phenomenon when the time has come, as do the secondary sex characteristics. Identity must be acquired through sustained individual effort. Unwillingness to work actively on one's identity formation carries with it the danger of role diffusion, which may result in alienation and a sense of isolation and confusion.

The search for an identity involves the establishment of a meaningful self-concept in which past, present, and future are brought together to form a unified whole. Consequently, the task is more difficult in a historical period in which the anchorage of family and community tradition has been lost. Hence, the present is characterized by social change, and the future has become much less predictable. In a period of rapid social change the older generation is no longer able to provide adequate role models for the younger generation. Mead (see Chapter 6) describes in detail the changing relationship of adolescents to parents as social change moves from post- to co- and prefigurative cultures. Keniston (1965) has even suggested that in a rapidly changing society, the search for an identity is replacing the socialization process, since the latter implies that there actually exist stable, socially defined roles into which the adolescent can be guided. Since the older generation no longer provides effective role models to the adolescent who is in the process of searching for a personal identity— or if they do provide them, the adolescent may reject them as personally inappropriate—the importance of the peer group in helping the individual answer the identity question "Who am I?" cannot be emphasized enough. The answer that will be found for this question depends on social feedback from others giving their perception and evaluation of the individual. Therefore, adolescents "are sometimes morbidly, often curiously, preoccupied with what they appear to be in the eyes of others as compared with what they feel they are and with the question of how to connect to earlier cultivated roles and skills with the ideal prototypes of the day" (Erikson, 1959: 89). Adolescents' preoccupation with the thinking of others is the basis of Elkind's theory of egocentrism (see Chapter 12).

Since an identity can best be found in interaction with significant other people, the adolescent may go through a period of almost compulsive peer group involvement. Conforming to the expectations of peers helps adolescents find out how certain roles fit them. The peer group, the clique, and the gang, even the lover, aid the individual in the search for a personal identity, since they provide both a role model and specific social feedback. The bull session and the seemingly endless telephone conversations, for example, serve a genuine psychological purpose by providing this kind of feedback. As long as the adolescent depends on role models and feedback, the in-group feeling that the peer group provides will remain quite strong. The ensuing clannishness and intolerance of "differences"—including petty aspects of language, gesture, hair style, and dress—are explained by Erikson as the "necessary defenses" against the dangers of self-diffusion that remain prevalent as long as the identity has not yet been achieved. Particularly during the time when the body image changes so rapidly, when genital maturation stimulates sexual fantasies, and when intimacy with the opposite sex appears as a possibility with simultaneously positive and negative valences, the adolescent relies on peers for comfort and companionship and as a sounding board. Eventually adolescents must free themselves from this new dependency on peers—which has just replaced their dependency on parents—in order to become themselves—that is, to attain a mature identity. Such an identity, once it has been found, gives the young adult "a sense of 'knowing where one is going,' and an inner assuredness of anticipated recognition from those who count" (Erikson, 1959: 118).

Pubescence, according to Erikson, is characterized by the rapidity of body growth, genital maturity, and sexual awareness. Because these changes are qualitatively quite different from those experienced during childhood, an element of discontinuity from previous development may be experienced during early adolescence. Youth is not only confronted with an internal "physiological revolution" that interferes with the establishment of a reliable body image but also with a "psychological crisis" that revolves around the issue of identity formation. Erikson maintains that the study of identity has become more important than was the study of sexuality in Freud's time. Particularly for the adolescent, identity—the establishment and reestablishment of sameness with one's previous experiences and a conscious attempt to make the future a part of one's personal life plan—seems to become subordinated to sexuality. Adolescents must establish ego-identity and learn to accept body changes and the new libidinal feelings as being part of themselves. The identity crisis depends at least in part on these psychophysiological factors. If ego-identity is not satisfactorily established during adolescence, there is the danger that role diffusion will endanger further ego development. "Where this is based on a strong doubt as to one's sexual identity, delinquent and outright psychotic incidents are not uncommon" (Erikson, 1950: 228).

Falling in love, a common occurrence at this age, is seen by Erikson not so much as a means of satisfying sexual needs, as it will be at a later age, but as an attempt to project and test one's own diffused and still undifferentiated ego through the eyes of the beloved person. The various love affairs through which adolescents pass contribute to the development of an identity; the feedback received in the love relationship aids the individuals in defining and revising their own self-definition and encourages them to clarify and to reflect on their own self-concept and their own definition of their ego. Thus, the numerous crushes and infatuations, not at all uncommon at the high school and even the college level, serve a genuine developmental purpose. "This is why many a youth would rather converse, and settle matters of mutual identification, than embrace" (Erikson, 1950: 228).

Of great concern for many adolescents is the issue of developing a vocational identity, and during the initial attempts some role diffusion is not uncommon. The problem—widely identified through empirical investigations—is that adolescents at this stage hold highly glamorized, idealized, and sometimes unrealistic conceptions of the vocational roles they dream about. Furthermore, goal aspirations are often much higher than the individual's perseverance and ability warrant. Frequently, the adolescent chooses vocational goals that are attainable by only a very few—models, actors, actresses, rock musicians, athletic champions, car racers, astronauts, and other glamorized "heroes." In the process the adolescents overidentify with and idolize their models and heroes to the extent that they yield their own identity and imitate the heroes. At this point youths rarely identify with their parents; on the contrary, they often rebel against parental dominance, value systems, and intrusions into their private life.

This is a necessary part of growing up, since they must separate their own identity from that of the family and develop autonomy in order to attain maturity.

The adolescent's search for a personal identity also includes the formation of a personal ideology or a philosophy of life that will give the individual a frame of reference for evaluating events. Such a perspective aids in making choices and guides behavior, and in this sense a personal identity based on a philosophy of life may greatly influence the individual. In a society such as ours, where many different ideologies compete for followers and new ideologies emerge constantly, the formation of a personal ideology that has both consistency and conviction is made increasingly difficult. While it is easy to adopt a ready-made existing ideology, such a philosophy is often less flexible and less effective than a personally developed one. The adopted ideology rarely becomes truly integrated into the personality and can, therefore, lead to foreclosure in identity development.

A positive outcome of the identity crisis depends on the young person's willingness to accept his own past and establish continuity with previous experiences. To complete the search for an identity the adolescent must find an answer to the question "Who am I?" He must also establish some orientation toward the future and come to terms with the questions "Where am I going?" and "Who am I to become?" The adolescent must develop a commitment to a system of values—religious beliefs, vocational goals, a philosophy of life—and accept his sexuality. Only through the development of these aspects of ego-identity can intimacy of sexual and affectionate love, deep friendship, and personal self-abandon without fear of loss of ego-identity take place and thus make possible the developmental advance to the next stage in the human life cycle: *intimacy vs. isolation*. The intimacy stage has been investigated in greater detail by Orlofsky (1978) and Orlofsky, Marcia, and Lesser (1973).

The adolescent who fails in the search for an identity will experience self-doubt, role diffusion, and role confusion; such an individual may indulge in self-destructive one-sided preoccupation or activity. He will continue to be morbidly preoccupied with the opinion of others or may turn to the other extreme of no longer caring what others think and withdraw or turn to drugs or alcohol in order to relieve the anxiety that role diffusion creates. Ego diffusion and personality confusion, when they become permanent, can be observed in the chronic delinquent and in psychotic personality disorganization. In its more severe form the clinical picture of identity diffusion may lead to suicide or suicide attempts. "Many a late adolescent, if faced with continuing diffusion, would rather be nobody or somebody bad, or indeed, dead . . . than be not-quite somebody" (Erikson, 1959: 132). The increase of suicide attempts among adolescents in the last decade is well documented and parallels the increase in identity diffusion.

INTIMACY VERSUS ISOLATION

Once a personal identity has been achieved, the need for personal intimacy moves into the foreground of the psychosocial development of the young adult. The conflict at the next higher level of development is between finding *intimacy or isolation* in interpersonal relationships. At this stage peer group conformity has lost much of its earlier importance. The peer group may aid in finding an identity and may even be helpful in making contacts with the opposite sex. Intimacy involves establishing emotional closeness to other people as a basis for enduring relationships. Physical closeness and sexual and affectional intimacy are only part of the issue. A basic theoretical insight emerges from the sequential order of Erikson's stages: the prerequisite for genuine and lasting intimacy is the achievement of an ego-identity, since intimacy implies the fusion of the identities of two people. It follows that ego-identity must be established before the possibility of marriage can be realistically considered. One must first find an answer to the question "Who am I?" before one can find a partner to match to this "I." As long as the "I" remains undefined or is still forming, the selection of a partner appears futile. "The giving of oneself to another, which is the mark of true intimacy, cannot occur until one has a self to give" (Constantinople, 1969: 359). If marriage is begun before one or both partners have established an identity, the chances for a happy, lasting marriage are low. This may explain why the divorce rate of teen-age marriages is much higher than for the population in general.

The conviction that emerges during the intimacy stage is: "We are what we love." The plural pronoun "we" rather than the singular "I" is a significant reflection of the mutuality of the relationship. The positive outcome of this stage in the human life cycle is intimacy, including sexual intimacy, genuine friendship, stable love, and lasting marriage. The negative outcome is isolation and loneliness, and if intimacy is not based on a permanent identity, divorce and separation may result. The young adult who still has basic uncertainties in his identity will shy away from interpersonal relationships or may seek promiscuity without intimacy, sex without love, or relationships without emotional stability. As a counterpoint to intimacy, detachment and distancing in interpersonal relationships may emerge—that is, "the readiness to repudiate, isolate, and, if necessary, destroy those forces and people whose essence seems dangerous to one's own" (Erikson, 1968: 136).

GENERATIVITY VERSUS STAGNATION

The developmental issue of adulthood is the achievement of *generativity;* the negative possibility is *stagnation.* This stage encompasses the productive years of the human life cycle, and generativity is the driving force in human behavior. Generativity is a productive creativity in terms of vocational and professional contributions to society. Marriage, giving birth to children, and guiding the growth of children are creative, productive activities. The successful resolution of the conflict implies that the mature person wants to be useful and productive, wants to be needed. The conviction that emerges is "I am what I create," or "I am what I can produce." The giving of oneself to another person, an ideal, or to one's work leads to an expansion of ego interests. If failure should occur at this stage, there would be no further development, and stagnation would be the outcome. Stagnation implies a routine repetition in vocational activities and social stagnation. The individual becomes egotistical, self-absorbed, and self-indulgent and in turn expects to be indulged. Stagnation means that "individuals begin to indulge themselves as if they were their own one and only child" (Erikson, 1968: 138).

INTEGRITY VERSUS DESPAIR

The last stage of the human life cycle encompasses old age and retirement from the productive years of life. The developmental task of this stage is between the achievement of *ego integrity versus disgust and despair*. The conflict here is between combining, integrating, and appreciating one's life experiences or becoming bitter, resentful, and negative. The successful resolution of the seven preceding stages culminates in *integrity*. The conviction that emerges is: "I am what survives of me." The positive outcome at this last stage in life is an acceptance of one's self and one's life without bitterness and regret and coming to terms with the approaching finality of life. Ideally, there is independence, autonomy, and maturity, rather than a regression to childlike dependency. Ego integrity is based on self-discipline and the wisdom that can give old age its positive quality.

The negative outcome, on the other hand, is a feeling that one's life was wasted—a basic discontentment with one's life, one's self, and others. There is fear of death and a regression to childhood dependency that characterizes the disintegration of old age, resulting in disgust and despair.

JAMES MARCIA'S EXPANSION OF ERIKSON'S CONCEPT "IDENTITY VERSUS ROLE DIFFUSION"

James Marcia's dissertation "Determination and Construct Validity of Ego Identity Status" and his subsequent research efforts (Marcia, 1966; 1967; 1968; 1976a; 1976b; 1980; Marcia and Friedman, 1970) constitute an interesting expansion and elaboration of Erikson's theoretical construct *identity vs. identity confusion*. Marcia identifies various patterns and common issues operating in youths who are coping with the adolescent identity issues. In addition, Marcia's conceptualizations have stimulated others to pursue identity status research relying heavily on Marcia's interview assessment technique. Especially noteworthy are, among others, the investigations by Andrews, Bob, Bunt, Cross, Donovan, Meilman, Schenkel, Toder, A. S. Waterman, and C. K. Waterman (see References).

According to Marcia, the criteria for attainment of a mature identity are based on two essential variables that had already been identified by Erikson: crisis and commitment. "Crisis refers to times during adolescence when the individual seems to be actively involved in choosing among alternative occupations and beliefs. Commitment refers to the degree of personal investment the individual expresses in an occupation or belief" (Marcia, 1967: 119).

In applying Marcia's criteria of the absence or the presence of crisis and also commitment to Erikson's developmental stage *identity versus role diffusion*, four identity statuses emerge. They provide the conceptual structure for Marcia's taxonomy of adolescence.

1. The *identity-diffused* or *identity-confused subject* has not yet experienced an identity crisis nor made any commitment to a vocation or a set of beliefs.
2. The *foreclosure subject* has not yet experienced an identity crisis but has made commitments. However, these commitments are not the result of personal searching and exploring; rather, they are handed, ready-made, to the individual by others, frequently parents. These superimposed commitments are accepted without the individual's raising of fundamental and searching questions about them.
3. The *moratorium subject* is in an acute state of crisis; he is exploring and actively searching for values to eventually call his own. In other words, this individual is actively struggling to find his identity but has not yet made a commitment or has only developed very temporary kinds of commitments.
4. The *identity-achieved subject* has experienced personal crises but has resolved them on his own terms. As a result of the resolution of these crises the individual has made a personal commitment to an occupation, a religious belief, and a personal value system and has resolved his attitude toward sexuality.

These four identity statuses may be perceived as a developmental sequence, but no one is necessarily and inevitably the prerequisite for the others, as is the case in Erikson's "Eight Stages of Man." Only the moratorium appears to be an essential and inevitable prerequisite for the achievement of an identity, since a true identity cannot be achieved without the kind of searching and exploring that is the defining characteristic of the moratorium. Any one of these identity statuses could become terminal, but the foreclosure subject is of course in greater danger of this than the moratorium subject. If the identity-diffused status becomes terminal, the probability of psychopathology or delinquency is especially great.

An individual in the process of moving to a higher status may well exhibit some of the characteristics of two or even three statuses at the same time. For example, a young man may already have developed a clear commitment to a vocation based on personal choices while still actively searching for a personal value system and remaining committed to a puritanical attitude toward sex indoctrinated by his parents. Marcia found that as students moved through the four years of undergraduate college experiences, the proportion of identity-diffused subjects declined significantly while the proportion of identity-achieved subjects increased steadily. This movement toward more mature identity statuses was not a function of college selectivity but of increased psychosocial maturity. Constantinople reports a "consistent increase in successful resolution identity, both from the freshman year to senior year across subjects and from one year to the next within subjects" (Constantinople, 1969: 367). In a more recent study, Meilman (1979) investigated the age changes in identity status and found, in accordance with Erikson's and Marcia's theoretical assumptions, that twelve-year-olds were identity-diffused (68 percent) or foreclosed (32 percent). Several studies have clearly demonstrated that with increasing age, adolescents steadily but slowly shifted toward a more mature identity status. Marcia (1980) believes that late adolescence (eighteen to twenty-one years) is the crucial period for identity formation. According to Meilman, by the age of twenty-four, the majority (56 percent) had achieved an identity, but the other statuses were still represented: moratorium, 12 percent; foreclosure, 8 percent; and identity-diffused, a surprisingly high 24 percent (Meilman, 1979).

In Marcia's research (1966; 1967; 1970; 1976a; 1976b) the individual's identity status is determined by means of an individual semistructured interview designed to assess the subjects' commitment to a vocation, a personal value system, and religious beliefs, the extent to which the subjects actually experienced a personal crisis in regard to any of these, and their attitude toward sexuality.

IDENTITY DIFFUSION

The identity-diffused individual has no apparent personal commitment to occupation, religion, or politics and has not yet developed a consistent set of personal standards for sexual behavior. He has not experienced an identity crisis in respect to these issues nor gone through an active struggle in terms of reevaluating, searching, and considering alternatives. Erikson (1968) maintains that identity diffusion is not a diagnosis of a psychological problem but a description of a normal developmental process—which, if it persists and only if it persists into late adolescence and adulthood, could become a diagnostic classification. Consequently, identity diffusion can encompass a variety of different behavior or personality patterns. This appears to be one reason why some of the research findings concerned with identity-diffused subjects are not always entirely consistent.

First, identity diffusion may exist due to a precrisis lack of commitment—not at all uncommon when entering early adolescence. Apparently, it is a kind of psychological chaos typically experienced by early adolescents, as the data by Meilman, cited above, clearly demonstrate. Thus, some degree of identity diffusion should be considered a normal characteristic of early adolescence. Second, there is also the narcissistic type of identity diffusion. These youths live and let live and in their selfish approach "use" others for their own pleasure and try to get for themselves whatever they can get away with. Apparently suffering from an unresolved ego crisis of Erikson's first stage, *trust versus mistrust,* and not being able to trust people, they use them. Third, identity-diffused subjects avoid anxiety, crisis, and confrontation by means of drugs or alcohol or by otherwise denying that crises exist. Finally, prolonged stagnation in the identity diffusion stage without further development may lead to personality disintegration, thus becoming a diagnosis of psychopathology that may lead to schizophrenia or suicide.

Identity-diffused subjects are in a state of psychological fluidity, still uncommitted to a personal value structure; consequently, they are open to all kinds of influences, and when opportunities arise they may take advantage of them, often without design or purpose. Such individuals may take a smorgasbord approach to ideological systems and be most influenced by and overly receptive toward whatever politician or minister was last heard. The diffused college student can become quite vehement in his demands on the college professor to tell him which of the various theories is best, which is right, or which one he is to believe in. Erikson (1965) maintains in *The Challenge of Youth* that the high rate of recidivism among young offenders can be explained by the fact that during identity formation, especially identity diffusion, these youth were forced by society into intimate contact with criminals.

 On Kuhn's (1954) Twenty Statement Test (TST) the identity-diffused subject may reveal confusion in answers to the question, "Who am I?" Some such answers might be "I am a nobody," "I don't know who I am," "I wish I weren't me," "I wish I knew who I am," "I am confused," "I am mixed up," "I am not me," "I am unsure of what I am," "I am dead," "I wish I were dead," "I am intelligent"/"I am stupid," "I am a child of God"/"I am a child of the devil." Identity in these responses is defined negatively by the lack of something, the reversal of an identity, the denial of an identity, death, and contradictory statements revealing confusion.

The classical example of identity diffusion in literature is Shakespeare's Hamlet. He is confused about his sex role: "Man delights me not, no, nor woman either." He is also estranged from love and procreation, as when he says: "I say we will have no more marriage." And finally he appears alienated from the ways of his country ". . . though I am native here, and to the manner born . . ." (Erikson, 1965: 6). In Arthur Miller's *Death of a Salesman,* Biff admits his identity diffusion quite succinctly: "I just can't take hold, Mom, I can't take hold of some kind of life."

Marcia's subjects were independently classified as to their identity status. In addition, personality tests were administered. Identity-diffused male subjects showed little resistance to self-esteem manipulation—that is, they quite readily changed their own opinions about themselves. They were vulnerable to evaluative feedback about themselves, since they did not have a firmly established identity. Gruen (1960), too, found that ego-diffused subjects were more willing to accept incorrect personality sketches about themselves than subjects who had achieved an identity. Marcia's subjects scored low on a stressful concept attainment task. They had lower self-esteem and experienced more difficulty than the other identity statuses in interpersonal relationships. Marcia and Friedman's (1970) identity-diffused female subjects were enrolled in the easiest college majors as compared to the other three identity statuses, even though they were no less intelligent. Females, too, obtained low self-esteem scores but high anxiety and authoritarianism scores. Block (1961) found a direct relationship between role variability and the individual's identity status. That is, subjects lacking a clear personal identity behaved quite differently in interaction with people having different roles, such as parent, lover, friend, coworker, boss, or acquaintance. Identity-achieved subjects, in contrast, revealed more internal consistency in their interpersonal behavior. Bronson (1959), contrasting those who have achieved an identity with those who have not, characterized identity-diffused subjects as:

1. Less certain about the relationship between the past and the present as it pertains to themselves and their self-concept. Their self-concept is not yet firmly rooted in earlier identifications.
2. Showing a high degree of internal tensions and anxieties.
3. Less certain about their own personality traits and showing considerable variability over a short period of time as to their own feelings about themselves. They have no clear definition of who they are and cannot estimate their own personality traits effectively.

FORECLOSURE

Foreclosure subjects are committed to goals and values, an occupation, and a personal ideology. Consequently, in everyday life they superficially may appear very much like identity-achieved subjects, with whom they actually have some characteristics in common. However, foreclosure subjects differ from identity-achieved subjects in that they have not experienced a psychological crisis or seriously considered other values and other alternatives as being applicable to themselves. The goals they aim for and the values they hold were determined by others—parents, religion, or peers. The foreclosure subjects frequently tend to become their parents' alter egos. When a young man is asked what he wants to become, he may answer, "I want to be a dentist," and when asked why he may respond, "Because my father is a dentist." And even further probing would not change the essence of the first response. No personal reason is given; no personal searching seems to have taken place. In talking to foreclosure subjects, it becomes difficult to distinguish between their own goals and those that parents have planned and emphasized for them. Foreclosure subjects were "socialized" by their parents in the sense that parents determined what they were to become. College serves mainly to reconfirm the childhood value system and provide an opportunity to attain the parents' goals rather than as a process by which to explore vocational options. The danger is that foreclosed subjects may become so solidified in their position and so authoritarian in their attitudes that the foreclosure status becomes terminal, and the subjects do not reach the status of identity achievement. There appears to be a certain rigidity in personality structure. If these subjects are not sufficiently challenged or guided to question their preprogrammed assumptions and values, foreclosure may become a permanent part of their personality structure.

On Kuhn's Twenty Statement Test (TST), foreclosure subjects seem to define their own identity in terms of relationships to other people or to see themselves as extensions of other people. The following responses of three college students from the author's files suggest foreclosure: "I am a daughter, a sister, an aunt, a sister-in-law, a niece"; "I am a girl, a daughter, my father's little girl"; "I am my mother's daughter, my father's daughter, my sister's sister, my brother's sister, my boyfriend's girl friend, my girl friend's friend, my next door neighbor's neighbor, my aunt's niece, my cousin's cousin."

Responses from Marcia's (1968) interview protocol may serve to illustrate the commitment of foreclosure subjects to parental values. One adolescent comments on his political affiliation with a Republican ideology quite similar to that of his parents: "You still pull that way, Republican, if your parents are that way. You feel like it is where you should be." Another foreclosed subject who holds the same religious beliefs as his parents states: "Maybe it's just a habit with me, I don't know. I have thought a lot and you meet all kinds of people here, but I really haven't changed any of my beliefs. . . . I plan to bring up my children in the church, just the way dad did with me" (Marcia, 1968: 329). Keniston seems to be referring to the foreclosure phenomenon when he writes that "total lack of conflict during adolescence is an ominous sign that the individual's psychological maturity may not be progressing" (Keniston, 1971: 364). Kubie and other psychiatrists have observed that an unusually smooth and conflict-free adolescence is often followed by mental breakdown or serious emotional problems in middle adulthood.

The foreclosure status is most frequently viewed as being shaped through the dominant influence of the subjects' parents. However, the dynamics do not necessarily involve the parents; they could be applied to other influential forces—such as the individual's peer group. For a certain developmental period, young adolescents may lose themselves and may lose their budding identity to the peer group. In this situation, foreclosure occurs because the individuals' identity submerges too readily and without questioning into the role prescribed for them by others. As a result they define themselves primarily by their group membership, and they act, dress, select food and entertainment, and use language and slang predominantly in the light of peer-group standards, expectations, and pressures. At the same time intolerance and even cruelty toward those who behave differently are not uncommon, especially in the junior high school years.

The youth group movement of totalitarian systems, such as the Hitler Youth in Nazi Germany, provides such group identity with uniforms, flags, rituals, beliefs, and even heroes as models. A similar vicarious identity is provided by belonging to a gang, a hippie subculture, and other less formal subcultural youth groups. Many junior high school students conform rather unquestioningly to the dress and behavior standards of their peer group in order to be accepted, to benefit from the feeling of group solidarity, and to boost their sense of identity through identification with the peer group. In the process, they often overidentify with the peer group, with its heroes and idols, to the extent that they may lose for some time their own personal value system and even the capacity to make independent decisions. According to Keniston, if the "conformity to peer group norms merely replaces conformity to parental norms . . . adolescent development is foreclosed before real self-regulation and independence are achieved" (Keniston, 1971: 377).

The youth group of the totalitarian system may serve as an illustration of political foreclosure, since the youth movement provides the adolescent with a ready-made system of beliefs and even a personal identity that the democratic society does not provide. The totalitarian system's appeal to many adolescents might be based on these considerations, since the totalitarian system supplies convincing and suitable identities—or symbols of identity—for this age group. Democratic identity has less extrinsic appeal and it is much harder to attain because it involves freedom of choice. Democratic values, rather than supplying a ready-made identity, insist on a self-made identity. Adolescent imagery, which frequently tends to classify into black and white, has an affinity to the totalitarian system, which supplies this kind of dichotomy. The democratic system allows for many different shades of ideological beliefs and therefore provides more ambiguity. It even is tolerant of totalitarian belief systems, such as the Moonies, which cater to the need of some adolescents for a ready-made totalitarian value structure. The democratic value structure requires that individuals develop their own ego-identity in order to withstand ambiguity and the persuasive arguments of totalitarian ideologies; the problem is that it provides little help to the individual in establishing an identity.

MORATORIUM

The word "moratorium," in a general sense, means a period of delay granted to somebody who is not yet ready to meet an obligation or make a commitment (Erikson, 1968: 157). The moratorium of the adolescent is defined as a developmental period during which commitments either have not yet been made or are rather exploratory and tentative. However, the concept implies that there are many crises and unresolved questions. The individual is in an active struggle to find an answer, explore, search, experiment, try out a different role, and play the field. It is in this sense that the moratorium is considered the adolescent issue *par excellence*. According to Marcia, about 30 percent of today's college students are in the moratorium stage.

Erikson and Margaret Mead (1961) both postulated that the adolescent period is a psychological moratorium, or an "as-if period" when individuals can experiment with different roles "as-if" they were committed to these roles. However, since it is only an "as-if period," they are not really committed and not held fully accountable for errors that might be made in trying out new roles. They can still change their values and commitments, and they frequently do so in the process of gaining experience and becoming more mature. Therefore, the as-if period is the delay society grants to its youth to try on different roles—like trying on clothes—to see which fits best. It is in this sense that the moratorium subject may try out radical political philosophies, try out new religious belief systems such as Oriental mysticism, or even try different vocational activities such as social work or the Peace Corps. The moratorium adolescent may try new and different sexual relationships, such as coed apartment living, bisexuality, or homosexuality.

If adolescents, while experimenting with moratorium issues, have sufficient opportunity to search, experiment, play the field, and try on different roles, there is a very good chance that they will find themselves, develop an identity, and emerge with commitments to politics, religion, a vocational goal, and a more clearly defined sex role and sexual preference. These final commitments are frequently much less radical than some of the tentative and exploratory commitments during the moratorium. According to Marcia, moratorium is truly an essential and necessary prerequisite for identity achievement. However, while the adolescent is in the process of searching and exploring, the world does not look very stable or predictable and does not appear to be a very desirable place; rather, the youth views the world and social institutions as badly in need of improvement. Moratorium subjects are inclined to express their disenchantment by challenging what they see. Their desire is to change government, politics, education—in short, "the system." While frequently very good diagnosticians and effective critics in pointing to the limitations, problems, and imperfections of the "system," they are not equally effective in producing viable, realistic alternatives because to do so requires identity, willingness to compromise, and a more permanent commitment.

In responding to Kuhn's (1954) test question "Who am I?" moratorium subjects typically reveal their lack of commitment, their uncertainty, and their search for an identity with such responses as: "I am searching, I am confused, I am thinking, I am wondering, I am calculating"; "I am a curious person, I am unsure of what I am, I am many people at different times, I seek new experiences to find out what I really am, I am looking for something, I am looking for myself."

Mead and Friedenberg have both expressed concern that in society's emphasis on success, progress, and production as symbolized by scout badges, good grades, promotion, honors, recognition, awards, and diplomas, we exert too much pressure on our youth and in the process deprive them of the opportunity to experience a moratorium, an "as-if period," without the pressure for accountability. It has been found that the need for a moratorium is reflected in the motives for volunteering in the Peace Corps.

IDENTITY ACHIEVEMENT

After an individual has experienced a psychological moratorium and has resolved the adolescent identity crisis and as a result has begun to develop lasting personal commitments, an identity has been achieved. Identity achievement contributes to an increment in ego strength. It means that adolescent development has been successfully completed and maturity has been attained. Successful adolescent development has been defined by Keniston (1971: 363) as ". . . integration of impulses into life . . . the humanization of conscience . . . the stability of a sense of self. . . ."

An identity has been achieved after the individual has seriously and carefully evaluated various alternatives and has considered different choices, and has come to conclusions and decisions on his own terms. Actually, it is not at all uncommon for such individuals to take a position that is fairly close to their parents' values; however, unlike the foreclosure subjects, they have considered various other options, tried more liberal or even more radical approaches, and finally accepted or rejected them on their own terms. This process contrasts with that of the foreclosure subject, who remains very close to parental values and expectations without ever making a genuine personal choice in the matter and without having seriously questioned parental values. The achievement of an identity gives the individual an awareness of and an acceptance of personal continuity with the past and a more stable orientation toward the future. Identity means that a new synthesis has been found which "will link the past, the present, and the future" (Keniston, 1965: 212). The function of this sense of identity is to create a new outlook toward the self which provides inner self-sameness and continuity and stabilizes values and purposes (Keniston, 1965). Once an identity has been achieved there is an increase in self-acceptance, a stable self-definition, a willingness to make commitments to a vocation, a religion, a political ideology and also to intimacy, engagement, and marriage. Orlofsky, Marcia, and Lesser (1973) were able to show that the identity-achieved subject had by far the greatest capacity for engaging in interpersonal intimacy; lower levels of identity had a much greater probability of being stereotyped, pseudointimate, or even isolate in their interpersonal relationships. To achieve a mature ego-identity the individual must overcome "his irrational rebelliousness as well as his irrational urge to conform" (Keniston, 1971: 364).

Individuals who have attained an identity feel in harmony with themselves, accept their capacities, limitations, and opportunities. Such an individual realizes "where he fits (or knowingly prefers not to fit)" into social situations in terms of his own personal development. Four college students' responses to the "Who am I?" test from the author's file may serve again to illustrate this sense of identity achievement: "the future Mrs. Jones, a future English teacher; a future resident of Colorado, a happy-go-lucky person"; "a woman, a potential wife, a potential mother, a student, a teacher"; "I am me, outgoing, well-liked, intelligent"; "a contained person, a free-willed individual, a leader, a self-sufficient young adult." These responses convey the feeling that adolescence has been or is about to be terminated. There is a sense of direction and a positive orientation toward the future, which is one of the characteristics of the identity-achieved individual.

RESEARCH FINDINGS ON IDENTITY STATUSES

A summary of the ego-psychoanalytically oriented identity research, based in part on review articles by Bourne (1978) and Marcia (1980), may show the extent to which Erikson's theory has stimulated contemporary research. Such a presentation may demonstrate the extent to which the concept of "identity statuses" has recently become a major research construct leading to the investigation of personality development in adolescents, including college students and young adults. Furthermore, this summary will demonstrate the broad range of issues and variables to which identity is related. Much of the identity research has been conducted with male subjects, hence the data presented are for males unless indicated otherwise. This section of the presentation will be organized by the major cognitive, educational, adjustment, and personality correlates of identity rather than by the identity statuses. Not all research specifically identifies Marcia's four identity statuses or uses Marcia's identity assessment technique; some studies contrast only the attributes of high- and low-identity subjects (La-Voie, 1976).

INTELLIGENCE

A frequently reported finding is that the four identity statuses are not systematically related to level of intellectual functioning or scholastic ability (Bob, 1968; Cross and Allen, 1970; Marcia, 1966; Marcia and Friedman, 1970; Schenkel, 1975). However, since many of these studies use college students as subjects, this finding may be influenced by the narrower range of mental ability characteristic of the student population.

ACADEMIC VARIABLES

Grade Point Average. Cross and Allen (1970) found that identity achievers received higher grade point averages than the other three identity statuses, even if scholastic ability is controlled; Waterman and Waterman (1972) found that identity achievers have better study habits. Donovan (1971), in contrast, found that the foreclosures, attuned to the values of their parents, obtained the highest grades.

College Major. Among female college students, the achievers and the foreclosures tend to choose more difficult fields of study than the other two identity statuses (Marcia and Friedman, 1970).

Achievement Motivation. Among a combined group of men and women, identity achievers and moratorium subjects showed a higher level of achievement motivation than the remaining two statuses (Orlofsky, 1978).

Fear of Success. Findings on Horner's "Fear of Success Variable" revealed a surprising reversal in the performance of the sexes. Among college women, the identity-achieved subjects and the moratorium subjects admitted greater fear of success; among college men, the foreclosure and the identity-diffused subjects showed more fear of success than the remaining two statuses (Howard, 1975; Orlofsky, 1978).

PERFORMANCE ON COGNITIVE TESTS

Concept Attainment. Marcia (1966) found that the identity achievers do better on a concept attainment task than the other three statuses. However, attempts to replicate this finding (Bob, 1968) have not been entirely successful—hence, the generalization is only tentative.

Performance under Stress. Identity achievers performed better on the concept attainment task when under stress than in nonstress conditions. When under stress, the moratorium and the diffused subjects did more poorly than in the nonstress situation. The performance of the foreclosures did not change as a function of stress (Bob, 1968). This finding is reminiscent of the observation that the foreclosures' level of aspiration did not change, even when confronted with failure experiences (Marcia, 1966).

Field Independence and Conformity. On a Witkin type field-independence task, college women who were identity achievers and foreclosures showed more field independence than those of the other two statuses (Schenkel, 1975); that is, they were better able to analyze and structure their experiences. This constitutes an implicit agreement with an earlier study by Toder and Marcia (1973) demonstrating that identity-diffused and moratorium women displayed the greatest degree of conformity in an Asch-type experiment. Apparently a lack of identity increases the need to conform in the identity-diffused subjects; however, in general it is assumed that foreclosures have a propensity toward accepting and conforming to traditional values.

Formal Operations. Studies investigating the relationship between Piaget's stages of formal operations and Marcia's identity statuses have been less conclusive than studies on many of the other variables, a finding consistent with the earlier reported findings of no differences between the identity statuses and intelligence. Cauble (1976) concluded that the four identity statuses did not show a significant distribution over several of Piaget's formal thinking stages. Wagner (1976) reported only scant evidence for a relationship between identity statuses and formal operational reasoning. Even the conclusions by Rowe and Marcia (1980), since based on a very small sample, can only be considered as tentative findings. They did report that subjects who were in an advanced stage of formal operations (IIIa or beyond) were also identity achievers. And a similar but less pronounced relationship existed for moratoriums.

Problem-Solving Stragegy. Identity achievers and moratoriums scored higher on a reflective problem-solving task; foreclosure and diffusion subjects were more impulsive (Waterman and Waterman, 1974).

PERSONALITY VARIABLES

In general, students who score high on measures of identity are as a group better adjusted, have a more integrated personality, and are more self-accepting than individuals who score low. This was demonstrated by LaVoie (1976) on measures of defensiveness, general maladjustment, personality disorder, neurosis, and personality disintegration. Donovan's

(1975) identity-achieved and moratorium subjects displayed highly developed ego functioning and independence.

Authoritarianism. A frequently replicated finding, well based in theory and equally obvious in males and females, is that foreclosures score as significantly more authoritarian and more conventional than all other identity statuses. They endorse authoritarian values, tend to be obedient, respect authority, and are loyal to conventional values (Breuer, 1973; Marcia, 1966; 1967; Marcia and Friedman, 1970; Matteson, 1974; Schenkel and Marcia, 1972). Foreclosures also showed a surprising willingness to administer a high level of electric shock to a victim in a Milgram-type obedience task (Podd, 1972). In contrast, the moratorium subjects scored significantly lower than all other identity statuses on authoritarianism; they seem to challenge traditional authority and question existing values.

Anxiety. Among the college males, the moratorium subjects are the most anxious of all the identity statuses (Mahler, 1969; Marcia, 1967; Oshman and Manosevitz, 1974; Podd, Marcia, and Rubin, 1970). One theoretical explanation is that they actually are in a developmental period of insecurity, vulnerability, and crisis, and hence anxiety would be quite natural. However, it could also be that they are more open with themselves and more willing to admit experiencing anxiety. Foreclosure males, in contrast, are rigid and defensive, and hence their self-reported anxiety scores are the lowest. The diffused males apparently have too much apathy or lack of commitment to experience a high level of anxiety. Among females, more in line with commonsense expectations, the diffused subjects display more anxiety than all other statuses (Marcia and Friedman, 1970); female foreclosures, like males, display the least amount of anxiety.

Affect. Identity-achieved and foreclosure women showed significantly less negative affect than the remaining two statuses (Toder and Marcia, 1973).

Self-Esteem. Quite surprisingly, since identity and self-esteem are related constructs, Marcia (1966) reported only a very low correlation ($r = .26$) between self-esteem and an overall identity score and no significant differences between the four identity statuses. However, Breuer (1973) did report that identity-achieved and moratorium subjects obtained higher self-esteem scores than foreclosure and identity-diffused subjects. Furthermore, LaVoie (1976), who compared high- and low-scoring mid-adolescents, was able to demonstrate that the former had significantly higher self-concept scores than the latter and showed that self-concept improves with age. Donovan (1975) also reports that his identity-diffused subjects "seemed to have the lowest sense of self-esteem."

In a study conducted by Marcia and Friedman (1970), women displayed a different pattern from that reported by Breuer for males. Foreclosure women obtained the highest self-esteem scores; identity-achieved women, surprisingly, scored lower on self-esteem than all other statuses. However, Dye, Marquiss, and LaVoie (1975) support only the earlier findings pertaining to foreclosure, challenging those related to identity achievement. They reported that identity-achieved and foreclosure women obtained significantly higher self-concept scores than either moratorium or diffused women. In this context it is important to recall that identity-achieved women also had the greatest fear of success. Apparently the identity statuses have a different meaning for males and females, as will be discussed in more detail later.

Self-Esteem Manipulation through Feedback. The identity achievers and the moratorium subjects appear to be little influenced by external feedback about their personality. They are secure in knowing who they are and where they are going. They are least likely to accept false personality sketches about themselves; hence, they are not as easily manipulated as the foreclosure and diffused subjects (Gruen; 1960, Marcia, 1967).

Internal-External Locus of Control (Rotter). Male identity-achieved and moratorium subjects scored significantly higher on internal locus of control than did foreclosure and diffusion subjects, who were externally oriented (Waterman, Beubel, and Waterman, 1970). Apparently, subjects with an established or developing sense of identity believe that they themselves are in control of the events that shape their lives. For women, the identity-achieved and the foreclosure subjects obtained higher internal locus of control scores (Howard, 1975). Again, as in the case of self-esteem, foreclosure women emerged with different—and more positive—attributes than males.

Cooperation versus Competition. Podd, Marcia, and Rubin (1970), using a prisoners' dilemma game, found no significant overall differences in the competitive versus cooperative responses to the four identity statuses. However, one situation arose in which moratorium subjects were not very cooperative—when playing with an authority figure rather than with peers. Their unwillingness to cooperate is understandable in the light of the above-discussed finding that the moratorium subjects scored lowest on measures of authoritarianism since they are obviously in a stage of rebelling against authority.

FAMILY ANTECEDENTS

Several studies (Cross and Allen, 1970; Donovan, 1975; Jordan, 1970; 1971; LaVoie, 1976; Marcia, 1976a) have investigated the relationship between identity status and adolescents' perceptions of their parents. The findings of these various studies are not entirely consistent, except for the following generalizations:

1. The moratorium subjects saw their parents as ambivalent. Parents appeared to be inconsistent from the moratoriums' point of view; that is,

parents were perceived as both accepting and rejecting. Among moratoriums the discrepancy between the parents and their son's point of view was great, as one might expect from the theoretical consideration that the moratoriums are actively questioning and challenging parental and established values. This discrepancy was greatest between sons and mothers.

2. The above statement also holds true for the identity achievers; however, for them the relationship had become more relaxed and more moderate. In a comparison of high- and low-identity mid-adolescents, subjects with a high level of identity did perceive less distance between themselves and their fathers and mothers than did subjects with low identity scores (LaVoie, 1976).

3. Foreclosure subjects were—as one would expect, based on the theoretical definition of foreclosure—very close to and felt highly valued by their parents. Foreclosure males reported an intermediate—neither too harsh nor too limited—degree of control from their fathers (Cross and Allen, 1969). Foreclosures perceived their parents as accepting and supportive but also as emphasizing strict superego functions. They saw their home as being loving and affectionate and had internalized their parents' goals for them (Donovan, 1975). The relationship between the foreclosure son and his father was especially strong. Apparently, the parents of foreclosure sons are quite effective in guiding them into the preconceived roles that they, the parents, have determined.

4. The parents of the identity-diffused subjects were perceived—again as suggested by theory—as detached, distant, uninvolved, and unconcerned. This observation was most noticeable in the father-son relationship. The diffused adolescents either didn't respect their parents or feared them and in general felt that there was a lack of understanding (Donovan, 1975). Identity-diffused students are more likely to come from broken homes than any of the other statuses (Jordan, 1970). Finally, it is interesting that college males who had grown up without a father attained lower overall identity scores than those who had come from intact families or whose mothers had remarried (Oshman and Manosevitz, 1974).

MORAL REASONING

The development of moral reasoning is closely related to the development of an ego-identity. The identity achievers and the moratorium subjects scored significantly higher than the other statuses on moral reasoning and functioned at postconventional levels of moral judgment. Rowe and Marcia (1980) demonstrated a highly significant relationship between identity achievement and Kohlberg's postconventional level of moral judgment (see Chapter 9). The identity-diffused subjects still intended to function at the preconventional level of moral reasoning and attained the lowest moral judgment scores. However, because there are obvious individual differences, it was not possible to classify each of the four identity statuses in terms of specific corresponding stages of moral reasoning as defined by Kohlberg (Podd, 1972; Poppen, 1974). Hayes (1977) reported, in a more general sense, that adolescents who had a high level of identity were also more highly ethical, empathetic, and socialized than low-identity adolescents.

AUTONOMY

Both the identity achievers and the moratorium subjects, male as well as female, accepted more responsibility for their own behavior than did the identity-diffused subjects (Neuber and Genthner, 1977). The orientation of high-identity males is toward independence and active achievement; low-identity subjects tended to be passive and more affective (Andrews, 1973). Josselson (1973) reported that females who had achieved an identity displayed better psychological adjustment and more autonomy than those who had not yet mastered the identity crisis. Orlofsky, Marcia, and Lesser (1973) found foreclosure and identity-diffused subjects to be low on self-directedness. The foreclosure subjects scored lowest in personal autonomy and highest in their need for social approval.

DRUG USE

Foreclosure subjects, committed to traditional values, are the most adamant nondrug users (Dufresne and Cross, 1972). Moratorium and identity-diffused subjects are more likely to use drugs; however, each may use drugs for somewhat different reasons. The identity-diffused subject may use drugs and alcohol in an attempt to avoid crises, loneliness, and the feelings of confusion and diffusion; their use serves a defensive function. Based on clinical case studies, Flynn reports that he frequently sees this kind of defensive use of drugs by young adolescents who are confronted with identity issues of aggression, sexuality, dependency on parents, and dating problems. ". . . They were using drugs and associated themselves with the drug using crowd as a kind of spurious identity in order to drop out, for a time, from the struggle for psychosocial and psychosexual maturity" (1970: 149). For moratorium subjects, in contrast, drug use may be a manifestation of their openness to new experiences, their concern with trying different life styles, and their exploration of their own sense of awareness. Thus, under the rationalization, "I will try anything once," they may try out a great variety of different substances.

SEX DIFFERENCES IN IDENTITY STATUSES

Several generalizations emerge from this review of the literature:
1. It appears obvious that on most variables of mental health, cognitive

performance, and life adjustment in general, the identity-achieved subjects score significantly higher than the identity-diffused subjects. This generalization applies to males as well as to females.

2. There exist sex differences in the personality correlates for these four identity statuses. However, the sexes also have much in common; in particular, the pattern for the identity-achieved and the identity-diffused is quite similar for both sexes. Sex differences become most obvious in the comparison of the foreclosure and the moratorium subjects. Apparently the route toward identity achievement follows a different course and may have different meanings for the two sexes—at least during the period when most of these studies were conducted.

3. Among men, identity achievers and moratorium subjects are often close together and perform better than the other two statuses on such variables as ego development, concept attainment, performance under stress, resistance to manipulation of self-esteem, internal reflectivity in decision making, and intimacy in interpersonal relationships.

4. Among females, identity-achieved and foreclosure subjects appear to be grouped together more often; they have higher self-esteem, show less conformity to peer group pressures, give evidence of a low level of self-reported anxiety, choose a more difficult college major, consider themselves straight rather than hip, and have attained higher levels of independence. One might further consider that there may be sex differences in the components that make up the identity of an individual. For example, Bell (1969) indicates that vocational identity plays a more central role in the identity of the male, and affiliation may play a greater role in the identity of the female (Douvan and Adelson, 1966). Erikson has emphasized that "... womanhood arrives when attractiveness and experiences have succeeded in selecting what is to be admitted to the welcome of the inner space" (1968: 283); for this reason, Marcia added a section about attitude toward premarital intercourse to the assessment of crisis and commitment in women as part of the identity interview. Schenkel and Marcia (1972) demonstrated that sexual ideology actually accounts for more variance in identity status than politics, occupation, and religion (which was second).

To interpret these reported sex differences is difficult, since earlier identity studies were primarily concerned with validating the construct "identity" and usually used males as subjects. Even later studies limited their population to either males or females and often investigated different variables. Nevertheless, all of these factors do not explain away the rather noticeable sex differences found in much of the identity research. Marcia and Friedman (1970) have suggested, based on social, cultural, and historical factors, that achievement and foreclosure are "stable" identity statuses for women, while achievement and moratorium are "stable" identities for males.

Most of our research with men suggested that *chronological proximity* to Identity Achievement was a crucial factor in the grouping of the statuses. That is, Moratoriums could be expected to behave most like Identity Achievements on measures involving general ego strength, while Foreclosures would perform most like Identity Diffusions. However, with women the *stability* of the identity status was emerging as the important issue. Identity Achievement and Foreclosure are both fairly stable statuses; both groups have an identity, even though one is achieved and the other foreclosed. Moratorium and Identity Diffusion are unstable statuses; neither one has a firm set of identity, although Moratoriums are moving towards it [Marcia, 1976b: 103].

It will be interesting to observe whether these relationships between sex and identity status will change as women become less traditional and more liberated in their pursuits of vocational careers, their striving for independence from their families, and their attitudes toward sexuality and sex roles. Schenkel (1975) suggests that such changes are taking place and that women make increasingly more demands for autonomy. Erikson does perceive some rather fundamental differences in the achievement of a mature identity for males and females.

Understanding of female development in adolescence is a far more complicated task than the understanding of male development. Female development is quieter, subtler. And because the end-points of female development are ambiguous, it is harder to identify markers along the way. . . . Because the Erikson stages of identity and intimacy are probably merged for girls . . . identity development proceeds at a deeper and less tangible level [Josselson, Greenberger, and McConochie, 1977: 162, 164].

EDUCATIONAL IMPLICATIONS

One basic issue regarding education during adolescence that emerges from Erikson's theory is: To what extent and how do educational institutions enhance youths' efforts in self-finding? Contemporary critics of the school system—Dennison, Friedenberg, Goodman, Holt, Silverman, and others—have maintained that schools require adolescents to suppress their creativity, individuality, and identity to the demands of the skill- and knowledge-oriented curriculum in order to succeed. Thus, schools seem to be encouraging foreclosure, since they demand conformity to the way things are and submission to authority, rather than aiding the adolescent in his search for a personal identity. Considering the Waterman and Waterman (1970) findings, it appears that foreclosure subjects were more comfortable in school and held more positive attitudes toward their educational experiences, while the uncommitted, searching, and experimenting moratorium subjects evaluated their educational experience rather negatively. Apparently, the structure of the school—the curriculum, schedules, grades, hall passes, and so on—encourages foreclosure rather than efforts toward self-finding and self-definition, which implies questioning and challenging existing patterns, values, and authorities. One might speculate whether the all-pervasive indifference toward school and the frequent discontent of adolescents with education and with their teachers are in part a result of the lack of concern on the part of many educators with what Erikson and Marcia consider a fundamental developmental issue, namely, the resolution of the identity crisis. It has long been recognized that the problem of the high school dropout is not simply a matter of lack of ability or even lack of achievement, but a desire for independence, a search without a goal, an expression of inner discontent and restlessness. Youth dissatisfaction with college, students questioning the value of their education, the increasing pattern of "dropping in and dropping out," as well as the increasing pattern of transferring from one college to another do make sense in view of Erikson's "identity crisis" concept and Marcia's assumption that a moratorium requires this kind of Wanderlust and exploration and is an essential prerequisite for the achievement of a mature identity.

   The cry for relevance in the curriculum and in the total educational experience might also be better understood in view of the moratorium issues: developing a sexual identity, finding religious values, selecting career goals, and developing a commitment to a political ideology. The adolescent often has difficulty in seeing the relationship among these burning personal issues and conjugating French verbs, studying ancient Rome, proving the Pythagorean theorem, and examining the finer points of Shakespeare's *Macbeth;* teachers are often remiss in making these relationships obvious, even in those content areas where they are most readily apparent. The junior high school student's and even the senior high school student's choices of different courses are limited, and the adolescent has relatively little to say about the curriculum. The curriculum should become more closely related to the adolescent's search for self-understanding by including more identity-relevant topics. This could include drug education and sex education, areas in which considerable misinformation exists even among sophisticated youth. Furthermore, such topics as human development, sociology, interpersonal relations, consumer economics, social organization, career opportunities in the future, ecology, gender roles and sex stereotypes, and a study of values could aid adolescents in developing a philosophy of life. All of these topics could be taught in a way that makes them academically respectable as well as personally meaningful. In their English courses, high school students could study the problems of adolescents as reflected in the literature dealing with adolescents. In addition, present teaching styles frequently include lecturing, rehearsing, reviewing, drills, quizzes, tests, and assignments—which means that even when these activities are meaningful, they are teacher-directed, and the learning activities are controlled by the authority of the teacher. Consequently, the high school student is often placed in a docile and submissive role; there is little opportunity to fulfill the needs of the moratorium subjects, and the foreclosure subjects are not encouraged to move out of their stagnation but may be rewarded for foreclosure behavior.

In contrast to Freud's emphasis on the dangers of frustration and the possible contribution of frustration to neurosis, Erikson distinguishes between meaningful frustration and neurotic frustration. Meaningful frustration can serve useful ends as an educational experience and implies that even though the adolescent initially does not see a possible solution to the teacher's question, problem, or assignment—and consequently feels frustrated—he can, with work and perseverance, find the solution by himself. The teacher who has become an effective frustrator does not contribute to neuroses but instead helps his students to develop frustration tolerance. Therefore, parents and teachers might introduce more culturally meaningful but frustrating challenges that the adolescent can resolve with effort. As part of the process of growing up, children must learn to accept some of the inevitable limitations and restrictions that may be frustrating. Erikson objects to a frustration-free educational environment—like Summerhill— in which children's natural tendencies and interests determine the learning activities and the curriculum. An educational policy characterized by the child's questioning his freedom to learn—as implied in the often quoted "Teacher *must* we do today what we *want* to do?" (Erikson, 1968: 127)— can be as detrimental to the establishment of a healthy identity as the traditional emphasis on duty, obedience, self-restraint, and arbitrary rules. Learning occurs more effectively and the development of identity is enhanced in an educational climate that avoids the pitfalls of both these extremes. Youth do benefit from being "mildly but firmly coerced into the adventure of finding out that one can learn to accomplish things which one would never have thought of by oneself, things which owe their attractiveness to the very fact that they are not the product of play and fantasy, but the product of reality, practicality and logic" (Erikson, 1968: 127). Consequently, meaningful ways of frustrating adolescents by challenging them with new ideas, problems, and subjects may increase their efforts to learn and master and, ultimately, contribute to their process of maturing.

In the past, societies—through puberty rites, initiation ceremonies, the apprenticeship-journeyman system, confirmation, bar mitzvah, and coming-out parties—have provided some fairly clearly defined social roles that gave the individual a kind of identity by providing self-definition and social status. As these social role definitions have virtually disappeared—and as confirmations and bar mitzvahs have become primarily private, religious matters—the individual's search for his own unique identity and for his place in society has become more pronounced and more of a burden is placed upon the individual. "Some of the adolescent difficulties in Western society may be better understood if one considers the adolescent as the marginal man who stands in a psychological no-man's-land without clear understanding of what is expected of him, struggling to attain adult status" (Muuss, 1970b: 113). The adolescent struggle to attain an identity and achieve adult status can be a frustrating experience, and society, educational institutions, and teachers may well ponder how they can make this experience more meaningful.

4: PETER BLOS' MODERN PSYCHOANALYTIC INTERPRETATION OF ADOLESCENCE

BLOS' THEORY: AN INTRODUCTION

Peter Blos (1904–   ) is a psychoanalyst in private practice in New York; he holds a Ph.D. rather than an M.D. and is a biologist by training. Blos has devoted a great deal of attention to the period of adolescence, both in his practical clinical work and in his theoretical formulations. More recently, he has "returned to his psychoanalytic beginnings," working with juvenile delinquents, as he did in the 1920s with A. Aichhorn in Vienna. His commitment to the period of adolescence is reflected in the titles of his numerous publications: *The Adolescent Personality* (1941), *On Adolescence: A Psychoanalytic Interpretation* (1962), *The Young Adolescent: Clinical Studies* (1970), and, more recently, *The Adolescent Passage* (1979).

Blos' theory of adolescent development has not been as widely accepted in the developmental literature as, for example, Erikson's theory, partly because it lacks popular concepts such as trust, autonomy, initiative, industry, and adolescent identity crisis; partly because emphasis falls on psychopathology; and partly because normal development is less systematically presented. Finally, the conceptual frame of reference is heavily laced with traditional psychoanalytic concepts such as the Oedipus complex, castration anxiety, penis envy, regression to the preoedipal and archaic mother. Most of Blos' efforts are devoted to a description of deviancy in development, juvenile delinquency, psychoanalytic treatment, and cases of psychopathology. His theory has therefore been more popular among psychiatrists than among developmental psychologists, whereas Erikson's theory (1950), with its emphasis on the normality of the "Eight Stages of Man," has in contrast had a more profound influence on education and psychology, especially child and adolescent development.

Blos' theory is not incompatible with the theoretical concepts advanced by Erikson, who added a psychosocial dimension but did not give up the basic Freudian psychosexual concepts. Both men emphasize different dimensions of adolescent development. Blos seems to have remained closer to the original writings of Freud, trying to expand and elaborate rather than modify fundamental psychoanalytic constructs, especially those pertinent to adolescence. However, he frequently cites Erikson and uses some Eriksonian constructs in his own writings.

In addition, Blos draws on the various constructs emerging from ego-psychology—the second individuation process, regression to earlier experiences in the service of ego development, separation from parents, and turning to peers as a necessary developmental progression—rather than on Freud's notion that conflict defines all developmental tasks. Furthermore, Blos accepts many of the basic psychoanalytic assumptions concerning the nature of man and the psychodynamics of development and utilizes Freudian constructs. Freud emphasized the revival of the Oedipus complex and the reawakening of castration fear during the genital period (adolescence). Blos relies on such ideas; however, he has developed a more elaborate system that views adolescence as the psychological adjustment to sexual and biological maturation. "Puberty is an act of nature and adolescence is an act of man" (Blos, 1979: 405).

Another concept that Blos stresses is the separation experience from parental dependencies and familial love objects as a crucial task for normal adolescent development, an idea he refers to as the second individuation process (Blos, 1979). This developmental process of adolescence requires a partial regression to earlier stages of development, which is necessary not as a defense mechanism but in the service of adolescent development (Blos, 1979). The Oedipus complex receives elaborate treatment and is used as a fundamental dynamic principle to explain drive and ego orientation during adolescence as well as sex differences in development. Throughout his writings, Blos emphasizes and describes how males and females differ in their development. More recently, Blos has written a paper, "Modifications in the Traditional Psychoanalytic Theory of Female Adolescent Development" (1981), in which he contrasts the classical Freudian theory of feminine development with more recent observations. Blos emphasizes that the orthodox psychoanalytic view of female adolescent development requires considerable realignment with more recent findings, and he suggests a need and a direction for further investigations. His purpose is to provide a new interpretation of the traditional psychoanalytical theory of the development of females during adolescence. On the basis of Green's (1975) behavioral observation of children, Blos maintains that a biologically determined male-female dimorphism exists that permits us to speak of a primary femininity and masculinity. It has been observed that newborn babies already show sex differences in their behavior patterns (Hamburg and Lunde, 1966), such as the much greater behavioral continuity of fearfulness in males when exposed to visual novelty (Bronson, 1973).

Freud identified adolescence as the genital stage and viewed it as the final developmental stage before sexual maturity is reached. Blos, in contrast, as an indication of his highly differentiated conceptualization of the period of adolescence, suggests six different adolescent phases, that is, if one includes latency as the preparatory stage for adolescence and postadolescence as the transition phase between adolescence and adulthood. These six phases are:

1. Latency
2. Preadolescence or prepuberty
3. Early adolescence or early puberty. (Phases 2 and 3 are sometimes treated as one stage and are then referred to as "Young Adolescence.")
4. Adolescence proper—middle adolescence or advanced puberty
5. Late adolescence—a phase of consolidation
6. Postadolescence—the transition from adolescence to adulthood

In addition to these six developmental phases, five phase-specific issues emerge and undergo reorganization in normal development and provide the structure for the discussion of each of the above phases:

1. Drive organization
2. Ego organization or ego function
3. Somatic maturation
4. Conflict formation
5. Conflict resolution

The overall pattern of these five phase-specific issues and six developmental phases is not readily identifiable at any one point in Blos' books but emerges sporadically throughout his writing, providing an underlying systematic theoretical structure of normal adolescent development.

One of the major distinctions between Blos' formulation and Freud's original conception of psychosexual development is that Freud emphasized that personality formation took place very early in life, primarily during the oral, anal, and phallic stages, and that personality formation was conceived to be almost completed once the Oedipus complex had been resolved. Such statements as "the personality patterns attained by the end of the oedipal period are seen as set and relatively unresponsive to changing conditions" (Wachtel, 1977: 51) have become commonplace in the developmental literature. In contrast, Blos, Erikson, and Sullivan, among others, placed an increasing emphasis on the importance of adolescence in personality development. Blos' major theoretical contribution is an identification of the reorganization and restructuring of personality during adolescence, a process he referred to as the second individuation process. Only after the second individuation process has been completed is a certain degree of permanence and stability reached within the personality structure. Only when writing about postadolescence does Blos (1962) speak of "developmental achievement of personality organization" (149), "harmonizing drive and ego organizations" (150), and "the organization of a stable self" (153).

At the close of adolescence, as I have remarked earlier, conflicts are by no means resolved, but they are rendered specific; and certain conflicts become integrated into the realm of the ego as life tasks. It remains the task of postadolescence to create the specific avenues through which these tasks are implemented in the external world [Blos, 1962: 150].

Before Blos' six phases of adolescence are presented, the second individuation phase and the impact of the Oedipus complex in adolescence must be considered. At this time, there is relatively little empirical research designed to assess the psychoanalytic propositions of Blos' theory. However, Fisher and Greenberg (1977)—discussed in more detail in Chapter 2—have reviewed an enormous amount of psychoanalytically oriented research that does support some but not all of Freud's theoretical assumptions. Considerable support was cited in support of the male's Oedipus complex. The support for the female oedipal situation was less positive; it is especially this part of the theory that Blos modifies and expands.

BLOS' SECOND INDIVIDUATION PROCESS

The first individuation process, a concept developed by Mahler (1963), is normally completed toward the end of the third year of life. Its completion is characterized by the attainment of "object constancy" and by the child's ability to distinguish between inside and outside reality—between "me" and "not me"—and between self and mother. "Mobility, language, and social experiences widen the child's life space and bring to his awareness the desirability of being like others, most importantly, like the parent or sibling" (Blos, 1962: 4). While the first individuation process aids in the differentiation between child and parent, it also contributes to the child's desire to model himself after the admired parent and contributes to the dependency of childhood. The first individuation process establishes independence from the concrete physical presence of the mother, and the mother becomes internalized. It is only in the second phase, at the dawn of puberty, that the "independence from internalized infantile objects" (Blos, 1979: 483) is attained.

By viewing adolescence as a recapitulation of psychoanalytically significant childhood experiences (e.g., a second Oedipus complex), Blos (1967) introduced as a major theoretical construct of adolescent development the "second individuation process"—a psychological weaning. It is initiated with the increase in the libidinal drive at puberty, continues until late adolescence, and reaches completion only when the adolescent can find external and extrafamilial love objects. As a result of the disengagement from parental control and from internalized, immature attachments of familial love and hate objects, the individuation process leads to a more realistic evaluation of parents and aids in the process of self-definition and ego maturity. Individuation involves "the shedding of family dependencies, [and] the loosening of infantile object ties in order to become a member of the adult world" (Blos, 1967: 163). The disengagement of childhood dependencies at the adolescent level takes place not only in relation to external concrete objects—as in the first individuation process—but also in relation to the internalized love objects of early childhood (Blos, 1979: 412). Only on completion of adolescence do these internalized self- and object-representations acquire firm boundaries and develop stability and resistance to change.

The adolescent individuation process helps to establish a personal, social, and sexual identity. It requires a turning away from parents and—because of still insufficient autonomy—a temporary turning toward the peer group. The peer group serves several functions—for example, helping the adolescent to resolve the oedipal conflict during this period and to sever parental dependencies. For several reasons the peer group may serve some functions better than the family:

1. The peer group helps adolescents to resolve internal conflicts within themselves and reduces anxiety, since peers can serve as a sounding board without arousing guilt or anxiety.
2. The peer group respects competencies—although these are often defined differently by adults and by various peer groups—as seen in the different emphases placed on social and athletic skills.
3. The peer group provides practical and personal guidance in social situations, especially in heterosexual relationships and behavior.
4. The peer group provides honest and critical evaluative feedback about the individual's behavior and personal attributes.

Since adolescents cannot find sexual gratification within their family of origin, and in order to sever family dependencies, they turn toward the peer group for support, values, and security. Security is found in the shared code of what constitutes adequate behavior and in the dependency on mutual recognition of sameness (Blos, 1962: 188). However, in the attempt to free themselves from the control and restrictions of parents, adolescents may fall prey to the tyranny of peers who require conformity to their standards in return for the security they provide. Ample research evidence (Brittain, 1966; Brownstone and Willis, 1971; Costanzo, 1970; Costanzo and Shaw, 1966; Iscoe, Williams, and Harvey,1963; Patel and

Gordon, 1960; Schmuck, 1963) has identified this developmental trend toward greatly increased conformity in early adolescence and continuing into adolescence proper, followed by a decline in conformity with increased maturity. Blos views this trend as a defensive denial of the adolescents' dependency needs and describes it as "uniformism." The importance of the influence of the peer group is nowhere more pronounced than in sexual behavior. Recent trends indicate that sexual intercourse is now being endorsed by the peer group and is considered mature behavior: "The peer group with its characteristic fostering of conformity has come to equate adolescent heterosexual behavior with independence, individualism, and adulthood" (Blos, 1979: 249). The peer group provides the kind of support that the adolescent often loses in the separation process from his own family: "stimulation, belongingness, loyalty, devotion, empathy, and resonance" (Blos, 1967: 177). For the time being, the adolescent too readily accepts the norms of the peer group as guides to regulate feelings, impulses, and sexual behavior. The peer group can become an emotional alternative to the family, a substitute family. One danger is that the family dependencies will be replaced by permanent peer group dependencies, with emotional independence remaining unresolved. The opposite danger, for the adolescent who does not want to fit into the model of uniformism, is to be "avoided, ridiculed, ostracized, or condescendingly tolerated" (Blos, 1962: 118).

The second individuation process requires a fundamental restructuring of drive organization and ego functions. During adolescence the ego becomes weaker relative to the id due to (1) the new urgency of sex drive intensity during puberty and (2) the rejection of parental ego support, which was available during latency as a legitimate ego extension. Individuation is not without negative manifestations, such as internal turmoil, heightened vulnerability in personality organization, and emotional complications. A sense of "discouragement, helplessness, despair, incompetent rage, weakness, and worthlessness" represents the emotions of abandonment and regression (Blos, 1970: 235). However, the experiences of these negative by-products are a developmental necessity before the individuation process can be completed. Adolescent turmoil is viewed as the sine qua non of development, the assumption being "that only through conflict can maturity be attained" (Blos, 1979: 14). For a new reorganization to take place, the old psychological organization needs to be loosened, resulting in temporary fragmentation, disorganization, instability, insufficiency, estrangement, and self-consciousness. To consolidate a new organizational structure necessitates experimentation, "the testing of the self by going to excess," as well as oppositional attitudes, rebellious behavior, and resistive strivings (Blos, 1962: 12). The resulting structural change will eventually become permanent personality attributes.

The second individuation process is a process in which both "regressive and progressive movements alternate" (Blos, 1967: 164), providing the psychological basis for the inner turmoil, external rebellion, unpredictability, and chaos that make adolescence a period of crisis. According to Blos, it is only during adolescence that developmental regression must be viewed as a necessary, integral, and healthy part of development. He speaks repeatedly of the regressive movement that is activated by the sudden increase in the sexual and aggressive drives and that creates anxiety. That anxiety is increased externally by the greatly increased social demands and expectations. The idea that adolescence typically is a period of heightened anxiety is generally acknowledged (Conger, 1977: 64–70). The idea received its empirical support through the work of Cattell, who maintains that "anxiety is very high in the adolescent, drops sharply as adulthood is reached, and continues to drop steadily throughout middle age until it rises very steeply again in old age" (1961: 262). Confronted with such demands and with internal conflicts related to sexual and aggressive drive, anxiety and conflict may be avoided by returning to more primitive responses, such as narcissism, oral greediness, and sadism, which were effective in earlier periods of life. Adolescent progress cannot take its normal path without this detour of regression; regression is seen as a precondition of progress, "without which emotional maturity cannot be attained" (Blos, 1979: 27). Individuation implies "a forward movement of the ego" and a "regression of the ego in the service of adolescent development." The meaning of these two apparently contradictory statements can best be illustrated by Nietzsche's famous aphorism, "They say he is going backward, indeed he is, because he attempts to jump." The backward movement manifests itself in an increase in narcissism, exhibited in arrogance, rebellion, defiance, and challenges to parents' authority (Blos, 1962: 91). Fantasies and acts of aggression are common during adolescence to an extent unusual among adults: "Rapaciousness, smuttiness, oblivion to unkemptness, dirtiness and body odors; motoric restlessness, and experimentation in every direction of action and sensation" (Blos, 1971: 964). However, the process of "disengagement from primary objects and the abandonment of infantile ego states" (Blos, 1967: 185) requires a regressive return to earlier periods of development.

> . . . the task of the psychic restructuring by regression represents the most formidable psychic work of adolescence. Just as Hamlet longs for the comforts of sleep but fears the dreams that sleep might bring, so the adolescent longs for the comforts of drive and ego gratification but fears the reinvolvements in infantile object relations. Paradoxically, only through drive and ego regression can the adolescent task be fulfilled [Blos, 1967: 171].

Failure to succeed in this emotional disengagement process interferes with the future task of finding extrafamilial ties of affection, impedes the movement toward autonomy and independence, and may contribute to deviant development and psychopathology. Difficulties in the successful completion of the second individuation process may manifest themselves in acting-out behavior, feelings of a lack of purpose, learning disorders, patterns of procrastination, moodiness, apathy, and negativism. In addition, some of the negative outcomes share with the individuation process the basic goal of adolescence, namely, a movement away from infantile dependencies without producing the necessary reorganization in psychic structure. Blos speaks of a "derailment of the individuation process" in which behavior and social roles are oppositional to parents' wishes and often constitute a more permanent break and unrealistic evaluation of these wishes.

THE OEDIPUS COMPLEX IN BLOS' THEORY

The Oedipus complex remains a core concept for understanding Blos' theory of adolescent development. Blos distinguishes between the familiar Oedipus complex toward the end of the phallic stage and the reemerging of a second oedipal situation during puberty. The resolution of the pubertal Oedipus complex is an important part of the second individuation process. In a developmental sense the Oedipus conflict is biphasic. The phallic-oedipal conflict constitutes the first phase. According to the psychoanalytic recapitulation theory, the revival of the second phase occurs during puberty with the increase in drive intensity. Adolescence is the completion and final resolution, not just a repetition of the Oedipus complex. Since the oedipal situation is different for boys and girls, sex differences must be taken into consideration.

The issues become further complicated by the distinction between a negative passive oedipal position and a positive aggressive oedipal situation. The former is referred to as the early oedipal position, during which the child is primarily receptive; the latter is the more commonly acknowledged oedipal conflict during which the child's love turns toward the opposite-sex parent. The term "negative" refers to the child's love for the same-sex parent, while "positive" implies a love relationship directed toward the opposite-sex parent. Oedipal love always implies a sexual component; however, oedipal love must be distinguished from nonsexual affection, admiration, respect, and loyalty, which children experience in relation to both parents.

During the negative oedipal-phallic period, the boy identifies with his mother while his passive-receptive libido is attached to his father. For example, the passive-receptive oedipal boy may fantasize or wish for a baby from his father. The early passive oedipal period terminates when the boy realizes that the female has no penis and when the more active mode of the phallic stage begins to prevail. The active, or positive, oedipal position brings forth a more aggressive, masculine, libidinal drive, now directed toward possessing the mother. Thus emerges the well-known triangular relationship in which the father is seen as the son's rival and competitor; both hostile impulses and fantasies are aimed at the father. The consequence is castration fear. Three factors eventually lead to the abandonment of the oedipal position: (1) fear of the father, especially in the form of castration anxiety, which exists simultaneously with (2) love for the father and (3) the boy's own immaturity (Blos, 1962: 26). The mother who does not encourage the symbolic seductive attention of her son also enhances the normal progression toward latency.

Blos distinguishes between two possible outcomes of the Oedipus complex: (1) to identify with the father and to attempt to become like him in the future or (2) to give up the competitive striving and regressively and passively submit to the mother. The first solution enhances the development of the ego and the superego during latency and brings forth an orientation in accordance with the reality principle. The second solution is a regressive return to the preoedipal mother; it enhances the id and the drive orientation directed towards the pleasure principle and leads to difficulties during puberty, when biological maturation reintroduces the oedipal situation once more.

With the beginning of puberty, the negative oedipal situation reemerges, resulting in a strong idealization and glamorization of the father. The father provides comfort and assurance, reviving "remnants of the boy's passive oedipal love for the father" (Blos, 1970: 221). The father is seen as the "protector against the pre-oedipal archaic mother," who represents the castrating threat during this phase (Blos, 1970: 154). This preadolescent castration fear generalizes and influences the boy's negative attitudes toward women. However, it also requires the adolescent boy to come "to terms with the homosexual component of pubertal sexuality" (Blos, 1979: 479). With the reorganization in libido drive from bisexual to heterosexual orientation on entering adolescence proper, the boy experiences the phase of the positive oedipal complex once more. Sexual attraction now turns to the mother while both fear and hostility are aimed at the father. In normal development, the social taboo against incestuous love has been internalized in the superego to the extent that the oedipal impulses are unacceptable, producing considerable guilt and anxiety. The resolution of the positive Oedipus complex constitutes a major developmental task during advanced puberty, and a successful resolution of this task becomes the necessary prerequisite for progression into late adolescence and adulthood.

The oedipal development of the girl contains elements that make the resolution of the conflict quite similar to that of the boy, and the four phases of oedipal development are the same. However, there are important variations that influence the different patterns in heterosexual development. Blos does not assume that the resolution of the male and the female oedipal situation is parallel. The difference lies in the necessity for the adolescent male to thoroughly resolve the positive as well as the negative aspects of the Oedipus complex in order to move more vigorously toward adulthood and maturity. "In contrast, the adolescent girl tolerates—within limits, to be sure—a far greater fluidity between the infantile attachment to both parents and her adult personality consolidation, without being necessarily encumbered in her advance toward emotional maturity" (Blos, 1981). In the prephallic stage the girl shares with the boy a passive receptive position vis-à-vis the active preoedipal mother. All children, regardless of their sex, see the mother as their first love object; in this situation the archaic mother is always active and, in relation to her, the child during the oral and anal phases is always passive and receptive. The sexes differ in that, for the male, the female always remains the ultimate love object, but the girl must abandon her first love object and turn toward the father and later toward other masculine love objects. Entry into the phallic stage brings about a change from the passive receptive mode to an active aggressive mode, the latter becoming more pronounced for the boy. This active phase emphasizes autonomy, initiative, and mastery of the world. "Femininity and passivity or masculinity and activity" are not synonymous, but are viewed as potential tendencies (Blos, 1979: 227). The girl's identification with the active mother during this early phallic stage ushers in the initial active, negative, oedipal situation for the girl. The stronger the attachment of the female to the mother during this period, the greater will be her dependence on the father later on. Curiosity, about the world in general and sexuality in particular, leads to the recognition of sex differences, an awareness that is burdened with meaning, encourages fantasy, and leads to body-damage anxiety. It is when the shift from active to passive takes place—due to disappointment with the mother who has not provided the girl with a penis—that the aim of instinctual libido shifts from the mother to the father, leading to the passive, or positive, oedipal position. It is this shift from the active (phallic) stance to the passive position that threatens the female with a return to the original infantile dependency position. "Only when the girl succeeds in abandoning her passive tie to the mother and advances to a passive (positive) oedipal position, can she be spared the adolescent regression to the preoedipal mother" (Blos, 1979: 227). The oedipal situation remains part of the emotional life of the girl during the latency period. "Girls remain in it [the oedipal situation] for an undetermined length of time; they demolish it late, and even so, incompletely" (S. Freud, 1933/1964: 129).

During preadolescence, the girl resists the regressive pull toward infantile passivity, which arouses anxiety. In contrast to the boy at this stage, she turns toward activity as a defensive maneuver against this regressive pull toward passivity and takes on a sexually aggressive masculine role, in which she becomes the sexual instigator and initiator.

Blos refers to this identification with the male role among girls as "the oedipal defense of the pre-adolescent girl" (Blos, 1970: 42). The preadolescent girl approaches heterosexuality more speedily and more directly than the boy. During adolescence proper, the girl takes on the positive passive role vis-à-vis her father and rejects her mother. However, as in the case of the boy, abandoning this oedipal position is the necessary step toward nonincestuous object finding and toward progression in development.

THE SIX PHASES OF ADOLESCENT DEVELOPMENT

The second individuation process and the second oedipal complex provide the basic framework within which Blos traces the epigenetic pattern of adolescent development. Normal development proceeds in an orderly progression identified by six adolescent phases: latency, preadolescence, early adolescence, adolescence proper, late adolescence, and postadolescence. Each of these phases represents phase-specific tasks and experiences, and the progression from one to the next is not just a matter of maturation but requires psychic restructuring. The transformations produce developmental characteristics that distinguish each phase from the one that follows or precedes it. Each phase, especially during the early stages, harbors the potential danger of "developmental derailment," leading to disturbances. However, the emphasis here, in contrast to Blos' original writing, will be on normal development rather than on the etiology and the dynamics of deviancy in development. The connecting and recurring issues around which the psychic restructuring of adolescent development takes place—and which Blos emphasizes, particularly in the description of the earlier phases—are drive organization, ego development, somatic maturation, conflict formation, and conflict resolution.

Drive Organization. Restructuring of drive organization refers to both the quantitative increase and the directional reorientation of libidinal and aggressive drive during puberty. According to Blos, drive intensification is equally strong for both libidinal and aggressive drives, a quantitative change that marks the progression from latency into preadolescence and early adolescence. The initial drive direction is diffuse, the bisexual orientation of childhood remains dominant into early adolescence and may include transitory homosexual experiences. A distinct restructuring of the direction of drive orientation characterizes the progression from early adolescence into adolescence proper with the advent of predominant heterosexual orientation. The movement from incestuous to nonincestuous object findings dominates drive organization in the late and postadolescent phase.

Ego Development. Ego development does not directly parallel modification in drive organization. The ego experiences an upsurge in maturity and strength during latency with a movement toward greater autonomy, increasing ego differentiation, and, in general, ego expansion. But with the onset of puberty, there is a flooding of the ego with the newly emerging instinctual pressures, leaving the ego relatively weak vis-à-vis the ascendency of libidinal and aggressive drives. The ego insufficiency during the earlier phases of adolescent development is partly responsible for some of the chaos, turmoil, and crisis. It is only later, as a result of the resolution of the Oedipus complex, that the ego once more asserts its autonomy in relationship to the id and the superego and the ego-ideal emerge out of the structure of the superego. The ego-ideal constitutes idealized goals and aspirations that lie in the future.

Somatic Maturation. The process of somatic maturation provides the physiological background for the progression in psychosexual development, and it is only against this biological aspect of development that changes in drive organization, ego development, the nature of conflict, and conflict resolution can be understood. Maturation is responsible for the profound changes in the primary and secondary sex characteristics; hence, the preadolescent and the early adolescent show much concern about these bodily changes. These concerns become obsessive and problematic when the adolescent discovers deviation in physical development—imagined or real. All of this contributes to an acute and heightened self-consciousness about the body. Pubertal maturation draws adolescents' attention particularly to the changing sex organs; they are curious about the functions of these organs and whether their own are normal and are anxious about their protection. "It is this preoccupation (unconscious and preconscious) with the sexual organs, their function, intactness, protection, and not the relationship theme of love and its fulfillment which stands out in the play construction of the preadolescent" (Blos, 1962: 58).

Blos is less specific in describing the maturational changes that take place in the body than, for example, Tanner (1962), who provides a detailed account of the process of somatic maturation. Blos sees it as his task to elaborate on the psychological consequences of these pubertal body changes, and he maintains that the "synchronicity between somatic and psychological changes," which is quite obvious during the early phases of adolescent development, disappears as the end of adolescence is approached.

Conflict Formation and Conflict Resolution. Each phase brings with it its own phase-specific set of conflicts requiring conflict resolution before normal progression to the next higher phase becomes possible. The more significant conflicts are the previously discussed negative oedipal conflict of preadolescence and early adolescence and the positive oedipal conflict of adolescence proper. Related to oedipal issues are the conflicts that emerge from the change from bisexuality during early adolescence to heterosexuality. The infantile dependency on parents produces conflict when heterosexual object choice becomes paramount. Conflicts are both essential and normative for developmental progress; only through conflict and conflict resolution can maturity be attained. "The formation of a conflict between generations and its subsequent resolution is the normative task of adolescence" (Blos, 1979: 11). It is only through the resolution of conflicts that normal movement through the adolescent phases is made possible, and this process is referred to by Blos as "the adolescent process."

In the remaining discussion of the six phases of adolescent development, an outline of this normal adolescent process will be presented and organized around the themes of drive organization, ego development, somatic maturation, conflict, and conflict resolution.

LATENCY

The latency period is viewed by Blos as an important preparatory phase for entry into adolescence, and much deviant development seems to emerge later from lack of success in ego consolidation—a major developmental task of latency. During latency, the libidinal drive—not entirely under cover—is less intense, more diffuse, and more easily diverted into constructive educational endeavors than during the oedipal periods that precede or those that follow it. The expansion of the ego renders the libidinal drive less dominant in the psychological structure. According to Blos, the latency period distinguishes itself from all other psychoanalytic stages of development insofar as no new instinctual aim or libidinal object emerges. The bisexual orientation of earlier developmental phases continues to be tolerated. The end of latency has arrived when the resurgence of libidinal drive is imminent. Indications that the transition between latency and prepuberty is taking place are the deterioration in manners, lack of concentration, decline in cooperativeness vis-à-vis authorities, and the increasing conformity to peer group pressures (Blos, 1970: 71).

Latency is a period of ego expansion, ego differentiation, and increased ego autonomy. The increased ego autonomy is accompanied by growth in several areas: cognition, judgment, logic, memory, empathy, anticipation, tension tolerance, self-awareness, the ability to distinguish between reality and fantasy, and a more precise differentiation between action and thoughts (Blos, 1970: 9). The confusion between internal and external, which is characteristic of early childhood—what Piaget calls the subjective and the objective—must be overcome before the end of the latency period. Healthy ego development during latency greatly facilitates the acquisition of basic knowledge and skills in school and contributes to the mastery of the environment, a major achievement of the latency period. The ego functions are also becoming increasingly resistant to regression and disorganization during latency (Blos, 1962: 57) and hence provide the necessary strength to deal effectively with the increase in drive intensity that will occur during the period of puberty.

During latency the body continues to grow at a fairly even and stable rate, without any dramatic changes in body configuration or body sensations. The growth in physical stature makes possible greater physical mobility and independence and provides the somatic basis for increasing mastery of the environment. There is now a decline in the expressive use of the body, for increased verbal facility results in separation of verbal expression from motor activity (Blos, 1962: 55). In general, the unselfconscious body spontaneity and body expressiveness of the younger child decline during latency, a decline that leads to the high degree of self-consciousness, body awareness, physical awkwardness, and body preoccupation observed through adolescence.

The latency period is relatively free of intrapsychic conflicts, especially if the conflicts surrounding the Oedipus complex during the phallic stage have been successfully resolved. During latency the boy represses the remaining oedipal attachments more successfully than the girl, rendering entry into latency somewhat more conflictual. For girls, the transition is smoother since the oedipal issues linger on and become part of the emotional life of latency; the oedipal conflicts do not require repression or a definitive conclusion but may actually continue into adolescence (Blos, 1962: 55).

Intrapsychic development is characterized by increasing ego autonomy and ego maturity, reducing conflict between id, ego, and superego. Thus, a successful latency provides the strength for successful conflict resolution in adolescence and contributes to the development of tolerance in handling conflictual and painful experiences. Deficits in ego development during latency make the later resolution of adolescent conflicts difficult, if not impossible, and may impede the "adolescent process."

PREADOLESCENCE

With the beginning of preadolescence, also referred to as prepuberty, the most significant change is a pronounced increase in the energy level of pubertal drive, both libidinal and aggressive (Blos, 1941: 196–197). This drive is still quite diffuse and not yet focused on one specific love object or an instinctual aim but rather is experienced in general tensions that demand to be discharged. These instinctual tensions manifest themselves in restlessness, moodiness, and an increase in aggression. Preadolescence typically is the time when delinquent behavior begins. The aim of the drive is still diffuse—literally anything can become sexually stimulating: fear, shock, anger, or general excitement, even if void of erotic content (Blos, 1962: 57). Girls during this stage often appear "horse crazy," and boys are more preoccupied with "dirty jokes" than with sex. The push toward genital organization is counterbalanced by a strong regressive movement toward infantile modalities—oral (overeating, oral greediness), anal (preoccupation with buttocks and the process of elimination), phallic (sadism) (Blos, 1970: 22). Traits such as smuttiness, neglect of body care, gluttony, and motor excitability emerge at this stage. The effects of the increase in drive energy manifest themselves in a growing intensity of affect, making for unpredictability and uncontrollability of affective responses (Blos, 1979: 195).

Temper tantrums, day dreams, bragging, swaggering, sulking and weeping, lying, cheating—these are the reactions of the small child faced by powers too strong for him, and these are the defenses to which he returns when the strains of adolescence are more than he can face. As temporary reactions they are usual and entirely to be expected at this time. Many types of behavior which would be considered dangerously neurotic during adulthood or middle childhood must be viewed as normal during the preadolescent period [Blos, 1941: 280].

The loss of responsiveness to parental control, already begun in late latency, continues. The preadolescent begins to withdraw from the family group, simultaneously entering the gang stage (Blos, 1941: 236–237). Parents often react with ambivalent feelings to this new attitude, revealing not only anger and resentment but also acceptance and support. Their inconsistency contributes further to the disturbance of adolescent-parent relationships. "Puberty constitutes a period of intensified stress and, as a consequence, it readily exposes certain inadequacies of psychic structure that were previously either nonexistent or seemingly irrelevant" (Blos, 1970: 9).

In preadolescence the demands for gratification of the increased instinctual tension meet the disapproval of the ego and the superego and thus introduce a disequilibrium in the psychic structure. Various mechanisms of defense are drawn on by the ego in order to deal with the tension between id and superego: repression, reaction formation, and displacement. (For definitions and illustrations of the various defense mechanisms, see Chapter 2.) In addition, there is "the revival of such primitive defenses as magical thinking, projection and denial, as well as all kinds of obsessive-compulsive traits, habits and thoughts" (Blos, 1970: 71). An illustration of reaction formation is the preadolescent boy who develops antagonism toward the opposite sex; he has no use for overt affection from his mother and avoids close contacts with females in general. The restructuring of the preadolescent ego is best characterized by the contradictory emotions: "the desire to go ahead" and "the fear of losing familiar ground" (Blos, 1970: xxi).

A qualitative maturational shift takes place with the beginning of pubescence and "pubertal maturation remains the biological initiator of adolescence" (Blos, 1971: 962). Some of the psychological restructuring of preadolescence actually precedes the physical changes of pubescence. The conflict of preadolescence emerges out of the changes in somatic maturation. The sudden increase in sex drive upsets the balance between ego and id and manifests itself in castration anxiety for boys and renewed penis envy in girls (Blos, 1962). Anxiety and worry about the possibility of injury to the sex organs are not at all uncommon, emerging partly from castration anxiety, and partly from guilt feelings as an accompanying emotion of masturbatory behavior.

The direction of psychosexual development, as well as the developmental time schedules of the two sexes, begins to take different routes with the onset of puberty. The spurt of physical development in girls takes place earlier; girls during puberty are actually more mature than boys, perform better in school, are superior in social development, show more mature interest patterns, and are superior to boys in introspection.

With the onslaught of pubescence, there is a rejection of the opposite sex, who are treated with derision and contempt. Instead, there is a turning toward the same-sex peer group. Sex differences in physical development are most pronounced at a time when the individual experiences a "heightened group- and self-consciousness" (Blos, 1941: 231), which has a significant influence on the social adjustment and the intellectual and emotional development of the adolescent.

During pre- and early adolescence, the boy directs his aggressive impulses and his castration fears primarily toward his mother but also toward females in general; actual conflicts with the father reach a low point. As a defensive reaction against castration fear, the boy shows an exaggerated idealization and aggrandizement of his father. During this negative passive oedipal phase of early puberty, it is the castrating mother rather than the father who is feared and avoided.

Preadolescent boys fear and even dream of the "phallic castrating, preoedipal mother" and develop a defense against female sexuality. During this phase boys may actually be repulsed by advances from the opposite sex, including affection for their mothers. The same-sex peer group provides a masculine identification and moral support, but at the price of conforming to its standard and values. Same-sex friendships often involve shared secrets, intimacies, and erotically tinted homosexual attractions and experiences, an idea also emphasized by Sullivan (see Chapter 5). Preadolescent boys avoid girls (Blos, 1962: 60), belittle them, and have no use for female sentimentality, "affection, endearment and amorousness" (Blos, 1979: 121). Fondling, kissing, protecting, and punishing by the mother are frowned upon and avoided, especially when it might be seen by peer group members.

Only later, during adolescence proper, with the reemergence of the positive aggressive Oedipus complex (about age fourteen to seventeen) does the hostile-aggressive impulse once more turn against the father and the sexual impulses toward the mother.

The female, as she enters the negative oedipal conflict of puberty, encounters a complex crisis, especially in relationship with her mother. Underlying this conflict is a fear of passivity, which stems from the girl's earlier relationship to her mother during the negative Oedipus complex in the phallic stage. As a defense against her fear of passivity and infantile dependency, she tends to overidentify with the male and aggressively turns toward the opposite sex. She "exaggerates her heterosexual desires and attaches herself to boys" (Blos, 1979: 110), and in the process she becomes either the "tomboy" or "the little woman." Attachments of this nature are defensive reactions against the pull toward passive, infantile dependencies and should be considered a necessary step in the movement toward mature femininity (Blos, 1981). Such heterosexual interest can lead to actual sexual involvement, which at this age lacks genuine personal-affectionate intimacy, in spite of the experience of passion. Blos, speaking of this thrust toward activity, refers to the preadolescent girl as being "boy crazy" and being an Amazon, pushing the boy into heterosexual social activities for which he is emotionally unprepared and in which he is not yet interested (Blos, 1962; 1979).

Girls are inclined to make demands on boys that boys cannot meet adequately and that merely force the boys into stronger defensiveness. As a result girls are likely to encounter defeat in their first heterosexual advances toward boys of their age group (Blos, 1941: 250–251).

If the girl should succumb to the regressive pull toward passivity during this stage, her drive orientation would more closely resemble that of the boy, since she too would experience homosexual yearnings and an antagonism toward the male.

EARLY ADOLESCENCE

Early adolescence, or early puberty, distinguishes itself from preadolescence by a higher degree of goal orientation of the libidinal drive and an increase in aggressive drive. The new goal consists of a beginning movement toward libidinous extrafamilial object finding, resulting in a more intense, richer, emotional life. With the onset of puberty, identification with parents declines rapidly and is replaced by an identification with others through friendship, admiration, hero worship, idealization, crushes, and infatuations. This developmental pattern of a frequently strong identification with parents and parental figures during latency, followed by a stage of identification with glamorized and romanticized persons during adolescence, and culminating in the identification with an imaginary character who is a composite of many desirable qualities during late adolescence has been demonstrated empirically (Havighurst and

MacDonald, 1955). These early adolescent identifications frequently have an erotic undertone; however, the libidinal love objects of early adolescence are not necessarily heterosexual in nature, since a strong bisexual tendency still prevails. The newly emerging drive manifests itself in "crushes" on sports and entertainment heroes of both sexes, people often considerably older than the adolescent.

Friendships with members of the same sex similarly take on an idealized quality, show a high degree of intimacy, which thrives on secrecy and may become eroticized and sexualized.

The phase of early adolescence is the time of friendship (still confined to the same sex) with unmistakably erotic overtones, either attenuated or more or less consciously experienced. Mutual masturbation, transient homosexual practices, mutually granted scotophilic gratification, shared transgression or crimes, idealization, feelings of bliss and elation in the presence of a friend—these are experiences in which the narcissistic object choice is manifested [Blos, 1965: 161].

The increase in the libidinal drive and the strong clash between the id and the superego during early adolescence leave the ego weakened, inefficient, and fumbling, because, even though independent from parental authority and control, the ego has also lost its legitimate support from the parental ego. In order to cope with the increasing internal conflicts with parents, which grew out of the oedipal situation and the reorganization of the emotional life—creating a feeling of chaos—the ego draws on various mechanisms of defense and "the gap between the ego and the superego" widens (Blos, 1962: 76).

Blos maintains that the continuing maturation of the pubertal drive toward heterosexual genitality eventually pushes the individual out of the preadolescent phase. In the male particularly there is a noticeable increase in masturbatory behavior and, while it produces tension reduction and drive gratification, the dynamic meaning relates to counteracting castration anxiety and fear of homosexuality, which are still prevalent during this stage of strong bisexual tendencies. "The adolescent boy's defensive reaction toward passive homosexual strivings or fantasies far exceeds in intensity anything we witness in an adolescent girl who might sense or become aware of lesbian feelings" (Blos, 1981).

The conflicts of early adolescence emerge from the bisexual nature that still prevails during that phase. Early adolescence is a state of chaos and conflict, since the newly emerging goal in drive orientation requires abandoning homosexual and bisexual tendencies, resulting in a total reorganization of the libidinal drive and the emotional life. This qualitative change in drive orientation toward genitality requires that the preoedipal and oedipal love objects be given up in favor of nonincestuous love objects. This process requires a detachment from parental dependencies and is often accompanied by outright conflict. "The conflict seems to focus on the mother and 'severance action' is required to resolve the passive dependency on the mother." At the same time the still-prevalent bisexual tendencies produce conflict in drive organization. In order to progress to the next higher stage, these tendencies will need to be replaced by a heterosexual orientation. The beginning of a sexual identity during early adolescence is the prerequisite to adolescence proper, which is based on a heterosexual orientation (Blos, 1970: 171). However, heterosexual orientation does not imply premarital sexual intercourse. Blos warns that too early a sexual initiation may interfere with ego development and the growth toward emotional maturity. Some empirical support for this assertion comes from the Jessor and Jessor (1975) study demonstrating that the transition from a virginal to a nonvirginal state, when it occurs in early adolescence, is commonly associated with deviant behaviors.

ADOLESCENCE PROPER

Adolescence proper, or middle adolescence, is characterized by a decline in bisexuality and a further modification in drive organization, which involves an intensification of the sexual drive as well as the aggressive drive. Libido is now directed toward new love objects, that is, the goal of the drive is heterosexual object finding. The recognition of the heterosexual tendencies of this phase requires both a separation from the family of origin and a new and final resolution of the positive oedipal conflict (Blos, 1962). This is a period of psychological restructuring (Blos, 1979), of chaos, of mood swings, of turmoil and crisis, of experimentation, and it manifests itself in the unpredictable, vacillating, and rebellious behavior typical of adolescents. Hence Blos uses the expression "proverbial adolescence" to characterize this period.

At about fourteen or fifteen, sometimes sooner or later, the pattern seems to shift. The child is still an unstable, moody, and rather unpredictable person—battling with adult authority and with himself—overanxious, self-conscious, and overconfident by turns, apparently sophisticated but frequently only on the verbal level, desperately wanting help and guidance but often quite unable to ask for it or accept it from those he likes best. Yet in many ways he is much more grown up than he was and much easier to teach. By this time his interest in the opposite sex is ordinarily open and frankly expressed. He is as meticulous about appearance and manners as he was careless a few years before; he is clean and more orderly again and considerably more responsible [Blos, 1941: 272].

Adolescence proper is not only a period of heightened turmoil and crisis but also a period of heightened ego experiences. The ego rather than restraining and diverting the libido, as in the two preceding stages, now joins the libido in its movement toward heterosexual object finding. This process involves a disengagement from the earlier family object ties and immature dependencies, a resolution of the second, positive Oedipus complex, and a movement toward heterosexuality.

Oedipal wishes and their attending conflicts come to life again. The finality of this inner break with the past shakes the adolescent's emotional life to the center; by the same token, this break opens up to him unknown horizons, raises hopes, and generates fears [Blos, 1962: 88].

The developmental task of this period is the emotional disengagement from parents. "The definitive resolution of the [Oedipus] complex is the inherent task of adolescence" (Blos, 1979: 325). The resolution of the pubertal Oedipus complex implies a distinct turn toward the achievement of a sexual identity and independence.

Somatic maturation continues into adolescence proper, also referred to as advanced puberty. With the movement away from bisexuality and toward heterosexual object finding, sexuality now becomes sensitive to stimuli that are exclusively heterosexual—erotic in nature—in contrast to the more diffuse and global expression in the nature of the jokes that fascinate early adolescents. Jokes, anal in content in the preceding stages, now reveal a distinct sexual and erotic flavor. Concurrent with this change in sexual sensitivity is the newly emerging experience of tender love, affection, devotion, and deep-burning emotions, as well as the idealization of the heterosexual love object.

However, as a counterforce restraining the movement toward extrafamilial heterosexual love, there is a fear of a new dependency on the love object especially at this point when the dependence on parents is just beginning to decline (Blos, 1962: 101). The adolescent often expresses this conflict by stating that he is fearful of getting "too involved," or "going too far" with his heterosexual love object. He is fearful of love and new dependencies because he is just beginning to escape from the intense emotional involvement with his parents. Anna Freud and Otto Rank speak of the adolescent's defense mechanisms of asceticism, intellectualization, and promiscuity as being based on the fear of a new emotional dependency on a heterosexual partner when dependency conflicts with parents are still lingering on. Even the striving for independence from parents is not without some ambivalence, since it not only contains a strong desire for adult freedom and independence but also an unacknowledged wish for childlike dependence and parental protection coupled with fear of loss of security and adult guidance. "The wish for independence augments the feeling of loss and of security as derived from the infantile parent image. The price of independence is the tolerance of loneliness, as well as the acceptance of personal limitations and of the temporality of life'' (Blos, 1970: 235).

The pubertal conflicts that began in preadolescence and early adolescence find their climax in the turmoil and the chaos of adolescence proper. The oedipal wishes reemerge once more, this time in their active positive form, which means that for the boy the active libidinal drive turns toward the mother and the aggressive, hostile impulses turn toward the father. Oedipal wishes emerging from the id collide with the superego when confronted with a relatively weak ego and increase internal conflicts. Guilt feelings and anxieties grow out of these oedipal desires. Oedipal thoughts, which are unacceptable to the superego, constitute the typical internal conflict of adolescence proper.

Somatic maturation, which reaches its peak during adolescence proper, not only intensifies the libidinal drive but also increases "the aggressive drive in equal measures." The aggressive drive manifests itself in quarrelsomeness and emerges in dreams and fantasies, including those of murder and suicide. "Aggression turns against the self, the object, or the nonhuman environment, indicating a fateful imbalance or defusion of the two basic drives" (Blos, 1979: 24). The reduction in bisexuality in drive orientation, which was characteristic of the earlier adolescent phases, contributes now to its very opposite—namely, a pronounced polarity of masculinity and femininity. Research evidence actually suggests that sex role conceptualizations, including sex role stereotyping, especially in terms of the opposite sex ideal, seem to reach their height in adolescence (Urberg, 1979).

LATE ADOLESCENCE

Drive organization during late adolescence continues to focus on heterosexual object finding and becomes more permanently entrenched in that position; however, some of the chaos, turmoil, reorganization, and restructuring that characterized adolescence proper has by now subsided. The ego emerges strengthened from the chaos of adolescence proper and begins to achieve more stable and lasting organizational structure. A new character synthesis begins to take place; the sexual identity is more firmly entrenched and becomes irreversible. There is a consolidation of social roles and personal identifications, which gives this phase its descriptive title, "personality consolidation." Blos identifies the developmental task of late adolescence as the "elaboration of a unified ego" and the achievement of a "stable ego organization," terms highly reminiscent of Erikson's notion of the achievement of an ego identity. "During normal adolescence the growing child uses his advanced cognitive faculty and somatic maturity to gain emotional, moral, and physical independence. This is a time when he forms his own view of his past, present, and future"

(Blos, 1979: 415). As the ego stabilizes there is decline in the experience of inner crisis, and many of the conflicts, the disorganizations, and the disunity that were so prevalent in the previous phase of development suddenly begin to decline (Blos, 1962).

The new ego organization is reflected in an integrated personality pattern in which id, ego, and superego are no longer in an adversary relationship. A more harmonious and cooperative personality structure is established in which both the id and the superego serve the purpose of the ego. Now the individual is able to conduct various daily interactions with the social and physical environment and satisfy basic needs within socially prescribed boundaries.

One major change in the tripartite structure of the id, ego, and superego takes place during late adolescence. According to psychoanalytic theory, the superego develops primarily after the resolution of the phallic-oedipal situation during latency. The function of the superego is that of prohibition (moral conscience). It sets boundaries and punishes the ego for transgressions through guilt and anxiety. As a result of the resolution of the pubertal-oedipal situation, the superego differentiates itself further, and the ego-ideal emerges as a new structure within the superego. The ego-ideal attains a clear and definitive structure within the superego during late adolescence. "The ego ideal becomes the heir to the regulatory function of the superego" (Blos, 1962: 152). It contains not only an individual component but a social component as well (Blos, 1979). It becomes the agency of aspiration and wish fulfillment, and its function is to set goals, to punish by shame and by lowering self-esteem.

The model of stages of ego development advanced by Loevinger (1976) does not readily fit Blos' theory of adolescent development. However, her stage five, defined as the conscientious stage, implies that morality has been internalized and that long-term goals and personal ideals have begun to emerge. The imperatives emerging from internalized moral values now take precedence over conformity to values sanctioned by the peer group. Loevinger's conceptualizations—not without some empirical support— appear to be quite analogous to the psychoanalytic notion of the ego-ideal and the conscience emerging out of the structure of the superego in the late adolescent phase. The differentiation of the superego into conscience and ego-ideal in psychoanalytic theory also appears to be a necessary prerequisite for the attainment of stage five (social contract orientation) and stage six (universal ethical principles orientation) in Kohlberg's theory of moral development (see Chapter 9).

The ego-ideal aims for perfection and sets goals that can never be fully attained; however, even the striving for perfection produces a sense of well-being. The ego must maintain a careful balance between the narcissistic internal self-idealization and the formation of realistic external ideals. The new ego-ideal of late adolescence is behind "the proclivity of youth for high ideals, for idealizations and ideologies'' (Blos, 1979: 320), including not uncommon personal vocational goals that lie beyond resources and/or capabilities. A Project Talent (Flanagan, 1979) investigation indicates, for example, that of those twelfth-grade boys who planned a career in law, 41 percent had academic aptitude scores below the overall average; similarly, of those who planned a career in mathematics, 33 percent scored below average in academic aptitude.

Late adolescence sees the resolution of instinctual conflicting tendencies that contributed to the turmoil and the chaotic disorganization of adolescence proper. Somatic maturation comes to completion during late adolescence, sexual needs reach their peak, and according to Kinsey, even ''sexual outlets'' reach an all-time high for the male adolescent. Drive and ego now combine in the search for a heterosexual love object, reducing ambiguous and conflictual emotions in the search for identifications and intimacies outside the family of origin (Blos, 1979).

Late adolescence is the consolidation phase of adolescent development during which most conflicts are resolved. The sexual identity takes on a final form and is no longer easily reversible. There is a gain in purposeful actions, behavior becomes predictable, self-esteem acquires stability, and emotions gain constancy. Recreational, avocational, vocational, and religious commitments and preferences emerge with greater stability (Blos, 1962).

POSTADOLESCENCE

Postadolescence marks the transitional phase between adolescence and adulthood and brings to completion the ultimate goal of the adolescent process, namely, the establishment of a stable drive organization that is in harmony with the ego organization and ushers in the final achievement of a stable self. Because self and object representation have developed firmer boundaries (Blos, 1979: 118), self-esteem becomes more constant and more stable. Self-esteem is less vulnerable to manipulation from outside sources and has come under control of the ego-ideal. Confronted with defeat, failure, or criticism, the ego, seeing itself now as separate from the ego-ideal, does not use rationalizations as defenses; it can nondefensively identify the boundaries between personal responsibility, situational circumstances, and unrealistic goals and can admit to errors and personal shortcomings. The completion of the adolescent crisis results in a more stable personality structure, and individuals can now reject false evaluations that do not correspond with their own self-evaluations (Gruen, 1960). Feelings become more consistent as a stable sense of self leads to a greater certainty about one's own personality characteristics, and there is a noticeable reduction in anxiety (Bronson, 1959).

The developmental task already begun during adolescence proper and late adolescence—that is, the attainment of identification, loyalties, and intimacies outside of the family of origin—becomes more urgent and more dominant at this point. With clearer boundaries established between self and object representation, the rebellious and conflictual elements that prevailed in these earlier phases subside and the adolescent's perception of the parents becomes more realistic, acknowledging, and accepting of positive as well as negative attributes. There are no more developmental road blocks to nonincestuous heterosexual object finding (Blos, 1962).

During postadolescence, the stabilizing tendencies of successful conflict resolution contribute to character formation. The ego has now become heir to the idealized parent of childhood. The adaptive and integrative functions of the ego continue to grow. What emerges during postadolescence is the moral personality, firmly anchored in society; there is a renewed experimentation with ego interests and with potential love objects. Postadolescence sees the emergence of a clearer conception of social roles, a sense of purpose, and a sense of direction.

EDUCATIONAL IMPLICATIONS

Blos recognizes the historical trend toward earlier physiological development and sexual maturation, described in more detail by Muuss (1970a), Tanner (1968), and others, but he remains dubious that the earlier sexual maturation of today's youth is accompanied by a corresponding acceleration in emotional, social, moral, and cognitive maturation. Hence, he warns that parents, schools, and other institutions should not simply allow and encourage this downward extension of adolescent heterosexual behavior under the rationalization of the typical American preoccupation with "the earlier and the faster, the bigger and the better." On the contrary, he feels that social institutions should retain their protective and containing functions rather than supporting or even rewarding this trend toward earlier and earlier heterosexual interest and involvement.

In addition, the physical and sexual maturation of boys and girls proceeds—as has been demonstrated by Tanner and others—according to very different time schedules. The earlier-maturing girls may make demands on boys, for which the less mature boys are totally unprepared. Because of these well-known sex differences in onset and speed of social-sexual development, the general acceleration of sexual development, the direction of sexual orientation, and the nature of conflict at the preadolescent and early adolescent phases (from the ages of about eleven to fourteen), Blos seriously suggests "that the separation of the sexes in school during these early years [not during the entire adolescent period] is, psychologically and biologically, well advised" (Blos, 1971: 970). During these years, when sex differences in intellectual, physical, social, and psychological development are most pronounced, boys and girls are poorly matched companions in work and play. Even Mead has expressed ideas quite similar to those of Blos: "The junior high school has become a forcing ground for inappropriate and socially maladjusted attitudes in boys and girls, laying the basis for hostility to females on the boys' part . . ." (Mead, 1961: 38). Blos, instead of identifying hostility as the crucial outcome, speaks of this situation as forcing boys into "stronger defensiveness." He continues his argument by pointing out that those boys who do develop a precocious preference for girls and bypass the strong identification with their own sex experience more concern about the adequacy of their own masculinity later in life while preadolescent and early adolescent boys who keep the company of boys of their own age seem to establish a firmer and more lasting masculine identity. This is a recurrent theme in several other theories such as M. Mead and Sullivan. Similarly, Blos views early sexual intercourse as severely interfering with the normal developmental and preparatory functions characteristic of this stage.

> We have ample evidence that an acceptance of the young adolescent as a self-directing, sexually active "young person" interferes severely with the preparatory functions of this stage. We can say that ego building at this time augurs more promisingly for the attainment of maturity than the early adolescent striving for a full sex life [Blos, 1971: 970].

Evidence for the assertion that frequent sexual intercourse during early adolescence interferes with ego development and is often associated with numerous other psychosocial problems emerges from such varied sources as Jessor and Jessor (1975), Loevinger (1976), and a summary review by Muuss (1982a).

One rather novel, insightful, and quite significant educational implication emerges from Blos' writings in regard to parents' methods of discipline, their socialization efforts, and their teaching of values. Blos calls into question the contemporary preoccupation with, and the all-too-ready absorption of, so-called expert advice by parents and educators. Blos maintains that with the gradual but radical change in family structure—and with the increasing significance of the mass media and commercialism— advertising and continuing education, the traditions of families in matters of childrearing, nutrition, learning expectations, values, manners, and moral stringencies have become replaced by a superabundance of so-called expert advice. Such expert advice flows freely and continuously into the home via newspapers, TV, magazines, books, lectures, films, PTA, and even church meetings. Thus, expert advice has replaced or is replacing established family traditions.

However, the various forms of expert advice are not based on a systematic, well-integrated, and uniform system of values; nor do they maintain an underlying coherent philosophy. Quite to the contrary, they come from very different and frequently even contradictory theoretical, philosophical, political, scientific, or religious systems. Furthermore, they often enter the home only in bits and pieces or as simplified and predigested summaries of serious work, presented by newspaper journalists or popular magazine writers. They sometimes support, sometimes contradict, and sometimes replace family tradition. Furthermore, today's expert advice may support, contradict, or replace yesterday's expert advice. Parents faithfully try out what they have heard or read today only to abandon that approach without having reaped the benefits of their efforts, replacing it a few weeks or months later with a quite different approach encountered more recently—one that sounds better or happens to be ''in.'' Parents who too eagerly, or even reluctantly, begin to apply this bewildering jumble of advice to their own offspring thereby ''abdicate their personal responsibility in favor of choices made by the expert.'' In this process parents by necessity surrender their own values and convictions as well as family tradition. ''This submission to the expert has drained ever larger sections of parental actions or attitudes of consistency, integration, and integrity'' (Blos, 1971: 972).

Childrearing has become ''synthetic'' and often inconsistent; hence, it is no wonder that parents have become confused and children unresponsive. Blos feels rather strongly that this strange mixture of so-called scientific advice concerning all areas of childrearing has itself become a major problem, contributing to family disorganization, alienation, ineffective childrearing practices, and unresponsive and recalcitrant children. Children, in turn, as soon as they can read and understand what is being said, get plugged into the expert advice circuit themselves and, as adolescents, pick out ideas and advice contradictory to that put forth by their parents. Thus, at an age when it is natural for adolescents to question and challenge parental values, adolescents quote expert advice on marijuana, smoking, dating, fashion, and sex to bolster their arguments, exposing their parents as ''old-fashioned,'' ''narrow-minded,'' ''past the time,'' ''out of it,'' or simply authoritarian. All these charges are based on the adolescents' claim that ''scientific evidence has shown that. . . .''

Schools seem to neglect an important responsibility in not teaching the adolescent about the phenomena of pubescence. It is a well-known fact that during adolescence the variations in somatic maturation are so pronounced that the identification of children by their chronological age is meaningless and sets up the incorrect notion that all twelve-and-a-half-year-old girls are in the same or even a similar stage of development. Actually, half of these girls are premenarcheal and half postmenarcheal; they espouse different values and different interests, prefer different types of activities, and have different degrees of feminine identification. The picture would be further complicated if one were to introduce twelve-and-a-half-year-old boys into the discussion. We know that the physical changes that accompany puberty pose a heavy emotional burden for the adolescent who is behind others in physical growth. Furthermore, adolescents are so preoccupied with physical normality that they are disturbed by even minor deviations. However, the adolescent usually does not know that most of these deviations that he observes in his own body and that disturb him are really quite normal. Thus, even minor or imagined deviations can become major psychological problems. The morbid preoccupation with normality, as well as curiosity about the function of sex organs and protection of primary and secondary sex characteristics, is most pronounced during pubescence. Since adolescents usually have little or no scientific basis by which to evaluate the actual adequacy of their own development, many uncertainties and anxieties arise, stemming primarily from furtive comparison with peers and peers' teasing comments, especially in the shower room. Any deviation from the "group average" can become a matter of concern and a source of worry. The emotional impact is magnified greatly when development does not progress in a sex-appropriate fashion—for example, when there are such sex-inappropriate characteristics as breast development or a feminine physique in boys, not at all uncommon during early adolescence. Boys especially are disturbed by such deviation from the normal course of development, even though most of these developmental "deviances" fall well within the normal range and are frequently only temporary. Such physical deviations negatively influence adolescents' social and emotional responsiveness and their general attitude toward themselves and toward life (Blos, 1941: 233). As a defense, during this phase an exaggerated preoccupation with maleness and masculinity emerges in boys. Some of the emotional significance of these well-known facts of very pronounced individual variations in the pubescent growth pattern and even the normality and the temporary quality of some sex-inappropriate secondary sex characteristics could be reduced through a well-timed educational program devoted to the psychological significance of the physiological changes during early adolescence.

5: HARRY STACK SULLIVAN'S INTERPERSONAL THEORY OF ADOLESCENT DEVELOPMENT

HARRY Stack Sullivan (1892–1949) proposed a social psychiatry theory of human development that highlights the importance of interpersonal relationships and communication. Unlike the traditional intrapsychic theories, which emphasize internal dynamics, his model accentuates the social component, the interaction between personality development and culture. He maintains—and therein lies one of his major contributions to personality theory—that the intrapsychic component of personality cannot be observed directly except through interpersonal interactions (which may take place in reality or in fantasy). His concern about interpersonal conflicts and tension extends far beyond individual and psychotherapeutic matters to include international conflict and prejudice as well as international understanding. He presented his most important paper on the topic of international understanding, entitled "Tension Interpersonal and International" (Sullivan, 1964), shortly before his death in Paris.

"Comfortable, successful interpersonal relationships are what life is all about," according to Sullivan. A complete understanding of Sullivan's ideas requires a conceptual framework of "field theory" (see Chapter 7). His view that psychiatry covers "much the same field as . . . social psychology, because scientific psychiatry has to be defined as . . . interpersonal relations" (Sullivan, 1953: 368) is unique. The social scientists C. H. Cooley and G. H. Mead exerted a strong influence on Sullivan. Especially noteworthy is Mead's idea that the self develops through the reflective appraisal of significant others; this became a major component of Sullivan's theory. His emphasis on the significance of interpersonal influences and his assertions that "every human being has as many personalities as he has interpersonal relations" (1964: 221) seems to anticipate the insights of W. Mischel and social psychology.

Sullivan underwent analysis with C. Thompson and participated actively in the American Psychoanalytic Association; however, his theory was most strongly influenced by sociological and anthropological thinking. He renounced many of the psychoanalytic constructs as insignificant explanations of human behavior and gave them a subordinate role in his theoretical model. In addition, he introduced his own unique terminology (e.g., defense mechanism = security measures) because he felt that many of the psychoanalytic concepts carried a heavy, specific burden of meaning. In contrast, the influences and terminologies of sociology, anthropology, and field theory permeate Sullivan's writing. He created a model that combines clinical, social-psychological, field-theoretical, and cognitive components.

Instead of explaining the primary forces in human development in terms of biological conditions, sexuality, internal conflicts, or aggression, Sullivan more than any other major theorist builds his developmental theory on the social context of human experiences. While he does not deny that constitutional factors play a role (as, for example, in schizophrenia), he plays down their significance because not much could change them. The social component of human development begins with a fundamental state of interpersonal relatedness in infancy and continues unabated throughout adulthood. Interpersonal relationships are the essential ingredients for normal human development; moreover, their destructive, anxiety-arousing manifestations provide explanations for immaturity, deviance, and psychopathology. The individual learns to behave in particular ways and learns to modify his behavior not because of biological imperatives but as a result of socialization. The major tenet of Sullivan's interpersonal theory, that a person does not and cannot exist without other people, becomes a recurring theme.

Sullivan's model of psychiatry is identified as "social psychiatry," and some commentators said that he really was a social psychologist whose specialty happened to be psychiatry. This model fits in well with our present concerns with adolescence: peer-group conformity, friendship patterns, peer pressure, and intimacy. Some current researchers of peer-group influences (Bronfenbrenner, 1986b; Kandel, 1986; Youniss, 1980) agree with Sullivan's theory that effective and meaningful peer relationships, especially during adolescence, are essential prerequisites for healthy and psychosocial development. Even the reverse receives much research support: that is, poor peer relationships contribute to poor mental health and depression. Furthermore, they are associated with delinquent behavior, poor school achievement, dropping out of school, running away from home, drug use, early sexual behavior, mental illness, and behavior disorder.

INTERPERSONAL RELATIONSHIPS

The quality and the nature of interpersonal relationships constitute the foundation of Sullivan's theory. *Interpersonal Theory of Psychiatry* (1953), his most important developmental book, posthumously published, is the major source for this chapter. According to Sullivan, interactions with other people are enormously important both in normal and pathological development. Sullivan's psychiatric research dealt with schizophrenic patients; however, his theories of normal development, especially adolescent development, will receive emphasis here.

Our relationships with other people influence how we develop and what we are. Sullivan defines personality as "the relatively enduring pattern of recurrent interpersonal situations which characterize a human life" (Sullivan, 1953: 111); this definition captures the significance of the "interpersonal," which is so prevalent in his theory. He perceives the satisfaction of interpersonal needs as even more important than that of sexual needs. Successful and positive interpersonal relationships are essential for a happy and satisfying life.

Sullivan virtually equates the personality of an individual with the recurring interpersonal relationships of that individual, almost to the extent of questioning whether a "unique individual self" independent of interactions with others actually exists. He is concerned that "entrenched feelings of independence and autonomy" have interfered with our understanding of interpersonal relationships, and he speaks of the "delusion of a unique individuality," an idea developed in "The Illusion of Personal Individuality" (1950).

The effects of interpersonal relationships can, of course, be both constructive and destructive. According to Sullivan (1953), the benefits of interpersonal contacts depend upon positive feedback. The knowledge that others value us and consider us attractive and worthwhile provides a feeling of security. However, when interpersonal relationships, especially in infancy and childhood, create a great deal of anxiety, the defenses we develop may impair our relationships with other people. Hence, almost by definition, social relationships are reciprocal in nature, and "one can find in others only that which is in the self" (Sullivan, 1947: 22). An adolescent who already has a low opinion of himself and feels inadequate tends to reject friendly overtures by others and remains hostile and distrustful. Positive, supportive, tension-reducing experiences with significant other people produce feelings of security. However, experiences that are negative, threatening, and anxiety-arousing create feelings of insecurity.

Depending on who they are interacting with at a particular time, individuals differ in the way they see themselves and in the way they behave. People can be understood only within the context of specific social interaction patterns. Thus, adolescents may—and often do—behave dramatically differently in their interaction patterns with parents, teachers, relatives, peers, valued friends, or members of the opposite sex. In other words, interpersonal relationships provide the most significant key to our understanding of human behavior.

THE SELF-SYSTEM

Closely related to Sullivan's general emphasis on interpersonal relationships is his specific use of the "self-system." Sullivan's notion of the self-system strongly reflects the influence of the social scientists concerned with the development of the self, especially C. H. Cooley and G. H. Mead. Since the self has a social origin, its theoretical primacy reflects the importance Sullivan accords to cultural and social as well as interpersonal experiences. Our sense of self is shaped by the manner in which "significant others"—people who are directly influential in our lives—see us and treat us. The self is first and foremost a social self, formed by others; in turn, the self becomes the instigator of social relationships. The self-system organizes life experiences within the personality. The self-system constitutes a very important part of personality, particularly important in fending off anxiety; however, it is only part of personality, not identical to it.

The self-system develops out of cultural, social, and interpersonal experiences; in the process it absorbs cultural values and becomes a "selective filter" through which experiences are incorporated in or excluded from awareness. "The origin of the self-system can be said to rest on the irrational character of culture or, more specifically, society" (Sullivan, 1953: 168). A self consists of the "reflected appraisal" by others. "If these appraisals were chiefly derogatory, as in the case of an unwanted child who was never loved . . . then the self dynamism will itself be chiefly derogatory. It will facilitate hostile, disparaging appraisals of other people and it will entertain disparaging and hostile appraisal of itself" (Sullivan, 1947: 22). The "reflected appraisal," the way significant people appraise the individual over an extended period of time, eventually becomes the way he appraises himself. There can be no standard for the evaluation of self other than the feedback received from others. In Shaw's play *Pygmalion,* Eliza Doolittle astutely describes this relationship when she says: "you see, really and truly . . . the difference between a lady and a flower girl is not how she behaves, but how she's treated. I shall always be a flower girl to Prof. Higgins, because he treats me like a flower girl . . . But I know I can be a lady to you, because you always treat me as a lady." Sullivanian analysis of Eliza's insight would go further. E. Doolittle is not only influenced by how others perceive her but also reacts to that perception (as the quote implies), which influences those who perceive her, which, in turn influences her . . . and so on. The relationship enters into an endless loop of continuing interactions.

According to Sullivan, "all that is the self-system arises in interpersonal relations" (1953: 200). The earliest experiences involve interactions with the "mothering one," experiences that can be tender and harmonious or forbidding and anxiety-arousing. As development progresses, both the kind of individuals with whom one interacts and the nature of the interactions increase in complexity. Furthermore, the self-system organizes these experiences and integrates them into a screening filter through which the individual perceives and evaluates events, especially whatever seems relevant to his self-appraisal. A human being without a self-system through which experiences are filtered is beyond imagination.

One of the important functions of the self-system is to provide satisfaction and to reduce the anxiety so often connected with the many experiences of disapproval or anticipated disapproval that accompany the socialization process. The self-system evolves in order to minimize anxiety in dealing with others (Sullivan, 1964). A coherent system which tends to perpetuate itself, the self-system is essential to the adjustment of the person in that it maintains self-respect, contributes to security, and is extremely important in warding off anxiety. After an equilibrium has been established in the self-system, it resists changes, because modifications can prove disturbing and threatening to the individual's sense of well-being. Unpleasant, anxiety-arousing experiences are dissociated from the self-system by a mechanism called "selective inattention." This mechanism renders us unable to observe the importance of those events that challenge established features of the self-system. Thus, while selective inattention reduces anxiety, it increases our "failure to profit from experiences." Because it resists change, the self-system can reduce anxiety; however, it can also interfere with an individual's ability to learn new but uncomfortable ideas, to try new approaches, and to live more effectively with others. Selective inattention also explains the great faith we have in our own prejudices: "The self-system is the principal stumbling block to favorable changes in personality . . . [but] also the principal influence that stands in the way of unfavorable changes in personality" (Sullivan, 1953: 169). Even though the self-system resists changes, Sullivan emphasizes repeatedly that it can and does undergo significant modifications, especially early in each of the transitions from one stage to another. Psychotherapy can offer another important route to self-system changes.

The self-system seeks the kind of information that contributes to self-protection and the maintenance of the equilibrium. Thus, it becomes of paramount importance in understanding the dynamics of interpersonal relationships. Not only is the self-system initially formed by the way important others treat us, but the reverse also holds true: our self-system guides our attention and influences how we perceive others. People with chronically low self-esteem inevitably anticipate that others also have unfavorable opinions about them. The self-system becomes the filter through which we evaluate our social environment and ourselves.

Healthy development is the process of transforming the undifferentiated and often anxiety-ridden self-system of the infant into the stable and secure self of the mature adult, in which various dynamisms are successfully integrated. The essential experience that makes this transition possible is based on mutually satisfying interpersonal relationships.

DYNAMISM IN SULLIVAN'S THEORY

Dynamism is a small component of the self-system. Sullivan defines dynamism as a "relatively enduring pattern of energy transformations which recurrently characterizes the interpersonal relations . . . which make up the distinctively human sort of being" (1953: 103). Both "enduring" and "recurrent," dynamism seems to approximate what in other systems has been referred to as "habit," "trait," "permanent attitude," or "consistent pattern of behavior." Dynamisms introduce an element of permanence, predictability, and stability into the self-system. Since dynamism is defined as a "pattern of energy," it does create tensions that disturb the individual. Furthermore, dynamisms do change over time, so that at various stages new patterns of interpersonal interactions develop. These changing patterns of interpersonal needs are the forces that move the child from one stage to the next. Actually, the deinvestment of energy from established interpersonal relationships allows the reinvestment of energy in new social endeavors. Particularly just before and during the early adolescent period do we see a deinvestment of energy from certain relationships (parents and family) and a reinvestment in new social relationships (chums and friends). The quality and nature of interpersonal relationships emerge and change as a result of being closely interwoven with dynamics.

All human beings basically have the same dynamism by which they try to maintain self-esteem and security; Sullivan emphasizes this similarity that all human beings—even psychotic patients—share, especially in contrast to other species. "Everyone is much more simply human than otherwise . . . the differences between any two instances of human personality—from the lowest-grade imbecile to the highest-grade genius— are much less striking than the differences between the least-gifted human being and a member of the nearest other biological genus" (Sullivan, 1953: 33). He has even spoken of the delusion of uniqueness and the illusion of individuality (1950). However, the extent to which humans reveal this dynamism and the way they do so demonstrate individual variations. Individual differences in the manifestations of dynamisms depend on earlier life experiences, on the developmental stage of the individual, and on the social, interpersonal context.

Sullivan refers to a great many different dynamisms that become important during development. However, the following distinctions need to be made: (1) the zones of interactions that are defined by specific areas of the body (oral dynamism, anal dynamism, etc.) and (2) the direction of interaction, which can be disjunctive, isolating, or conjunctive.

A *disjunctive dynamism* produces repetitive destructive energy patterns—for example, the dynamism of malevolence, in which the individual habitually behaves hostilely or aggressively toward other people.

An *isolating dynamism* moves the individual away from other people because it becomes detached from interpersonal relations—for example, the lust dynamism, which seeks sexual gratification primarily through masturbation or without regard to the partner's feelings.

The *conjunctive dynamism* involves behavior patterns that benefit the self-system, contribute to the expansion of the self, and build constructive interpersonal relationships. Examples of conjunctive dynamism include a nurturing dynamism, expressed by a recurring desire to care for others; an affinity dynamism, characterized by seeking close friendships with other people; and an intimacy dynamism, which develops during preadolescence and implies a very close relationship with just one other person.

TENSION: NEEDS, ANXIETY, ENERGY TRANSFORMATION

Sullivan views personality as an energy system whose goal is to reduce tension. The emphasis on energy and tension reduction is also a major tenet of the psychoanalytic model. Tensions arise from such basic needs as food, water, oxygen, sleep, and so on, but they also result from anxiety-provoking interpersonal situations. The alternating pattern of increasing and declining tensions creates an impetus toward development. Tensions fall along a continuum. At one extreme is absolute tension, a rarely observed state of panic, as when one suddenly faces the possibility of injury or death. At the other extreme is absolute absence of tension, experienced as utter well-being or euphoria. The illustration that Sullivan provides for absolute absence of tension is the infant in a state of deep sleep. The relationship between tension and euphoria is inverse: the higher the level of euphoria, the lower the level of tension of anxiety, and vice versa.

Tensions provide the organism with the potential for action; some tensions arise out of biological needs (e.g., oxygen, water, food, etc.). Tensions lead to energy transformations that dissipate the tension and create a mental state of satisfaction. The tension, by way of energy transformation, finds its outlet in work or overt action, when one is fully aware of what one is doing. Energy transformation may also take place in less obvious ways, as in scratching one's head, when there is no awareness of that particular behavior. Many patterns of tension and energy transformation are learned; they are culturally based and depend on what is socially approved and expected.

There are several kinds of tensions. Some arise from general, usually physical needs (hunger, thirst, etc.). Others, called zonal needs, emerge from specific body zones (oral, anal, etc.). Still others, which arise from anxiety, originate from social difficulties. Whereas general and zonal needs usually lead to integrative behavior, tension arising from the anxiety of interpersonal difficulties may lead to disjunctive or disintegrative behavior.

Anxiety is a particularly significant tension because it always interferes with the reduction of other needs and the achievement of a feeling of satisfaction. The anticipation of unfavorable evaluation of one's current behavior by significant others whose opinion we value creates anxiety. It always relates to what Sullivan (1953) calls "the whole interpersonal field." Anxiety is created by the way in which other people meet, or—more importantly—fail to meet the needs of the individual. Anticipatory anxiety is an emotion that we create in anticipation of negative events that may never happen or are very unlikely to happen. The distinction between fear and anxiety is important in this context. The origin of fear (such as fear of a biting dog) is known, but the origin of anxiety is unknown. Fear increases performance in the form of fight or flight; anxiety (often accompanied by loss of energy, memory, and the ability to concentrate) interferes with performance. Fear can be postponed, especially while we are struggling with the object of fear. Anxiety is not postponable except through security measures (defenses). Although the negative emotions felt in both instances are similar, these concepts cannot be used interchangeably.

Human beings seek security more than any other state. Sullivan elevates striving for "freedom from anxiety" to be the major motivating force in humans, an idea most clearly expressed by the existential philosophers, especially Kierkegaard. From the early experiences with the "mothering one," anxieties evolve out of interpersonal relationships, and anxiety remains the most pervasive interpersonal force in the human life cycle. The corollary is also true: an imagined threat to one's security produces anxiety. The more severe the threat, the greater the anxiety. As our anxiety level increases and our ability to benefit from experience, to plan ahead, and to communicate decreases, we resort to private, symbolic emotional fantasy or nonsymbolic responses. Anxiety can create disintegrative behavior; it blocks communication, which, in turn, increases the level of anxiety.

The reduction of needs is a transformation of energy that dissipates tension and produces a feeling of satisfaction (Sullivan, 1950: 85). Adolescents frequently experience a clash between various tensions, such as the desire for sexual behavior and the need to be free of anxiety. The sexual activities, to the extent that they are socially disapproved, increase anxiety. However, even if encouraged by the peer group, they may create anxiety in regard to interpersonal intimacy or in anticipation of other events (pregnancy, AIDS, etc.). To avoid this anxiety, therefore, means to avoid the sexual activity.

MODES OF EXPERIENCE

According to Sullivan, experience—and basically all cognition—occurs in one or more of three modes. These modes (the prototaxic, the parataxic, and the syntaxic) represent the elaboration of events in inner thought: they emerge in a developmental pattern that becomes increasingly complex. However, at times of difficulty, we all return to more primitive patterns of thought. Psychiatric patients commonly function at these lower levels.

The prototaxic mode is the crudest, most primitive, simplest, and—developmentally speaking—lowest form of awareness; it is also very common. It involves sensory experiences that are discrete, momentary, and unconnected to other events. Dreaming is a good illustration of the prototaxic mode. Prototaxic thinking is presymbolic and incapable of formulation or conceptualization. Communications by "emotional contagion or empathy," as between mother and child, are prototaxic. This mode involves primitive feelings of body states, sensations, and emotions that are not lost but become part of the unconscious. For example, tactile sensations from my buttocks inform me that I am sitting in a chair and also that I have been in that position too long.

The parataxic mode is more differentiated; however, it is primarily private in that the experience makes sense to the individual but not necessarily to others. Events are connected in a temporal sequence, as when a feeling of hunger leads to the anticipation of feeding. The parataxic mode involves private thought, private speech, fantasies, magical thinking, daydreams, and superstitions. Autistic speech is a typical manifestation of the parataxic mode, as is the belief that "the black cat crossing the street will cause me bad luck." Distortions that we hold about other people or groups of people—in terms of stereotypes, prejudice, or personifications—represent parataxic thinking.

The syntaxic mode involves language that clearly conveys thoughts to other people. The child now understands physical and spatial causality. Syntaxic symbols and syntaxic language can be illustrated by gestures and speech that have been consensually validated. They are logical and rational, and others have no difficulties in following the ideas expressed.

PERSONIFICATION

"Personification" refers to the mental image that a person has of himself or herself (e.g., good-me, bad-me, not-me) or of another individual (e.g., good-mother, bad-mother). Such mental pictures may have some correspondence to reality; however, they may also be distorted by the individual's needs, disturbed experiences, and/or anxieties. These mental pictures develop from a group of interrelated attitudes, emotions, and evaluations that grow out of experiences such as praise, support, tenderness, need satisfaction, threats, criticism, punishment, and anxiety. Based on experiences with the "real" mother, the infant differentiates her into two personifications.

The good mother emerges as a differentiation of the good and satisfactory nipple (being nursed and cared for). She provides tenderness, love, security, and satisfaction. More generally, any satisfaction of basic needs without undue anxiety tends to create a "good" image of the caregiver. On the other hand, *the bad mother* is the symbolic representation of the mother whose presence arouses anxiety. She punishes, scolds, criticizes, disapproves, makes forbidding gestures, and provides the "anxious" nipple.

The differentiation of the "me" results in three kinds of personification: the good-me, the bad-me, and the not-me, all of which grow out of the child's increasing awareness of his body. *The good-me* is based on interpersonal experiences conducted in a way that invites tenderness, love, appreciation, and encouragement from others. Later, actions that receive social approval produce the good-me awareness. Good-me personifications are conscious and find expression in "I am . . ." statements completed by positive attributes. *The bad-me* forms by habitually being the recipient of negative comments, punishment, criticism, and anxiety. As others consistently disapprove certain of the child's behaviors—such as touching certain parts of her body or refusing to eat certain foods—bad-me feelings are produced; eventually, just the impulses toward such behaviors may create bad-me feelings. *Not-me* has a different quality and consists of dissociated behavior that lies outside of conscious awareness. Experiences of being totally disapproved, feelings of being unwanted, or overwhelming anxiety contribute to the development of a "not-me" personification. Unacceptable behaviors that we do not recognize as "ours" are not-me, as are parts of ourselves so alien or so hideous that they must be denied. When an individual does or says things of which he has no awareness or knowledge, "not-me" dissociation is at work. It is a common experience during dreams, especially nightmares, rage, severe temper tantrums, or drunkenness. Similarly, thought processes during severe schizophrenic episodes are examples of "not-me" dissociations.

Personification provides the individual with helpful guidelines for coping with other people who show attributes that are similar to, for example, the bad-mother. Any demanding and authoritarian male may be perceived as a symbolizing part of the "frightening father," and any nurturing and warm female is recognized as a representation of the "good-mother." These personifications guide the child's behavior toward such people. Personification, therefore, can help the infant and later the child in coping with anxiety and guiding behavior when confronted with social complexity. However, later in life these earlier personifications may be retained, even when they have become too simplistic and are no longer appropriate. The result is that distorted attitudes stemming from experiences in the past are transferred to people in the present; such attitudes are parataxic.

Personifications shared by a larger group of people are referred to as *stereotypes*. They are the generalized attitudes that we often express by using such derogatory classifications as "dumb blond," "irresponsible student," "obnoxious teenager," "absent-minded professor," and so on.

SULLIVAN'S HEURISTIC STAGES OF DEVELOPMENT

Like many of the major theorists of development, Sullivan assumes that human development progresses through a sequence of stages from infancy to adulthood. However, in line with his fundamental social science orientation, he readily admits that his stages are primarily applicable to Western societies; he makes no claim to universality. In addition, his division of the stages differs from that of other theories. For example, the "latency period" is subdivided into two important stages that receive special attention. The terms commonly used to describe children of different ages provide the names of most of Sullivan's stages; they seem devoid of any heavy theoretical message. Each of these developmental stages has a unique quality of interpersonal relationships. The movement from one stage to another involves a shift in the orientation toward "significant others." In each stage, a specific person or group has a predominant influence on the child's self-evaluation: infancy (mother), childhood (family + parents), juvenile era (school + peer group), pre-adolescence (chum), early adolescence (friends, beginning opposite-sex orientation), and late adolescence (lover).

According to Sullivan, the forces that propel the child from one stage to the next are not primarily sexual (Freud), or maturational (Gesell), or cognitive (Piaget), nor do they constitute social crises (Erikson). Instead, they are based on the child's growing ability to cope with basic feelings of anxiety that are the inevitable result of changing interpersonal relationships. Maturation, the child's social experiences, the development of new interpersonal needs and new social relationships—all these play an important part in the process. Sullivan highlights "the interpersonal dimension of human existence," and the crucial experiences for this interpersonal orientation are very much a function of preadolescent and adolescent events.

As in Erikson's psychosocial theory, so in Sullivan's interpersonal theory of development: the mastery of tasks, especially the learning of interpersonal skills, influences the success of development in the following stage. Important developmental deficits from earlier stages can produce problems in future stages. But successful or supportive encounters (e.g., with a chum, a peer group, an understanding teacher, or a psychotherapist) can correct such deficits, facilitate readjustment, and redirect the individual toward normality and health.

Anxieties begin early in life when parents disapprove of some behaviors in their infants; the reduction of tension by avoiding disapproval is a major motivating force. However, the quality and nature of interpersonal relationships give each stage its unique meaning and specific interpersonal focus. Social forces produce interference or enhance the progression from one stage to the next. This focus on the socialization process reflects Sullivan's belief that interpersonal needs are more important than biological needs. The process of socialization, which depends on absorbing social values from significant other people, contributes greatly to the process of development. The movement from one stage to the next occurs because the skills and characteristics acquired in early stages suddenly become "actually inadequate" as new, more complex social relationships develop. For example, during early adolescence, as the social needs of friends change, friendships become vulnerable to breakup. As interest patterns diverge, former partners require different kinds of interpersonal relationships; as a result, new friendships are formed, often in rapid succession. In order to succeed in becoming a normal, civilized human being, an individual's social relationships must become increasingly more complex and differentiated. Sullivan's stages of development reflect this increasing interpersonal complexity and the process of social differentiation that occurs between infancy and adulthood.

INFANCY

Infancy is the period between birth and the maturation of "articulate speech, however uncommunicative or meaningless" (Sullivan, 1953: 33). The infant's basic drives, its need for food and bodily comfort, and more global needs for security create tension that can be satisfied only by other people, especially the "mothering one." The manner and extent to which these fundamental needs are satisfied become the determining factor in the development of the individual's self-system. If the mother is tender, supportive, and responsive to the infant's basic needs without arousing anxiety, the infant will feel secure—even "euphoric"—and will develop a good-me personification. Experiences based on the deprivation of bodily needs becomes the initial catalyst for the development of anxiety as a personality characteristic. Furthermore, through gesture, tone of voice, or behaviors, the mother will communicate her own inevitable anxieties, creating bad-me feelings in the infant. Sullivan states this idea as a theorem: "The tension of anxiety, when present in the mothering one, induces anxiety in the infant" (1953: 41). This process is "empathy," which means the infant can "read" the mother's feelings. The transfer of anxiety is further complicated because even the infant's crying increases the mother's anxiety. (This is especially true if she cannot account for the infant's discomfort. Her increased anxiety then, in turn, is communicated back to the child.) By way of this empathic linkage, the infant's crying may contribute to its own anxiety. From such early anxiety-arousing experiences with the "mothering one," tension and anxiety later evolve in the course of interpersonal relationships.

CHILDHOOD

Childhood is the period from the beginning of meaningful speech to the appearance of a need for interaction with playmates or compeers—that is, of companions or cooperative individuals of approximately one's own status. The major developmental accomplishment during this stage is the emergence of symbolic capacity in the cognitive area. The child begins to use words, language, and gesture in such a way that the meaning is understood; however, language is still used in a parataxic way. The learning of language, in particular, facilitates the formation of the self-system and enables the child to identify and express emotional states. At this stage, the child has a very active imagination. In the absence of actual interpersonal relationships or the presence of loneliness, the child may turn to a rich fantasy life, create imaginary playmates, and have imaginary conversations. To the extent that children play with other children, they tend to interact in an egocentric, basically self-centered way. They are primarily concerned with their own welfare, their own pursuits, and their own needs.

Parents now increase pressure toward socialization and teach their values, thereby directing the child in the acquisition of acceptable cultural patterns and attitudes. The most significant accomplishments of this stage are the learning of cooperation in interpersonal relationships, carrying out instructions, and doing simple chores in order to avoid anxiety. Mastery of these social skills places the child on the threshold of the next higher stage. However, to the extent that she does not live up to her parents' expectations, she may experience disapproval and feel fear and shame, which contribute to the internalization of parental standards. The experience of obedience and approval—being called cute, clever, smart, or charming, for instance—contributes to the good-me personification. Repeated disapproval creates anxiety, until eventually the breaking of a social rule arouses anxiety even if the parents are not present.

The child learns some of these skills and attitudes through punishment, which may be effective as long as the child perceives the chastisement as fair. Nevertheless, in this process, the child may also learn to conceal from authority figures those events that are known to bring on punishment or anxiety. These efforts at concealment take on the form of "verbal excuses" and private fantasy, but they can also create a "social distance" and, to the extent that they reflect low self-esteem, may lead to social isolation. Punishment perceived as unfair, as well as disapproval (being called bad, clumsy, stupid, naughty, etc.), leads to rebelliousness and the development of the bad-me personification.

If the punishment is severe, callous, degrading, and arbitrary, the child will feel that he lives among adversaries and will not trust people. The punished behavior may eventually be concealed, dissociated from the personality, no longer recognized as part of the self, and submerged into the not-me personification.

THE JUVENILE ERA

The juvenile era is a period characterized by the broadening of social and interpersonal relationships. During this stage the need for playmates emerges and develops. Chronologically, the juvenile era encompasses the early elementary school years. It ends when, due to maturation, the child desires to deepen social relationships. The young person then longs for deep, intimate interpersonal relationships, usually with just one person of a status comparable to his or her own.

Sullivan ascribes extraordinary significance to this period: "The importance of the juvenile era can scarcely be exaggerated, since it is the actual time for becoming social" (1953: 227). The youth moves away from the family into the larger social world and enters school. He has opportunities for a variety of new social experiences, but he also becomes vulnerable to socialization efforts and social pressures from peers. In the course of learning true cooperation in play activities as well as sharing and communicating experiences with peers, the youth comes to adopt the syntaxic mode. However, since the compeers have now become a particularly significant reference group, the "threat of ostracism" and the fear of being excluded by them become powerfully felt threats to security and self-esteem. The widely recognized individual differences in development, as well as other factors, contribute to the formation of "in-groups" and "out-groups." Being a member of the out-group creates considerable anxiety, arousing fears of ostracism, isolation, loneliness, exclusion, and harassment. "Most people have had in the juvenile period an exceedingly bitter experience with their compeers . . . the fear of being accepted by no one of those whom one must have as models for learning how to be human" (Sullivan, 1953: 345).

Because many of the earlier social experiences occur with parents, older or younger siblings, or imaginary playmates, the child has had relatively little opportunity to develop a sensitivity to the actual feelings of personal worth in peers. They, therefore provide such experiences and, in the process, contribute a different kind of socialization experience. In addition, compeers contribute some corrective experiences for those children who were overprotected as well as those who were petty tyrants, overly docile, or overly obedient at home. Thus, during the juvenile era and under favorable circumstances, peer groups can still help to correct serious distortions carried over from childhood. At times, the peer group's efforts are not benevolent and its socialization pressures—in the form of teasing, bullying, and ostracizing—increase anxiety and pain and may become debilitating themselves. The juvenile peer group calls for the acquisition of habits of competition, cooperation, compromise, and teamwork toward some common goal; such requirements are seldom imposed in the same way by parents. Peer disapproval can be more devastating than that of parents. The juvenile faces opportunities to compare the values, attitudes, and behaviors of family members with those of peers and other people. As the circle of social contacts outside the home enlarges, young people are likely to question parental infallibility and to change their perceptions not only of their families but also of themselves.

In a process Sullivan refers to as learning "social subordination," the child learns to respect and obey the demands of new authority figures, such as teachers, coaches, and Cub Scout leaders. Later, there are further contacts with people who are, think, or behave differently and who thereby expand the youth's horizons. Such interactions teach tolerance toward social diversity and give rise to a more differentiated self-image.

One of the outcomes of training by parents and other authority figures during the juvenile era is the emergence of stereotypes. That means taking from others the inadequate and often inappropriate mental picture of a group of people—one that is not based on observation, experience, analysis, or some form of personal validation. Stereotypical thought provides shortcuts that simplify social complexities, but it remains at the parataxic level. "Overemotional—just like a female" or "another aggressive, competitive male" both illustrate this parataxic mode. One particular stereotype that is quite prevalent during the juvenile and the preadolescent periods is the blind acceptance of the peer group's idea of the opposite sex. Sullivan explains that "in spite of all experience which was contrary to the stereotype, you almost had to adopt, by the time you were on the verge of preadolescence, what might be described as the juvenile stereotype of the "girls" or the "boys"—whichever the other sex was—and govern yourself accordingly—publicly at least" (1953: 238). The juvenile peer group holds distorted ideas of what the opposite sex is like, creating animosity and social distance that can interfere with opposite-sex intimacy later on. Since stereotypes include prejudicial attitudes, they foster intolerance, fear, hatred, aversion, and revulsion toward an alleged class of people, and they encourage the juvenile to disregard personal experience and to ignore individual differences. Unfortunately, once such stereotypes have become a more permanent fixture of the self-system, they are resistant to change. They interfere with the establishment of successful and satisfactory interpersonal relations with members of the stereotyped class. Sullivan expresses concern not only with the individual aspects of stereotypes but also with their social and international implications. The emphasis on this period finds expression in Sullivan's division of the latency period into two distinct stages: the juvenile and preadolescent eras. These years between childhood and adolescence include the period that is commonly referred to as the "latency period." Psychoanalytic theory considers latency a period of consolidation and superego development, but it receives less attention than the periods that precede or follow it. By contrast, Sullivan regards this period as one of paramount importance, not only for learning social skills, developing social sensitivity, learning social subordination and social accommodation, and developing academic and intellectual skills but also for very important personality changes. According to Sullivan, personality is not fixed in the first few years of life; rather, it continues to remain open to modification: "Everything that has gone before becomes reasonably open to influence; this is true even in the organization of the self-system, which . . . is remarkably inclined to maintain its direction" (1953: 227).

PREADOLESCENCE

In Sullivan's theory, preadolescence is depicted as an exceedingly important period, even though, chronologically speaking, it is of short duration. It begins with a powerful change in social orientation, a newly emerging need for an intimate one-to-one relationship with a playmate of the same sex. Preadolescence ends "with the eruption of genital sexuality" as a result of puberty.

The individual now moves away from the broad need for a larger group of playmates that prevailed during the juvenile era. A new need emerges— for interpersonal intimacy and the intimate sharing of thoughts, feelings, and ideas with just one playmate who is similar to oneself. Sullivan defines intimacy as the "type of situation involving two people which permits validation of all components of personal worth" (1953: 246). Intimacy always involves interpersonal closeness but not genital contact. This best friend—a "chum" who also becomes a confidant—would be of the same sex, the same social status, and approximately the same age. Thus, the preadolescent experiences, often for the first time, genuine love, loyalty, opportunity for self-disclosure, and intimacy, but in an atmosphere still uncomplicated by the lust dynamism. As Sullivan explains, "The quiet miracle of preadolescence, the changes of character of interpersonal relations . . . includes an interest in the satisfactions and security of another person which approaches . . . one's interest in one's own satisfaction and security" (Sullivan, 1950: 103). In this new chum-relationship, the two friends find themselves more and more able to talk about those things and to express those thoughts that they had learned during the juvenile era never to discuss. The chum becomes of great importance to the self in almost every area. There emerges a new quality of deeper interpersonal mutuality that was lacking in the juvenile era. The youth, in confronting the views held by the valued playmate, acquires information about himself that can help to correct autistic ideas, fantastic perceptions, and distorted personifications. Sullivan maintains that because of this corrective influence of the "chum," many individuals avoid serious mental disorders. The fact that someone approves of her and finds her attractive and worthwhile may counteract the low opinion she has of herself or that others have. In addition, this process of revealing virtually everything about oneself (things that had previously been kept secret) can relieve the sometimes morbid, egocentric thought: "I am quite different from everyone else." As the preoccupation with the chum relationship gains in importance, the preadolescent tends to distance himself from the family. He begins to look at them more objectively, often more critically, and shares this new perception with his chum.

Sullivan describes this relationship revealingly:

> All of you who have children are sure that your children love you; when you say that, you are expressing a pleasant illusion. But if you will look very closely at one of your children when he finally finds a chum—somewhere between eight-and-a-half and ten—you will discover something very different in the relationship—namely, that your child begins to develop a real sensitivity to what matters to another person. And this is not in the same sense of "what should I do to get what I want," but instead "what should I do to contribute to the happiness or support the prestige and feeling of worth-whileness of my chum." So far as I have ever been able to discover, nothing remotely like this appears before. . . . Thus the developmental epoch of preadolescence is marked by the coming of the integrating tendencies which, when they are completely developed, we call love, or, to say it in another way, by the manifestation of the need for interpersonal intimacy [1953: 245].

Later on, heterosexual adjustment may be impaired if intimacy with a chum of the same sex and same age is not experienced, if loneliness is never dispelled before puberty brings the lust dynamism into the foreground during the early adolescent stage. Sullivan maintains that almost all adult males who have difficulties in relating to other men—who are unaware of what members of the same sex are thinking about them—never had the opportunity to benefit from such a chumship during preadolescence. The integration of the lust dynamism with the intimacy dynamism in late adolescence will be impaired if intimacy in relation to a chum is never experienced. Achieving such a deep, intimate relationship with a member of the same sex, therefore, is the major developmental task of the preadolescent period. To repeat, this is essential because once true intimacy with a chum has been learned, heterosexual relationships become possible. Chumship also provides the opportunity to work through the problem of loneliness and to validate one's own personal worth. Blos (1962, 1965), Erikson (1950, 1968), G. H. Mead (1934), and M. Mead (1961) agree that genuine friendship between same-sex friends in childhood and early adolescence serves an important purpose in the development of a healthy self and facilitates the development of a positive identity. Early same-sex friendships contribute significantly to the emergence of love and intimacy in heterosexual relationships later on. Gilligan (1982) also feels that the intimate friendship between girls in early adolescence is a better preparation for love and heterosexuality than too early and often shallow involvement with boys.

The preadolescent's great need for intimacy and love must be viewed against its opposite force, which also reaches its peak during this period—loneliness. Since human beings are basically social creatures, they experience throughout life a recurrent need to be with others. This need may take on various qualities and involve numerous people, including imaginary playmates; nevertheless, to seek contact with others remains a powerful force at all ages. The infant craves tenderness and physical contact, the child wants adult participation in play activities, the juvenile has a need for compeers, the preadolescent craves a chum, and the adolescent pines for sexual intimacy and love. The lack of satisfying personal contacts is experienced as loneliness, which the individual feels with great intensity during preadolescence and which, later in life, may become even more terrible than anxiety. Although the lonely child often has a rich fantasy life, this leads to social isolation, which increases anxiety about the process of seeking companionship. In the juvenile era, reporting one's fantasies to peers can invite ridicule, ostracism, and avoidance, all of which tend to perpetuate social isolation. This leads to more fantasy and creates a vicious circle that discourages a reality orientation vis-à-vis other people and contributes to the derailment of the socialization process. Sullivan himself, because of his Irish Catholic background, his homosexual tendencies, and his life on an isolated farm in an all-Protestant rural community, in all likelihood experienced an acute sense of loneliness as well as ostracism; he was probably in the "out group" as an adolescent.

EARLY ADOLESCENCE

Puberty and the eruption of genital maturity determine the onset of early adolescence. As a result, the individual experiences a conflict and collision between the intimacy dynamism and the newly emerging lust dynamism. Early adolescence ends when interest shifts from a person of one's own sex to one of the opposite sex.

A zone of the body that until now was experienced primarily in terms of excretion suddenly becomes significant for exciting interaction in physical interpersonal intimacy. In addition, the genital drive in its pure form is now experienced as a feeling of lust, resulting in tension. Out of this lust dynamism emerges a growing desire to attain intimacy with a member of the opposite sex, following the pattern established during preadolescence.

In the normal pattern of social development, especially in early adolescence, a need emerges that requires a shift in the object of intimacy. For the preadolescent, that object is an "isophilic choice," someone quite like oneself, the chum. During adolescence, that changes to a "heterophilic choice," someone who, in very significant ways, is quite different from oneself. However, this move toward opposite-sex intimacy initially involves a great deal of insecurity, fumbling, and wishful thinking; it is complicated not only by the usual adolescent anxieties but also by the stereotyped views of the opposite sex acquired during the juvenile stage. In actuality, there is much wishful thinking about the opposite sex, but the individual may still spend a great deal of time with same-sex chums and friends.

Thus, three highly significant and powerful but, at this stage, still incompatible needs begin to collide during early adolescence; it is usually not until much later that these needs are effectively integrated and become compatible. Their collision provides some real understanding of the various interpersonal difficulties so commonly experienced during this period. These still separated needs are (1) the new need for sexual satisfaction, (2) the preadolescent need for intimacy, and (3) the need for personal security in the form of freedom from anxiety. A collision of these needs may occur on different levels.

Lust, which, as a result of puberty, emerges as a new dynamism in the self-system of early adolescence, collides with the already established security dynamisms in the personality. The most powerful conflict is created through "the collision between one's lust and one's security." Security encompasses self-esteem, a feeling of personal worth, and the absence of anxiety. The threat to one's security comes from general cultural patterns as well as from earlier established personal values such as embarrassment, humiliation, puzzlement, and shame. The genitals until now were not an incorporated and integrated part of an approved and worthy social self. Thus, a revision of the self-system is required, because the feeling of arousal and sexuality has to become an accepted component of the self-image. But there also exist, at least in some individuals, more serious primary phobias in relation to the genitalia; these generally stem from the parents' punitive efforts to prevent the child from handling, exploring, or showing these body parts.

In addition, "the intimacy need may collide with the need for

security." Often the family brings pressure to bear against the establishment of intimacy with members of the opposite sex, a pressure that was not
applied against earlier preadolescent chum relationships. These pressures
may take a variety of forms, from objecting, criticizing, nagging, and
threatening to ridiculing; they can be very powerful and devastating threats
to one's security. In addition, anxiety involves the fear of disapproval—
disapproval from the opposite sex being a strong possibility in the mind of
the early adolescent. Thus security needs are threatened by the often quite
awkward initial attempts to find a suitable opposite-sex partner. Many an
invitation is never extended because the young adolescent fears rejection
more than he or she desires intimacy.

Finally, there is the "collision between intimacy and lust." Sullivan
identifies four types of awkwardness that contribute to conflicts between
these two dynamisms in early adolescence: first, the awkwardness in
interpersonal situations commonly experienced during early adolescence
(when lust is not yet a fully integrated part of the self); second, lack of
self-confidence; third, excessive precaution in an unknown situation (see
Chapter 7). All these factors make intimacy highly unlikely if not
impossible. The fourth type is characterized by an exaggerated confidence,
leading to particularly crude advances toward the desired object of
intimacy. This approach is often so obnoxious that it prompts embarrassment and withdrawal in the person being approached and thereby precludes
any further development.

Failure to integrate the lust and the intimacy dynamisms may lead to the
splitting of these motives into two separate forces, which are then directed
toward two different types of people. For the young man, one of these is
the "good girl," who can provide friendship, love, and untarnished
intimacy; she may be seen as a potential marriage partner. The other is the
"bad girl," the prostitute or the "sexy" female, who satisfies genital
needs but not the need for intimacy. The opposite sex is divided into two
groups, one that can help overcome loneliness, reduce anxiety, and
provide intimacy and another that can satisfy lust. However, this arrangement occurs at the expense of self-esteem, because a boy cannot have an
affair with a "bad girl" without loss of self-respect. Such an arrangement
precludes the easy integration of the genital needs into the personality,
"which is in itself an extremely unfortunate way of growing up"
(Sullivan, 1953: 269). The conflicts experienced in the fumbling attempts
to establish intimacy with the opposite sex are not only "internal" but also
the result of interpersonal difficulties, stereotypes, and communication
problems. Observation of middle-school boys and girls in cafeterias,
hallways, or other gathering places gives testimony to the teasing—the
clumsy, awkward, and sometimes exaggerated attempts to capture the
attention of the opposite sex.

Sullivan observes both the delay that some individuals experience in the timing of puberty and the very serious personality disturbances that may result if being out of step developmentally becomes a major issue in establishing acceptance and friendship in the peer group. The effects of maturation can become a major threat to one's self-system because of negative evaluation by peers. Furthermore, during early adolescence girls are quite advanced in the developmental progression through puberty, to the extent that, when the boys finally awaken to an interest in girls, "most of the girls are already fairly wound up in their problems about boys" (Sullivan, 1953: 266).

Early adolescence continues until a way has been found to satisfy lust or the genital drive. Inability to resolve the conflict between security, intimacy, and lust creates crisis and feelings of loneliness. Masturbation appears to be the only easy solution to tension created by the lust dynamism.

LATE ADOLESCENCE

Late adolescence begins when the individual has established a pattern by which to satisfy his genital needs. It ends when the capacity to reproduce and the need for tenderness and intimacy begin to merge and the task becomes the integration of both into a mature interpersonal relationship. When all the partially developed aspects of personality fall into their proper place and form a more integrated pattern, including a vocational identity, the individual is ready to leave adolescence behind. In adulthood, lust and intimacy have been fused and the individual can now form a stable, lasting relationship based on love; this means that the other person has become "as significant, or nearly as significant, as one's self" (Sullivan, 1953: 34).

Sullivan believes that "late adolescence extends from the patterning of preferred genital activity through [numerous] . . . steps to the establishment of a fully human or mature repertory of interpersonal relations, as permitted by available opportunity, personal and cultural" (1953: 297). During late adolescence, people explore what they prefer in terms of genital activity and how it will fit into their lives. Sullivan assumes that genital activity is essential to the establishment of mature, intimate interpersonal relationships based on mutual respect. The late adolescent needs to experiment with all of the components of the self-system in order to form a functioning unity.

A disjointed or compartmentalized self is like living behind a "mask." According to Sullivan,

The adolescent may begin the "life behind a mask" that tends to characterize numbers of urban denizens. The mask, however, requires so much energy for its successful maintenance that personality growth is apt to end with its successful construction. As the necessities for masking certain motivations vary from one interpersonal situation to another, it may be easier to avoid further integration of the self, and to develop, from this point onward, specialized accommodations and interest for various groups [1972: 210].

In order to become an adult, the individual must institute effective security measures that help him or her to cope with anxiety and sublimate tension. This task is "all-absorbing, all-frustrating" and requires the development of effective mechanisms for coping with anxiety and achieving a sense of respect for self and others. A major obstacle to further development occurs if the individual attempts to escape the anxiety of adult responsibility by avoiding reality-oriented behavior and engaging in daydreaming and fantasy or, more seriously, through disassociation from personal and social difficulties. Late adolescence can also become the precipitating event of personality disorder, especially for those who suffer from loneliness, low self-esteem, anxiety, or who enter the period inadequately prepared by preceding inappropriate interpersonal events.

The demarcation between early and late adolescence is not biologically determined but does involve an achievement: "the achievement of adequate and satisfactory genital activity" (Sullivan, 1953: 297). Religious, legal, political, and personal restrictions can create obstacles to the achievement of this progression; hence, not everybody reaches late adolescence. Interpersonal problems experienced earlier in life can contribute to a poorly developed affectional growth pattern and may produce a major stumbling block in interpersonal relationships. In late adolescence, the capacity to reproduce should merge with the capacity for tenderness and intimacy.

To the extent that tasks of late adolescence are mastered successfully, there is "great growth in the experience in the syntaxic mode." Colleges and universities especially foster the expansion of the syntaxic mode of thinking by providing extraordinary opportunities for the widening of cognitive and symbolic horizons. Mastery of these late-adolescent tasks prepares for the successful entry into adulthood.

RELATIONSHIP TO OTHER SYSTEMS

Sullivan is able to effectively integrate rather diverse psychological, psychiatric, anthropological, field-theoretical, and sociological thoughts into a systematic statement about the nature of human development that emphasizes the importance of the adolescent and preadolescent periods. Nevertheless, his theory hardly seems to have received the attention it deserves. In part, this neglect has resulted because his system is quite complex and does not easily fit existing models; it integrates clinical, social, and cognitive psychology in unconventional ways. Finally, the richness of his thought is not matched by the clarity of his writing style. Sullivan was aware of this: "Some of my critics say that I do not write clearly" (Perry, 1982: 212).

Since Sullivan presents a new interpersonal theory of development, it appears appropriate to contrast some of his basic ideas with other systems, especially psychoanalysis. Although Sullivan identified with the psychoanalytic movement, he was hardly a psychoanalytic thinker in the traditional sense. He refused to compare his theory with psychoanalysis. When asked whether his self-system corresponded to the Freudian ego or the superego, Sullivan basically rejected such parallels because his self-system and Freud's contributions are based on fundamentally different assumptions. The ego is an intrapsychic construct while the self-system is social and interpersonal. Obviously, Sullivan's self-system cannot easily be translated into the id, ego, superego model. Nevertheless, he conceded that there may be some commonalities; he left it to others to define them.

Sullivan did not deny that biology plays an important role in human, especially adolescent, development (puberty); nevertheless, he emphasized the socialization process and acculturation—the nature and quality of interpersonal relations—much more than almost any other theoretical system except social learning theory (see Chapter 13). Sexuality is not seen as the major driving force in human behavior; a much more important motivating force is the continuous struggle to overcome the feeling of anxiety. According to Sullivan, anxiety is the central motivating force in human behavior. Since anxiety is the result of interpersonal difficulties, interpersonal needs appear to be more significant than sexual needs. Infantile sexuality is not a major issue in Sullivan's theory, while the ability to establish an intimate personal relationship from infancy on—and especially during preadolescence and adolescence—becomes a major factor in the movement toward maturity, adulthood, and adult sexuality. In general, Sullivan deemphasized past events; he regarded as much more important the "here and now" of the contemporary interpersonal field. Interpersonal relationships, communication, and social factors promote or thwart the individual's advancement from one stage to the next. Rather than emphasizing trauma, conflict, and crisis, Sullivan placed greater emphasis on the positive forces in development. Furthermore, he saw development as continuous. Even the names of his stages imply more continuity than the body zones that give libido satisfaction (Freud) or the psychosocial crises that need to be resolved (Erikson). Sullivan believed that important personality changes may occur, certainly up to and including adolescence, but under favorable circumstances even later in life.

Sullivan's theory of development was written, as were many of the other major developmental theories, primarily from the male's viewpoint. The uniqueness of the female experience of adolescence especially seems to have been neglected. Female development, or at least the experiences of the female that correspond to those described for the male, are seldom mentioned and never made as explicit as those of the male. One gets the impression that there are many similarities in the development of the sexes but also that important differences exist. Neither similarities nor differences are made sufficiently clear. In the development of the characteristics of each of the stages, Sullivan was unequivocally concerned with the male, especially in his description of the two stages that precede adolescence. Sullivan made a revealing statement that, although written in a very specific context, seems to be an appropriate self-critique about the general attention given to female development in his theory: "I am confining my remarks to male . . . because the female picture is more complicated and I have less material on it" (1953: 248). Many of Sullivan's reviewers and critics took him to task for not having sufficiently developed in his writing his thoughts on female development. However, Mullahy (1970) claimed that Sullivan "possessed keen insight into feminine psychology."

The last quote makes particularly good sense in view of Carol Gilligan's (see Chapter 10) research on sex differences in moral judgment. She was able to show that females make moral judgments differently than males. Compared to males, females are guided much more by their concern and empathy for other people, their efforts to communicate, and, in general, their emphasis on interpersonal relationships than by their focus on abstract universal priniciples. Kandel (1986) too has observed that girls are more receptive to interpersonal influences than boys. Looking at Sullivan's theory from Gilligan's and Kandel's perspectives implies that his theory has much greater relevance to a "psychology of women" than do the traditional psychoanalytic theories, with their emphasis on the primacy of genitality and sexuality. Many authors have claimed that for the female—as in Sullivan's theory—the interpersonal quality of an intimate relationship is much more important than the lust dynamism. For Sullivan, anxiety grows out of actual or anticipated interpersonal disapproval, and sexuality reaches maturity only when it involves intimacy and concern for the other person. Regrettably, Sullivan did not make some of the feminine values that are implied in his theory more explicit in his writing.

6: CULTURAL ANTHROPOLOGY AND ADOLESCENCE

BIOLOGICAL VERSUS CULTURAL DETERMINISM

In the early part of the twentieth century, there arose a major controversy about human nature. It stemmed from research in cultural anthropology and had substantial implications for developmental theory. That is, cultural anthropology emerged as a major theoretical contender in the controversy regarding "biological destiny" versus "cultural destiny." The issue over which the battle was being fought is relevant to the theme of this book: Is adolescence a biologically determined period of *Sturm und Drang* (storm and stress), or is adolescent turmoil and crisis a reaction to social and cultural conditions?

Biological determinism had its roots in Darwin's theory of biological evolution (see Chapter 1), which Sir Francis Galton, through his ideas of "race improvement," had applied to humans. At about the same time, the rediscovery of Gregor Mendel's work on heredity and Henry Goddard's (1914) work on the Kallikak* family advanced the powerful eugenics movement and influenced the passage of sterilization laws. Eugenics had as its goal the improvement of the human race through selective breeding. Numerous states actually passed laws calling for the sterilization of the retarded and the deviant—laws that had strong racial overtones. These ideas, fairly prevalent in the United States, found their most despicable expression in Hitler's Eugenic Sterilization Laws (1933). All these legal measures to influence heredity were based on assertions like those of the English scientist Sir Francis Galton, who claimed that nature is five times as influential as nurture.

---

* Goddard researched the family tree of Kallikak (a fictitious name of Greek origin, meaning good-bad). Kallikak, a Civil War soldier, first conceived a child with an ill-reputed barmaid. Eventually, this union gave rise to 480 descendants, most of whom became alcoholics, prostitutes, or criminals; many were mentally retarded. Later, Kallikak married a respectable and socially prominent "good" woman; their offspring became the social and political leaders in New Jersey. Goddard's books contributed greatly to the belief in heredity.

In psychology, the trend toward biological determinism found expression in the belief in instincts (William McDougall). Freud, who had claimed that his developmental stages were universal, emphasized biology. G. Stanley Hall's (see Chapter 1) influential theory of adolescence was based on evolutionism. Adolescence—a period in which "storm and stress," "crisis," "turmoil," and "conflict" were the inevitable effects of the process of physical and sexual maturation—was natural and hence biologically determined. Hall's thinking had a profound influence on Gesell's maturational theory of development. Freud's biologically rooted theory greatly influenced the psychoanalytic thinkers who followed, particularly Blos and, to a lesser extent, Erikson, who combines psychoanalytic theory with insights obtained from anthropology and the social sciences.

Franz Boas, professor of anthropology at Columbia University, was influenced by the German philosopher Immanuel Kant and the liberal and enlightened ideals of the German revolution of 1848, in which his uncle had participated. Boas most strongly opposed the supremacy of biology. His theory of extreme cultural determinism postulated "the independence of cultural achievement from race" and claimed that "the social stimulus is infinitely more important than the biological mechanism"; he took a point of view opposite to Galton's. These statements constituted a major intellectual and theoretical challenge to the thinking prevalent at about 1917 and eventually led to the separation of cultural anthropology from biology. However, Boas' theory had never been empirically tested. The testing ground for the validity of cultural determinism became adolescence, and, specifically whether adolescence proved a universal period of storm and stress, turmoil and crisis (biologically determined), or whether a "negative instance" could be found to demonstrate that adolescence could be a smooth, happy, carefree time (culturally determined). The task fell upon Margaret Mead (1901–1978), a doctoral student of Boas, who undertook a field study in the South Seas to provide such a negative instance, that is, a counterexample in which adolescents did not categorically experience crisis or storm and stress. With the goal of establishing whether adolescent turmoil was biologically or culturally determined, Mead landed in 1925 in Pago Pago. However, upon her findings rested the fundamental claim of cultural determinism, namely that "human behavior could be explained in exclusively cultural terms" (Freeman, 1983: 48). Her purpose became the demonstration that human behavior is intelligible only in the context of social and cultural patterns. Theories of adolescence became the battleground on which these issues were fought, even though the findings pervaded our conception of human nature.

MARGARET MEAD'S SAMOA AND FREEMAN'S CRITIQUE

The classic example of a society in which many of the behavior, attitudes, and values of the average adolescent were allegedly almost the opposite of what was reported as the natural pattern in the United States was Samoa. Mead's famous report of her field investigation, *Coming of Age in Samoa* (1928/1950), became the most widely read anthropological book ever published (sixteen translations and millions of copies sold). Samoa became the earliest and most powerful demonstration of Franz Boas' theory of "cultural relativism," in which he had maintained that environment, culture, and socialization are the primary determinants of human personality and behavior. Boas' theoretical position began as a reaction against the biologically based developmental, psychological, and psychiatric theories of that period. He emphasized that the diversity of child-rearing, family, and cultural patterns exerted an influence much greater than had been believed and that a uniform, universal, biologically based human nature simply did not exist. Mead's field study of adolescents in Samoa (1925–1926) was the first major anthropological investigation to report about a society in which the transition from childhood to adulthood appeared fundamentally different from the expected and, presumably, natural pattern in the United States. Quite widely accepted as proof, Mead's findings seemed to demonstrate that whether or not adolescence becomes a period full of stress, conflict, and sexual difficulties or one of harmonious, pleasurable, sexually uninhibited experimentation depends entirely on the cultural context. Hence, Mead defended "cultural relativism."

Mead's observations of adolescent girls in Samoa have been used to demonstrate that the turmoil, crises, sexual frustration, and storm and stress associated with growing up in the United States—and considered universal by many of the major developmental psychologists of that time—far from being an inevitable, universal condition, actually resulted from cultural setting, social environment and child-rearing practices. Mead's description of Samoa (1928/1950) presents a life characterized by carefree, unpressured, and harmonious interpersonal interactions where "a lack of deep feeling . . . is the very framework of all their attitudes toward life" (133), where life is devoid of jealousy and stress. "Love and hate, jealousy and revenge, sorrow and bereavement, are all a matter of weeks" (132). The relationship between adolescents and their parents seemed easygoing—like life in Samoa—where "disagreements between parent and child" end with "the child moving across the street" (132). Mead described the transition to adulthood as smooth and unencumbered by conflicts. Samoan society, she said, encouraged free love and uninhibited sexual exploration among the youth; hence, sexual expressions and sexual experimentation occurred without fear, shame, guilt, or social sanctions. In Samoa "sex is a natural, pleasurable thing" (134). Mead explained the differences between Samoa and the United States in terms of the lack of competitiveness, the low level of violence, the easygoing, carefree nature of Samoans, and the "general casualness of the whole society" (132).

In a more general sense, Mead described Samoa as a patient, gentle, and peaceful society where "no one is hurried along . . . or punished harshly" (132). Samoans experienced no religious or sexual conflicts and no jealously; by extension, Mead concluded, the carefree behavior of the adolescent can and must be explained strictly in terms of cultural learning, child rearing, and socialization. Cultural conditioning, and thereby "nurture," became the principal mechanism by which to explain human diversity.*

In a highly critical analysis entitled *Margaret Mead and Samoa: The Making and Unmaking of an Anthropological Myth* (1983), Derek Freeman questions the validity of many of her findings and sets out to show that *Coming of Age in Samoa* seriously misrepresents the Samoan culture and the character of the Samoan people. An Australian professor of anthropology who spent six years in Samoa (Mead was there for only nine months), Freeman maintains that many of her assertions "are fundamentally in error, and some of them preposterously false" (1983: 288). Mead's findings about Samoa had been criticized before. However, Freeman not only questions the validity of her specific findings but also develops a picture of Samoa and Samoan youth that is diametrically opposite to Mead's. Freeman demonstrates that, indeed, as much if not more violence, competition, guilt, and repressed sexuality permeate Samoan culture as many Western cultures. Samoan parents beat their children and continue to beat them if they do not stop crying. Vividly describing the significance of the official deflowering of the virgin bride during her wedding rites, Freeman speaks of a "virginity cult" and maintains that virginity is of great social importance—not something to be casually and carelessly done away with, as Mead would have us believe. On the basis of official documents, Freeman shows that Samoans do have a surprisingly high rate of homicide, rape, and assault and that they are prone to jealousy.

The discrepancy between these two accounts speaks to the vulnerability of anthropological research. We cannot know how the late Mead might have defended her findings. In any case, the controversy aroused by Freeman's book has once again brought the issue of "nature versus nurture" to the fore. Those who tend to ascribe greater significance to the environment attempt to defend Mead against Freeman's painstaking

---

* In the previous editions of *Theories of Adolescence*, more space is devoted to both the theory and a description of the idyllic, natural, and appealing experience of growing up on a South Sea island.

collection of evidence, while the hereditarians praise Freeman's work "as a masterpiece of modern scientific anthropology" (Nikolaas Tinbergen, 1973 Nobel Prize winner).

Some of the factors that may have influenced Mead's research are well known. A young anthropologist who went to Samoa at the age of twenty-three, Mead was philosophically committed to the cultural determinism advanced by her mentor, Boas. Obviously, he conceived of Samoa as the proof of his contention that what we may think of as human nature is not common at all. And since Mead was the first of the emerging scientists of anthropology to provide substantial evidence for the theory of cultural relativism, Boas praised her lavishly in his foreword to *Coming of Age in Samoa:*

> The anthropologist doubts the correctness [of the idea that adolescence is a period of unavoidable difficulty], but up to this time hardly any one has taken the pains to identify himself sufficiently with a primitive population to obtain an insight into these problems. We feel, therefore, grateful to Miss Mead for having undertaken to identify herself so completely with Samoan youth that she gives us a lucid and clear picture of the joys and difficulties encountered by the young individual in a culture so entirely different from our own. The results of her painstaking investigation confirm the suspicion long held by anthropologists, that much of what we ascribe to human nature is no more than a reaction to the restraints put upon us by our civilization [Boas, 1928/1950].

Besides Mead's determination to find evidence for Boas' cultural relativism, other factors raise questions about her methodology and findings. Because she did not speak the language when she arrived in the South Seas, Mead had to rely on interpreters. Rather than opening her inquiry with an overall assessment of the Samoan culture, Mead started immediately with her research, focusing on adolescent sexual adjustment. She did not live among the natives but with expatriate Americans. Girls from three villages often came to the naval medical dispensary where Mead had her headquarters; she talked to her informants in this setting. Samoan teen-agers may have let fantasy color their reports of what happened in the bushes, just as adolescents in our society often exaggerate their sexual adventures in reporting them to others. Perhaps these teen-agers teasingly misled Mead. According to Freeman (1983), teasing or duping someone is a pastime that greatly appeals to Samoans; it seems to be a reaction against "the severity of the authoritarian society." Samoans are prone to *tau fa'ase's*, which literally translated means "to cause to slip" or "to dupe." And Samoans who remember Mead's visit to their villages explain her findings, so contrary to their own experiences, in the context of this pastime. As a woman, Mead was excluded from the meetings at which chiefs discussed important issues. Freeman, in contrast, became the adopted son of Lauvi Vainu'u, a senior talking chief; later, a chiefly title was bestowed on Freeman himself, allowing him to participate in the meetings of the chiefs. His claim that he has "yet to meet a Samoan who agrees with Mead's assertion that adolescence in Samoan society is smooth, untroubled, and unstressed" (Freeman, 1983: 259) devastates Mead's conclusions. Furthermore, he cites numerous educated and knowledgeable Samoans who, appalled by Mead's account of their society, offer evidence that Samoan culture is full of stress and strain. Freeman had access to substantial and diverse historical and anthropological data—documentary evidence as well as official crime records. In a special effort to avoid the problem arising from the fact that he visited Samoa many years later than Mead, Freeman traces the major Samoan traits discussed by Mead from 1830 to 1980.

Thus, in Hegelian terms, one can look at the biological determinism espoused by Darwin, Galton, Mendel, Goddard, McDougall, Hall, and Freud as the thesis. Boas, Mead, and Benedict challenged this thesis and advanced cultural determinism as the antithesis. Freeman argues for a synthesis "in which there will be, in the study of human behavior, recognition of the radical importance of both the genetic and the exogenetic [cultural] and their interaction, both in the past history of the human species and in our problematic future" (Freeman, 1983: 302).

Freeman's critique of Mead's work is effectively documented and well reasoned, but his argument for a synthesis between biological and cultural determinism seems to come too late to have a major impact. The synthesis has already taken place. Although proponents of culture or biology may emphasize one more than the other, most contemporary theorists view development as an interaction between nature and nurture. Adolescent turmoil, storm and stress, and crises are no longer considered inevitable, not even for adolescents growing up in the United States. And regardless of whether or not Mead was correct about Samoa, other anthropologists have observed societies in which adolescence is *not* turbulent. Thus, the physiological changes of puberty and sexual maturation alone are not categorically responsible for adolescent difficulties. Anxieties, insecurities, social pressures, social expectations, and cultural, educational, and family factors may all contribute to adolescent stress.

RUTH BENEDICT'S THEORY OF CULTURAL CONDITIONING

Ruth Benedict (1887–1948), in "Continuities and Discontinuities in Cultural Conditioning" (1938/1980) and *Patterns of Culture* (1934/1950), advanced a theory of development from the perspective of cultural determinism (sometimes also referred to as cultural relativism)—a perspective particularly well suited to illustrating the transition from childhood to adulthood from an anthropological point of view. This theory of cultural conditioning is based on various field investigations conducted by Margaret Mead in the South Seas. By combining the theoretical writings of Benedict with these anthropological field studies, we derive a systematic statement concerning the importance that the early cultural relativists ascribed to environmental and social factors in the developmental process. "Cultural relativism" is a term more appropriately applied to the earlier writings of Mead, when she firmly supported the sovereignty of culture over biology in shaping the raw material of human personality. In her later writings she modified her extreme position to give some limited credence to the importance of biology. That is, she recognized universal aspects of development (e.g., an innate pattern of growth, menarche as a biological event of social significance, the incest taboo). Mead's earlier findings—despite Freeman's challenge—did contribute the revolutionary idea that adolescence is not a biological but cultural phenomenon. Benedict, a contemporary of Mead and also a student of Boas, wholeheartedly endorsed the emphasis on the importance of environment and socialization and expressed these ideas cogently in *Patterns of Culture* (1934/1950).

Benedict argued that human beings show far greater plasticity and modifiability than do animals. She accepted the Boasian principle that humans, above all, were from birth onward conditioned by their cultural setting. This ability to adapt, in Benedict's view, accounts for the progress the human species has made as well as for wide intercultural differences. The human constitution does not determine particular patterns of behavior; chromosomes and genes do not transmit culture. Cultural relativists claim that few if any human traits are universal; even if there are universal traits, they may not be biologically determined.

Benedict (1938/1980) offers as a theoretical construct "continuities and discontinuities" as a means of analyzing the socializing influences of a given culture on the development of individual personality. If it were uninfluenced by social-environmental forces, Benedict felt, natural growth would be a gradual, smooth, and continuous process; however, to the extent that social groups introduced requirements, restrictions, differential treatment, and expectations, discontinuities would emerge. Newborn infants depend on other people for support and survival. From this early infantile dependency, they must grow into a state of relative independence; as adults, they must function to maintain themselves and must provide for and protect their own offspring. The patterns by which the child reaches independence vary from one culture to another. In some cultures, such as the American, the difference between a child and an adult—and even among adolescents of different ages—is emphasized sharply, by legal definition, by different schools, and by different grades for different ages. This Benedict refers to as an *age-graded society*. Advancing from one grade or one group to another, and especially from one type of school to another, introduces anxiety and insecurity; it often requires the formation of new interpersonal relationships. This creates discontinuity in social, emotional, and personal processes. The famous cross-cultural study of crime by Bacon, Child, and Barry (1963) supports Benedict's claim of the disadvantage of discontinuity by showing that the abruptness of transition (discontinuity) as an approach to facilitate independence training in children is accompanied by an increased frequency of personal crime. Lewin (see Chapter 7) also accounts for many adolescent adjustment problems in terms of the cultural dichotomy between children and adults. Lewin conceptualizes adolescence as having only a "marginal" status between these groups.

One example of this discontinuity in our society—at least in the past—involved the exclusion of sex from the child's life as opposed to the sexual orientation of the adults. Children never, or very rarely, witnessed childbirth, sexual intercourse, or death; with pregnancy camouflaged, evacuation prudishly veiled, breast-feeding hidden, and girls sometimes reaching menarche without knowing anything about it, they had few or no opportunities to learn about such realities. TV has changed much of this, but only in a vicarious, impersonal, and out-of-context way. Children still receive a fragmented account of the sexual life cycle, and emerging sexual feelings during puberty still clash with prevailing social values, thus producing discontinuity. The sexual explicitness of the mass media from *Playboy* to prime-time TV stimulates sexual feelings and may clash with the preachings of parents and church.

In contrast, children in some primitive societies follow a relatively continuous growth pattern. Youths have an opportunity to observe birth and death near or in their own homes. They may have seen a partly developed fetus and occasionally stolen glimpses of adult sexual activity. They would certainly have observed copulation among animals. Considered natural and pleasurable, sex is not repressed in some societies. Thus, some societies provide a relatively gradual, continuous sequence of experiences without severe interruptions or restrictions, making for continuity in the developmental process. By contrast, many experiences approved for or tolerated among adults in Western societies remain restricted from, forbidden to, or hidden from children. Attitudes, values, and skills that children have learned must be unlearned when they become adults. Such transitions may be stressful.

Benedict discusses three specific aspects of discontinuity versus continuity in cultural conditioning. The major changes relevant to these three occur during adolescence in Western society. They are:

1. Responsible versus nonresponsible status role
2. Dominance versus submission
3. Contrasted sexual roles (Benedict, 1938/1980: 15)

The issue of work and play demonstrates the difference between continuity and discontinuity in behavior from *responsible to nonresponsible status roles.* In American society, especially in urban areas, work and play are considered separate and distinct. A child rarely makes labor contributions to the subsistence of the family and is protected by law from employment outside the family. But when young men and women graduate from high school or college, they must compete—sometimes for the first time—on an equal basis with other adults and suddenly assume dramatically different roles. In the small family-owned farm of the nineteenth century, this transition proved much more continuous. Play and work were not mutually exclusive activities; for example, turning the hay, harvesting potatoes, or driving the cows to the fields involved playfulness and fun as well as some work, and this work increased as children grew older. In many contemporary primitive societies, development from a nonresponsible to a responsible status role similarly proceeds gradually. Play and work are not necessarily separated; they often involve the same activities. Among the Cheyenne Indians, a boy receives a bow and arrow at birth. As he grows, he receives larger and larger bows. His relatives will feast to celebrate his first contribution of a snow bird to the family meal. The boy's contribution has value to the family even if his father brings home a buffalo. Nor will the boy's status change when he finally brings home a buffalo himself. The family will regard his killing of the buffalo as part of a natural, predictable sequence.

In Samoa, girls, sometimes as young as six or seven years old, accept responsibility for caring for and disciplining their younger siblings. Thus, each girl is socialized to develop responsibility by her early involvement in family duties. The boys too, at an early age, learn the simple tasks of reef fishing and canoeing, while the girls, after they are released from their duties as nursemaids, work on plantations and help carry food to the village. There is no basic change during the adolescent period; the degree of responsibility and the amount and quality of work increase as the child grows and matures. In our society (especially in urban and suburban communities), the transition from nonresponsible play to responsible work is often experienced as a rather sudden shift; it can create anxiety and even conflict in adolescents, since they must now enter a heretofore unknown field. In addition, employment requires a redefinition of essential roles.

The difference between *dominance and submission* is also extreme in our culture. The individual must relinquish childhood dependency and submission and adopt its very opposite—dominance—in adulthood. Often, hard-to-break emotional attachments perpetuate submission to parental authority. Our emphasis on respect for parents and elders creates strong elements of discontinuity because the submissive child must eventually become a dominant parent. Nowadays, people even undertake "assertiveness training" to unlearn submissive behavior.

During adolescence, a rather sudden shift from submission to dominance takes place. Frequently, only a short time elapses between the era when adolescents submit to parental wishes or demands and that during which they leave home to begin their own families. At times, adolescents who are ready to leave home consciously experience this change as discontinuity, but they have typically received little or no training for independence. As a result, they may become homesick or actually return home. In contrast, some primitive societies have patterns of continuous conditioning in respect to submission-dominance. Benedict reports a case among the Crow Indians in which a father boasted "about his young son's intractability even when it was the father himself who was flouted; 'He will be a man' his father said. He would have been baffled at the idea that his child should show behavior which would obviously make him appear a poor creature in the eyes of his fellows" (Benedict, 1938/1980: 17). In Samoan society, the seven-year-old girl dominates her younger siblings as their nursemaid, but she herself may still be under the dominance of older sisters. As the child becomes older, she dominates and must discipline younger children; in turn, older children restrict and discipline her. If a youth gets into a conflict with his parents, he may move to his uncle's house without stigma or emotional trauma. Parents have only limited influence over their children because discipline is the job of an older sibling. As a result, the intensely emotional conflicts between dominance and submission so common in our society remain relatively unknown in Samoa.

Another important discontinuity in the life cycle in our culture involves the child's need to learn to assume a sexual role leading to parenthood. Benedict does not deny that *the discontinuity in sex role* has an important biological root, based on the distinction between sterility before and fertility after puberty. However, whether the contrasted sex roles of child and adult are experienced as continuous or discontinuous is determined not only by physiological maturation but also by social expectations and cultural patterns that alter the influence of physiological factors. Our culture emphasizes the discontinuity of the sexual role. Childhood sexual experiences are legally prohibited, socially disapproved, and sometimes labeled sinful. Although practiced only to a limited extent, virginity and sexual abstinence until marriage are upheld as social ideals. Clinical evidence suggests that the virginal bride frequently cannot make a good sexual adjustment after her wedding because she has failed to unlearn lessons about the "danger" and "evil" of sex that she was taught while growing up. Benedict defines continuity in the sexual roles to mean "that the child is taught nothing it must unlearn later" (Benedict, 1938/1980: 19). Mead's account of Samoa has, for fifty-five years, offered an alluring picture of a society in which happy, uninhibited, carefree sexual experimentation and free love among the young ensured continuity in sexual development. Mead concluded that Samoan adolescents have the smoothest and happiest sexual adjustment possible anywhere on earth and do not experience maladjustments, moral conflicts, or "adolescent turmoil." However, Freeman (1983) proves that many of Mead's conclusions were "fundamentally in error." He questions whether sexual adjustment in puberty can ever be totally smooth, harmonious, and anxiety-free; he also suggests that the Tahitians are sexually less inhibited than the Samoans. Even when we confine ourselves to the Western societies, we find a more open and accepting attitude toward sexuality among Swedes and Danes—one that contrasts sharply with the puritanical attitude of many Americans.

Benedict (1938/1980) maintains that significant discontinuity in child rearing necessarily results in emotional strain, whereas cultural conditioning characterized by continuity is more likely to promote smooth, healthy, and harmonious growth. Western societies that are based on discontinuous cultural patterns foster conflict, crisis, turmoil, and storm and stress during adolescence. Primitive societies that are continuous in their child-rearing patterns—where the child does not have to unlearn anything in the course of maturing and becoming an adult—foster happy, healthy, conflict-free development. Societies that emphasize discontinuity are identified as *age-graded societies,* which means that those from whom we expect similar behavior or the learning of similar material are grouped together. Presumably, these groups of children have distinct characteristics and approximately the same skills. In age-graded societies, stages in development become observable because social institutions and the law expect or demand different behaviors at different age levels. Children in a certain age grade are grouped in formal institutions such as schools, scout troops, and in informal play and peer groups. Their activities are organized around behaviors considered appropriate for that age; the more formal training a society requires, the more discontinuity ensues. Individuals often "graduate" from one group or school to another; they receive certificates, social recognition, and—at a clearly demarcated point in time—become legally entitled to drive, to buy cigarettes, or to vote. All this introduces elements of discontinuity.

MEAD'S POSTFIGURATIVE, COFIGURATIVE, AND PREFIGURATIVE CULTURES

Relevant to the consideration of peer-group versus parental influences on the individual adolescent (issues that will be discussed in Chapter 15) and also relevant to some of the fundamental changes in the structure of the modern families—identified by Bronfenbrenner (1986b)—is Mead's conceptualization of "postfigurative," "cofigurative," and "prefigurative" cultural patterns. These terms require definition: the prefixes "post" (the past), "co" (the present), and "pre" (the future) refer to the type of world youth will inherit when they grow up. "Figure" is a model or representation of that world. Thus, a postfigurative culture is one in which the adolescent will grow into a world that is very much modeled after the past; the idea of a postfigurative culture is related to the concepts "folk society" or "preindustrial society." The cofigurative culture is modeled after the present world; sociologists would identify it as an "industrial society." Mead's prefigurative society represents the emergence of an unknown future, an idea expressed among sociologists by the term "postindustrial society." These patterns, concerned with the speed of cultural change and the transmission of cultural information from the older to the younger generation, are crucial to an understanding of adolescence. Adolescents stand on the boundary between childhood and adulthood, where the individual moves from the younger to the older generation. In addition, the adolescent is the cultural connecting link between tradition (the past) and innovation (the future).

POSTFIGURATIVE CULTURES

The historically earlier and preliterate cultures are described as *postfigurative*. They are basically static, experiencing relatively little or no change. In such cultures, children and adolescents grow up in a world that is very much the same as the world of their parents and grandparents; it will still be the same when these adolescents have themselves become grandparents. Postfigurative cultures depend on the presence of three generations who live in the same village or abode. Frequently, the children follow in their parents' footsteps vocationally. Parents and adults possess the basic knowledge, skills, and values required to function effectively in such a stable and unchanging world; therefore, they are seen as knowledgeable and respected for knowing how to live. The requirements for the young person to become a self-governing adult are quite clear because they remain easily identifiable. A different future lies literally beyond imagination. The parents are the most experienced guides, able to pass on this information—these skills, ideas, and vocational roles—to their offspring. Children and adolescents cooperate through their willingness to absorb the skills, knowledge, and values passed along by their elders; their future depends on that transmission. Finally, a stable cultural pattern emerges in which adolescents are adult-oriented. Often, they enter adulthood relatively early. Puberty rites play a particularly significant role in postfigurative societies. Clarifying at what point youth is prepared to take on adult roles, the rite makes this transition socially visible.

A postfigurative culture is one in which change is so slow and imperceptible that grandparents, holding newborn grandchildren in their arms, cannot conceive of any other future for the children than their own past lives. The past of the adults is the future of each new generation; their lives provide the ground plan. The children's future is shaped in such a way that what has come after childhood for their forebears is what they, too, will experience after they are grown [Mead, 1970: 1–2].

Examples of such cultures include the mountain Arapesh of New Guinea, the Australian aborigines, as well as many of the preliterate and basically unchanging cultural groups. And even within our own societies, there are postfigurative communities that emphasize tradition and resist change, such as the Amish in Pennsylvania or the Hutterites in North Dakota.

COFIGURATIVE CULTURES

Because of migration or religious conversion, as technology advances and intercultural contact and commerce increase, a break in the postfigurative system occurs and cultural patterns begin to undergo modification. *The cofigurative culture* experiences a moderate rate of social change. The assumption that life for the the new generation will differ from the life of the old generation begins to take hold. The family structure changes from the extended (three-generation) family pattern to a nuclear family pattern, and the influence of grandparents diminishes even if they live in the home. The peers and age cohorts rather than the elders begin to represent the future for an adolescent. The sense of interconnectedness and mutual respect and support between older and younger generations prevalent in the postfigurative family declines and is replaced by isolation. Parents no longer provide the sole or even major models for teaching important skills, knowledge, attitudes, and values that will be useful in the future. The function of passing along cultural knowledge and skills becomes increasingly supplemented and eventually replaced by schools and formal education. The actual introduction of formal education for all inevitably accelerates the rate of social change. In addition and no less important, the same-age peers provide informal teaching-learning opportunities. The adolescent shifts in orientation away from the parents, who are no longer perceived as models or as the source of wisdom; increasingly, the adolescent looks to peers for guidance and information. Peers become the models, at least in those areas of life that are particularly relevant to social adaptation outside the home—areas of which adults may have little knowledge and experience. Illustrations from our cofigurative culture would include the use of drugs, adolescent fashion, athletics, and adolescent entertainment and music, as well as topics about which parents are unwilling to communicate, such as heterosexual relationships, sexual behavior, sexually transmitted disease, and so on. Mead describes the relationship between the older and the younger generation in the cofigurative culture in the following terms:

In . . . cofigurative cultures the elders are still dominant in the sense that they set the style and define the limits within which cofiguration is expressed in the behavior of the young. There are societies in which approbation by the elders is decisive for the acceptance of new behavior; that is, the young look not to their peers, but to their elders for their final approval of change. But at the same time, where there is shared expectation that members of a generation will model their behavior on that of their contemporaries, especially their adolescent age mates, and that their behavior will differ from that of their parents and grandparents, each individual, as he successfully embodies a new style, becomes to some extent a model for others of his generation [Mead, 1970: 32–33].

As a result of these changes, adolescents express less interest in the past, in terms of both family tradition and of cultural history, and more in the future. Hence, a gap develops between the parents, who often cherish the past and tradition, and adolescents, who value the future. Different thinking along generational lines has divided many families, especially after the turn of the century and most intensely the post-World War II family. Cofiguration is most pronounced in first-generation immigrant families, where parents still try to hold onto Old World tradition and to maintain control. Adolescents in such families are often particularly anxious to adapt to the New World; they perceive their peers as better and more knowledgeable models than parents and resent their control.

THE PREFIGURATIVE CULTURE

As the pace of technological and social changes accelerates—consider the splitting of the atom, the invention of the computer, the birth-control pill, space travel, the disintegration of the traditional family, urban blight, and the slow but steady destruction of the environment—new cultural patterns emerge with increasing rapidity. Major events are communicated around the world instantaneously, reaching almost every village on the globe; as a result, a world community develops—a community united ''by shared knowledge and danger''—creating a situation that has never existed before. For this new world community the future no longer exists as a predictable extension of the past. The role of parents as models declines further because their skills, knowledge, and values have become dated. *The prefigurative culture* is a conception of the future, an era that—at least in some segments of our society—we are about to enter. Family disintegration continues to erode family support and cohesiveness, propagating rootlessness and alienation. The older generation becomes isolated from the younger and has less and less to offer in terms of guidance, advice, and values. Mead does emphasize that love, trust, and dependence remain important, at least for the younger child. Even though the future is all important, its great uncertainty means that the young have to chart their own course without much guidance from the parents. The past no longer has much meaning and provides no answers: ". . . it will be the child—and not the parent and grandparent that represents what is to come" (1970: 88). A feeling prevails that nothing out of the past is meaningful. Cofigurative parents used to say: "You know, I have been young and you have never been old" (1970: 63). Prefigurative youth may respond: "You never have been young in the world I am young in, and you never can be" (1970: 63).

Adolescents—if they attend effective schools—now actually know more and are more up to date on current scientific advances than are their parents. Learning begins to take place without the guidance and sometimes even without the understanding of the parents. Roles begin to reverse, and adults learn much from their young. The best illustration is computer technology, where parents, if they understand anything about computers, come to their children for advice. But even in other eras of life—fashion, entertainment, sexual behavior—adults begin to imitate their offspring rather than the other way around. Parents can no longer advise children or help them solve problems; they may even respond helplessly to questions by saying, "You better figure that one out for yourself." As new patterns of cultural change and cultural transmission emerge (changes that differ fundamentally from the postfigurative and cofigurative changes), inevitable clashes between values, groups, ideologies, and beliefs may take on violent forms. A clear illustration involves the clash between those who unyieldingly and with dogmatic fervor oppose abortion and hold onto the idea of the sanctity of life, no matter how and under what circumstances conception took place. At the other extreme are those who view abortion as no more than a belated, just slightly more expensive form of birth control.

> As I see it, children today face a future that is so deeply unknown that it cannot be handled, as we are currently attempting to do, as a generation change with cofiguration within a stable, elder-controlled and parentally modeled culture in which many postfigurative elements are incorporated [Mead, 1970: 62].

According to Mead, while we still retain some of the characteristics of the cofigurative culture and maybe even remnants of the postfigurative culture, we are moving slowly but inevitably into a prefigurative culture. In education, change affects not only who instructs whom and where information may originate; the very mode of learning changes from the "what" (knowledge) to the "how" (the method of discovery). The ability to cope with change becomes of paramount importance. Education shifts from a product to a process orientation. To face an uncertain future, flexible problem-solving strategies are the most important tools that the older generation can give to the young.

SEX-ROLE PATTERNS IN DIFFERENT CULTURES

Prior to World War II, Mead studied the sex-role patterns in three primitive societies in New Guinea. Quite in line with her theoretical commitment to cultural relativism (which means that the attitudes and characteristics of adolescents vary greatly from one cultural group to another), Mead challenged the belief that masculine and feminine traits are based on biological factors. Basically, she attacked the "cultural assumption that certain temperamental attitudes are 'naturally' masculine and others 'naturally' feminine" (Mead, 1935/1950: 14). Instead, she tried to demonstrate that particular gender-role behaviors are a function of the social and cultural conditions under which children and adolescents grow up. Her findings contribute greatly to our understanding of sex-role development because she did present evidence to show that certain masculine and feminine traits that are considered typical are actually less "natural" and more culture-bound. The comparison to follow will focus on Mead's *Sex and Temperament* (1935/1950), which identifies three distinct patterns, all different from our own. She focuses on the relationship between the sexes and sex-role development in three New Guinea tribes: the Arapesh, the Mundugumor, and the Tchambuli.

THE MOUNTAIN ARAPESH

The Mountain Arapesh live in a steep, inhospitable, and unproductive mountain region of New Guinea. Poor and undernourished, they have to struggle to produce enough food. Food-gathering efforts become a major preoccupation because the possibility of starvation is always present. Because of this threat, they spend much of their time helping their neighbors; men and women display equal commitment to such group efforts. Their major interest is in growing things: children, pigs, and coconut trees. They treat an infant as a "soft, vulnerable, precious little object to be protected, fed, cherished" (Mead, 1949: 65). Among the Arapesh, both males and females display some of the characteristics that in Western societies are often associated with the feminine gender role. Mead describes the Arapesh of both sexes as cooperative, unaggressive, peaceful, noninitiatory, warm, docile, contented, and responsive to the needs of others.

Boys and girls absorb these social values and move into adolescence with happy, trustful, confident attitudes. Sex differences during adolescence are few, though boys enjoy somewhat greater freedom in expressing aggression and girls learn to be more passively accepting of the way things are. The major adjustment crisis for an Arapesh girl does not occur during adolescence but when she loses her husband or her husband's affection. Such an event makes her most vulnerable, because she has been supported and protected all her life. As the children reach puberty, they become conscious of their sexuality and observe the cultural taboos. For the still growing young Arapesh, sex is forbidden—not for moral reasons but because it is believed to stunt growth and therefore to be dangerous for the young. Sex is good, but only for adults, who have completed their growth.

THE MUNDUGUMOR OF THE YUAT RIVER

The Mundugumor are cannibals who live on the banks of the swiftly flowing Yuat River in the jungles of New Guinea. Their food-gathering expeditions lead them downriver, where they prey upon the malnourished bush people, who live on poorer land, to capture "fresh meat." The Mundugumor illustrate a social organization where both male and female are trained to display exaggeratedly masculine characteristics. Both men and women are ruthless, quarreling, aggressive, assertive, competitive, domineering, and unresponsive to the needs of others. Except for rare cooperative interludes for ceremonial occasions and against a common adversary, it is each man's hand against the other man's. The social structure of the Mundugumor is founded on mutual hostility among all individuals. Assisted by boys, women provide much of the food, go fishing, harvest sago, and climb coconut trees, leaving the men free to plot and fight. Women despise the rearing and bearing of children; they do not cherish their maternal roles. While men do a little hunting and fishing, they carve, paint, and ornament wooden figures much of the time.

The culture into which a Mundugumor child comes is hostile, a world where welcome is always uncertain, where maternal rejection is likely. Emphasizing individuality, the treatment from the beginning is harsh and hostile, the training Spartan. The youth learns that success in life depends on one's capacity to defend oneself, to fight, and to be able to revenge an insult. Society places a value on virginity; once a girl is known to be no longer a virgin, her value declines. Passion without tenderness characterizes love affairs among the unmarried youth. Such affairs remain short, secretive, and impersonal because of the ever-present danger of discovery. Foreplay is expressed by violent scratching and biting, which produce maximum excitement in a minimum of time.

THE LAKE-DWELLING TCHAMBULI

The Tchambuli, a very small tribe, build their houses on the shores of the beautiful Lake Tchambuli, which is connected to the Sepik River in New Guinea. Though they have gardens, they depend mainly on fishing and the barter of foods. Among the Tchambuli, the women perform most of the labors. Therefore, Tchambuli society may serve as an illustration of the reversal of gender roles typically found in Western societies. The

Tchambuli are an agricultural and artistic tribe. However, the stern, dominant, matter-of-fact, determinedly busy, and impersonal women pursue fishing, weaving, planting, harvesting, cooking, and the rearing of children. Their attitude toward men is one of kindly tolerance, but women hold the positions of real power: "Tchambuli women, brisk, unadorned, managing and industrious, fish and go to market; the men, decorative and adorned, carve and paint and practice dance-steps" (Mead, 1949: 54). Slender, narrow-bodied, submissive, emotionally dependent, involved in petty bits of insult and gossip, the men are less responsible than the women but more responsive to the needs of others. They stay at home, creating new dances, fixing their hair, pursuing various forms of artistic endeavor, and planning the ceremonies.

Surprisingly, in Tchambuli society, where the sexes behave so differently, boys and girls, until the age of six or seven, receive identical treatment from the women who train them. The girls learn womanly skills and responsibilities and fairly soon form a solid identification with their own sex. Boys between seven and twelve have no clearly defined role but do begin to join the men. A ceremonial but painful cutting of patterns on a boy's back emphasizes this transition, but often young males return and take refuge with the women. They find themselves on the edge of society, often excluded from the men's activities, sitting around on logs, sulking and quarreling with each other and sometimes getting chased away by bigger boys. There is a piecemeal admission to the "secrets," which turn out to be very little more than what they already knew. However, this experience of exclusion and neglect may become a male pattern that prevails even later in life, so that men remain sensitive, easily hurt, and quick "to burst into hysterical vituperations." As they grow older, they learn to play the flute and to pursue the other artistic endeavors of men.

HISTORICAL CHANGES IN GENDER-ROLE PATTERNS

These illustrations from New Guinea offer vivid illustrations that gender role is not determined solely by biology and can be modified. On the other hand, societies such as the Arapesh, Mundugumor, and Tchambuli are the exception, not the rule. The more common gender-role patterns, even in preliterate societies, are similar to our own: males tend to be more dominant and do the heavy work, while females tend to be more nurturant, cook, do the housework, garden, and care for the children. However, gender roles in our own society are in a process of continuous change. What is socially accepted, appropriate behavior, demeanor, and apparel for males and females has changed substantially over time and continues changing at an accelerated rate. At the time of the American Revolution, a man, especially a gentleman of status, did wear hose, a powdered wig, and even a lace-trimmed shirt. This clothing did not appear odd or feminine. Women in the early part of the century could not smoke in public and did not cross their legs; nubile girls did not go out with males unchaperoned. On the plantations in the South, when nubile unmarried young females stayed overnight, all unmarried males had to move for that night into another building.

These changes, under the influence of the Women's Liberation Movement, have intensified in the last two decades. The trend today is toward greater equality and increasing overlap of gender roles, a phenomenon referred to as *androgyny,* which means combining, accepting, and expressing both masculine and feminine traits regardless of one's own sex. In terms of vocational choices, this means that adolescent males may become nurses, househusbands, and caregivers for the young. Adolescent females today aspire to become bus drivers, astronauts, and business executives. A girl may join the previously all-male wrestling team in her high school and win the match.

As a result of these social changes, the assumption that males should act "masculine" and females should act "feminine" has been questioned. However, many people, adolescents in particular, continue to be committed to some degree of sex-role differentiation. On the other hand, an overly rigid identification with the traditional role of one's sex may be associated with negative psychological characteristics. The especially feminine female tends to show more signs of anxiety, low self-esteem, and low self-acceptance. While the overly masculine adolescent may initially be less disadvantaged, he is, later in life, more likely to show anxiety, neuroticism, and low self-acceptance.

Even among technologically advanced societies, substantial sex differences have been observed. Communist and socialist countries have advocated equality and encouraged women to enter the labor force. They often provide child care and even household assistance. Actually, less gender-role differentiation has been observed in Sweden and Denmark as compared to the United States (Block, 1973). However, even in the Soviet Union, where sexual equality is a political goal and women have entered many of the so-called masculine jobs, females often end up in the lower-paying positions and are not proportionally represented in the leadership roles. For example, in typically male professions, 36 percent of the engineers (but only 12 percent of the plant supervisors), 72 percent of the schoolteachers (but only 23 percent of the school directors), and 45 percent of the scientists (but only a small proportion of the members of the Soviet Academy of Science) are women. In Japan, by contrast, women's roles have changed more slowly. They still find themselves in the more traditional roles of housewife and secretary, while higher education remains less accessible to them.

Obviously, the patterns of gender-role differentiation or similarity very much reflect the influence of historical and social changes, environmental and cultural factors; biology may play less of a role than has been assumed.

EDUCATIONAL IMPLICATIONS

M. Mead (1961) and R. Benedict (1938/1980) were convinced that cultural, social, and environmental factors account for the difficulties of American adolescents, such as the "discontinuities of cultural conditioning" and even the "contradictions and unevenness of physical puberty." Since identifiable conditions in the United States produce stress, strain, crisis, anxiety, and instability in the adolescent, Mead suggests modification of these conditions through social planning and education.

In modern Western societies, which Mead considers "prefigurative cultures," the rate of social and technological change has accelerated rapidly. Adolescents confront many—often too many—alternatives and choices with little, often inadequate, guidance. Consequently, problem situations involving genuine choices with far-reaching consequences arise more frequently than they do in primitive societies. The possibility of inappropriate choices is always present. Adolescent difficulties in complex societies relate to "the presence of conflicting standards and the belief that every individual should make his or her own choices, coupled with a feeling that choice is an important matter" (Mead, 1928/1950: 154). This conflict of choice becomes intensified and further encumbered because physiological puberty now occurs earlier than in the past and because a number of behaviors involving important choices (such as dating, partying, smoking, drinking, drug use, and sexual intimacy) arise with increasing frequency at earlier ages. At the same time, expectations for prolonged and advanced education are increasing. The earlier and earlier imitation of "adultlike" behavior among adolescents, in combination with an extended period of education and the prefigurative rapidity of social change, have increased the duration of social adolescence and created a "mass adolescent culture pattern" in which the influence of parents has declined—"today the elders can no longer with certainty present moral imperatives to the young" (Mead, 1970: 82)—and the significance of the peer group as guides and models has increased.

Mead feels that junior high school has especially contributed to the adolescent's increased anxiety* and insecurity about growth, body image, peer acceptance, and appropriate sexual behavior. Since females mature significantly earlier than boys, the slower-maturing male suffers special vulnerability to anxiety. He may be pressured into premature romantic

---

* Cattell and Scheier (1961) found that anxiety reaches its peak at about fifteen and returns to such height again only in old age.

associations with members of the opposite sex at a time when he is not yet psychologically or physiologically ready. The formation of deep personal friendships and associations with members of his own sex would help him to develop his own masculine identity, an idea that Mead, Blos, and especially Sullivan emphasize. These theorists perceive intimate same-sex friendship in early adolescence as prerequisite for heterosexual adjustment later. Consequently, Mead feels that boys and girls begin too soon to depend on each other for "social and intellectual companionship" (1961: 44). Mead postulates that, because of premature and early heterosexual intimacy, the young adolescent learns to distrust his male companions as competitors in the dating process. Because junior high school invites and the peer group expects early interest in the opposite sex, junior high may contribute to the development of negative attitudes and hostility between the sexes. It lays "the basis for hostility to females on the boys' part and, on the girls' part, pressure toward marriage combined with contempt for males" (Mead, 1961: 38).

With Erikson (1968) and other contemporary writers, Mead maintains that the major task facing adolescents is the search for a personal identity. This task is immeasurably more difficult in a modern, heterogeneous society than it is in primitive cultures. The behavior and values of parents in a prefigurative society no longer provide adequate models, since these elders are often seen as out of step with the models provided by the mass media. Furthermore, adolescents, in the process of freeing themselves from dependency, are not only unresponsive but also often antagonistic to their parents' admonitions. Since adolescents have learned to evaluate their behavior against that of their age mates, they often discard or ignore the advice of parents and exchange their parents' values for those of their friends. The rapidity of social change, exposure to various secular and religious value systems, and modern technology make the world seem overwhelming to the adolescent—far too complex, too relativistic, unpredictable, and dangerous to provide a stable frame of reference for the future. In the past, society provided adolescents with a period (e.g., apprenticeship, travel, trying a job without commitment) that both Erikson and Mead called a "psychological moratorium" or "as if" period, during which youth could tentatively experiment with various options without being asked to show "success" and without emotional, economic, or social commitment. The adolescent's loss of such an experimental period during which to explore various identity issues makes establishing an identity more difficult. As a substitute for a personal identity, youth may, therefore, utilize peer-group symbols, establishing a semi-identity by way of special clothing, hairstyles, and attitudes, most dramatically illustrated in our time by the "punk" subculture. Identity formation is difficult today because education has become functional, compulsory, and success-oriented. Consequently, the goals and values of adolescents are directed toward economic success, security, immediate gratification of desires, conformity, and social acceptance, with little room for "playing the field," "fooling around," experimentation, idealism, utopianism, or personal martyrdom. "Failure to adopt our educational and social system . . . may be held responsible for . . . negative identities . . . characteristic of this present group of young people" (Mead, 1961: 49).

Mead criticized the American family for its too intimate organization and its crippling effect on the emotional life of the growing youth. She believed that overly strong family ties handicap individuals in their ability to live their own lives and make their own choices. She suggested that "it would be desirable to mitigate, at least in some slight measure, the strong role which parents play in their children's lives, and so eliminate one of the most powerful accidental factors in the choices of any individual life" (Mead, 1928/1950: 141). However, even though she objected to the pattern of the American family, feeling that it produces too much conformity and dependency in children, she considered the family an important social institution and demonstrated that it is almost universal. Mead felt that there was no better way to produce wholesome individuals than through a tolerant family system in which father and mother could disagree without quarreling and adolescents could challenge their parents without losing love and self-respect or exacerbating emotional tensions.

Mead also demanded more emphasis on mental and physical health in the classroom. Making choices has become an important component of growing up in America, especially for adolescents, who experience growing sexual urges long before sexual behavior is seen as appropriate. The adolescent will be increasingly confronted with conflicting choices in sexual as well as in many other matters. The lack of a definitive, generally accepted social canon in American society—and the conflicting advice of parents, teachers, peers, and the mass media—complicate this situation considerably. Consequently, many situations calling for choices produce anxiety for the adolescent. To help overcome this dilemma, a special educational effort designed to train adolescents to think critically and to consider options, alternative solutions, and consequences when confronted with a question of choice ought to be made. "Children must be taught how to think, not what to think" (Mead, 1928/1950: 161). The new model of education should teach adolescents "not what to learn, but how to learn and not what they should be committed to, but the value of commitment" (Mead, 1970: 92).

Returning to the theory of continuities and discontinuities in cultural conditioning, the implications are self-evident: our educational practices in the home as well as in school should emphasize continuity in learning so that the individual acquires the same set of values and behaviors in childhood that will be appropriate in adulthood. Children should be taught nothing that they will have to unlearn later in order to become mature adults. The implementation of this idea is obviously difficult in a modern, age-graded, complex society. Our culture expects each of us to change behavior, often to an extent that constitutes a discontinuity, as we move from elementary school to high school, from college into the marketplace, and from the suppression of sexuality before marriage to sexual bliss thereafter.

7: FIELD THEORY AND ADOLESCENCE

KURT Lewin (1890–1947) was a disciple of the early Gestalt school of psychologists at the University of Berlin. He was also influenced by Freud's psychoanalytic theory, particularly in regard to motivation in human behavior. However, Lewin's theory of adolescence is conceptually quite different from any of the theories discussed so far. Lewin's field theory—especially as it relates to social psychology and learning theory—is widely known and frequently discussed in the psychological literature, but comparatively few references are made to his theory of adolescent development, which is explicitly stated in "Field Theory and Experiment in Social Psychology" (1939). His field theory explains and describes the dynamics of behavior of the individual adolescent without generalizing about adolescents as a group. His constructs help to describe and explain, and—if the field forces are known—to predict the behavior of a given individual in a specific situation. In a sense, the field theory of adolescence is expressed explicitly and stated more formally than other theories of adolescent development. At the same time, however, Lewin's theory strongly opposes those conceptual schemes that require placing the phenomenal world in rigid and mutually exclusive categories.

Lewin assumed the "lawfulness" of all psychological events, even those that occur only once. He maintained that general psychological concepts and laws derived on the basis of frequency of occurrence created a dilemma, since these laws are abstracted from many individuals and are true in terms of probability only. Such laws may or may not apply to a specific individual. Therefore, no individually useful application results from these generalizations except by way of probability.

DEVELOPMENTAL CONCEPTS OF FIELD THEORY

One of Lewin's core concepts is the law "that behavior (B) is a function (f) of the person (P) and the environment (E), $B = f(PE)$, and that P and E in this formula are interdependent variables" (1951: 25). How a child (P) perceives his environment (E) depends on the stage of his development, his personality, and his knowledge. An unstable psychological environment during adolescence brings about instability in the behavior of the individual. Therefore, to understand a child's behavior, one must consider the child and the environment as a constellation of interdependent factors. The sum total of all environmental and personal factors in interaction is called the "life space" (LSp), or the "psychological space." Behavior is a function of the life space and not only of the physical stimuli, $B = f(LSp)$. The life space includes physical-environmental, social, and psychological factors, such as needs, motives, goals, and obstacles, all of which determine behavior. To demonstrate the dynamics of the life space, Lewin introduces two constructs that are to represent the situation of a particular individual at a particular time in a particular environment:

1. A map or geometrical representation of the life space, in which the person, available goals, and possible barriers between an individual and his goals are depicted (see Figure 5).
2. A representation of the forces that act on the individual and bring about locomotion toward or away from a goal.

Within the life space, objects or goals can have a positive (attraction) or negative (repulsion) valence. If goals allow the fulfillment of needs and desires, they have a positive valence; barriers that interfere with the attainment of a goal have a negative valence. If the attracting and repulsing forces are in balance, a person experiences conflict. If the forces are not in balance, they produce locomotion and the individual moves, psychologically speaking, toward or away from the goal. When several forces act simultaneously, the locomotion is called a "resultant." A barrier between an individual and the goal may increase the individual's efforts to reach the goal, but it may also result in frustration.

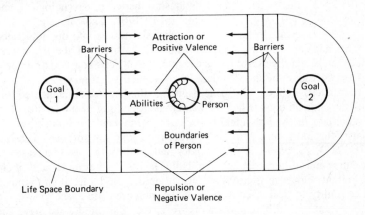

FIGURE 5. An Individual's Life Space in a Conflict Situation.

In Figure 5, the person (P) is strongly attracted to the goal (G1), such as passing a course or getting a good grade in high school. However, to reach this goal various barriers having negative valences—for instance, quizzes, exams, papers, and reports, which require effort and time—must be overcome. If another attractive goal (G2), wanting to earn money, is operative at the same time and also requires overcoming barriers—namely, mowing the lawn, washing the car, and so on—the adolescent may experience conflict if the forces are in balance. Actual behavior would be determined by the strength of the forces, as one individual may be more attracted to earning money, or less repulsed by mowing the lawn, whereas another may be more interested in passing the course or may actually enjoy writing the required paper.

The psychological field, or the life space, includes the individual with his biological and psychological dimensions as well as the environment with its social relations and physical objects. Since person and environment are seen as a constellation of interrelated factors, this theory achieves harmony among the many aspects of development by combining biological, sociological, environmental, and psychological factors in the concept life space. Field theory has successfully integrated the biological and sociological factors, which are frequently considered contradictory (for example, the nature-nurture issue). Lewin made explicit his position on this issue in several of his publications: "the social aspect of the psychological situation is at least as important as the physical" (Lewin, 1946: 793); "the psychological influence of environment on the behavior and development of the child is extremely important" (Lewin, 1931: 94); "psychology in general [is regarded] as a field of biology" (Lewin, 1935: 35). "Psychological ecology" is seen as the biological science that deals with the relationship between the organism and its environment or, as Lewin states the issue, "the relationship between psychological and non-psychological factors" (Lewin, 1951: 170). Thus he attempts to combine biological, social, and environmental forces into one integrated system, and he accomplishes this with the construct of the life space, which can be readily illustrated as a map of the objects, goals, and valences that are operative on an individual in a specified situation.

In infancy, a child's life space is unstructured and undifferentiated; the child depends on outside help and external structuring of the environment by other people. An individual's space of free movement is limited by "(a) what is forbidden to a person, (b) what is beyond his abilities" (Lewin, 1936: 217). As the child grows older and as the life space increases in structure and differentiation, the child learns to be more and more self-reliant. Fewer restrictions are placed on the child's freedom to move; hence ability to deal effectively with the increased life space grows. To acquire maximal differentiation of life space, the child must have the freedom to advance into new regions, to explore and include new experiences. Lack of freedom of movement will place restrictions on the child's attempt to expand his life space; psychological rigidity of personality will result. Conversely, if the life space, especially in early childhood, remains unstructured, the personality will lack integration and organization. Thus Lewin not only emphasizes the child's developmental need for independence but also adds the idea of a developmental need for a kind of dependency that provides the child with structure and guidance toward favorable personality development. The importance of the dependency need and the structure in the home contributing to the socialization of the child is a major concern of social learning theory discussed in Chapter 13. Research findings reported by Harris (1958) support this idea. Studies were made of the feelings, attitudes, and ideas of adults who, as children, attended the University of Minnesota Nursery School in the late 1920s. Those who had been reared in structured situations were decisive, confident, self-accepting, and achievement-oriented. Those raised in an unstructured home situation were indecisive, distrustful, pessimistic, and perceived success and failure in terms of good or bad luck. Similarly, Bronfenbrenner observed that adolescents from egalitarian, permissive families received lower ratings than those from structured (patricentric or matricentric) families in terms of responsibility and self-reliance.

The space of free movement—that region in the physical and psychological life space that is accessible to an individual—differs from person to person both in scope and nature, thus providing for a conceptualization of different experiences and thereby explaining individual differences (see Figure 6). But even more important are the restrictions that limit free movement. Individual differences in forbidden and permitted regions are important in understanding the achievement of independence which is a crucial factor in healthy personality development. As the adolescent's life space increases, many more regions become potentially accessible (see Figure 7). But often it is not at all clear to adolescents whether or not they are supposed to enter these regions. Sometimes they enter such a forbidden activity when they are not supposed to and experience conflict; at other times they do not enter a new region when they are supposed to and experience reprimand. The difficulty arises because these regions are no longer "beyond their ability"; because these regions may not be explicitly allowed or explicitly forbidden, they are part of the space of free movement but remain undefined and unclear. If they are forbidden, adolescents realize that these regions are not forbidden for some of their peers, and hope that their own restrictions will soon be lifted. Consequently, the definition and redefinition of the space of free movement in the adolescents' life space may take innumerable hours of discussion and argumentation between them and their parents. This uncertainty of the undefined space of free movement illustrated in Figure 7 is the psychological construct by which field theory explains the unpredictability of

FIGURE 6. Comparison of the *Space of Free Movement* of Child and Adult. The actual activity regions are represented. The accessible regions are blank; the inaccessible shaded. (a) The space of free movement of the *child* includes the regions 1–6, representing activities such as getting into the movies at children's rates, belonging to a boy's club, etc. The regions 7–35 are not accessible, representing activities such as driving a car, writing checks for purchases, political activities, performance of adults' occupations, etc. (b) The *adult* space of free movement is considerably wider, although it too is bounded by regions of activities inaccessible to the adult, such as shooting his enemy or entering activities beyond his social or intellectual capacity (represented by regions including 29–35). Some of the regions accessible to the child are not accessible to the adult, for instance, getting into the movies at children's rates or doing things socially taboo for an adult which are permitted to the child (represented by regions 1 and 5).

From Kurt Lewin, The Field Theory Approach to Adolescence. *American Journal of Sociology*, 1939, *44*, 868–897. Reproduced by permission from The University of Chicago Press.

some adolescent behavior. The undefined regions in Figure 7 are "new psychological situations."

Lewin speaks of developmental stages, but his conceptualization of stages is quite different from the stages of Freud, Erikson, Blos, and Piaget. Lewin's stages relate to differences in the scope of the life space and the degree of life space differentiation. In accordance with the all-inclusive definition of the life space, these developmental differences are

FIGURE 7. The *Space of Free Movement* of the *Adolescent* as It Appears to Him. The space of free movement is greatly increased, including many regions which previously have not been accessible to the child, for instance, freedom to smoke, returning home late, driving a car (regions 7–9, 11–13, . . .). Certain regions accessible to the adult are clearly not accessible to the adolescent, such as voting (represented by regions 10 and 16). Certain regions accessible to the child have already become inaccessible, such as getting into the movies at children's rates, or behaving on too childish a level (region 1). The boundaries of these newly acquired portions of the space of free movement are only vaguely determined and in themselves generally less clearly and sharply differentiated than for an adult. In such cases the life space of the adolescent seems to be full of possibilities and at the same time of uncertainties.

From Kurt Lewin, The Field Theory Approach to Adolescence. *American Journal of Sociology*, 1939, *44*, 868–897. Reproduced by permission from The University of Chicago Press.

concerned with the psychological environment as well as with the individual, his body, his goals, and his self-perception. According to Lewin, the differences between developmental stages manifest themselves in the following ways:

1. An increase in the scope of the life space in regard to
   a. what is part of the psychological present
   b. the time perspective in the direction of the psychological past and the psychological future
   c. reality-irreality dimension
2. An increasing differentiation of every level of the life space into a multitude of social relations and area of activities
3. An increasing organization
4. A change in the general fluidity or rigidity of the life space [Lewin, 1946: 797–798].

Figure 8 illustrates the change in life space as a function of age, comparing the child's (a) life space with that of an adolescent (b). Several important developmental differences become obvious from this comparison. (1) The main difference is the increased differentiation in the life space of the adolescent as compared to the undifferentiated and

FIGURE 8. The Life Space at Two Developmental Stages. Figure 8a represents the life space of a younger child. Figure 8b represents the higher degree of differentiation of the life space of the older child in regard to the present situation, the reality-irreality dimension, and the time perspective. C, child; R, level of reality; I, level of irreality; Ps Past, psychological past; Ps present, psychological present; Ps future, psychological future.

unstructured area of the child's life space. Both the child and his perception of the environment become differentiated and structured in the developmental process. This holds true in respect to many different aspects of development, such as language skills, social relations, and emotions, as well as the child's understanding of his world. The adolescent knows more people, is familiar with a wider geographic area, and has more and better social, physical, and intellectual skills than the child. Change in the differentiation of the life space occurs slowly at certain times and more rapidly at other times. Slow changes result in harmonious periods of development, whereas rapid changes are more likely to result in periods of crisis. Adolescence is characterized by a relatively rapid change in the structure of the life space, and the rapidity of the growth of the life space during adolescence may be responsible for the so-called adolescent crisis. (2) The comparison between (a) and (b) makes clear that the time perspective has expanded, since it now includes a more distant future and a more distant past. Such change in time perspective is a fundamental aspect of development; it has far-reaching consequences for education, the curriculum, and vocational planning. The adolescent develops the ability to understand the past, adopt a new outlook toward the future, and plan his own life more realistically. (3) Since the life space differentiates and the time perspective expands, the reality-irreality level also takes on new dimensions. The reality-irreality dimension is an important concept of Lewin's (1946) theory. "Irreality" refers to fantasies, dreams, wishes, fears, and certain forms of play. Young children are not able to distinguish clearly between wishes and facts, hopes and expectations. As they grow older, their understanding of reality enables them to distinguish with increasing accuracy between truth and falsehood, perception and imagination. One characteristic of adolescents is that they have learned to distinguish between reality and irreality.

KURT LEWIN'S THEORY OF ADOLESCENT DEVELOPMENT

Fundamental to Lewin's theory of development is the view that adolescence is a period of transition during which adolescents must change their group membership. While both the child and the adult have a fairly clear concept of how they fit into the group, the adolescent belongs partly to the child group, partly to the adult group, without belonging completely to either group. Parents, teachers, and society reflect this lack of clearly defined group status; and their ambiguous feelings become obvious when they treat the adolescent at one time like a child and at another time like an adult. Difficulties arise because certain childish forms of behavior are no longer acceptable. At the same time some of the adult forms of behavior are not yet permitted either, or if they are permitted, they are new and strange to the adolescent. The adolescent is in a state of "social locomotion," moving into an unstructured social and psychological field. Goals are no longer clear, and the paths to them are ambiguous and full of uncertainties—the adolescent may no longer be certain that they even lead to the desired goals. Such ambiguities and uncertainties are illustrated well by the boy asking or hesitating to ask for his first date. Since the adolescent does not have a clear understanding of his social status, expectations, obligations, or how to cope with rejection, his behavior reflects this uncertainty.

A life space—as illustrated in Figure 5—has different regions that are separated by boundaries with varying degrees of permeability. For example, the adolescent is confronted with several attractive choices that at the same time have relatively impervious boundaries. Driving a car, smoking pot, dropping acid, having sexual relations are all possible goals with positive valence, and thus they become part of the adolescent's life space. However, they are also inaccessible because of parental restriction, legal limitations, or the individual's own internalized moral code. Since the adolescent is moving through a rapidly changing field, he does not know the directions to specific goals and is open to constructive guidance, but is also vulnerable to persuasion, seduction, and group pressure. Unfamiliar situations cause crises that can produce withdrawal, sensitivity, and inhibition as well as aggression, inappropriate emotional outbursts, rebellion, and radicalism. Consequently, because of a lack of cognitive structure, the adolescent frequently is not sure whether certain behavior will lead toward or away from a particular goal. This concept of "lack of cognitive structure" helps explain the uncertainty in adolescent behavior.

The self-image of individuals depends on their bodies. During the normal developmental process body changes are so slow that the self-image remains relatively stable. The body image has time to adjust to these developmental changes so that individuals know their own bodies. During adolescence changes in body structure, body experience, and new body sensations and urges are more drastic, so that even the well-known life space of the body image becomes less familiar, unreliable, and unpredictable. Adolescents are preoccupied with the normality of their bodies and how their bodies are perceived by others; they are concerned about and may actually be disturbed by their body image. They spend considerable time studying their image in the mirror and are concerned about the development of primary and secondary sex characteristics in relationship to age-mates. This is understandable; obviously, the body is especially close to and vital to one's feelings of attractiveness, stability, security, and one's sex role. Negative feelings about one's own body are related to a negative self-concept and may lead to emotional instability that can change one's orientation toward life. Due to these uncertainties, adolescent behavior is characterized by an increased plasticity of personality that can lead to personality changes and even religious conversions.

The change in a child's life space from being limited in scope but relatively structured to the increased but less structured and often unknown regions of the adolescent's life space includes not only more extensive social relationships, a new body image, and expanding geographic surroundings, but also an increased perception of the future and a better understanding of his own past.

Field theory defines adolescence as a period of transition from childhood to adulthood. The possibility of moving from one social group to the other is determined informally by one's physique: looking like an adult makes it easier to get adult privileges. Formally, adult privileges and responsibilities are determined by law and come at legally established ages. This transition is characterized by deeper and far-reaching changes, a faster rate of growth, and differentiation of the life space as compared with the preceding stage of late childhood. The transition is also characterized by the fact that the individual enters a cognitively unstructured region that results in uncertainty of behavior. Transition from childhood to adulthood is obviously a universal phenomenon, since children become mature adults in all societies. However, the shift from childhood to adulthood can occur in different patterns. It can take the form of a sudden shift, such as has been observed in primitive societies in which the puberty rites end childhood and signify the beginning of adulthood. Mead reports, for example, that for the Manus girl, puberty "means the beginning of adult life and responsibility" (Mead, 1953: 107). There can also be a gradual shift, especially if the child group and the adult group are not as clearly separated and defined as they are in our society. Thus development would be continuous and the adolescent crisis would be mild. If the transition period is prolonged and if the children as a group are clearly distinguished from adults, as they are in Western societies, adolescents find themselves in a social situation in which their group membership is not clearly defined. The adolescent in such an in-between situation is referred to by Lewin as the "marginal man," and the adolescent's in-between standing is represented in Figure 9 by the overlapping area (Ad) of the child region (C) and the adult region (A). The assumption of the marginal-man concept is that the adolescent no longer belongs to the social group of children and does not want to be considered a child; yet he is not yet accepted into the social group of adults, and to the extent that this in-between situation is operative in his personal life space, his behavior will reflect this marginality. Being a marginal man implies that the adolescent may at times act more like a child, often when he wants to avoid adult responsibilities; at other times he may act more like an adult and request adult privileges. Parents and teachers, too, may interpret the marginal-man situation in their own way; however, they are more likely to remind the adolescent to be mature, grown-up, and adultlike when the issues involve responsibilities, chores, work, and study. They perceive their charges as "still so young" and "immature" when it comes to adult rights and privileges. Such a situation is most characteristic of youth in Western society, and it is partly responsible for some of Western society's "adolescent difficulties." The marginal man, topographically speaking, stands on the boundaries that separate two groups. "They are people who belong neither here nor there, standing 'between' the groups" (Lewin, 1948: 179). Marginality, even in other social situations, increases social tensions. Minority group members may find themselves in such a situation when they attempt to establish close personal relationships within the majority group—that is, by changing their group belonging. The psychological problems confronting the marginal man are both internal—instability, uncertainty, and self-hate—and external—a constant conflict over group belonging and a lack of role definition, with ostracism by either group possible.

From these basic assumptions about the nature of human development,

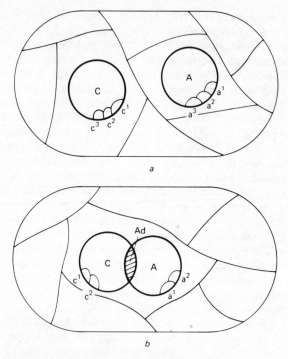

FIGURE 9. The Adolescent as a Marginal Man. (a) During childhood and adulthood the "adults" (A) and "children" (C) are viewed as relatively separated groups, the individual child (c^1, c^2) and the individual adult (a^1, a^2) being sure of their belonging to their respective groups. (b) The adolescent belonging to a group (Ad) which can be viewed as an overlapping region of the children's (C) and the adults' (A) group belonging to both of them, or as standing between them, not belonging to either one.

From Kurt Lewin, The Field Theory Approach to Adolescence. *American Journal of Sociology*, 1939, *44*, 868–897. Reproduced by permission from The University of Chicago Press.

Lewin (1939) derives a number of statements that describe, explain, and if the field forces are known, predict adolescent behavior:

1. The adolescent may show shyness and sensitivity but at the same time aggressiveness, mainly because of the unclearness of the situation and the disequilibrium in the life space.
2. As a marginal man, the adolescent experiences a continuous conflict among different attitudes, values, ideologies, and life styles, since he is shifting his orientation from the childhood group to the adult group, but he really does not belong to either. Therefore, he experiences lack of social anchorage except in relationship to his peer group.

3. These conflicts in values, attitudes, and ideologies result in increased emotional tension.
4. There is a predisposition in the adolescent to take extreme positions and to change behavior drastically; consequently, one can find radical, rebellious attitudes and actions side by side with sensitivity and withdrawal tendencies.
5. "Adolescent behavior" can be observed only if and to the extent that the structure and the dynamics of the life involve the following: (1) expansion and differentiation of the life space; (2) marginal-man standing in relationship to childhood and adult groups; and (3) biologically determined changes in the life space, as a result of body changes. The particular type of behavior that emerges and the degree of "adolescent behavior" depend greatly on the strength and nature of these conflicting forces. Above all in importance is the amount of difference between—and the factors that separate—adult society and child society in a particular culture.

The question of universality of the adolescent phenomenon is one of statistical frequency. Lewinian field theory (1935) considers this question irrelevant as well as the question of whether heredity or environment is the greater influence on development. Both nature and nurture can be depicted in the life space of an individual, and one can be more important than the other for a particular goal or a particular behavior.

> What is . . . important to the investigation of dynamics is not to abstract from the situation, but to hunt out those situations in which determinative factors of the total dynamic structure are most clearly, distinctly, and purely to be discerned. Instead of a reference to the abstract average of as many historically given cases as possible, there is a reference to the full concreteness of the particular situations [Lewin, 1935: 31].

The dynamic aspect of adolescent behavior and the individual situation, not the statistical frequency of one event or another, is the concern of field theory.

According to Lewin, specific characteristics of individuals cannot be classified in categories of overt behavior. Field theory moves away from classification systems; it assumes that there are great individual differences and sees as its objective the systematic explanation of these differences. Sensitivity to environmental influences varies greatly among people. The speed with which the differentiation and structurization of the life space take place also varies considerably in different people. Therefore, we must expect great individual variations in behavior. Furthermore, since sensitivity as well as rate of change in the life space increases during the adolescent period, we must expect that behavior changes also will differ widely and probably be more noticeable than at other times.

Moreover, field theory assumes not only individual differences, but cultural differences as well. Thus, while the life space varies from individual to individual within a given culture, the differences from culture to culture are even greater. Two aspects that will be relatively stable within a given culture but quite different from culture to culture are (1) the ideologies, attitudes, and values that are recognized and emphasized and (2) the way in which different activities are seen as related or unrelated; for example, religion and work are more closely related in Mennonite society than in American society as a whole (Lewin, 1942).

Another factor that may account for cultural differences in adolescent behavior is the varying length of the adolescent period from culture to culture and from social class to social class within a culture. Furthermore, the degree to which the child group and the adult group are differentiated in a given culture has far-reaching consequences for adolescent behavior. The more clearly the groups are separated, the more difficult the transition.

EDUCATIONAL IMPLICATIONS

Adolescents and their problems are related to the change in group belonging. They no longer belong to the child group and are no longer considered children. Nor do they yet belong to the adult groups and receive their privileges, even though adult activities may have a positive valence for them. Thus, adolescents are in a stage of social locomotion; they are transferring from one group to another but do not belong to either one. The term "marginal man" implies that adolescents are "social outcasts," to use a somewhat extreme term. This condition necessarily makes them more dependent on their own age group for support, inspiration, fellowship, and idols than either children or adults are dependent on their age groups. These insights gained through field theory may be used as psychological arguments in favor of the junior high school, since this is the age group in which the accelerated change in body maturity and the shift in group belonging are most obvious. Counterarguments concerning the negative psychological effects of the junior high school are advanced by Mead and were presented in the previous chapter.

An important factor in adolescent development is the enlargement, differentiation, and conceptualization of the time perspective. The young child lives mainly in the present; the past and the future include only a few days or weeks and have relatively little effect on behavior. As a child grows older, and especially during the adolescent period, he develops a time concept that makes the past significant; historical occurrences can now be understood in their chronological sequence. Lewin's concept of the enlargement of the time perspective during adolescence coincides with the teaching of history at the onset of adolescence and has been supported by research studies. But the time concept expands not only into the past but also into the future, which now becomes meaningful for the individual, who begins to form a life plan and set goals. The older child has to make choices in training and preparing for a vocation. This bespeaks the necessity for vocational guidance.

Adolescence is a period in which reality and irreality should be clearly distinguished, even though irreality will not necessarily disappear completely from the thought of the adolescent. It is important for the educator to emphasize the understanding of reality and to confront the adolescent with facts when responses become fabrications based on fantasy or irreality.

Adolescents' social awareness of group belonging undergoes great change, as do their bodies and body images. The child "knew" his body or showed little interest in it, but sexual maturity disturbs the adolescent, and the new bodily dimensions, qualities, and functions are sometimes threatening. Thus, a very close and vital part of life space, one's own body, becomes foreign and produces tension. Since body image is a fundamental region in the life space, this change leads to confusion, conflict, and uncertainty of behavior. Preoccupation with one's body and body image disturbances in their extreme manifestations take pathological forms, such as anorexia nervosa and bulimia (Muuss, 1985; 1986). Education probably will not be able to overcome all the difficulties related to body change, but it can at least prepare the adolescent boy and girl for these changes by helping them understand human growth and by giving them knowledge of the great normal variations in physical development.

The infant and the child must have their life space structured by their parents and other adults. But as they grow older, the restrictions and limitations should be removed slowly so that young adults are allowed to structure their own world. From an educational point of view, this means that the adolescent should be encouraged to develop independence and responsibility by setting his own goals and choosing his own methods to reach them.

Field theory presents the total situation, with all the aspects that make up the child's life space. If teaching is to be successful and produce the maximum amount of learning, the activities involved should have a positive valence for the student. Field theory holds that success in teaching depends on all of those conditions of learning that have been singled out by one or another educational theory—the social atmosphere, the amount of security, the interest and meaningfulness of the material, its psychological appropriateness for the developmental level of the learner, and the atmosphere in which the material is taught.

Lewin suggested, as do other phenomenological oriented psychologists, that what is more important psychologically speaking is the subject's perception of an event rather than the objective reality. This implies that a teacher must make a genuine effort to understand the student's perception of the situation—that is, to try to empathize with the adolescent's point of view. An illustration is the not uncommon observation that two students perform about the same on an examination and both receive a B grade. However, their psychological experience of success or failure is not so much dependent on the objective reality of their performance, but on their expectation. The student who expected an A is disappointed and perhaps even angry. The student who feared a C or worse is encouraged and feels elated. Understanding behavior is only possible through a reconstruction and understanding of the perceptual field of the behavior. Facts acquired in this way may be quite different from those obtained by an objective approach. Psychoanalysis, clinical psychology, Gestalt psychology, and field theory have applied this method within its natural limitations. The phenomenological point of view means that, within the obvious limits of this approach, the educator and the counselor would attempt to see and understand the world of the adolescent from the adolescent's perspective.

8: JEAN PIAGET'S COGNITIVE THEORY OF ADOLESCENCE

JEAN Piaget's (1896–1980) contribution to our understanding of human development is reflected in the increasing attention that psychologists—especially those with a cognitive development orientation—have devoted to his theory. In his earlier work, Piaget emphasized the cognitive development in infancy and childhood; only in his later research did Piaget give systematic attention to the more advanced levels of cognitive reasoning characteristic of adolescents. The book most explicitly designed to describe cognitive development in adolescence is *The Growth of Logical Thinking from Childhood to Adolescence* (Inhelder and Piaget, 1958).

After completing his dissertation, Piaget worked in Paris on the standardization of intelligence tests. Even though Piaget showed little interest in the psychometric and statistical procedures essential for test construction, he became fascinated with the underlying reasoning that children revealed while trying to solve test problems, and he found their explanations of incorrect responses particularly fascinating. The Geneva group still feels that standardized test questions frequently lead to stereotyped responses that do not fully disclose the underlying thought structure. They instead gather data through a "clinical method" that assesses thought processes rather than knowledge and allows children to explain the reasons for their thinking. In the meantime Piaget-type cognitive assessment batteries have been developed by Pinard and Laurendeau (1964), Furth and Wachs (1975), Patterson and Milakofsky (1980), and others. In general, the emphasis in such procedures is not so much on the answers given and whether or not they are correct as on the reasons for the answers. Piaget's preoccupation with qualitative changes in children's thought processes is obvious in much of his work. However, the lack of statistical analysis, noticeable in his earlier work, has long been a source of criticism.

Among contemporary schools of psychology, Piaget takes a relatively unique and independent position. There are no immediate predecessors with whom Piaget studied or whose ideas he expanded. Nevertheless, Piaget was influenced by a number of thinkers. Philosophically, he was influenced by Kant's epistemology and Bergson's metaphysics. Piaget read

Freud, but references to Freud appear only in his earlier work. Piaget did not share Freud's interest in the subconscious, in conflicts, in dynamics, or in the affective aspects of development. Instead he focused on the conflict-free and rational side of development and emphasized thought processes, the structure of intelligence, and the development of logical thinking. Nevertheless, Piaget's concept of "egocentrism" (see Chapter 12), which characterized the language, thought, and social judgment of developing children, is quite compatible with some psychoanalytic notions, such as the subject-object differentiation. Piaget also stimulated the present concern with moral judgment (see Chapter 9) and social cognition (see Chapter 11).

In certain respects, Piaget's theory (1947b) appears to be closer to the German school of Gestalt psychology, and Piaget once said that if he had studied with the Gestalt psychologists in Berlin he probably would have become a Gestalt psychologist himself. His kinship with Gestalt psychology is especially clear in his emphasis on the patterns of organization, the structural whole, and the total system. Piaget was concerned with the relationship between the parts and the whole. However, he disagreed with several Gestalt assumptions. For example, Gestalt principles do not seem to be useful in explaining the "logical operations in thought" that Piaget attempted to discover. Furthermore, he emphasized structural changes as a function of development, whereas Gestalt psychology maintains that the "laws of organization" and "perceptual structure" are independent of age.

Piaget, who has been characterized as a "zoologist by training, an epistemologist by vocation, and a logician by method," is best known for his contributions to developmental psychology. He regarded himself as an interdisciplinary thinker and can best be identified as a "genetic epistemologist." Epistemology is the branch of science concerned with the methods, the limits, and the validity of knowledge. The term "genetic" implies that the acquisition of knowledge is influenced by genetic or biological factors; however, Piaget was not a maturationalist but is better characterized as an "interactionist." He emphasized that development is an interaction between biology and environment. Coming from philosophy and biology, his methodology as well as his theoretical conceptualizations initially were unique and even suspect, but they have slowly and steadily been integrated into the mainstream of psychological thought and have become a dominating influence in cognitive and developmental research in the last twenty years. The popularity of "cognitive psychology" as a new field is, in part, a result of Piaget's contributions.

THE MAJOR DEVELOPMENTAL CONCEPTS OF PIAGET'S THEORY

Piaget's theory of development contains two components which, even though closely interrelated, can be analyzed separately: the stage-dependent and the stage-independent theory (Flavell, 1963a). The elements of the stage-dependent theory are the four well-known developmental stages: sensorimotor, preoperational, concrete operational, and formal operational stages. In addition, Piaget advanced a system of interrelated concepts, borrowed primarily from biology, that make up his stage-independent theory of development. The important constructs of the stage-independent theory are: schema, structure, operation, assimilation, accommodation, adaptation, equilibrium, and disequilibrium. These ideas cut across all levels of the stage-dependent theory and are as applicable to early motor development as they are to the advanced logical thought processes of the mature adult.

The first two concepts of the stage-independent theory, schema and structure, appear to be almost interchangeable. A schema is a generalized or established behavior pattern of meaningful and repeatable action patterns, such as the sucking schema, the grasping schema, and later in adolescence, the "all-other-things-being-equal" schema of reasoning. As children continuously interact with their environment, the simple schemata become broadened and modified and combine with other schemata. Schemata, therefore, are not static, but are continuously growing and are even referred to as "mobile schemata." When referring to the thought processes of adolescents, Piaget uses such terms as "cognitive schema," "operational schema," "anticipatory schema," and "logical schema." It is in these latter instances that schema and structure become synonymous, except that schema is the behavioral equivalent and structure the internal thought patterns. The structures are the organizational properties of thought that determine the nature of the child's actions, especially the more complex cognitive responses. Thus, the theory focuses on the qualitative changes of intellectual structure from birth to maturity. Each structure is built on earlier, simpler, less mature structures. The integration of older, lower-level structures into new, more advanced structures provides the continuity for cognitive development (Flavell, 1963b).

According to Piaget, when schemata and structures have developed to the extent that they can be used by interrelated systems of logic, they are called "operations." Piaget defines an operation as a reversible action or a reversible transformation of one structure into another. Consequently, operations are more complex and more differentiated than schemata and begin to approximate a logical model. It is possible to apply operations to a much wider spectrum of related problems. For example, memorized formulas that a student applies to a series of identical problems correspond to schemata. But when a student is able to solve related or similar problems in a different context, or by using different symbols, or can understand the relationship of each piece of information to the whole problem, he demonstrates operational thinking. In this situation the reliance on the memorized formula becomes unnecessary because the meaning of the problem is understood. To the extent that operations have become meaningful parts of the cognitive structure, they show resistance to forgetting. "Operations," to which Piaget devotes considerable emphasis in his theory, have two characteristics:

1. Operational thought is reversible. Logical operations can be reversed by cancelling an operation. The operational child understands that subtraction can cancel the process of addition just as division can cancel multiplication. The addition $6 + 7 = 13$ can be cancelled by its reversal $13 - 7 = 6$. One can reverse an operation by reciprocity and return to the starting point. A clay ball can be made into a clay sausage or a clay pancake and again be reversed into the original form of a clay ball.

2. Operational thought is associative. Thought is not limited to only one avenue, but has the flexibility and the freedom to pursue a problem by way of different routes, detours, and by way of a variety of methods and approaches. For example, the problem 25×25 can be solved in a number of ways: $(25 \times 20) + (25 \times 5)$; or $20^2 + (2 \times 20 \times 5) + 5^2$; or $25 \times 100 \div 4$; and so on.

The distinction between operational and preoperational thought constitutes the fundamental dividing line in Piaget's stage-dependent theory. Since such systems of logical operations, reversibility, and associativity of thought do not emerge until about the age of seven, Piaget speaks of the child prior to this age as the *preoperational child,* who relies predominantly on perception and intuition. After the age of seven the child enters the *operational stage of development.* Operations are seen as internalized actions that constitute a system of organized and related thoughts and correspond to the operations of mathematics and logic. Piaget speaks of logical operations, such as addition, multiplication, and reciprocity; and uses mathematics and logic as the models for his analysis of the thought of the operational child.

The three variables primarily responsible for development in general and cognitive development in particular are:

1. The maturation of the nervous system
2. Experiences gained through interaction with physical reality
3. The influence of the social environment

The maturation model of development constitutes only a general background for Piaget's equilibration-equilibrium model, which places major emphasis on the dynamic interaction between the developing child and his physical and social environment.

Cognitive adaptation to the environment takes place by way of assimilation and accommodation. The child's environmental experiences are first assimilated; that is, the new experience or event is structured or restructured to fit into the present intellectual organization. To intellectually assimilate "reality is to construct that reality, and to construct it in terms" of one's existing cognitive structure (Flavell, 1963a: 48). Accommodation refers to the process of internal change in the cognitive structure, a change brought about by utilizing and incorporating—that is, accommodating to the new experiences that were just assimilated. Piaget borrowed the terms assimilation-accommodation from biology, and biology provides an appropriate analogy. The organism assimilates food by chewing, swallowing, and breaking it down. In this process food is restructured to fit the biological needs of the organism. However, in the process the organism also changes. The organism accommodates food by incorporating (digesting) it into its own structure. As a result, the organism itself is restructured; it has more energy and it grows. Assimilation and accommodation are complementary processes. They bring about conceptual adaptation and cognitive growth through their continuous interaction. It is through this process of assimilation and accommodation that the intellectual structure expands. When a balance between assimilation and accommodation has been accomplished, a state of equilibrium exists.

Equilibrium is the harmony between sensory information and accumulated knowledge, or harmony between the individual and the environment. As new sensory information—in the form of questions, problems, and issues—disturbs existing, incomplete, or incorrect knowledge, the equilibrium is thrown into a new disequilibrium, and a new assimilation-accommodation process begins. As these questions, problems, or issues are taken into the existing structure (assimilation) and the existing structure grows, changes, and expands in the process (accommodation), a new, higher-level equilibrium is attained. The accommodation of new experiences produces modifications in the structure and the schema, which means that the child has gained something that allows him to make more sophisticated observations, to solve more difficult problems, or to advance higher-level generalizations. Thus the theory allows for continuous progressive cognitive development. Assimilating and accommodating environmental experiences lead slowly but steadily to cognitive growth. Piaget views children as active participants in their own development. This active conception of the nature of the child is well expressed in the often quoted statement by Piaget, "Every time we teach a child something, we keep him from reinventing it. On the other hand, every time a child discovers it for himself, it remains with him for the rest of his life."

The concept of equilibrium is essential in Piaget's definition of intelligence as a "form of equilibration . . . toward which all functions lead" (Piaget, 1962: 120). Equilibration is defined as a compensation for an external disturbance. Intellectual development becomes a continuous progression moving from one structural disequilibrium to a new, higher, structural equilibrium. Intellectual operations never function in isolation but are regulated by organizing principles that relate to the total system. Consequently, Piaget frequently draws parallels from the basic cognitive structures of thinking to the child's level of moral judgment (1932b), language development (1932a), reasoning, and conceptions of the world (1929), or physical causality (1930), or numbers (1952a), or space (1967). "It is possible to discern synchronized structures of operational development manifesting themselves in such diversified fields as logic, space, time, etc." (Inhelder, 1966: 304).

PIAGET'S STAGES OF COGNITIVE DEVELOPMENT

Piaget's theory originally focused on infancy and childhood but was later expanded to include adolescence. The interrelationship of the various facets of Piaget's theory makes it necessary to discuss briefly the characteristics of the earlier stages of development. The preadolescent and adolescent periods, which are characterized by operational thought, will be described in more detail and become the primary focus of this chapter. The following stage-dependent theory has to be understood in the light of the continuing disequilibrium-assimilation-accommodation-equilibrium process just discussed.

THE SENSORIMOTOR STAGE

The *sensorimotor stage of development* (from birth to two) is subdivided into six developmental phases. The first phase (birth to one month), the *reflex* phase, consists primarily of exercising inborn reflexes such as the sucking reflex, which, as it becomes modified to meet the demands of different situations, becomes the sucking schema. During the second phase (one to four months), which Piaget calls the phase of *primary circular reactions,* reflexes are slowly replaced by voluntary movements. The child may tirelessly practice an emerging schema, such as grasping, since he is motivated by "function pleasure"—a concept quite different from the behavioristic notion of "drive reduction" or "reinforcement." In the third phase (four to eight months), that of *secondary circular reactions,* infants begin to pursue objects and events unrelated to themselves—for example, following the slow movement of an attractive toy. Or, if an infant learns through trial and error to grasp a cord and make a bell jingle, he may repeat such behavior. That such an action can be repeated is evidence of the beginning of intentionality and even an incipient form of goal-directed behavior. The fourth phase (eight to twelve months), that of *coordination of secondary schemata,* is characterized by the emergence of means-ends relationships. The child reaches for a box in order to obtain the toy that is inside the box. The child will begin to search or look for a toy hidden under a blanket, indicating that the concept of "object permanence" is beginning to emerge. During the fifth phase (twelve to eighteen months), that of *tertiary circular reactions,* the concept of "object permanence" becomes more stable. The child will search for and find the object even though in the process of hiding it, it may have been moved through a series of displacements. That is, the object may have been placed first under a blanket, then under a pillow, and finally under a box. The last of the six phases (twelve to twenty-four months) is that of *internalization of sensorimotor schemata.* The child begins to use foresight and symbolic representation in solving sensorimotor problems. For the first time, the child may investigate whether a hole is big enough before attempting to push an object through it, thus giving evidence that the strictly sensorimotor approach to problem solving is being replaced by thought.

THE PREOPERATIONAL STAGE

The second period of development (two to seven years), called the *preoperational stage,* is a transition period from the predominantly egocentric and motor stage of early childhood to the early forms of social behavior, sociocentric speech, and conceptual thought, all of which become more obvious as the child approaches the end of the preoperational stage. This stage is subdivided into two distinguishable phases. The first, that of *extracting concepts from experiences,* covers the years from two to four. Children learn new concepts on the basis of direct, first-hand sensory experiences—that is, they are still at the mercy of their own perceptions. Reality is what they perceive; no other alternatives are available to them. When a chocolate bar is broken up, they think there is more chocolate, because the pieces look more than the solid bar. During this phase, children's language develops at a phenomenal rate. From the rather rudimentary forms of language usage at the age of two, children normally develop language ability to such an extent that they are able to communicate their thoughts by the age of four. The words they hear and use become associated with objects and relationships and thus contribute to conceptual growth.

The second, more advanced phase of the preoperational stage (four to seven years) is that of *intuitive thought,* or intuitive use of concepts. The differentiation from the previous stage is a fine one; the judgments are still intuitive and subjective, but they deal with more complex issues than in the previous stage. The child now can manipulate objects, tools, and toys much more effectively and the ability to communicate with others is enhanced by language development. Therefore, it becomes possible for children to make more systematic interrogations. Nevertheless, accurate judgment is limited by three factors:

1. Basically, children are still dependent on sensory experiences.
2. They cannot consider two or more dimensions at the same time;

rather, they focus on one aspect and consequently neglect to consider the other.
3. They cannot rearrange or reorganize information in their minds.

Since these children are too dependent on sensory impressions, they do not yet comprehend the *principle of conservation:* that a given quantity remains the same, even though the way that quantity has been arranged has changed. The typical example is the clay ball being changed into a long clay sausage. The preoperational child thinks it is more "because it looks longer." Neither does he think in terms of a hierarchy of classes and supraclasses. A child may maintain, "We are not in Baltimore, we are in Maryland," not yet comprehending that one can be included in the other.

THE CONCRETE OPERATIONAL STAGE

At approximately age seven or eight, a major shift in the child's conceptual development takes place. He now begins to perform logical *concrete operations* in his mind. This period (from seven or eight to puberty) is referred to as the *operational stage in logical thinking.* Chronologically, this period extends into the preadolescent period.

During the operational stage, the child learns to master the basic logical and mathematical operations, using concrete content. "Concrete" in this context does not mean that the child can only deal with tangible objects but that the problems have to be tied to reality. The major limitation evident in the thinking at this level is the inability to think abstractly about a problem. Since concrete operations can be performed mentally, overt trial and error becomes unnecessary. For the first time, the child begins to think in accordance with a model of logical reasoning. The important elements of concrete logical operations are:

1. *The logic of classes,* which is based on an understanding of whether or not an object belongs or does not belong in a given class. This enables children to solve problems of classification. They become concerned with the relationship between the parts and the whole. Understanding and classifying the parts that belong together helps them to gain a better understanding of the whole, the supraclass. Their ability to hold several pieces of information in mind and to reverse their thinking enables them to understand a hierarchy of classes and supraclasses. The operational child may actually become preoccupied with systems of classification.

2. *The logic of relations,* which makes it possible to order and organize several things in relationship to one another, according to specific criteria such as size. In a test situation, the child is asked to rank order a series of objects, such as dolls or sticks, according to their size. Such an "operation of serializing" is similar to the classification of a hierarchy, since it involves some understanding of the structure of the whole. "There is no

class without classification; there is no systematic relation without serialization" (Piaget, 1962: 126). The logic of relations gets elaborated when the child is asked to set two series of objects into correspondence with one another. An example would be to match a series of dolls with a corresponding set of hats or sticks. The operational child, possessing the "logic of relations," is able to order objects according to their size, height, or weight as long as objects are presented concretely. It is not until adolescence that such operations can be performed on an abstract level.

The operational child now begins to develop an understanding of the *principle of conservation*, realizing that changing a clay ball into a sausage or flattening it out into a pancake does not change its mass, weight, or volume. The concept of conservation of mass is established first, weight is of intermediate difficulty, and volume is the most difficult and may not emerge in the concrete operational stage (Elkind, 1961a; 1961b). Elkind (1961b) showed that the conservation of volume concept appeared later in American adolescents than suggested by Piaget; however, he did agree with Piaget that formal operations are necessary for the attainment of the conservation of volume concept.

An understanding of the principle of conservation leads to an awareness of the reversibility of thought processes. Reversibility is defined as "the permanent possibility of returning to the starting point of the operation in question" (Inhelder and Piaget, 1958: 272). The child can construct a chain of colored beads, copying the original pattern in reversed order. Awareness of the concept of reversibility is critical to operational thought. "An operation is an action capable of occurring internally and of which . . . the essential characteristic is its reversibility. Cognitive activity becomes operational when it acquires a mobility such that an action (or transformation) can be annulled in thought by an inverse action or can be compensated for by a reciprocal action" (Inhelder, 1966: 302). The ability to return to the starting point of an operation—which is implied in the concept "reversibility"—constitutes an important milestone in the intellectual development of the child. Operational children use addition and can reverse the findings by subtraction. They can judge the distance between point A and point B and conclude it to be the same as between B and A. Alice in Wonderland, after eating one side of the mushroom, demonstrates the idea of reversibility by nibbling on the other side in order to reverse her height. As a result of having reversible operations, the operational child can use various approaches to solutions of a problem without becoming committed to any one as the only one.

At the same time that the concrete operations emerge, the child's language, which has been predominantly egocentric until the age of seven, becomes primarily sociocentric. Sociocentric language implies a genuine effort to understand other people and to communicate thoughts objectively. "The child really exchanges his thoughts with others, either by telling his hearer something that will interest him and influence his actions, or by an actual interchange of ideas by argument or even by collaboration in pursuit of a common aim'' (Piaget, 1932a: 9–10). Research does not substantiate the shift from egocentric to sociocentric speech as neatly as the shift from preoperational to operational thought as the theory does, but the research does support the more general idea that with increasing age the proportion of egocentric speech decreases and sociocentric speech increases.

The change from egocentric to sociocentric thought is not only reflected in the child's language, but permeates his thought processes as well. The sociocentric child can place himself in the situation of another person and take that person's point of view. When confronted with a model of three differently shaped mountains, he can identify correctly what they would look like from other positions (see Figure 10). He can rotate objects in his mind and might spontaneously ask, ''What does the other side of the moon look like?''

Piaget identifies the properties of concrete operations and applies the term ''elementary groupings,'' or ''group-like structures,'' to the different ways in which the child's thought processes can manipulate classes and relations. Since Piaget postulates a direct relationship between logic and the child's cognitive processes, the concepts he introduces are conveyed in terms of logic and mathematics. An important set of four concrete operational groupings follows:

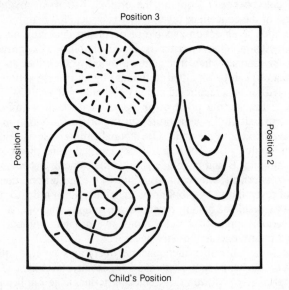

FIGURE 10. Schematic Presentation of the Three Differently Shaped Mountains. The question is, When can a child accurately identify what the mountain range looks like from positions 2, 3, and 4?

Combinativity. Two or more classes can be combined into one larger, more comprehensive class. For example, all men and all women equals all adults. Logical relationships such as A is larger than B and B is larger than C can be combined into a new statement that A is larger than C. The ability to combine subclasses into supraclasses is essential to the understanding of a hierarchy of classifications.

Reversibility. Every operation is reversible. Every operation has an opposite operation that reverses it. Supraclasses can be taken apart, so that the effect of combining subclasses is reversed. All adults except all women equals all men. The child's ability to reverse thought processes is an important indicator of cognitive development.

Associativity. The child whose operations have become associative can reach a goal in various ways, making detours in thought, but in such a fashion that the results obtained by these different routes remain the same. For example, $(3 + 6) + 4 = 13$, and $6 + (3 + 4) = 13$.

Identity or nullifiability. An operation that is combined with its opposite becomes nullified. Illustrations of nullifiability in mathematics are: give 3 and take 3 away results in null, or 5 times X divided by 5 equals X. All Americans except those who are American equals no one. If I drive one mile west and one mile east, I am where I started; my actions are nullified.

Primary groupings make combinativity, reversibility, and associativity in thought possible and thus aid the child in achieving an equilibrium that is considerably more mobile and flexible than the thought process of the preoperational child. Thus, the approach to problem solving is no longer intuitive or impulsive but rational and logical. However, reasoning is not yet integrated into a single total system of interrelated propositions.

THE FORMAL OPERATIONS STAGE

The final stage of cognitive development in Piaget's theory is the *stage of formal operations,* which is characterized by the use of propositional thinking, combinatorial analysis, and abstract reasoning. The concept "formal" implies that what matters is form rather than content. The major source of information about adolescent cognitive development is *The Growth of Logical Thinking* (Inhelder and Piaget, 1958). Piaget subdivides the stage of formal operations further into substages III-A, almost full formal function (eleven or twelve to fourteen or fifteen years), and III-B, full formal function (fourteen or fifteen years and up). This division of the adolescent period at the age of fourteen or fifteen implies another restructuring and a disequilibrium, which then leads to a higher level of equilibrium and intellectual structure during late adolescence. In this division III-A—the earlier substage, corresponding to early adolescence—appears to be a preparatory stage in which adolescents may make correct discoveries and handle certain formal operations, but the approach is still cumbersome, and they are not yet able to provide systematic and rigorous proof for their assertions. By the time adolescents reach substage III-B they have become capable of formulating more elegant generalizations and of advancing more inclusive laws. Most of all, they are now able to provide spontaneously more systematic proof for their assertions, since they understand the importance of the method of control. The difference in approach and reasoning of adolescents in substages III-A and III-B may be illustrated by actual responses.

In one experiment, "The Law of Floating Bodies . . .," the subject is presented with a variety of objects. The problem is to distinguish those that float on water from those that do not and to provide proof.

Jim (12; 8) classifies floating or sinking objects according to whether they are *"lighter or heavier than water."*—"What do you mean?"—*"You would have to have much more water than metal to make up the same weight."*—"And this cover?"—*"When you put up the edges, there is air inside; when you put them down, it goes down because the water comes inside and thus makes more weight."*—"Why does the wood float?"—*"Because it is light."*—"And that little key?"—*"No, this piece of wood is heavier."*—"So?"—*"If you measure with a key* [= with the weight of a key], *you need much more wood than lead for the weight of the key."*—"What do you mean?"—*"If you take metal, you need much more wood to make the same weight than metal"* [Inhelder and Piaget, 1958: 38].

The subject who has reached substage III-B sees the problem more specifically in terms of units of measurements that are provided and uses the measures spontaneously. Furthermore, the subject appreciates that the weight of the object in relationship to the weight of the water that it replaces determines whether it floats or sinks. There is a reduction in trial-and-error reasoning, and proof is provided with greater elegance and precision, as the following protocol illustrates.

Lamb (13; 3) correctly classifies the objects that sink: *"I sort of felt that they are all heavier than water. I compared for the same weight, not for the same volume of water."*—"Can you give proof?"—*"Yes, I take these two bottles, I weigh them . . . Oh!* [he notices the cubes] *I weigh this plastic cube with water inside and compare this volume of water to the wooden cube. You always have to compare a volume to the same volume of water."*—"And with this wooden ball?"—*"By calculation."*—"But otherwise?"—*"Oh, yes, you set the water level* [in the bucket]; *you put the ball in and let out enough water to maintain the original level."*—"Then what do you compare?"—*"The weight of the water let out and the weight of the ball"* [Inhelder and Piaget, 1958: 44].

As these illustrations show, the reasoning from substage III-A to III-B becomes increasingly more abstract and shows a more sophisticated mastery of the formal operations. Since Piaget postulates a direct correspondence between the structure of logic and the structure of cognitive operations, there is a developmental approximation of the operational thought process of the adolescent to the formal system of modern logic. The significance that Piaget attaches to the change from concrete operations to formal operations is even reflected in a change in the symbols of logic; for example, A + B used for concrete operations, changes to the symbols of logic "p o q" for the same operation. These changes in thought processes are seen as being directly related to maturational changes in the cortex that accompany puberty. While the child at the concrete operational stage is able to reason on the basis of objects, the adolescent begins to reason on the basis of verbal propositions. The principal difference between the operational and the formal operational stages is that the adolescent gains the ability "to reason in terms of verbally stated hypotheses and no longer in terms of concrete objects and their manipulation" (Piaget, 1980: 72). The adolescent can now make hypothetical deductions and entertain the idea of relativity. "Formal thought reaches its fruition during adolescence. An adolescent, unlike the child, is an individual who thinks beyond the present and forms theories about everything, delighting especially in consideration of that which is not" (Piaget, 1947b: 148).

Adolescents not only think beyond the present but analytically reflect about their own thinking. Piaget calls this kind of reasoning "second-degree thinking"; it involves operations that produce "thinking about thinking," "statements about statements," or more significantly, "operations on operations." The adolescent's theories may sometimes still seem to be oversimplifications of reality. Nevertheless, most adolescents in substage III-B have social and political theories and at least some also have religious, philosophical, and scientific theories. Formal operations give the adolescent the ability to understand and even form theories and "to participate in society and the ideologies of adults; this is often accompanied by a desire to change society and even, if necessary, destroy it (in his imagination) in order to elaborate a better one" (Piaget, 1980: 72). This preoccupation with theory can even be applied to the dreams girls have of their future husbands; these dreams are frequently quite "theoretical," as is their understanding of married life (Inhelder and Piaget, 1958).

In their thoughts adolescents can leave the real objective world behind and enter the world of ideas. They now control events in their minds through logical deductions of possibilities and consequences. Even the directions of thought processes change. Preadolescents begin by thinking about reality and attempt to extend thoughts toward possibility. Adolescents, who have mastered formal operations, begin by thinking of all logical possibilities and then consider them in a systematic fashion; reality has become secondary to possibility, reality now being reduced to a subset of possibility. To emphasize this point further, one could say that in operational thinking reality is the foreground and possibility remains in the background. In formal operational thinking, this relationship is reversed—possibility has become the foreground and reality has become simply one of the many possibilities. "The most distinctive property of formal thought is this reversal of direction between *reality and possibility;* instead of deriving a rudimentary type of theory from the empirical data as is done in concrete inferences, formal thought begins with a theoretical synthesis implying that certain relations are necessary and thus proceeds in the opposite direction. . . . This type of thinking proceeds *from* what is possible *to* what is empirically real" (Inhelder and Piaget, 1958: 251). This reversal of the direction of thought between reality and possibility constitutes a turning point in the development of the structure of intelligence, since it leads to an equilibrium that is both stable and more flexible.

An illustration may serve to contrast preadolescent reasoning based on concrete operations with adolescent reasoning based on verbal propositions. The nine-year-old can arrange a series of dolls according to their height and can even supply each doll with a stick of a corresponding size from a series of different size sticks, even if the sticks are presented in reverse order. But not until the formal operations have developed can a similar, abstract problem be solved: "If B is not as bad as C, and C is not as good as A, then who is worst?"

The attainment of formal operations is not an all-or-nothing proposition. Between the ages of eleven or twelve and fourteen or fifteen, considerable modification, systemization, and formalization of thought processes can be observed. The complexity of the problems that the individual can handle increases substantially during these years and reaches an equilibrium after substage III-B has been attained.

Piaget distinguishes between the concrete elementary, or primary, groupings discussed earlier and formal, or second-degree, groupings characteristic of the formal stage. He also refers to these more advanced groupings as operations to the second power, or the proposition-about-proposition attribute. Implied in the proposition-about-proposition concept is the idea that adolescents think about their own thoughts in a reflective way (see Chapter 12). Turning to a description of the formal operational schemata, one ought to remain aware that adolescents, even though they think operationally, do not have a basic understanding of the kind of *formal logic* by which Piaget analyzes and describes adolescent thought processes. The two important theoretical foundations of the formal logic are:

1. *The combinatorial system of operations,* defined as "the matrix of all possible combinations of all possible values of all possible variables inherent in the problem" (Dulit, 1972: 288).
2. *The INCR group of operations,* to be discussed later.

These two theoretical "building blocks" are comparable in significance to the "logic of classes" and the "logic of relations" in the operational stage.

COMBINATORIAL SYSTEM OF OPERATIONS

Formal operations allow adolescents to combine propositions and to isolate variables in order to confirm or disprove their hypotheses. They no longer need to think in terms of objects or concrete events but can carry out symbolic operations in their minds. This first grouping to be presented constitutes a combinatorial system of operational schemata characterized by propositional operations. The formal-operational thinker can make the following logical combinations.

1. Combine by conjunction. "Both A and B make a difference." The subject was asked to determine why certain objects float and others do not. In solving this problem the subject has to realize that "both weight and volume make a difference" before being able to comprehend the notion of density, which emerges once the relationship between weight and volume is understood. As long as the subject attempts to explain the phenomenon of floating or sinking on the basis of either weight or size—as the concrete operational child commonly does–he fails to make the correct generalization.

2. Combine by disjunction. "It's got to be this or that." In order to solve a problem, variables have to be identified and tested so that a hypothesis can be confirmed or rejected. In one of the experiments, the subject is presented with a simple pendulum (see Figure 11). The variables that can be manipulated are the length of the string, the weight, the point at which the weight is released, and the force of the push. The problem is to discover what factors affect the frequency of the oscillation. Once the subject reasons, "It's got to be this or that" (length of string or weight), he begins to approach the solution hypothetically. By experimenting with each of these two variables independently, the subject discovers that weight is irrelevant and the length of the string is the important variable.

3. Combine by implication. "If it is this, then that happens." Once a relevant variable has been identified, a specific explanation can be tested and stated. "If the string is short then the swing is fast; if the string is long then the swing is slow." That is in essence what one of Inhelder and Piaget's (1958) sixteen-year-old subjects concluded, even though he initially believed that all four variables were involved. The hypothetical nature of the propositional thinking finds a clear expression in the declining frequency of operational statements, such as: "This is true, therefore . . ."

FIGURE 11. The Pendulum Problem. The pendulum problem utilizes a simple apparatus consisting of a string, which can be shortened or lengthened, and a set of varying weights. The other variables which at first might be considered relevant are the height of the release point and the force of the push given by the subject

From *The Growth of Logical Thinking from Childhood to Adolescence,* by Bärbel Inhelder and Jean Piaget, © 1958 by Basic Books, Inc., Publishers, New York and Routledge & Kegan Paul, Ltd., London. Reproduced by permission.

and an increase in hypothetical deductive statements, such as: "If this were true, then. . . ."

4. Combine by incompatibility. "When this happens, then that does not." In the pendulum experiment, increasing and decreasing the weight does not change the oscillation of the pendulum and thus serves to eliminate a hypothesis that is incompatible with the actual observation. A commonly made incorrect assumption in this experiment is that weight does make a difference. Consequently, the ability to combine by incompatibility appears relatively late in the operational stage.

Initially, in substage III-A adolescents cannot yet reason out the whole range of intrapropositional combinations, which means that they cannot produce systematic proof of their response by way of the schema, "all other things being equal." It is only at substage III-B that subjects can spontaneously use this method. They are now capable of holding all other variables constant and can systematically change one variable at a time to study the effects of each variable in isolation. As a result they not only advance hypotheses but subject them to empirical verification. As their thought processes simulate the controls of a scientific experiment, their proofs become more rigorous and their generalizations gain in precision.

Contrasting the responses of two adolescents in an experiment that involves five variables may illustrate the difference in reasoning of a subject in substage III-A with a III-B subject, only the latter apparently being able to use the important schema, "all other things being equal."

The apparatus consists of a vertical holder with clamps from which brass and nonbrass rods of different sizes and shapes can be horizontally suspended. The holder actually stands in a large basin of water. The subject is to determine the flexibility of the rods and to identify under what circumstances they would touch the water. The flexibility of the rods is dependent on the following variables:

1. The material (steel or brass)
2. The length of the rods (they can be shortened or lengthened)
3. The thickness of the rods (7mm^2, 10mm^2, 16mm^2)

FIGURE 12. The Flexibility Experiment. Diagram A illustrates the variables used in the flexibility experiment. The rods can be shortened or lengthened by varying the point at which they are clamped (see B for apparatus used). Cross-section forms are shown at the left of each rod; shaded forms represent brass rods, unshaded forms represent nonbrass rods. Dolls are used for the weight variable (see B). These are placed at the end of the rod. Maximum flexibility is indicated when the end of the rod touches the water.

From *The Growth of Logical Thinking from Childhood to Adolescence*, by Bärbel Inhelder and Jean Piaget, © 1958 by Basic Books, Inc., Publishers, New York and Routledge & Kegan Paul, Ltd., London. Reproduced by permission.

4. The cross section, or form (round, square, rectangular)
5. The weight attached to the end of the rod (100g, 200g, 300g)

The problem is to determine under what circumstances the rod touches the water level and to provide proof for the assertions made.

Pey (12; 9) speculates that if the rod is to touch the water it must be "long and thin." After several trials he concludes: *"The larger and thicker it is, the more it resists."*—"What did you observe?"—*"This one* [brass, square, 50cm long, 16mm^2 cross section with 300 gram weight] *bends more than that one* [steel; otherwise the same conditions which he has selected to be equal]: *it's another metal. And this one* [brass, round] *more than that one"* [brass, square; same conditions for weight and length, but 10 and 16mm^2 cross section].—"If you wanted to buy a rod which bends the most possible?"—*"I would choose it round, thin, long, and made of soft metal"* [Inhelder and Piaget, 1958: 56–57].

The ability to combine the results of each pair of comparisons lead to an understanding of the "structured whole" and—in contrast to the one-by-one comparisons of earlier stages—demonstrates the operation of formal thought. Such an approach is "under construction" in substage III-A (as demonstrated above), not becoming fully operational until substage III-B, when it makes the process of verification much more convincing, as evidenced by the following protocol:

Dei (16; 10): "Tell me first [after experimental trials] what factors are at work here."—*"Weight, material, the length of the rod, perhaps the form."*—"Can you prove your hypotheses?"—[She compares the 200 gram and 300 gram weights on the same steel rod.] *"You see, the role of weight is demonstrated. For the material I don't know."*—"Take these steel ones and these copper ones."—*"I think I have to take two rods with the same form. Then to demonstrate the role of the metal I compare these two* [steel and brass, square, 50cm long and 16mm^2 cross section with 300 grams on each] *or these two here* [steel and brass, round, 50 and 22 cm by 16mm^2]: *for length I shorten that one* [50 cm brought down to 22]. *To demonstrate the role of the form, I can compare these two"* [round brass and square brass, 50 cm and 16mm^2 for each].— "Can the same thing be proven with these two?" [brass, round and square, 50cm long and 16 and 7mm^2 cross sectional].—*"No, because that one* [7mm^2] *is much narrower."*—"And the width?"—*"I can compare these two"* [round, brass, 50cm long with 16 and 7mm^2 cross sectional] [Inhelder and Piaget, 1958: 60].

The elegance of reasoning demonstrated here is based on the systematic verification of one variable at a time with "all other things being equal."

And if one were to give substage III-B a theoretical name, it ought to contain this "all other things being equal" quality.

INRC GROUP OF OPERATIONS

A second set of formal groupings that develop as part of the propositional logic of the adolescent is made up of four transformations, referred to as the INRC group. Each of these letters represents one of the logical transformations that can be performed on a proposition, changing it into a different operation. The acquisition of the INRC group is an important step in the development of logical thought in adolescence. An understanding of these four transformations is necessary in order to solve problems of proportionality and equilibrium.

1. "I"—Identity or identity transformation. The identity transformation refers to the starting operation that was initially given. This transformation is also referred to as the null transformation, since it results in no basic changes; the original proposition retains its identity. One of Piaget's experiments may provide an illustration. In a balance-type weighing scale, different size weights can be attached to several points on the crossbar (see Figure 13). The problem is to develop an understanding of the concept of equilibrium, which is based on an awareness of proportionality. In an "I" transformation, the subject may simultaneously increase the weight and the distance in such a way that the balance itself remains unaffected. Any change would be of such a nature that the basic relationship between the elements—the equilibrium of the scale—retains its identity.

2. "N"—Negation or inversion. A negative transformation means an undoing of the original operation. In an N transformation, everything in the initially given proposition is changed into the opposite of the original proposition. "All assertions become negations, and vice versa, and all conjunctions become disjunctions, and vice versa" (Flavell, 1963a: 216). The inverse to

FIGURE 13. The Balance Scale Used to Assess Children's Concepts of Proportionality. Different weights can be hung at different points on the crossbar.

"all vertebrates" is "all nonvertebrates." Inversion or negation cancels out an operation and consequently constitutes one form of reversibility. Reversibility by inversion or negation means that the result of an operation is annulment. For example $+ 6 - 6 = 0$, or $+ n - n = 0$ (Piaget, 1980). In the crossbar experiment, an N transformation would be to "reduce the distance while increasing the weight or diminish the weight while increasing the distance or diminish both" (Inhelder and Piaget, 1958: 178).

3. "R"—Reciprocal or reciprocity. Reciprocity transformation means undoing the results of the original operation; however, in this transformation it is accomplished by changing some other variable in the system. The reciprocal of a proposition transforms the proposition without changing the conjunction or disjunction that joins the part of the proposition. "A is twice as large as B" in an R transformation becomes "B is twice as large as A." Reciprocity does not cancel a factor in the sense that negation does; rather, it neutralizes one factor, which makes it possible to vary the other. It allows for systematic testing of hypotheses and makes experimental manipulation of variables possible. In the crossbar experiment, "R compensates I by increasing both weight and distance on the other arm of the balance" (Inhelder and Piaget, 1958: 178). Reversibility by reciprocity involves operations of relationships. "For example, if A = B, then B = A, or if A is to the left of B, then B is to the right of A" (Piaget, 1980: 71). A good illustration is Piaget's ring experiment, in which the subject is given a screen, a light source, a board with holes, and a series of different size rings with pegs. The task is to place two rings on the board, producing only one shadow on the screen. Ring size and distance from the screen bear a reciprocal relationship. One must compensate for the increase in the size of the ring by increasing the distance from the light source.

4. "C"—Correlative. Correlative transformation simply means the negation of a reciprocal. Piaget refers to the correlative as the "inversion of the reciprocal," or the "reciprocation of the inverse"; in other words, the relationship of C to R is the same as that of N to I. This transformation changes the conjunction or disjunction that joins the parts of the proposition but does not transform the remainder of the proposition. In the crossbar experiment, "C cancels R in the same way that N cancels I" (Inhelder and Piaget, 1958: 178).

The availability of propositional logic and the ability to make these transformations is one important aspect of formal thought. Another important dimension—closely interrelated with propositional operation—is the appearance of combinatorial operations. In an experiment conducted to illustrate the close relationship between propositional logical and combinatorial systems, the subject is exposed to five bottles:

1. Diluted sulfuric acid
2. Water

3. Oxygenated water
4. Thiosulfate
5. A bottle with a dropper, containing potassium iodine, called "g."

The bottles are labeled 1, 2, 3, 4, and g. The subject does not know the chemical elements in each flask. While the subject is watching, the contents of three of these containers are mixed and produce a yellowish-brown liquid. Adding the contents of a fourth container returns the liquid to its original colorless state. The subject's problem is, first, to reproduce the yellow color using any combination of the bottles 1, 2, 3, 4, and g and then to return the liquid to its colorless state.

The approaches of concrete operational children are characterized by two forms of behavior: first, they systematically add "g" to all liquids since this is what they saw the experimenter do; second, they appear to think that color is attributed to only one of the elements, and this reveals the difference between a noncombinatorial and a combinatorial structure of intelligence.

Gay (7; 6) also limits himself to $4 \times g$, $1 \times g$, $3 \times g$, and $2 \times g$, and discovers nothing else. "Could you try with two bottles together?"—[Silence.]—"Try."—[$4 \times 1 \times g$] *"It doesn't work."*—"Try something else."—[$3 \times 1 \times g$]—*"There it is!"*—"And that one [2], do you think that it will be as yellow?"—[No trial.]—"What do you think makes the color, the three together or only two?" *"Here"* [3].—"And that one?" [1]—*"There isn't any color."* "And that one?" [g].—*"Yes, it's there inside."*—"Then what good are 1 and 3?"—*"There isn't any color"* [Inhelder and Piaget: 1958, 111].

Gay follows the pattern of the early operational child. He adds "g" to all combinations and ascribes the quality of color to one particular liquid, first to 3 and later to "g."

In substage III-A, systematic combinations become possible. In addition, even when III-As find the correct solution, $1 + 3 + g$, they are not satisfied and try other combinations. Their interest reaches beyond a solution of the problem to an understanding of the total structure and the total number of combinations.

Sar (12; 3): "Make me some more yellow." —*"Do you take the liquid from the yellow glass with all four?"*—"I won't tell you."—[He tries first with $4 \times 2 \times g$, then $2 \times g \times 4 \times g$] *"Not yet.* [He tries to smell the odor of the liquids, then tries $4 \times 1 \times g$] *No yellow yet. Quite a big mystery!* [He tries the four, then each one independently with g; then he spontaneously proceeds to various two-by-two combinations but has the feeling that he forgot some of them.] *I'd better write it down to remind myself: 1×4 is done; 4×3 is done;*

and 2 × 3. Several more that I haven't done [he finds all six, then adds the drops and finds the yellow for 1 × 3 × g]. *Ah! it's turning yellow. You need 1, 3, and the drops."*— "Where is the yellow?"—. . .—"In there?" [g] — *"No, they go together."*—"And 2?"—*"I don't think it has any effect it's water."*—"And 4?"—*"It doesn't do anything either, it's water too. But I want to try again; you can't ever be too sure* [he tries 2 × 4 × g]. *Give me a glass of water* [he takes it from the faucet and mixes 3 × 1 × water × g—i.e., the combination which gave him the color, plus water from the faucet, knowing that 1 × 2 × 3 × 4 × g produce nothing]. *No, it isn't water. Maybe it's a substance that keeps it from coloring* [he puts together 1 × 3 × 2 × g, then 1 × 3 × 4 × g]. *Ah! There it is! That one* [4] *keeps it from coloring."*— "And that?" [2].—*"It's water"* [Inhelder and Piaget, 1958: 116–117].

Substage III-B, while not basically different from III-A, manipulates these materials more systematically, more quickly, and with an eye toward proof. Piaget describes this approach as a "generalization of substitution and addition."

Eng (14; 6) begins with 2 × g; 1 × g; 3 × g; and 4 × g: *"No, it doesn't turn yellow. So you have to mix them."* He goes on to the six two-by-two combinations and at last hits 1 × 3 × g: *"This time I think it works."*— "Why?"—*"It's 1 and 3 and some water."* —"You think it's water?"—*"Yes, no difference in odor. I think that it's water."*—"Can you show me?"—[He replaces g with some water: 1 × 3 × water.] *"No, it's not water. It's a chemical product: it combines with 1 and 3 and then it turns into a yellow liquid* [he goes on to three-by-three combinations beginning with the replacement of g by 2 and by 4—i.e., 1 × 3 × 2 and 1 × 3 × 4]. *No, these two products aren't the same as the drops: they can't produce color with 1 and 3* [then he tries 1 × 3 × g × 2]. *It stays the same with 2. I can try right away with 4* [1 × 3 × g × 4]. *It turns white again: 4 is the opposite of g because 4 makes the color go away while g makes it appear."*—"Do you think that there is water in [any of the] bottles?"—*"I'll try* [he systematically replaces 1 and 3 by water, trying 1 × g × water and 3 × g × water, having already tried 1 × 3 × water]. *No, that means 3 isn't water and 1 isn't water."* He notices that the glass 1 × 3 × g × 2 has stayed clearer than 1 × 3 × g. *"I think 2 must be water. Perhaps 4 also?* [He tries 1 × 3 × g × 4 again] *So it's not water: I had forgotten that it turned white; 4 is a product that makes the white return"* [Inhelder and Piaget, 1958: 120–121].

Another illustration of the same principle of combinatorial operations is suggested by Hunt (1961). His example is particularly relevant, since it clearly demarks the preadolescent thought processes from those found in the stage of formal operations. The task is to describe and identify *all possible combinations of animal life* on a newly discovered planet. The assumption is that animals on the planet can be classified into two basic classes: (1) vertebrates (V) and their inverse, invertebrates (I), and (2) those animals that live on land, terrestrial (T), and those that live in water, aquatic (A). The concrete operational child in all probability would answer with the following four classes of animal life:

1. (VT) vertebrates, terrestrial
2. (VA) vertebrates, aquatic
3. (IT) invertebrates, terrestrial
4. (IA) invertebrates, aquatic

The adolescent who possesses formal operations and can bring combinatorial analysis to bear on the problem might be able to conceive of sixteen possible groups of animal life that are considered to be the inevitable outcome of combining two such propositions by logic.

1. No animals at all
2. Only (VT)
3. Only (VA)
4. Only (IT)
5. Only (IA)
6. (VT) and (VA), but not (IT) or (IA)
7. (VT) and (IT), but not (VA) or (IA)
8. (VT) and (IA), but not (VA) or (IT)
9. (VA) and (IT), but not (VT) or (IA)
10. (VA) and (IA), but not (VT) or (IT)
11. (IT) and (IA), but not (VA) or (VT)
12. (VT), (VA), and (IT), but not (IA)
13. (VT), (VA), and (IA), but not (IT)
14. (VT), (IT), and (IA), but not (VA)
15. (VA), (IT), and (IA), but not (VT)
16. All four classes (Hunt, 1961: 232)

The concrete grouping structure of the operational child does not possess the combinatorial system necessary to select the total number of possible combinations that produce the "structured whole." Concrete operations readily identify the four multiplicative classes VT, VA, IT and IA; but to reason beyond these four concrete combinations requires an understanding of the structured whole and a combinatorial method that sees the relationship between the classes vertebrates and terrestrial as more than multiplicative. The fully operational adolescent can consider all possible combinations of all variables and work them out in a systematic fashion.

Formal operations are necessary to see these four classes as the factors that, taken n-by-n, produce the sixteen possible combinations.

EVALUATION OF PIAGET'S FORMAL THINKING STAGE

An important question is being raised with increasing frequency: that is, what proportion of all adolescents do actually attain the full ability to perform the kind of logical operations that Piaget so skillfully described in *The Growth of Logical Thinking from Childhood to Adolescence*? Both Arlin (1975) and Kuhn (1979) cite the widely demonstrated estimate, according to which only approximately 50 percent of the adult population actually attain the full stage of formal thinking (III-B). Kuhn (1979) suggests, based on a review of the relevant literature, that the formal operations stage of adolescence, quite in contrast to the preceding childhood stages of Piaget's theory, may never be attained by a significant proportion of the general adolescent population, and many adults do not solve the above cited "animal-life-task" correctly. Piaget (1980) readily admits that the subjects of his study were "from the better schools in Geneva" and that his conclusions were based on a "privileged population." However, he ascribes differences between his own studies and those of others to "differences in speed of development without any modification in the order of succession of the stages." In spite of evidence critical of his assumptions, he maintains that "all normal individuals are capable of reaching the level of formal operation" (1980: 75) as long as the environment provides the necessary cognitive stimulation. However, he does admit to a differentiation in cognitive aptitude with increasing age, depending on interest, motivation, and environmental stimulation, so that some adolescents may show their operational skills in logic, mathematics, or physics, while others may show it in literature, linguistics, or artistic endeavor, and still others in practical skills such as are performed by the carpenter, the locksmith, or the mechanic. However, in spite of this concern, it is important to keep in mind that Piaget's theory has been studied, tested, and developed in the adolescent age range primarily with content material that came from science and mathematics. Piaget has shown little concern with the question of how formal operations might manifest themselves in artistic and literary endeavors. Gallagher (1978) has expanded the investigation of formal thought research to include analogy and metaphor. Gardner even suggests that formal operations might actually interfere with artistic development:

> Formal operations may even at times serve to hinder artistic development, since the tendency to focus on underlying content, to abstract meaning, to be sensitive to the explicit demands of a task, to proceed in a systematic exhaustive manner, and, above all, to translate problems and questions into logical-propositional terms may all militate against the sensitivity to detail and nuance and the

faithfulness to the particular properties of object and medium that are so vital for the artist [1973: 308].

Dulit (1972), utilizing Piaget's experiment, claims that among his group of average older adolescents only 20 to 35 percent actually functioned at the full formal level (III-B), and even in a selected group of scientifically gifted older adolescents that figure is only 75 percent. Actually, it is very difficult if not impossible to compare the various percentages reported in the literature for the presence or absence of formal operational reasoning ability. The problem is that Inhelder and Piaget never spelled out the methods they used in administering these tasks nor the exact criteria used for scoring. This lack of standardardized procedures has plagued the formal operations research (Kuhn, 1979). Dulit, Kuhn, and others question the validity of the impression created by Piaget that the attainment of the formal-stage thinking is the norm in the same way that the attainment of the earlier Piagetian stages is apparently the rule for all younger children. Inhelder did report to Dulit that "not all cases were reported." The intent of the study was not to speak to the issue of "frequency" or "incidents"; rather, specific protocols were selected as illustrations of the theory. Dulit's own empirically derived frequency data throw serious doubts on the generalization that the full formal-stage thinking is the common or typical pattern in middle and late adolescence. He concludes that adolescence is indeed the characteristic age of the onset of formal operations, but such reasoning structure is not attained by all, or even by the majority, of adolescents. "Thus for adolescents the formal stage is more of a *characteristic of potential* only sometimes becoming an actuality" (Dulit, 1972: 298). The fully operational formal-stage reasoning ability must be viewed as an ideal kind of cognitive equilibrium. However, it is far from being normal or typical among adolescents. "It is more ideal than typical, more potential than actual."

Another related question is whether and to what extent changes in the subjects' problem-solving approach on the various cognitive problems (e.g., the pendulum, the floating bodies, colorless chemicals, the projection of shadows, the flexible rods, and others) develop synchronously—or to state it differently, whether the performances on these Piagetian tasks correlate with one another. If they do correlate or change synchronously, one could assume that such changes are the result of changes in the underlying cognitive structure. In general, the reported correlations for intertask performances vary, but fall in the $r = .30$ to $.40$ range, not a very convincing piece of evidence for the existence of a coherent, underlying, and generalizable formal structure. Bart (1978) had hypothesized, in agreement with Piaget's theory, that the content of a test of formal reasoning should have little or no effect on formal reasoning performance. However, contrary to his hypothesis, he found that the correlations between three formal reasoning tests, quite different in content but structurally equivalent, were not between 1.0 and .9 as expected, but were actually only .46, .51, and .65. He concludes that formal reasoning, therefore, is not necessarily generalizable across content areas. Since the performance on Piaget's formal tasks has not been studied longitudinally, we do not know to what extent changes in reasoning are synchronized. Finally, there is the additional question whether and to what extent performance on Piaget's formal operations tasks correlates with more traditional measures of intelligence. If the correlations between various Piaget-type tasks were significantly larger than between such tasks and IQ, this again might add weight to the argument that solving Piaget-type problems has some uniqueness that might indeed relate to formal operations. Again the evidence is not very convincing.

IS THERE AN ADULT STAGE OF COGNITIVE DEVELOPMENT?

The question has been raised whether there exist cognitive structures that extend beyond and are different from those of the formal operational stage, moving the end of cognitive development into adulthood. Such a notion would place into question Piaget's statement that the formal operations of adolescence constitute the "final equilibrium" in cognitive development. Arlin (1975) contrasts, on the basis of theoretical considerations as well as some empirical evidence, the "problem-solving stage," identical to the formal operations, with the "problem-finding stage," which is assumed to constitute a new level of reasoning more advanced than the stage of formal operations. Such a problem-finding stage is described as a creative stage, and involves the ability to raise new questions and to discover. If such an assumption were proven, the stage of formal thinking would lose its special status as the "final equilibrium," since cognitive growth would continue in adulthood. However, the evidence for such a proposition is not entirely convincing and has been challenged on theoretical as well as empirical grounds.

EDUCATIONAL IMPLICATIONS

In his interaction with children in various experimental situations, Piaget observed that children often show resistance to learning from traditional instruction. Apparently, the subject's cognitive structure determines the degree of understanding that the individual can bring to the solution of a problem. Piaget was very skillful in challenging his subjects, by way of his clinical methods, to the limits of their understanding. Nevertheless, children seem incapable of being guided even through careful questioning beyond these limits. And even if correct answers with explicit explanations are provided, children appear to return to their own level of cognitive functioning as indicated by their earlier responses rather than to produce any generalized cognitive growth that would readily transcend the earlier established limits. Lovell (1961) investigated the influence of teaching on the child's ability to solve Piaget-type problems and the long-range benefits of such strategies. Apparently, the knowledge that a child might acquire before developing the corresponding cognitive structures either disappears very rapidly or, if it is retained, is retained as rote memorization without real understanding.

The interaction between a child and the experimenter, as reported by Piaget (1963: 294–295), may serve to illustrate the subject's resistance to change as a result of information that is still beyond his cognitive structure. The child is presented with an open box that contains twenty wooden beads; eighteen of these beads are brown and two are white. The child is asked: "Which are there more of, brown beads or wooden beads?" The preoperational child—who cannot yet classify and cannot consider two dimensions of a problem simultaneously—cannot distinguish brownness as a subclass to woodenness as a supraclass and consequently is most likely to answer: "There are more brown beads, because there are only two white ones."

Following such a typical preoperational response, Piaget might go to great length explaining the situation and the task to the child. Introducing an empty box he might ask: "If we were to put all the wooden beads in the box, how many would be left?" Whereupon the child might reply: "None, because they are all wooden." It thus becomes apparent that the child knows all beads are wooden. So Piaget continues: "Now, if we were to put all the brown beads in this box, how many would be left?" The child's reply would be: "These white ones," or "Two." Apparently the subject now clearly understands the situation that all beads are wooden, that most of the beads are brown, and that two are white. After these teaching efforts, the initial question is asked once more: "Which are there more of, wooden beads or brown beads?" The child may hesitate, indicating that he is more aware of the nature of the problem; nevertheless his response remains the same: "There are more brown beads, since there are only two white ones." Even though the elements necessary for solving the problem have been explained, the child before age six to seven is still unable to consider both the color and the woodenness of the objects and is unable to free his thinking from the perceptual dominance of the many brown beads.

Development is seen as an increase in complexity, mobility, and systematization of schemata and logical structures, which result from equilibrium-equilibration processes, but which cannot be substantially accelerated by instruction. Obviously, in the assimilation-accommodation process, education plays a very significant role. However, the assimilation-accommodation process must move in very small logical steps in order to enhance learning. If the gaps in the presentation of educational material are too large or too advanced for the child, as they apparently are in the incident just cited, the individual cannot accommodate. The teacher has to be skillful in maintaining the proper level of tension between assimilation and accommodation, in starting at the child's level and in progressing in small steps in order to foster genuine conceptual and cognitive growth. On this particular issue Piaget appears to be very close to a maturational interpretation of development and reveals a somewhat conservative outlook on education. His objection to what he referred to as the American question, "How can we accelerate the child's progression through your developmental stages?" is that to do things faster or earlier is not necessarily a desirable thing and may be even worse than doing nothing.

Interestingly enough, it is on this issue that some of Piaget's close associates seem to depart from his interpretation. Bruner, who was influenced by Piaget's theory, seems to take almost the opposite point of view when he says: "We begin with the hypothesis that any subject can be taught effectively in some intellectually honest form to any child at any stage of development" (Bruner, 1960: 33). On the other hand, Bruner quotes and appears to agree with Inhelder's statement that it may be worthwhile to devote two years of schooling "to a series of exercises in manipulating, classifying, and ordering objects in ways that highlight basic operations of logical addition, multiplication, inclusion, serial ordering, and the like" (Bruner, 1960: 46). Such an approach implies a rather direct structuring of the school curriculum in accordance with Piaget's theory.

Some research does provide evidence that Piagetian-type problems can be taught and that teaching such concepts does accelerate cognitive growth. Ojemann and Pritchett (1963) have shown that guided learning experiences, such as teaching preadolescents the reasons why objects sink or float, significantly affect the child's thought structure. Aebli (1963), a former associate of Piaget, has taken his teacher's theory of development and expanded it toward an education theory. Aebli uses the sandbox in which the subject looks at three mountains of different shapes and is asked what the scenery would look like from different angles (see Figure 10). He demonstrated that the method of presentation and the number and nature of significant cues were as important as the child's cognitive structures in facilitating solutions to the problems and learning. He varies the complexity of the problem by providing the subject with the following: (1) the contours of the mountains only, (2) contours and surface structure of the mountains, and (3) contours, surface structure, and color of the mountains.

Aebli and Bruner do not maintain that the child's logical structures can easily and substantially be accelerated through educational procedures. They are, however, somewhat more optimistic than Piaget in attributing a greater importance to the curriculum material and the methods of teaching, since they feel that complex concepts can be simplified and presented so as to fit the logical structure of the child. The task of the teacher then becomes that of the "translator" who has to present the curriculum content on such a level and in such a way that it corresponds to the cognitive structure of the child; the goal is to correlate systematically the curriculum to the child's ability to assimilate and accommodate the material. Such a translation implies that, for any learning problem, the preoperational child should be presented with the problem in the form of direct sensory experiences, whereas the preadolescent would be able to work with concrete problems, and the adolescent could master abstract ideas, verbal propositions, and combinatorial analyses. More specifically, the formal operations found in the adolescent constitute the prerequisite for teaching geometry, proportionality, propositions, and probabilistic reasoning. A Piagetian approach to teaching would make it mandatory for the educator to assess the operational structure of pupils. Piaget-type assessment and test materials (Burk, 1973; Furth, 1970; Patterson and Milakofsky, 1980; Pinard and Laurendeau, 1964; Uzgiris and Hunt, 1976) and curriculum material constructed with Piaget's developmental and educational theory in mind (Furth and Wachs, 1975; Lavatelli, 1970; Petrone, 1976; Sund, 1976; Weikart et al., 1971) have become available and have been used in educational settings. Elkind (1978) reports that the rather dramatic upsurge of interest in Piaget-type curriculum and materials in the elementary schools peaked in the sixties when humanistic and child-centered values were cherished in education. This child development orientation has subsided as a result of the recent emphasis on basics, accountability, competence, and a more generally conservative attitude in American society. The effect of these trends, as well as some other factors, "such as ignoring the basic premises of Piaget's research and theory," has been the abandonment of Piaget-type elementary curriculum. However, on a more hopeful note, Elkind adds:

> Interestingly enough, where Piaget is now having a major impact is at the secondary level. Those concerned with physics and chemistry are, for example, examining the sequencing of materials, and the logical substructure (the requisite mental operations) of their tasks. Moreover, what is exciting about this work is that it is empirical rather than reflective. Various instructors are trying out different sequencing and ways of presenting materials and they are sharing their findings through meetings and journal articles. This to my mind is the way Piaget should be used in producing curriculum materials [1978: 2].

The ages that Piaget provides for the various developmental stages in some of his books are only approximations, or at best generalizations, and not statistical averages. Piaget is concerned with fundamental questions of genetic epistemology and the sequence and orderliness of cognitive changes and not with the variables that have always been of concern to the educational and developmental psychologist: individual differences, sex, socioeconomic class, IQ, reading level, and so forth. Piaget's theory has stimulated considerable research into these traditional developmental variables. For example, sex differences on Piagetian problems have been demonstrated (Keating and Schaefer, 1975; Dulit, 1972), especially on spatial processing tasks (Jamison and Signorella, 1980; Liben, 1974; 1975; 1978; Liben and Golbeck, 1980; Ray, Georgiou, and Ravizza, 1979; Thomas and Jamison, 1975; Thomas, Jamison, and Hummel, 1973). From childhood into early adulthood, males perform consistently better than females on Piagetian-type horizontal (judging the position of liquid in a tilted container) and vertical (judging the position of plumb lines in an oblique context) spatial tasks. Liben and Golbeck conclude that the persistence of such "sex differences suggests that there are actually competency differences in males and females" (1980: 596).

Piaget himself devoted little attention to such variables. He never denied that they might exist; he simply focused on a different set of questions. "The order of succession of these stages has been shown to be extremely regular and comparable to the stages of an embryogenesis. The speed of development may vary from one individual to another and also from one social environment to another . . . but this does not change the order of succession of the stages through which they pass" (Piaget, 1980: 70–71). It is the order of succession in the acquisition of knowledge that was the focus of Piaget's research. However, knowledge of Piaget's theory gives the educator insights into the limitations and abilities of children at various stages in their cognitive development. Piaget made it clear that children think differently at various age levels and think quite differently from adults. Did it occur to anyone that children might think—assuming equality exists—that there is more milk in a thin, tall glass than in a wide, low glass before Piaget's experiments became widely known?

Not only the content of Piaget's theory and the substance of his findings but also his methods are relevant to the educator. He collects data by what is frequently referred to as the "clinical method," which means that the child actively searches for the solution to the problem. The examiner stimulates and challenges the child to reflect and elaborate on the answers and to use this discourse as a means to clarify thinking. Piaget believes in the autonomy of children and in their active participation in their own cognitive growth—an idea he shares with John Dewey. "There are two basic and correlated principles from which an educator inspired by psychology can never depart: (1) That the only real truths are those that one builds freely oneself and not those received from others, and (2) that moral good is essentially autonomous and cannot be prescribed" (Piaget, 1947a: 248). Through this method, Piaget skillfully questioned children and provided for learning, pushing them to the limits of their operational structure without giving them ready-made answers.

Applying Piaget's findings about children's cognitive growth to teaching would have a revolutionary impact on curriculum planning. The content itself would be influenced, or more important, the logical processes by which we think and by which we attempt to solve problems could become a major area of focus in any educational endeavor. Thus there would be more emphasis on classification, reversibility, logical transformations, and the process of logic.

9: LAWRENCE KOHLBERG'S COGNITIVE-DEVELOPMENTAL APPROACH TO ADOLESCENT MORALITY

PIAGET'S CONTRIBUTION TO AN UNDERSTANDING OF CHILDREN'S MORAL JUDGMENT

Jean Piaget, in *The Moral Judgment of the Child* (1932b), postulated that the development of children's moral judgment follows the same basic pattern as that of cognition. The moral schemata develop out of existing cognitive structures, and the moral judgment is always based on the necessary level of conceptual-cognitive development. The development of moral reasoning depends on such cognitive skills as the perception of reality, the organization and evaluation of experiences, the ability to take the other person's point of view, and—during adolescence—the ability to think abstractly.

Piaget and Lawrence Kohlberg were primarily interested in moral judgment, which differs significantly from moral behavior. Moral judgment refers to the intellectual or reasoning ability to evaluate the "goodness" or "rightness" of a course of action in a hypothetical situation. Moral behavior involves the individual's ability, in a real-life situation, to help others and to resist the temptation to steal, cheat, lie, or commit other immoral acts. Piaget and Kohlberg have assumed that the structure underlying verbal moral judgment and actual moral behavior, while related, are not identical. Because people can identify morally right behavior intellectually does not guarantee that they will actually behave in accordance with moral principles. Various research studies have demonstrated that the correlation between moral judgment and moral behavior is not very high (Hartshorne and May, 1928–1930); however, some positive relationships have been observed (Coady, 1986; Rubin and Schneider, 1973), and juvenile delinquents rather persistently score lower on cognitive moral reasoning tasks than do their nondelinquent peers (Fodor, 1972; Hains and Miller, 1980; Kohlberg, 1969).

Piaget has observed that a remarkable change in the quality of children's moral reasoning takes place when they progress from preoperational to operational and later from concrete operational to formal operational thinking. He identifies the morality of the preoperational stage, before the age of about seven, as a "morality of constraint" or "moral realism" and describes a child at this stage as showing blind obedience to authority. The child perceives justice as resting in the person of authority. (This idea is referred to as an "ethics of authority.") The moral concepts of children develop out of parental teachings about right and wrong. Preoperational children do not have the intellectual structure to consider other alternatives, nor do they have the emotional capacity to empathize with others. Children at this stage are not yet able to decenter—that is, they do not yet have the capacity to move from one point of view to another or to take the view of another person into account. They cannot, symbolically speaking, "walk in the moccasins of another person."

With the shift from preoperational to operational reasoning, the ability to decenter increases. Children become more altruistic and more aware of the needs of others in orientation and behavior (Rubin and Schneider, 1973). While preoperational children approach moral dilemmas from an "objective" viewpoint—that is, they are primarily concerned with the objective amount of damage resulting from an act rather than with the intent or the motivation of that behavior—the moral judgment of the operational child, "morality of cooperation," reflects the change to a social orientation, an "ethics of mutual respect." Moral judgments shift from an objective to a subjective orientation: of major concern is no longer simply the objective amount of damage caused by the immoral act but also the intent or motivation. Children begin to take the viewpoint of others into consideration and to appreciate the reciprocity of relationships. In one of Piaget's stories, children must decide who is naughtier: John, who opens a door and accidentally breaks fifteen cups that were behind the door, or Henry, who tries to snatch some cookies, climbs on a chair, and in the process breaks one cup. Preoperational children judge John to be naughtier because they are primarily concerned with the objective amount of damage. Operational children feel that Henry is naughtier because the subjective intention receives more weight than the objective damage.

The moral judgment of preoperational children has two basic characteristics: moral realism and immanent justice. Moral realism implies that moral rules have an existence of their own and cannot be changed (Piaget, 1932b). Immanent justice involves the child's belief that immoral behavior inevitably brings pain or punishment as a natural consequence of the transgression. For example, if a child steals and later, on the way home, falls and hurts himself, he may see the fall as punishment for the stealing. The transition from moral "realism" to moral "relativism" takes place when the child no longer blindly follows orders but considers the intent of any act rather than the letter of the law. The child realizes that the law, or the rules that govern behavior, can be changed by consensus.

For Piaget, the highest stage of moral development, characteristic of adolescence, is "moral autonomy." Dependent on the attainment of formal or abstract reasoning ability, moral autonomy begins at puberty. In a game situation, the adolescent reveals interest not only in the rules of the game but also in anticipating all possible alternatives to which these rules would apply. Since abstract thought is possible, the adolescent begins to develop a sense of ethical and moral responsibility based on abstract principles of what is right or wrong:

> The same is true of the concept of social justice and of rational, aesthetic, or social ideals. As a result of the acquisition of such values, decisions, whether in opposition to or in agreement with the adult, have an altogether different significance than they do in small social groups of younger children. . . . The possibilities opened up by these new values are obvious in the adolescent, who differs from the child in that he is not only capable of forming theories but is also concerned with choosing a career that will permit him to satisfy his needs for social reform and for new ideas [Piaget and Inhelder, 1969: 151].

KOHLBERG'S THEORY OF MORAL DEVELOPMENT

Kohlberg (1927–1987), inspired by Piaget's cognitive developmental approach to moral development, expands the structural cognitive approach through longitudinal, cross-cultural, social class, and educational research (Blatt, 1959; Kohlberg, 1963, 1969; Kohlberg and Blatt, 1972; Kohlberg and Kramer, 1969; Turiel, 1966, 1969). From his findings, Kohlberg develops a more inclusive and systematic theory of moral judgment than Piaget. Initially, Kohlberg based the theory on the moral reasoning responses of seventy-two male subjects aged ten, thirteen, or sixteen. For Kohlberg, the adolescent years rather than those of childhood become the critical time for the development of advanced levels of moral reasoning.

Kohlberg bases his classification of stages of moral reasoning on various ways of resolving moral dilemmas. The following story, entitled "Heinz's Problem," illustrates one of these: A woman is dying of cancer. The local druggist has discovered a new drug that could save her life. The druggist, who has not invested much in this cure, sells it for $2,000, an amount that is ten times greater than his cost. The sick woman's husband, Heinz, tries to borrow money but can raise only $1,000. He approaches the druggist, asking him to sell the remedy for half the price or to let him repay at a later time, but he is refused. In desperation, the husband breaks into the store and steals the medicine. Should he have done so? Why? In exploring the rightness or wrongness of the husband's decision, the subject must consider the rights of the druggist, the duties of the husband, the appropriate punishment for the husband, and the obligations that an individual may have toward relatives and nonrelatives.

Kohlberg based his classification of responses not on the particular solution the subject proposed but on the moral reasoning that led to the proposed answer—in other words, on the moral structure underlying the response. This means that all classifications depend on the subject's verbal reasoning and may not be related directly to actual moral behavior. Other stories (there are a total of twelve) place the conflict between satisfying a personal need and keeping a promise, respect for an individual versus concern for the group, obedience versus keeping a promise, and so on. Most of Kohlberg's dilemmas, as critics have pointed out, do not involve typical, everyday adolescent issues and conflicts.

STAGES OF MORAL DEVELOPMENT

Kohlberg's theory distinguishes three basic levels of moral development: the preconventional or premoral level, the conventional or moral level, and the postconventional or autonomous level. Moral development begins in young children as an undifferentiated, selfish, and egocentric idea; but, with increasing maturity, as the individual moves through specific stages of moral thinking, it becomes more sophisticated and sociocentric. In some individuals, moral judgment may reach an awareness of both universal values as well as ethical principles of justice. Kohlberg subdivides each of these three general levels into two stages to create a highly differentiated and elaborate theory of moral development consisting of six stages. Each stage of moral reasoning represents a distinct moral philosophy that has implications for social and political organization and can serve as a typology of moral orientation even among adults.

Level 1: The Preconventional Level of Moral Reasoning. This is most prevalent during childhood and is concerned with external, concrete consequences to the self. It is common in children aged four through ten but may characterize the moral reasoning of some adolescents and even adults. Children at this level respond to the definitions of good and bad provided by their social reference group. Although the children are often well behaved, their moral structure is still undeveloped and undifferentiated; indeed, the reasons underlying the moral judgments of those at the preconventional level are different from the reasons of those who have advanced to higher levels. At this level, moral decisions are primarily egocentric, hedonistic, and based on self-interest, fear of punishment, anticipation of reward, or material considerations. Individuals at this level interpret behavior as good or bad in terms of what Piaget has termed "objective judgments."

Level 1, Stage 1: The Obedience and Punishment Orientation. At the lowest level of moral reasoning, the main motivation for obeying a rule is to avoid punishment and achieve gratification. "Good" and "bad" are defined by the obedience and disobedience of authorities and rules. The child's conscience is based on a primitive, egocentric fear of punishment.

Children at level 1 manifest submission to superior power and try to avoid trouble. Still unclear about human values and human life, they value people in terms of the benefits they can provide. The actual physical damage of an act rather than the underlying intent becomes primary in the child's evaluation of goodness or badness. This confusion of the physical with the social-moral world corresponds to what Piaget calls "moral realism." If the man in the previously described dilemma operated at this level, he would fear that God would punish him if he let his wife die.

Level 1, Stage 2: Instrumental Relativism Orientation. At this stage, children can distinguish between physical damage and psychosocial intent; however, they still confuse individual needs with what they think is right or wrong. At stage 2, which involves a hedonistic orientation, morally right behavior depends on what satisfies one's own personal desires. A major motivating force becomes the manipulation of others in order to obtain the desired reward—for example, being good before Christmas in order to maximize the number of gifts one will get. The notion of reciprocity is beginning to emerge; consequently, under circumstances when it will be to one's benefit, the needs of others receive consideration. Reciprocity, then, depends on an exchange of powers and favors rather than on considerations of loyalty and justice. The prevailing philosophy seems to be "You scratch my back, I'll scratch yours." Fairness, reciprocity, and sharing do exist, but exclusively in pragmatic and utilitarian terms. The episode in which Tom Sawyer whitewashed the fence provides a classic illustration of this level of moral development. The criterion for making moral decisions depends on selfish desires, as in the case of the child who believed that Heinz should steal the drug for his ill wife because, if she died, nobody would take care of Heinz's needs. Stage 2 subjects cannot decenter their thinking sufficiently to consider the position of another person objectively.

Level 2: The Conventional or Moral Level. At this level, children become concerned about meeting external social expectations. They base their moral orientation on an acceptance of the existing social order and a clear recognition of the rights of others. Kohlberg describes the child at this level as conforming to social conventions, desiring strongly to maintain, support, and justify the existing social order. Most adolescents and even the majority of adults function on the conventional level. As an individual progresses into adolescence, the association of a specific chronological age with a specific level of moral reasoning becomes increasingly difficult. Many adults continue to function primarily at the conventional level, while some mature adolescents reason at the postconventional level. However, Kohlberg believes that "little development occurs after the early twenties" (Kohlberg and Kramer, 1969).

Level 2, Stage 3: Interpersonal Concordance Orientation. This is the first stage of the conventional level of moral judgment in which the egocentric orientation is replaced by one that is sociocentric. Kohlberg refers to stage 3 as the "good boy–good girl" approval-seeking orientation in moral development. Personal needs and morality can be distinguished, but the confusion is now between social approval and right and wrong. Living up to the expectations of others becomes more important than "goodness." Good behavior now becomes that which pleases or helps others, and children will try to behave *not* because that is the right thing to do but in order to win the approval of others. Because the ties that individuals have to their social group now define morality, adolescents may break the laws of the larger society in order to win the approval of their peers. Actions are "right" if they win approval and "wrong" if they elicit disapproval from significant others.

The need to win the approval of the immediate social group and to live up to the perceived expectations of significant others becomes the yardstick for moral decisions in smoking, alcohol and drug use, sex and abortion. Subjects conform to what they believe to be majority opinion on "natural behavior." In an Ash-type* experiment, seventh-grade adolescents in stage 3 conformed more than age mates who had attained higher as well as lower levels of moral reasoning (Saltzstein, Diamond, and Belenky, 1972). Like individuals in Piaget's subjective stage, those in stage 3 judge behavior by the underlying intentionality, a perspective frequently expressed by the adolescent's explanation that "he means well." Often, like Charlie Brown in *Peanuts,* adolescents overuse this argument. Stage 3 also includes the Mary Poppins type of morality. Both as adolescents and as adults, females remain at the stage 3 level longer than do males, a finding that has been reported for other societies as well (Reid, 1984) and will become a major issue in the following chapter on Gilligan's theory of moral reasoning in females.

Level 2, Stage 4: Orientation toward Authority, Law, and Duty. Characteristic of morality at stage 4 is a strong belief in "law and order," with support for the existing social order as a primary value. Moral rules and a focus on duty become distinguishable from feelings of approval. However, rather than involving abstract principles of justice, at stage 4 the rules are concrete: "Thou shalt not. . . ." One obeys and respects the laws to avoid the penalty that legitimate authority can impose; one also realizes that others have legitimate rights. Breaking the law produces guilt. Therefore, both personal guilt and fear of legitimate censors motivate moral behavior. The moral orientation involves believing in existing authority, obeying the law, doing one's duty, showing respect for authority, and maintaining the social order at any price. This emphasis on duty motivates Colonel Saiti in *The*

---

* In Ash-type experiments, subjects are asked to select the longer of two lines of obviously different length (A is longer, B is shorter). About 10 subjects are stooges and instructed to say, for everyone to hear, that B (which is shorter) looks longer to them. The experimental subject, who is naive, is asked last. The question is: Does the naive subject trust his own perception and report that A is longer, or does he yield to the group and say B is longer?

Bridge over the River Kwai; the colonel rigidly maintained his lifelong orientation toward duty, authority, and the social order, even when this was no longer appropriate and even counterproductive. According to Kohlberg, "Life is conceived as sacred in terms of its place in a categorical moral and religious order of rights and duties" (1970: 184). In Heinz's moral dilemma, an example of stage 4 reasoning might be: Since marriage is an institution essential to society and is based on law, Heinz should consider it his duty to steal the drug.

Level 3: The Postconventional or Autonomous Level. The individual at this level is primarily concerned with self-chosen moral principles. At this advanced level the approach to moral problems—no longer based on selfish needs or on conformity to others or the social structure—depends on autonomous, universal principles of justice that retain validity even beyond existing laws, social conventions, or one's personal social reference group. At this highest level of moral reasoning, moral judgment and behavior reveal more congruence than at earlier levels.

Level 3, Stage 5: The Social Contract Orientation. Moral reasoning at this postconventional level depends on fundamental principles such as individual rights, equality, human dignity, contractual agreement, and mutual obligation. Consequently, Kohlberg refers to this stage—which is based on formal, abstract, operational thinking ability—as the principled stage of moral thinking. Moral behavior reflects a concern for the welfare of the larger community and a desire for community respect. Because the individual believes the law should preserve human rights and serve the larger community, it follows that unfair or unjust laws must be changed. Laws and rules for behavior are not right in and of themselves. In contrast to the individual at stage 4, the postconventional thinker views the law as modifiable and works to change the law as long as such change reflects consensus and follows rational deliberations and considerations of social utility. Stage 5 reasoning is represented by the moral philosophy underlying the U.S. Constitution. However, although democratic government is philosophically based on the moral judgment identified as stage 5, Kohlberg estimates that only 20 to 25 percent of adult Americans actually reach this level of moral development. In literature, Shakespeare's Prince Hamlet reveals a postconventional level of morality when he challenges the legitimacy of King Claudius' claim to the throne. The individual at stage 5 may decide that Heinz should steal the drug in order to save his wife, perhaps reasoning that the couple have promised to love each other regardless of the circumstances; furthermore, society sanctions their moral commitment to each other.

Level 3, Stage 6: Universal Ethical Principles Orientation. In his earlier writings, Kohlberg gave greater emphasis to stage 6. He has omitted it as a distinct stage in some of his more recent material because it is neither universal nor invariant. It seems to emerge primarily in Western democratic societies that espouse a "liberty and justice for all" philosophy, but very few adolescents (or adults) ever get that far (Turiel, 1974). Morality at this most principled stage of moral reasoning assumes a conscience that is based on self-chosen ethical principles which place the highest value on human life, equality, and dignity. Rules are binding only to the extent that they represent these ethical principles. The concept of justice at stage 6 goes beyond any particular existing social order. Consistency, logical comprehensiveness, and universality characterize the ethical principles of stage 6 subjects. These principles are abstract: for example, the Golden Rule or Immanuel Kant's categorical imperative (. . . so act, that the principle of your action could be a universal law. . .). They are not specific moral rules, such as the Ten Commandments. No one can attain the individual principled level without having operated first at the social contractual level or having clearly understood the basic contractual nature of the existing social order.

The individual governed by universal ethical principles may practice civil disobedience—not out of disrespect for the law but in the name of a morality higher than the existing law. Unjust laws will be broken because level 6 morality is grounded in ethical principles of justice and respect for the rights of the individual, not in legality. In practicing civil disobedience, the individual willingly accepts the penalty in order to demonstrate to society at large that principles of justice, human rights, and human dignity are more important than the law. The stage 6 individual feels that no law, contract, moral obligation, or possible punishment can interfere with his desire to save those he loves. As the husband in the dilemma, he will steal the drug—first, to save the life of his wife; second, to demonstrate to society that the right to live is so fundamental that it must and should take precedence over the right to make a profit; and third, to exemplify his willingness to accept the penalty. Visionaries and moral leaders like Joan of Arc, Abraham Lincoln, Henry David Thoreau, Nelson Mandela, Hans and Sophie Scholl, and Claus Schenk von Stauffenberg seemed to have accepted universal ethical principles that challenged the existing morality of their societies and times.

The thinking of an individual oriented toward universal moral principles receives clear expression in an excerpt from Martin Luther King's "Letter from Birmingham Jail":

> I do not advocate evading or defying the law, as would the rabid segregationist. That would lead to anarchy. One who breaks an unjust law must do so openly, lovingly, and with a willingness to accept the penalty. An individual who breaks a law that conscience tells him is unjust, and who willingly accepts the penalty of imprisonment in order to arouse the conscience of the community over its injustice, is in reality expressing the highest respect for the law [King, 1964: 86].

The empirical basis for the two postconventional stages is much less secure than that for the first four stages, which have received substantial support during the two decades that followed their introduction. The postconventional stages, therefore, do not represent a natural, inevitable, universal developmental progression; they are advanced forms of meta-ethical and philosophical reflection on moral reasoning. Kohlberg's (1978) revised scoring manual omits stage 6 (presented here for completeness' sake). The theoretical basis for the postconventional stages has become problematic: more recent empirical data have failed to support the universality and the naturally occurring, inevitable upward progression that a developmental theory requires.

A much-debated, commonly observed phenomenon is that well-educated, intelligent, late adolescents who had already scored at the postconventional level of moral reasoning later regressed, during their sophomore college year and sometimes even later in life, to a more contextual relativism. They were then more likely to include contextual properties in their moral reasoning, such as "they would have to know more about who these people were and where they lived—that is, about the contingencies of their particular lives and social circumstances" before making a judgment (Gilligan, 1981: 153). According to Kohlberg's scoring criteria, this would involve a regression from principled moral reasoning. However, Murphy and Gilligan (1980) advance a strong argument that "contextual relativism" constitutes not a regression to lower levels of moral judgment but a different and equally valid form of postconventional morality, often based on real-life experiences in making moral choices. They propose that two distinct types of postconventional moral reasoning exist: Kohlberg's principled solutions and a relativistic conceptual solution.

THE INVARIANT DEVELOPMENTAL SEQUENCE IN MORAL REASONING

Kohlberg (1970) claims that these stages of moral judgment represent an invariant developmental sequence because they are universal and the thinking of any one moral stage remains fairly consistent in a variety of situations. Development inevitably progresses from the lower to the higher stages in an invariant sequence; the child moves sequentially and inexorably step by step through these stages. Theoretically, according to Kohlberg, these stages are constant, and normal development requires that each occur in sequence. However, in actuality, Holstein (1976) found that some individuals do skip a stage while others regress to lower levels of moral reasoning.

According to Kolhberg, the age at which a child reaches a specific stage may differ from individual to individual and from culture to culture, but the individual cannot function at stage 5 without having previously moved through all the preceding stages. If children become fixated at one stage, they will not progress any further; however, if and when they do move on, the development would continue in an upward step-by-step progression. Because children and adolescents do move through these stages with varying speeds, the relationship between chronological age and stage of moral development is less and less synchronized as the individual grows older. Age approximations after the individual has left stages 1 and 2, those generally associated with childhood, are generally not reliable. Although the moral reasoning of stages 3 through 5 occurs during adolescence, many adults also operate at this level. In fact most adults never reach the postconventional level. Postconventional thinking most often develops in college-educated middle-class youth, and even they may regress to earlier stages of moral development after their education has been completed. Only about 10 percent of American adults reach stage 6, and the largest proportion continue to function at the "law and order" stage. Postconventional morality does have as a prerequisite the attainment of abstract formal operations in cognitive development. One cannot easily associate any one stage of moral development with adolescence. However, since adolescence is a period accompanied by progression through several of these stages, and since progress commonly ceases in the early twenties, all of Kohlberg's stages are highly relevant to a discussion of theories of adolescence.

As previously mentioned, Kohlberg maintains that these stages are universal. He believes that the moral structure reflected in the decisions with which people respond to his dilemmas do not involve mastery of cultural values. He argues that the sequential patterning of these stages occurs under varying cultural conditions and that the principles of justice reflected in postconventional reasoning are free from culturally defined content.

Consistency in moral reasoning does not imply "moral character" or a moral trait. There is, however, a high degree of consistency within a particular moral stage and from one moral stage to another. The moral reasoning of about 50 percent of the subjects tested reflected a single stage, even though the subjects responded to a variety of moral dilemmas. Subjects who were apparently in the process of moving from one stage to another typically responded partly at stage 3 and partly at stage 4 (not at all uncommon during adolescence), but rarely simultaneously at stages 2 and 5. Thus, in conclusion, Kohlberg perceives the development through these stages as an invariant, sequential, universal progression.

CROSS-CULTURAL, SOCIOECONOMIC, AND POLITICAL DIFFERENCES IN MORAL REASONING

In support of his claim of universality in moral reasoning, Kohlberg (1964; Nisan and Kohlberg, 1982) and others have conducted research with adolescents not only in the United States but also in the Bahamas, Great Britain, Canada, Honduras, India, Israel, Kenya, Mexico, New Zealand, Nigeria, Taiwan, and Turkey. Although the sample includes few truly primitive societies, the findings support his claim of the universality of the developmental stages. In all the societies studied, the prevalence of stage 1 and 2 thinking declines sharply as a function of age, especially in early adolescence. The thinking representative of stages 3 and 4 increases at least until middle adolescence, and in the more primitive societies until late adolescence, when it begins to level off. Moral reasoning representative of the postconventional level shows a slow increase during adolescence primarily in the Western democratic societies, although the total percentage of even late adolescents reaching the principled stages remains very small. This leveling-off trend is especially pronounced in the educationally and technologically underdeveloped societies (Kohlberg, 1970). Patterns of increasing moral reasoning (at least through the conventional level) with advancing age apparently remain the same in all the cultures Kohlberg studied. Education plays a major role in the development of moral reasoning, and individuals who terminate their formal education tend to remain at the level of moral reasoning they attained while in school.

Kohlberg reports that cultural anthropologists had warned him that he would have to throw out his culture-bound dilemmas and his moral stages. In a dilemma in which the wife is starving to death and the husband has no money to buy food and thus must choose between stealing or letting his wife die, Taiwanese adolescents typically gave stage 2 responses: the husband should steal, because if he lets his wife die, he must pay for her funeral. In the Atayl village, where funerals are not so expensive, the typical stage 2 response differed in details: the husband should steal because he needs his wife to prepare his meals. Thus, while the specific content of responses is culture-bound, the underlying moral reasoning is basically the same.

Kohlberg did observe that cultural differences exist in the ages when adolescents progress from one moral stage to the next. In general, these advances occur earlier in technologically more advanced societies and later in more primitive societies. For example, in Yucatan, more sixteen-year-olds remained at the preconventional level and fewer had advanced to the postconventional levels than in the United States. In preliterate village or tribal communities, individuals rarely attain postconventional levels.

The findings comparing social class differences within the United States seem to follow the same pattern: "middle-class children were found to be

more advanced in moral judgment than matched lower-class children''
(Kohlberg, 1970: 154). The reason may be that middle-class children tend
to take the social perspective of others and are more likely to be involved
in debate surrounding legal, political, and economic issues. However,
middle- and lower-class subjects—even though they may progress at
different rates—subscribe to basically similar moral values.

In general, moral development is slower and less likely to reach the more
advanced level of moral reasoning in primitive, less educated, rural, more
traditional, and lower-class communities. Situational factors obviously influence moral judgment. Among adolescents and adults, those who are
politically conservative tend to endorse a law-and-order morality, to argue
for the maintenance of the existing political system, and to make moral
judgments characteristic of level 4. Individuals in stage 3 tend to emphasize
''conformity to stereotypes'' and to think in terms of stereotypical roles,
such as ''dumb blondes,'' ''preppies,'' ''hardhats,'' ''drug addicts,'' ''red-
blooded Americans,'' ''bankers,'' and ''women's libbers.'' Liberals and
moderates tend to utilize stage 5 moral reasoning. Revolutionary and radical
subjects seem strangely divided between highly idealistic postconventional
and egoistic stage 2 responses (Hampden-Turner and Whitten, 1971). Individuals who reason at the postconventional level provide for innovation,
experimentation, and change in social values, since they are likely to
challenge existing values. Individuals at the conventional level of moral
reasoning represent the conservative elements in society; they would like to
maintain the status quo.

RELATIONSHIP OF KOHLBERG'S THEORY OF MORAL REASONING TO OTHER THEORIES

According to Kohlberg, there is a conceptual relationship between his
stages of moral judgment and Piaget's stages of cognitive development.
The concrete operations in Piaget's model correspond to the preconventional level of moral development. The early interest of the operational
child clearly relates to the punishment/obedience orientation in moral
thinking. The concrete reversibility of thought patterns, part of Piaget's
operational stage, has its analogue in Kohlberg's stage 2 of an instrumental
relativism orientation. The shift from childhood to adolescence involves a
dramatic shift from concrete to abstract thought processes, just as the shift
from preconventional to conventional morality constitutes the basic difference between the child's and the adolescent's moral structure. Piaget's
earlier substage of formal operations, concerned with relationships involving the inverse of reversibility, corresponds to Kohlberg's interpersonal
concordance orientation (stage 3). Piaget's more advanced substage III-B
of abstract operations—which encompasses Kohlberg's stage 4 orientation
toward authority, law, and order—makes the more advanced postconven-

tional stages possible. Of a group of sixteen-year-old adolescents, 60 percent had attained abstract operational thinking but only 10 percent had reached the postconventional level of moral reasoning. However, all those who had reached the postconventional level of morality were able to think in terms of logical, abstract, formal operations. The relationship between these two theories is such that the attainment of Piaget's cognitive stages is a necessary precondition for the attainment of the corresponding level of moral thought. However, mastery of the thinking skills of any given stage does not guarantee that the individual has necessarily attained the same level and stage in moral reasoning. The latter, though frequently lower, is never higher.

Kohlberg's stages of moral development have also been related to Marcia's stages of ego-identity. Podd (1972) classified students into Marcia's four identity statuses: identity achievement, moratorium, foreclosure, and identity diffusion (see Chapter 3). He independently assessed the same individuals about their moral development and classified them as preconventional, conventional, or postconventional; he also added a fourth group: transitional. While the findings do not provide simple, clear-cut relationships, interesting relationships between identity and moral development do emerge. Podd had hypothesized that the most mature level of moral reasoning would be found among students who had already achieved an identity. Actually, about two-thirds of the morally principled subjects on Kohlberg's test were classified as having a mature identity. None of the subjects who were transitional in their moral thinking had achieved a mature identity, but approximately two-thirds were identity-diffused. Apparently, a person who is undergoing an identity crisis is also unstable and inconsistent in the ability to solve moral problems. Before an individual can effectively question the conventional morality of his society, he must first have questioned his own identity—that is, he must first have resolved his own personal moratorium issues. Of the subjects subscribing to a conventional level of morality, 40 percent had actually achieved a mature identity, while 30 percent of the conventional subjects were still in the foreclosure stage. As the theory suggests, foreclosure subjects showed a strong tendency to use a conventional mode of moral reasoning.

Kohlberg's Moral Judgment Scale was administered to a large group of students, including student activists who had participated in demonstrations at the Berkeley campus of the University of California (Haan, Smith, and Block, 1968). Distinguishing between arrested, participating, and nonparticipating students revealed the following thinking patterns: stage 6 subjects indicated that protest reflected their morality and that they were very much concerned with civil rights, civil liberties, and the relationship between students as a group and the university as a community. Of stage 6 subjects, 80 percent were arrested. For stage 5 subjects, that issue seemed less clear, and only 50 percent were arrested. To students at the conventional level of morality (law and order), the issue again was quite clear, but this group opposed the protest and only 10 percent participated in the sit-in leading to arrest. However, due to their participation at the protest, students at stage 2 were at risk of arrest almost to the same degree as those at stage 6. Of stage 2 subjects, 60 percent were arrested; however, their protest stemmed from egoistic personal reasons and revenge, not autonomous morality. They experienced more concern for their own personal rights than for the community or for human rights. Those who responded with stage 2 solutions to moral dilemmas tended to use the protest movement to fight their own personal battles with society. This study demonstrates clearly that moral structure is not identical with moral behavior and that not all civil disobedience arises from postconventional principled morality. College activists include individuals at both the highest and the lowest levels of moral development. While protest may be a sign of mature and principled morality, it can also be a sign of an immature, selfish stage 2 orientation: "Protest activities, like other acts, are neither virtuous nor vicious; it is only the knowledge of the good which lies behind them that gives them their virtue" (Kohlberg, 1970: 159).

EDUCATIONAL IMPLICATIONS

Though Kohlberg's theory of moral development has stimulated much thinking and discussion about moral education in the classroom, it has not resolved many of the controversial issues that surround the teaching of morality. Parents fear that educational systems may impose arbitrary values upon their unsuspecting children, or, worse, that the values taught in school are the sort that they might oppose for religious, political, or philosophical reasons. Consequently, the teaching of moral issues often becomes disguised in such "value-neutral" approaches as mental health, life adjustment, personality development, and, more recently, "value clarification." Other parents, partly because of their own confusion as to what is right and partly because of their inability to teach the moral values that they accept, increasingly demand that values and moral behavior be taught in school. However, there is little consensus as to what those values are and how they should be imparted. This is illustrated by the current discussion of sex education, obviously a controversial moral issue. Teachers and schools have been reluctant to teach moral values, partly because the teaching of middle-class values may confuse or offend the child who is exposed to lower-class values at home and partly because of the wide endorsement of a relativistic moral philosophy, not only among adolescents ("do your own thing"), but also among theologians in the form of "situational ethics." A teacher might say: "I will expose my children to my moral philosophy, but I will not impose it upon them. Who am I to say that I am right and they are wrong?'' Obviously, no easy solution to this dilemma seems likely.

The relativist philosophy of ''doing your own thing'' questions the school's right and obligation to teach morality. Historically speaking, American schools have progressed from the formal teaching of Christian moral values in the strict Puritanical tradition of the seventeenth century. A more subtle and indirect approach to morality appeared in the form of moral fables; in the McGuffey readers in the middle and later part of the nineteenth century, misbehavior inevitably resulted in painful consequences, an idea that Piaget identified as ''immanent justice.'' During the early part of the twentieth century, emphasis fell on the teaching of virtues such as honesty, service, duty, and self-control. More recently, schools and teachers have declined the role of teaching virtues and values, especially when ''values'' seem to mean only ''white middle-class values.'' Some have seen the Supreme Court's interpretation of the First Amendment concerning school prayer as meaning to eliminate not only religious education but also any form of moral and ethical education from public schools (Ball, 1967). By contrast, Kohlberg (1967) believes that the school can no more be committed to value neutrality than can the law, the Constitution, or the government. Two people obviously have the right to hold different values, but that does not mean that both attitudes are equally valid. Indeed, to believe that because a person maintains a sincere commitment to a set of values these values are necessarily valid, sound, mature, or beneficial involves an egregious fallacy. Public schools have a commitment to the development of the idea of justice, and Kohlberg attempts to make this commitment explicit. Furthermore, schools frequently do have a ''hidden moral curriculum'' that becomes obvious in the kinds of behaviors that teachers reward and punish. Students learn to be obedient, to wash their hands, to avoid disturbing neighbors, to avoid fighting. The underlying moral assumptions regarding what behavior to reward and what to punish may actually remain unconscious on the teacher's part, involving no recognition of the reinforcement of explicit moral values.

The early version of moral education consisted of teaching a ''bag of virtues.'' These included honesty, service, self-control, friendliness, and truthfulness. Aristotle had already proposed a similar cluster of virtues including temperance, liberality, pride, good temper, and justice. More recently, the Boy Scouts have advocated honesty, reverence, cleanliness, and bravery.

Traditionally, children were encouraged to practice virtuous behavior. They learned about the benefits and rewards of good behavior and about the harm or the punishment that would come if they were not virtuous. To illustrate the point, teachers used didactic stories in which good little children received rewards and bad ones received punishment. According to

Piaget and Kohlberg, this experience amounts to training for an immature (stage 2) level of moral development, since in more mature reasoning the abstract moral principle is more important than the material reward. The bag-of-virtues approach to moral education cannot be effective because virtue is not a psychological trait; virtues, such as honesty, are labels for abstract qualities that are not consistently reflected in behavior. The famous Hartshorne and May study (1928–1930) demonstrated that participation in the character-education program as provided in schools, churches, and Scouts did not contribute to improved moral behavior as measured by simulated situations involving honesty, self-control, and service. For example, almost all children cheated, no matter what their moral education had been. Far from being a consistent trait, cheating depended upon the situation and the likelihood of being caught. Though some children cheated in one situation, this did not predict their behavior in other situations. Follow-up studies have supported this observation that moral knowledge and moral behavior often show low correlations. Children who did cheat were just as likely to say that cheating was wrong as those who did not cheat. When asked "How can one teach morality?" Kohlberg answered as Socrates might have answered: "You must think I am very fortunate to know how virtue is acquired. The fact is that far from knowing whether it can be taught, I have no idea of what virtue really is" (Kohlberg, 1970: 144).

Kohlberg believes that educational procedures can facilitate moral reasoning; some of these have been tried experimentally. The goal of this approach is to aid children to take the next step to greater moral maturity, to assist them in developing the natural tendency toward which the child is already predisposed. Kohlberg's suggestions as to the teaching of moral values represent radical departures from those used in teaching a "bag of virtues" (which included preaching, rewarding, punishing, cajoling, and demanding). Instead, Kohlberg sees morality as an understanding of justice; consequently, schools must become concerned with moral development and moral reasoning.

Prior to Piaget and Kohlberg, the belief that moral development functioned as part of the socialization process dominated. Kohlberg assumes that progress from one stage to the next—like development in Piaget's theory—results from adaptation to a cognitive disequilibrium. The advance from one moral stage to the next is not simply a matter of socialization, of more or better understanding, but a reorganization and restructuring of earlier modes of moral thinking. Cognitive disequilibrium can result from moral challenges, from working through moral conflicts that often emerge in interactions, and from debate with peers. Consequently, social interactions with peers centering on conflicts to be resolved can facilitate moral development, especially if the moral ideas and ideals of one's peers are slightly ahead of one's own conceptual development. In addition, Kohlberg (1969) sees moral development as a function of role-taking ability. Through role-taking, people learn to restructure their own moral schemata and incorporate those of others. Consequently, role-taking opportunities and interaction with peers will facilitate moral development. Keasey (1971) investigated these hypotheses and found that the stages of moral development of early adolescents showed a positive relation to the degree to which individuals rated highly in social participation and social interaction. Adolescents with significant peer group involvement, role-taking opportunities, and social interaction advanced more rapidly through the moral stages than children who were withdrawn and lacking in opportunities for social participation. Selman (1971a), too, found that "the ability to understand reciprocal social perspectives"—that is, role-taking skills—related positively to higher levels of moral thought and constituted one precondition for progression in moral development (see Chapter 12).

The teaching of moral values involves several steps. First, creating in students a feeling of dissatisfaction about their concept of good and bad, right and wrong. This cognitive disequilibrium results from exposing adolescents to situations involving moral conflicts for which they have no readily available solutions or which contradict their own point of view. The second step is to engage them in a discussion with their peers, a discussion in which different interpretations, disagreements, and conflicts are freely expressed, thereby inviting role-taking. Ideally, the moral arguments advanced should be one stage beyond the subject's own moral development, since arguments two or three stages ahead are not easily assimilated and sometimes not even fully understood. Children and adolescents can understand the moral argument of all stages preceding their own and actually prefer the moral reasoning that they can comprehend (Rest, 1973); however, they rarely comprehend an argument that is more than one stage ahead of their own (Turiel, 1966, 1969). By creating a cognitive dissonance and having the subject listen to the arguments of others, one can communicate aspects of the moral dilemma that were inaccessible to the subject before. As adolescents think about the problem, they are likely to incorporate into their thinking suggestions proposed by others. Cognitive conflict brings about the advance to the next level, since resolution of conflict leads to a reorganization of structure—an idea not unlike Piaget's progression from equilibrium through disequilibrium to a higher level of equilibrium (Turiel, 1966, 1969) in cognitive development.

Research (Blatt, 1959; Kohlberg and Blatt, 1972) utilizing this technique has demonstrated that 50 percent of the experimental subjects moved up one stage and an additional 10 percent moved up two stages. In a control group not exposed to such teaching of moral thinking, only 10 percent moved up one stage in the same period of time. Follow-up data suggest that the gain in moral structure was permanent. An experiment involving juvenile delinquents (Hickey, 1972)—who originally, at the preconventional level, espoused an "If I'm not getting nothing, I'm not giving nothing" philosophy—showed that most had moved to a stage 4 law-and-order morality after exposure to this method of creating cognitive dissonance.

Kohlberg is concerned that schools themselves often do not espouse a very highly developed institutional moral philosophy in their actual day-to-day operation. All too often, school management seems to blend a fear of punishment (stage 1) with an ever-present concern for law and order (stage 4).

10: THE FEMINIST PERSPECTIVE: CAROL GILLIGAN'S REVISED THEORY OF SEX DIFFERENCES IN MORAL REASONING

THERE is increasing awareness and increasing evidence that most major developmental theories, written as they are from the male perspective, may reflect a gender bias. The reasons are numerous: partly because the creators of these theories have been predominantly male; partly because the theoretical models have been based on research data collected from males; partly because female data have not easily fit into the established male model (see Chapter 3); and partly because cultural prejudice and stereotypes may have influenced psychological and developmental thinking in the past.

Initially, like many of the developmental theorists who preceded him, Lawrence Kohlberg conducted his research on moral development with male subjects and developed his scoring method from male responses. Based only on males' resolutions of moral dilemmas, Kohlberg's theory is necessarily biased against females. At a later point, Kohlberg administered the moral dilemmas to females as well and did find sex differences in the development of moral judgment. However, he identifies these differences primarily in quantitative, not qualitative terms. Kohlberg and Kramer (1969) and others have rather consistently observed—and cross-cultural data support their observations—that the average adolescent female attains a moral judgment rating corresponding to stage 3 (the good boy–nice girl orientation); frequently, this becomes the terminal stage for females. In stage 3, the stage in moral development referred to as "interpersonal concordance," the subject perceives morality in terms of interpersonal relationships, where goodness implies helping or pleasing others. Adolescent boys of the same age typically score approximately one whole stage higher, with an average at stage 4 (the law-and-order orientation). In stage 4, subjects base their moral judgments on whether the behavior maintains or violates the existing social order. In addition, according to Kohlberg and others, more male than female adolescents move beyond stage 4 to the higher postconventional level of development in their moral judgment. This sex difference has commonly been explained as a deficiency in the female's ability to apply advanced principles of moral judgment. To put the argument in different terms, Kohlberg's system appears to penalize women for their greater sensitivity to others and their caring attitude and to reward males for their ability to abstract principles of justice.

Explanations for these sex differences in moral development have been suggested elsewhere. Douvan and Adelson (1966) and others have observed that females as a group tend to be somewhat more conforming, more attuned to others, less autonomous, and less inclined to develop an independent, well-defined, and firm personal creed. Researchers have interpreted all this to mean that females are more sensitive to others and more willing to please others, thus contributing to a good boy–nice girl orientation. However, a more basic theoretical explanation had already been proposed in Freud's early psychoanalytic conceptualizations of sex differences. Girls, because of the incomplete resolution of the Oedipus complex, were labeled as deficient in superego development, with the result that their moral development suffered. The following statement by Freud has been quoted extensively; however, it deserves repetition here because it highlights the ensuing argument and provides insight regarding the origin of theoretical understanding and psychological reasoning:

> I cannot evade the notion (though I hesitate to give it expression) that for women the level of what is ethically normal is different from what it is in men. Their superego is never so inexorable, so impersonal, so independent of its emotional origins as we require it to be in men. Character-traits which critics of every epoch have brought up against women—that they show less sense of justice than men, that they are less ready to submit it to the great exigencies of life, that they are more often influenced in their judgment by feelings of affection or hostility—all these would be amply accounted for by the modification in the formation of their super-ego which we have inferred above [Freud, 1925/1961: 257–258].

The underlying attitude of denigrating women's intellectual ability while praising their caring for others has historical roots. The German philosopher Schopenhauer wrote: "The weakness of their reasoning function also explains why women show more sympathy for the unfortunate than men." Such attitudes have had detrimental effects on women's social, legal, political, and economic opportunities.

Carol Gilligan's research and theorizing provide a major impetus for the rethinking of both developmental theory and the role of sex differences in our theoretical conceptualizations. For a number of years, Gilligan was associated with Kohlberg; she participated in his earlier research on moral judgment. Not until her more recent research did Gilligan redefine Freud's and Kohlberg's notion that what is ethically normal in females "is different from what it is in men," postulating a new theoretical conceptualization of women's moral development. Gilligan does not deny that sex differences exist: quite the contrary, she develops her theoretical model in an effort to explain these sex differences and goes so far as to say that we really need two different theories to describe both sexes accurately. However, she differs significantly from Freud, Kohlberg, and others because she does not conceptualize these sex differences as "lower" or "higher," "better" or "worse," but as complementary. In Gilligan's system, the fact that feelings for the other person influence women's judgment is not at all a moral deficit but a moral quality, a unique and valuable moral asset. She writes:

> Yet, herein lies the paradox, for the very traits that traditionally have defined the "goodness" of women, their care for and sensitivity to the needs of others, are those that mark them as deficient in moral development. The infusion of feeling into their judgments keeps them from developing more independent and abstract ethical conceptions in which concern for others derives from principles of justice rather than compassion and care [1977: 484].

Thus, Gilligan redefines the issue: the female level of moral judgment is not "lower" than that of men but does require a different theoretical explanation.

Gilligan has demonstrated that males and females approach moral and several other issues—such as the expression of violence and their perception of danger—from fundamentally different perspectives. They construct their relationships to self, others, and society in different ways. Men tend to organize social relationships in a hierarchical order and subscribe to a morality of rights in their judgments. Based on repeated responses to the Kohlbergian dilemmas, men respond to "an injunction to respect the rights of others and thus to protect from interference the right of life and self-fulfillment" (Gilligan, 1977: 511). In contrast, oriented toward interpersonal connectedness, females base their morality on care, sensitivity, and responsibility to people rather than on abstract principles of justice. For females, the moral imperative that recurs in Gilligan's interview protocols involves "an injunction to care, a responsibility to discern and alleviate the 'real and recognizable trouble' of this world" (1977: 511).

Gilligan designed a series of studies to define more precisely the nature of these sex differences, the divergent male and female developmental patterns, the female perception of morality and the way in which females make moral choices. Gilligan uses her findings to construct a theory quite different from those of her male predecessors—a feminist theory.

GILLIGAN'S TWO MORAL VOICES

In all human experience and human judgment, Gilligan maintains, two different voices utilized by the majority of males and females emerge. One of these voices, the one most commonly identified with the masculine world, speaks of preserving rights, exercising justice, obeying rules, and upholding principles; logical and individualistic, this male voice advocates equality, reciprocity, autonomy, and individuation; in short, this represents the justice orientation. The other voice, more dominant in women than in men, speaks of caring for others, sensitivity to others, concern for others, connectedness to others. It emphasizes responsibility to human beings rather than to abstract principles and advocates avoiding hurt and violence, maintaining relationships and attachments even if self-sacrifice becomes necessary. In short, this female voice represents the "interpersonal network" or care orientation. As the titles of Gilligan's book (1982) and article (1977) imply, these two voices represent different ways of viewing the world, people, self, and morality. According to Gilligan, in our theory of moral development, the first voice, the masculine voice, which represents the justice orientation, has become the standard for evaluating both males and females: Gilligan argues against this as prejudice to women. Since the interpersonal network or care orientation tends to be more salient in women, researchers in the past have portrayed women as deficient or even deviant in moral judgment because they have evaluated everyone against the masculine justice orientation.

In summarizing six studies, including four longitudinal investigations, Gilligan (1984) reports that 90 percent of the combined pool of subjects from all six studies actually reveal both orientations in their moral reasoning. However, 65 percent of the total sample rely more heavily on one of the two. Gilligan reports that of the women 92 percent include the interpersonal-network or care orientation, 62 percent preferred it, and 8 percent excluded it in their moral reasoning. Among the men, 62 percent included, 7 percent preferred, and 38 percent excluded the interpersonal-network orientation. For the justice orientation, this trend was reversed. Of the men, 100 percent used the justice orientation, 93 percent preferred it, and none excluded it in their moral reasoning. Among the women, 77 percent included the justice orientation, 38 percent preferred it, and 23 percent excluded it.

These data illustrate the existence of two very different ways to view the world. The statistics make it obvious that males generally reveal a strong preference for the justice orientation, while females prefer the interpersonal-care orientation. However, closer inspection also reveals that females are less one-sided in their reliance on the interpersonal-care orientation than males are in their reliance on the justice orientation. Perhaps this explains why females experience more ambiguity in evaluating multiple perspectives. Males tend to be more one-sided in their preference for the justice orientation. Particularly noticeable is the large group of men (38 percent) who exclude the interpersonal-care orientation altogether.

Rather than using either of these approaches as "the" correct orientation, Gilligan has sought interpretations that accept both perspectives as viable.

Gilligan maintains that justice and care must both receive attention for a moral choice to be perceived as tragic. Thus, the avoidance of tragic confrontation requires an appreciation and a utilization of both perspectives. Gilligan suggests that only by integrating these complementary male and female orientations—justice and care—will we ever be able to realize our full human potential in moral and general development. In a different context, such a position has become known as androgyny.

SEX DIFFERENCES IN PERCEPTIONS OF VIOLENCE

Pollak and Gilligan conducted an interesting, related research study entitled "Images of Violence in Thematic Apperception Test Stories" (1982). Stories written by college students in response to four TAT (Thematic Apperception Test) pictures were analyzed for violence, which was defined as inflicting actual harm—such as homicide, suicide, accidental death, rape, forcible violation, physical assault, and so on—on others.

Two of the four TAT pictures used as stimuli represent "affiliation themes" and depict people in close interpersonal relationship: (1) a man and a woman sitting next to each other overlooking a river; (2) a man and a woman in a trapeze act with the woman in midair, grasping the man's wrist. The remaining two pictures, representing "achievement themes," show (3) a man alone at his desk in a high-rise office building with a picture of his wife and children on his desk and (4) a group of women in white coats working in a lab with an older woman in the background supervising the group.

The stories were scored in two different ways. First, the researchers looked for the presence or absence of violent imagery in each of the situations depicted. Second, an independent score was based on whether, in the violent stories, the subject associated danger with the affiliation or with the achievement situations. Horner (1972), in her research, had observed that women often wrote violent endings to situations exhibiting competition for academic success. Pollak and Gilligan found that men often created violent stories for pictures suggesting affiliation and possible intimacy. From these initial observations about sex differences, Pollak and Gilligan developed the hypothesis that men are more likely to experience "fear of intimacy," to see danger in interpersonal closeness, and to project violence into situations that depict affiliation and intimacy. In contrast, if women experience "fear of success," they are more likely to see danger in being alone and to project violence into competitive achievement situations.

The findings supported the existence of sex differences both in the quantity of aggression and in the distribution of violent imagery in response to affiliation or achievement themes. As expected, and as has been reported elsewhere, the occurrence of violence in the stories of college men was much more common (51 percent portrayed violence in at least one story) than it was in women (22 percent). However, more interesting than these expected quantitative differences are the sex differences in violence elicited by affiliation versus achievement themes. Pollak and Gilligan based their scoring criteria on the situations depicted in the pictures. The male students' responses to the two pictures showing interpersonal affiliation and possible intimacy revealed more violence (26 percent of the men's stories) than the females' stories (only 6 percent). For the pictures suggesting achievement themes, these findings were reversed. In response to the achievement pictures, 16 percent of the women created violent stories as compared with only 6.8 percent of the men. In addition, some men but no women perceived violence in both the affiliation and the achievement situations. Pollak and Gilligan assert that these data support an interpretation of qualitative differences between the perception of violence among males and females.

A somewhat different scoring approach was used in analyzing the content of the stories in terms of where males and females perceive danger. In general, these independently derived data follow the same trend as those found in violence studies, but they demonstrate even more dramatic sex differences. In the affiliation situations, 26 percent of the men but none of the women perceived danger. In contrast, in the achievement situations, 12 percent of the women but only 1.1 percent of the men perceived danger. In the stories of both the men and the women, the victims of the violence tended to be females, a trend that was even more pronounced for women, who seldom created stories in which the victim was a male.

Pollak and Gilligan concluded from these data "that men and women perceive danger in different situations and construe danger in different ways" (1982: 164). In a more general sense, and quite consistent with the overall theme of Gilligan's research and her emerging theory, men seem more likely to see danger in interpersonal connectedness and may fear being entrapped, rejected, humiliated, or betrayed; men perceive competitive achievement as less dangerous than do women. Women, in contrast, see danger in the separation from others that comes with competitive success; they fear being left alone, isolated, or separated from others. Gilligan speaks of the tremendous sensitivity to abandonment in women, who tend to view interpersonal affiliation and intimacy as safe and nonthreatening. For many women, interpersonal care and intimacy are very important personal goals, and the interpersonal network is something that needs to be protected.

Thus, this study of college students' violent imagery and their perception of danger complements the moral judgment studies summarized above and gives additional credence to the theory that men and women structure their environment differently, show different orientations to affiliation and achievement situations, and speak with "different voices."

TEENAGERS MORAL REASONING ON SEXUAL DILEMMAS

Most of the past research concerned with moral judgment utilizes Kohlberg's standard moral dilemmas, such as "Heinz's Problem." Only an expensive drug can save Heinz's dying wife, but Heinz cannot afford the price demanded by the pharmacist. Critics of Kohlberg's methodology have suggested that the content of the dilemmas and the nature of his moral problems are such that they remain far removed from the daily experience of the average adolescent. In other words, Heinz's dilemma and others like it seem quite unrelated to the decisions and choices that people actually have to make. Therefore, one may question whether or not the exercise constitutes detached intellectual reasoning with a moral content or whether it really assesses a personal, existential moral judgment. This issue is crucial because the assessment of moral development depends on the subject's actual rather than hypothetical choices.

The question underlying this distinction involves whether or not adolescents can apply their impersonal moral reasoning skills equally effectively in a context that may correspond to real-life situations. Gilligan, Kohlberg, and several others conducted a study to investigate this issue. The researchers developed three new, more personally applicable sexual dilemmas describing situations with which teen-agers are more likely to identify, situations that they might actually experience.

The following sexual dilemma, for example, with abbreviated questions to assess moral reasoning, illustrates the relevance of this issue:

A high school girl's parents are away for the weekend and she's alone in the house. Unexpectedly, on Friday evening, her boyfriend comes over. They spend the evening together in the house and after a while they start necking and petting.
1. Is this right or wrong? Are there any circumstances that would make it right (wrong)?
2. What if they had sexual intercourse? Is that right or wrong? Why?
3. (If applicable:) Why do you think petting is OK but sexual intercourse is wrong?
4. Are there any circumstances that would make sexual intercourse right (wrong)?
5. Suppose the girl is less willing than the boy to have sexual intercourse. The girl thinks sex before marriage is OK for boys but not for girls. What reasons does she have for thinking that way? What is your thinking about this?
6. The girl's parents return and find out that the couple had sexual intercourse—what should the parents do?

7. Do you think these issues about sex have anything to do with morality and immorality?
8. Where do you think your ideas about what's right and wrong come from?
9. There is a lot of talk these days about the new morality and the sexual revolution. What do you think about this? [From: Gilligan, Kohlberg, Lerner, and Belenky, 1971: 151–152].

Three such sexual dilemmas, along with Kohlberg's standard moral dilemmas, were administered to 25 male and 25 female high school juniors from a higher and a lower academic group of a suburban high school. As critics had suggested might be the case, the Moral Maturity Scores (MMS) on Kohlberg's standard dilemmas were significantly higher than on the sexual relationship dilemmas, with which adolescents are more likely to identify personally. On the standard MMS, subjects scored about halfway between stages 3 and 4; on the sexual dilemmas, however, they clearly scored at stage 3. Half the subjects reasoned at the same stage when working out both sets of problems; however, of those who demonstrated any changes, 80 percent exhibited a lower level of reasoning when asked to respond to the sexual dilemma. This was equally true for both sexes; but comparing the two types of dilemmas, the boys showed greater differences than the girls. For example, 13 boys dropped two stages and 6 dropped three stages, but none of the girls dropped more than one stage. The evaluations for girls on the sexual dilemmas remained closer to their general MMS than those for boys. Girls in general tended to be somewhat more conservative in their reasoning on the sexual dilemmas, a characteristic that, in this hypothetical situation, appeared to be in their own best interest.

The decline in moral reasoning from stage 3.5 to stage 3 is both statistically and theoretically significant. Stage 3 implies a great deal of influence of significant others, peer group pressure, conformity to those who matter in one's life and desire to be accepted by doing what others expect. Obviously, in a situation involving sexual temptation, these kinds of pressures can influence practical decisions. Gilligan et al. conclude that "the affective involvement of the adolescent with sex depresses his ability to reason at a level comparable to that shown on more abstract issues" (1971: 149).

ABORTION AS A MORAL DILEMMA

In a related study, Gilligan and Belenky (1980) examined the moral reasoning of young women involved in making a personal, existential decision regarding abortion, a very difficult moral choice. The abortion issue, obviously a central one in women's moral choices, emphasizes the conflict between self-interest and concern for others.

Abortion and pregnancy counseling services referred to the investigators 29 women whose pregnancy had been confirmed and who were seriously considering an abortion. Their ages ranged from 15 to 33, and they represented diverse ethnic and social class backgrounds. The researchers administered several of Kohlberg's standard hypothetical moral dilemmas to them and interviewed them in some depth about their reasoning in regard to whether or not to terminate a problematic pregnancy. The issue was not whether they decided to abort or to have the baby but the moral reasoning that led to their eventual choices. Using criteria based on Kohlberg's theory, the investigators scored the subjects' responses according to the underlying level of moral reasoning.

The first interview took place during the first trimester of the pregnancy, followed by a similar interview with 24 subjects of the initial group one year later. These data allowed the analysis of several related issues:

1. The relationship between the level of impersonal moral reasoning on Kohlberg's dilemma (Moral Maturity Score = MMS) and the level of moral reasoning underlying their personal abortion decision.
2. The changes in moral reasoning that took place between the first interview and the second interview a year later and how the patterns of relationship identified under item 1 related to changes in moral reasoning.

Three different groups emerged from the data:

1. For one group of women, the MMS and the abortion reasoning scores were about the same. These women applied their moral reasoning equally effectively to impersonal issues and to their own personal abortion dilemmas.
2. For a second group of women, reasoning about personal decisions operated on a more mature level than more generalized moral reasoning.
3. A third group of women scored higher on the impersonal, traditional moral dilemmas and lower in respect to their own personal abortion decisions. Apparently, they were unable to apply their moral reasoning ability when they themselves were directly and personally involved in the issue. This third pattern corresponds to that of many of the adolescents responding to the sexual dilemmas, whose scores dropped lower when confronting more personal problems.

Group 2, those for whom the reasoning about their own personal abortion issues had scored higher than the more traditional MMS, experienced the greatest growth in moral reasoning during the intervening year. Apparently, working through a personal moral issue facilitated maturation; in addition, the more general life circumstances of those in this group had also improved during the intervening year.

For the remaining two groups, (1) traditional and abortion reasoning on the same level and (3) traditional reasoning higher than the abortion reasoning there was no significant downward or upward trend in moral reasoning during the intervening year. Their level of moral reasoning had remained unchanged. Even though they did not experience a change in overall moral reasoning ability, the third group (whose MMS had been significantly higher and level of abortion reasoning lower) did give evidence that they were unhappy both about life in general and the abortion decision in particular. They also experienced a decline in emotional and mental health during the year following the initial interview.

A THEORETICAL CONSOLIDATION: THE FEMALE STAGES OF MORAL REASONING

On the basis of an analysis of the moral reasoning of women confronted with the abortion issue, as well as several of the other related studies of females (some used Kohlberg's traditional moral dilemma situations), Gilligan suggests that we replace Kohlberg's male-oriented preconventional, conventional, and postconventional levels of moral reasoning with different constructs for females. These redefined female levels are based on interpersonal relationships in women's moral reasoning, not on Kohlberg's principles of justice based on the moral judgment of males. What follows is a summary of Gilligan's female levels of moral reasoning:

LEVEL 1: THE ORIENTATION TOWARD SELF-INTEREST

At the simplest level of moral reasoning, women are pragmatically and egocentrically preoccupied with self-interest and survival. Females perceive morality as a matter of obeying restrictions imposed upon a helpless subject by society. The pregnant woman's major concern is with taking care of herself; often, she perceives herself as being alone in relation to this issue. When asked about her plans after she found herself pregnant, an eighteen-year-old stated: "I really didn't think anything except that I didn't want it. (Why was that?) I didn't want it, I wasn't ready for it, and next year will be my last year and I want to go to school." When asked about a right way to make a decision, she answered, "There is no right decision. (Why?) I didn't want it" (Gilligan, 1982: 75). At this level, moral consideration would enter the reasoning process only if the subject's own needs were in conflict. If that were to happen, she would have to weigh which was more important to her. The desire for "having my very own baby'' could counterbalance an opposing wish, such as being able to get out of the house more often. The decision would be based on what, under the circumstances, would be best for the subject, without consideration for anyone else.

THE FIRST TRANSITION: FROM SELFISHNESS TO RESPONSIBILITY

In the transition period, the individual begins to become aware of the difference between what she wants (selfishness) and what she ought to do (responsibility). This implies a more mature and a more differentiated self-concept than the strictly egotistical reasoning characteristic of level 1. This growth from egocentric selfishness to an emerging concern for others is the first major step from childhood toward a more mature level of moral reasoning. One of Gilligan's subjects expressed the ordering of selfishness in relation to a beginning sense of responsibility in the following words: "Sometimes what is necessary comes before what you want, because it might not always lead to the right thing" (1977: 494).

LEVEL 2: IDENTIFICATION OF GOODNESS WITH RESPONSIBILITY FOR OTHERS

During adolescence, there is often development leading to the next higher level of moral reasoning and allowing a societal perspective to emerge. Self-interest falls into the background and the need to please others, to do what others demand—even at the price of ignoring the voice within—surfaces. The woman thus moves from selfishness to a concern for others, an overriding sense of responsibility for others, and the capacity for self-sacrifice. A young woman might agree to an abortion because that is what her husband, her lover, her lover's wife, or her parents want; she might realize that bringing a baby into the world would be unfair ("it would not be a good life for the baby"), even though she despises herself for consenting to the demands of others. In this stage, the young woman equates goodness with self-sacrifice and with pleasing or caring for others. When a problem cannot be resolved in the best interest of everyone, she will sacrifice her own preferences to redefine the problem in terms of care and responsibility to others. Thus the decision to abort can actually stem from concern for pleasing others. The exclusion of her own values from the decision-making process creates an inequality in interpersonal relationships, because the young woman subordinates or sacrifices the self to please others. The ability to value and to assert oneself implies danger because it can lead to criticism and even abandonment by others. Survival remains a primary concern, which the young woman views as requiring dependence on and approval from others. Actually, a common theme in the abortion reasoning of women at this level is the fear that "my boyfriend would leave me if I did not have the abortion."

In the past this orientation of pleasing others at almost any price has been the socially expected role for women; the men in a woman's life would take charge, care for her, make decisions for her, protect her—but with the expectation that she would do as she was told. The woman herself, at this level of reasoning, justifies her action by believing in the value of choosing a life of self-sacrifice to please those for whom she cares.

THE SECOND TRANSITION: FROM CONFORMITY TO A NEW INNER JUDGMENT

A beginning critical questioning about her own value characterizes the second transition. The young woman begins to wonder whether her concerns are really selfish or whether considering one's own values and needs, not only those of others, might actually be responsible. Is it possible to avoid hurting the other person and remain true to oneself? Does the reconciliation between hurt and care require compromise? Thus, the young woman questions all the assumptions that, heretofore, she had so readily accepted. The essence of this transition is the change "toward a new conception of goodness which turns inward in an acknowledgment of the self and an acceptance of responsibility for decision" (Gilligan, 1977: 500). However, the individual's perception of her self-worth is still too uncertain to allow her to claim full equality with others.

LEVEL 3: FOCUSING ON THE DYNAMICS BETWEEN SELF AND OTHERS

At the third level of moral reasoning, which many never attain, the individual develops a universal perspective. In reasoning about their abortions, level 3 women assert their own independent rights but simultaneously give equal consideration to their responsibilities to others. Thus, the primitive selfishness of level 1 reemerges in a restrained way: "I have rights that are equal to those of others"—an assertion combined with a modified desire to please others and to be sensitive to their needs. There now emerges a condemnation not only of exploitation but also of unnecessarily hurting others or being hurt. A level 3 woman no longer sees herself as submissive or powerless; she has become an active and equally valid participant in the decision-making process. The question now becomes what action would minimize hurt for others as well as for the self. However, the woman herself has retrieved the judgmental initiative, so that the realities and consequences for all concerned enter into her reasoning process. She has learned to "verify her capacity for independent judgment and the legitimacy of her own point of view" (Gilligan, 1977: 502). The woman's criteria for decision making are predicated upon a transformed understanding of interpersonal connectedness and on care for others. The moral foundation of this system is the young woman's commitment to nonviolence and the duty to minimize pain for all concerned. Gilligan asserts that "Care then becomes a universal obligation, the self-chosen ethic of a postconventional judgment that reconstructs the dilemma in a way that allows the assumption of responsibility for choice" (1977: 504).

Gilligan assumes that these developmental stages—and this is her major contribution to the revision of Kohlberg's theory—have greater validity for the moral reasoning advanced by females. Obviously, Gilligan's three female levels of interpersonal care morality share similarities and have parallels to Kohlberg's stages of moral judgment. His preconventional level parallels Gilligan's level of self-interest, and selfishness is a major issue for both. Kohlberg's conventional level encompasses much of what Gilligan describes as responsibility and self-sacrifice. The conformity to social expectations and societal conventions is a recurrent theme for both. Finally, the postconventional level corresponds to the maintenance of balance between the inner self and responsibility to others. Personal autonomy in moral reasoning is the common issue for Kohlberg and Gilligan at this level. Besides these structural parallels, however, are fundamental differences in focus and orientation that have "to do with the subordination of the interpersonal to the societal definition of the good" (Gilligan, 1977: 489), a characteristic particularly relevant in the transition from Kohlberg's third to his fourth stage of moral development. Gilligan's premise is not that her theory is "better" than Kohlberg's. Far from claiming that her theory should replace his, Gilligan argues that these two theories are distinctly different and equally valid. Indeed, the highest form of moral reasoning can utilize, combine, and integrate both the masculine orientation toward rights and justice and the feminine attitude toward responsibility and an interpersonal network of care.

CRITIQUE OF GILLIGAN'S THEORY AND INFERENCES ABOUT OTHER THEORIES

Intriguing as Gilligan's theory is, the empirical basis, especially the empirical support from researchers whose primary concerns are sex differences in moral judgment, is weak. The invariant and developmentally sequential nature of her stages has not yet been clearly established. Critics have even questioned Gilligan's basic assumption that female children and adolescents score consistently lower on the traditional moral dilemmas Kohlberg originally developed. Existing research data are much less clear-cut in supporting Gilligan's notion that males' moral judgments tend to be governed by a principled justice orientation and that the moral judgment of females shows more empathy, altruistic concern for the other person, and a greater interpersonal orientation. The relevant evidence is too extensive—including over a hundred research studies—to be reviewed here; however, the interested reader is referred to the following review articles: Brabeck (1983); Krebs (1970; reviewing seventeen studies on sex differences in altruism); Rest (1979; data on gender differences from twenty-two studies using the Defining Issue Test); and Walker (1984; reviewing seventy-two Kohlbergian research studies concerned with sex differences). However, the argument is not conclusive; there has been a rebuttal to Walker's argument (Baumrind, 1986) and a rejoinder to the rebuttal (Walker, 1986).

These reviews and the meta-analyses of a considerable amount of evidence suggest that Kohlberg's theory of morality (based on universal principles of justice) and Gilligan's theory of a female moral orientation (based on interpersonal connectedness, care, and nonviolence) appear to be much less sex-specific than the way they are presently perceived, particularly in college textbooks and the popular press. The empirical research does not identify as neat, consistent, unequivocal sex differences as Gilligan's theory implies. Gilligan's ultimate contribution may lie not so much in her discovery of a new feminist theory of moral reasoning, no matter what the continuing assessment of her research reveals, as in her broadening of our assumptions and her refining of our understanding that the really moral person must integrate the concept of abstract justice and the concern for particular others.

Gilligan presents data relevant to her basic argument in four areas: moral judgment, sex differences in violence, sexual dilemmas, and the abortion decision. However, by inference, much of what Gilligan has to say about the limited applicability of Kohlberg's theory to the development of moral judgment in females suggests that similar shortcomings may exist in most or all the theories of adolescent development presented in this book. Gilligan suggests that past models of human development have often failed to give the female experience its unique place and its proper value in our theoretical conceptualizations. By extension, Gilligan suggests that we might need to theorize differently for males and females.

Sullivan's theory (see Chapter 5) is relevant to this discussion. His stages—specifically what happens just before and during adolescence—do seem to present primarily a male perspective. However, his remarkable and continuous emphasis on the significance of others, of interpersonal relationships, and of communication and care seems to have anticipated many of the elements that Gilligan now identifies as central to the female experience.

11: SOCIAL COGNITION. PART 1: ROBERT SELMAN'S THEORY OF ROLE TAKING

SOCIAL COGNITION

The concept of social cognition has rapidly gained popularity, recognition, and respectability, both as a popular research topic and as an important theoretical construct. In contrast to most developmental theories, the theory of social cognition is not associated with one particular person, or even one psychological school of thought; rather, it constitutes a new synthesis of several psychological positions. As a result, the concept of social cognition seems to suffer from diversification and a mushrooming of independent, interrelated minitheories and submodels. Because the important social cognition concepts come from different authors, different theories, and different research orientations, they do not have the unifying cohesiveness of theories developed by one person, such as those of Erikson or Piaget. Thus, social cognition theory constitutes the integration of several trends in the study of cognitive and social development.

Several major influences have contributed ideas to the theory of social cognition. On the one hand, there is the obvious influence of the vast literature concerned with the process by which children acquire their knowledge about the physical world, a process commonly referred to as cognitive development and heavily influenced by the writings of Jean Piaget, Heinz Werner, and Jerome Bruner. Even more relevant is Kohlberg's theory of moral development, which covers one aspect of social cognition (see Chapter 9).

On the other hand, the vast literature on social development and social psychology also makes a significant contribution to the "social" side of social cognition theory. There is an extensive accumulation of information, much of it empirical in nature, about the developmental changes that take place in the social behavior of children and adolescents. The theoretical background for this approach is influenced by social learning theory and also by psychoanalytic theory, and new theoretical perspectives are emerging (see Chapter 14).

Social cognition focuses on the processes by which children gain knowledge about their social world and their social reasoning processes. Underlying all social cognition issues is the assumption that adolescents apply cognitive abilities and cognitive skills to interpersonal situations and social problem-solving tasks (Youniss, 1975), such as anticipating or predicting how another person may feel or behave in a social dilemma. However, social cognition theory asks some important questions: How does the child learn to understand what children and adolescents think about one another's behavior? And how does the individual conceptualize the thinking of others?

The theoretical concept of "social role taking" as a significant construct in social and developmental psychology goes back to the writings of George Herbert Mead (1934). Two concepts from Piaget's developmental theory are directly related to social cognition: egocentrism and decentering. Both will be treated in more detail in Chapter 12. Egocentrism and decentering are applicable to impersonal tasks such as Piaget's famous mountain range where the child has to determine what the silhouette of the mountains looks like from a different position. However, egocentrism and decentering apply equally to interpersonal issues, such as putting one's self into another person's position. In Piaget's view, the emergence of role-taking ability must be viewed as a by-product of social and cognitive decentering.

An important question must be raised: "Are social objects and physical objects known in the same or in different ways?" (Youniss, 1975: 173). Much information about social behavior, like much information about the physical world, will be acquired through observation, trial and error, exploration, direct first-hand experiences, and discovery. There also appears to be some parallel in the structural changes that accompany the development of impersonal and interpersonal cognition. Byrne (1974), for example, was able to demonstrate a close relationship between logical stages, moral stages, and role-taking stages. A certain level in logical thinking appears to be necessary before the equivalent stage in moral judgment is reached, and a certain level in role taking is a prerequisite for the corresponding level of moral judgment. "Logical stages may be in evidence without the equivalent role taking or moral stage, but the role taking or moral stage rarely occurs without the corresponding stage of logical thinking" (Byrne, 1974: 5647B).

However, as Piaget (1932b) pointed out, there is one important distinction between physical knowledge and social understanding: Scientific knowledge is objective and factual and can be proven or disproven through the scientific method. Social knowledge, in contrast, is arbitrary, and appropriate social behavior is determined to a very large extent by the specific social situation, as well as by social, cultural, and even subcultural definitions and expectations.

> Because of the arbitrary nature of social rules and social protocol, the child will have to acquire some knowledge by direct instruction from adults or older children, by observing the behavior of mature people in the environment, and by experiencing approval and disapproval for appropriate and inappropriate behavior [Moore, 1979: 54].

Because social rules are less uniform, less specific, and more situation-dependent than physical phenomena, they are less predictable and more complicated to understand.

There is considerable debate in the literature about whether and to what extent physical knowledge and social cognition are correlated and about whether scientific problem-solving skills and social problem-solving skills are correlated or two relatively independent entities (Keating, 1978; Keating and Clark, 1980). At this point we are not justified in assuming that cognitive problem-solving skills can easily be transferred and applied to social problem-solving skills. Many writers have claimed that social problem-solving skills function independently of and are different from intellectual problem-solving skills and need to be taught in their own right. Shure and Spivack (1980) provide evidence that the cognitive abilities involved in interpersonal problem solving are not the same as those measured by the conventional IQ test. Furthermore, the improvement in social adjustment that resulted from interpersonal skills training programs was not dependent on the child's level of intellectual functioning. Selman (1976b) reports that when a poorly adjusted clinical group of preadolescents was compared to a matched group of normally functioning peers no differences in level of cognitive functioning were found, but the poorly adjusted group was substantially below the normal group in the domain of interpersonal and moral reasoning. The individual with a deficient ego, according to psychoanalytic theory, has greater difficulty in differentiating between physical and social reality. Such individuals are often surprisingly capable of figuring out problems posed on an impersonal, factual level, but they are unable to solve corresponding problems of social living or to see that their own aggressive behavior might have a negative impact on the group. Our present knowledge about the relationship between physical knowledge and social knowledge can best be summarized by a quote from Selman: "The development of social conceptions, reasoning, thought—social cognition—is distinct from, though not unrelated to, the development of nonsocial cognition" (1980: 14). Therefore, the investigation of social cognition development, independent of reasoning ability, is justified and potentially a fruitful contribution to developmental psychology.

Although many writers on social cognition refer to the works of Piaget, Kohlberg, Bruner, and Heider, new and more specific social cognition theories of development have emerged, particularly in the writings of Flavell (1974; 1977), Shantz (1975), and Selman (1976a; 1976b; 1977; 1980).

Flavell's model of social cognition is not strictly developmental; rather, it is a "general information processing model." He identifies four components that are necessary for drawing inferences about the perspectives of other persons: the existence component, the need component, the inference component, and the application component (Flavell, 1977). The *existence component* simply implies a subject's recognizing the existence of psychological experiences or events in the other person and realizing that the other person's perspective of such experiences or events may differ from one's own. "There scarcely can be any thinking about social-cognitive phenomena if the very existence of such phenomena is not yet represented by the thinker" (Flavell, 1977: 20). The *need component* expands and includes the idea that the goal-directed behavior of another person is now understood as being motivated by a need. Other people are now being seen as having existence, feelings, and needs. The *inference component* leads to the construction of a representation of another person's subjective experiences. In other words, there is an attempt to figure out what the specific nature of the other person's needs or feelings may be. This kind of social thinking requires observing clues, integrating the clues, and probabilistic reasoning. The *application component* is the subject's adjusting behavior—as in game strategies or through verbal compliments—to apply the information obtained from the inference. A decision about an interpersonal problem must go through all of these steps.

For example, assume an adolescent boy riding in a train is sitting next to a teen-age girl reading a book. He first becomes aware of her and finds her attractive. His interest increases until he is aware of little else. To assess her need component he may begin to observe whether and how much she is absorbed in her reading, what she is reading, what she is wearing, whether she is wearing an engagement ring or other evidence of being attached; whether or not she looks at him, the openness and closedness of her body posture, and so on. He infers that she might be interested in talking to him.

The young man may never dare to make the necessary application and talk to her, in which case he will never know the correctness or incorrectness of his inferences. If he does complete the fourth step and makes the application by saying, "Hi, I see you are interested in science fiction—so am I," he may find out whether his inferences about her were correct. She may look at him, smile, and respond. He also may be forced to reassess his initial inference if, for example, she abruptly turns the page or stares away from him without responding.

Shantz (1975) develops her theory around five related questions that address the fundamental issue of social cognition:

1. What is the other person seeing? This calls for the ability to make inferences about a person's visual perception of objects in space.
2. What is the other person feeling? The focus here is on understanding the emotional state of the person; it involves empathy.
3. What is the other person thinking? At issue is the ability to make inferences about the thought processes of other people and to distinguish them from one's own.
4. What is the other person intending? This particular social cognition skill requires inferences about the motivation of the person.
5. What is the other person like? This social cognition skill involves person-perception and can deal with overt (physical characteristics) and covert (personality traits) aspects of the other person.

The insights that can be ascertained from these social cognitive developmental issues provide a model for understanding social behavior and social development (Selman, 1980). The discussion that follows will focus primarily on the contribution of Robert Selman, who has developed a social cognition theory that considers preadolescence and adolescence in more detail than anyone else. Taking the social perspective of someone else—which his theory emphasizes—appears to be at the very core of social cognition.

DEFINITION OF SOCIAL OR INTERPERSONAL COGNITION

Social cognition can be defined as "how people think about other people and about themselves," or how people come to know their social world. Social cognition is concerned with the processes by which children and adolescents conceptualize and learn to understand others: their thoughts, their intentions, their emotions, their social behavior, and their general point of view. Social cognition involves role taking, perspective taking, empathy, moral reasoning, interpersonal problem solving, and self-knowledge. Shantz has provided a formal definition of social cognition: "the child's intuitive or logical representation of others, that is, how he characterizes others and makes inferences about their covert inner psychological experiences" (Shantz, 1975: 1). Implied in the concept of social cognition is an ability to make inferences about other people's capabilities, attributes, expectations, feelings, and potential reactions. These inferential processes of social cognition are referred to as role taking or perspective taking. Selman differentiates between role taking and social-perspective taking. The former involves the question of what social or psychological information may look like from the position of the other person. Social-perspective taking more broadly involves an "understanding of how human points of view are related and coordinated with one another" (Selman, 1980: 22).

The defining characteristics of social cognition may be highlighted by a statement from Tagiuri, which captures the essense of that concept and focuses on the events and classes of objects toward which the efforts of social understanding and social problem solving are directed:

> The observations or inferences we make are principally about intentions, attitudes, emotions, ideas, abilities, purposes, traits, thoughts, perceptions, memories—events that are *inside* the person and strictly psychological. Similarly, we attend to certain psychological qualities of relationships *between* persons, such as friendship, love, power, and influence. We attribute to a person properties of *consciousness* and *self-determination*, and the capacity for *representation of his environment*, which in turn mediates his action [Tagiuri, 1969: 396].

Social or interpersonal cognition or social intelligence cannot be perceived as one uniform, consistent, theoretical construct. Under the umbrella "theory of social cognition," a variety of minitheories, constructs, and models have emerged. The various social cognition constructs have stimulated considerable research to investigate these constructs, the interrelationship between the various social cognition concepts, and their relationship to the more general concepts of cognitive, moral, and social development. To provide the reader with a general overview of the multidimensional quality of social cognition theories and an understanding of some of the major conceptual constructs, as well as some references to the research literature, a summary of information is provided in Figure 14.

Most of these studies used only children as subjects and therefore cannot be reviewed; however, the study by Montemayor and Eisen (1977) does focus on changes in self-conception from childhood through adolescence and hence deserves a more detailed review. The authors utilize Kuhn and McPartland's (1954) "Who Am I" techniques, and the results are based on Gordon's (1968) thirty response classification categories. Responses at age levels ten, twelve, fourteen, sixteen, and eighteen show a significant increase in the following response categories: occupational role (e.g., I want to become a teacher); interpersonal style (I am lonely); psychic style (I am happy); a sense of unity (I am in harmony); a sense of self-determination (I

Social Cognition Topics	Research References
Role taking	Byrne (1974); Chandler (1973); Flavell (1968); Selman (1971a; 1971b); Selman and Byrne (1974)
Perspective taking	Kurdek (1978); Selman (1971b)
Understanding the feelings of others	Feshbach (1973; 1975)
Understanding the motives of others	Berndt and Berndt (1975)
Interpersonal understanding	Selman (1980)
Interpersonal awareness	Selman, Jacquette, and Lavin (1977)
Social and interpersonal reasoning	Damon (1980); Keating and Clark (1980)
Social relations such as friendship and authority	Damon (1977)
Interpersonal acts such as kindness	Baldwin and Baldwin (1970); Youniss (1975)
Interpersonal problem solving skills	Spivack and Shure (1974); Spivack, Platt, and Shure (1976)
Social rules and conventions	Turiel (1975; 1978)
Moral judgment and behavior	Flavell (1977); Kohlberg (1969); Rest (1974)
Social institutions	Furth, Baur, and Smith (1976); Furth (1978)
Social competency	Elardo (1974)
Communication skills	Gluecksberg, Krauss, and Higgens (1975)
Empathy	Eisenberg-Berg and Mussen (1978); Feshbach (1973); Hughes, Tingle, and Sawin (1981); Hoffman (1976)
Self-recognition	Flavell (1978); Hill and Tomlin (1981)
Attribution theory	Kelley (1973); Weiner (1974);
Egocentrism	Elkind (1967); Elkind and Bowen (1979); Looft (1971); Muuss (1981); Rubin (1973)
The self's own thought processes (Metacognition)	Flavell (1977; 1978)
Person perception	Livesley and Bromley (1973); Montemayor and Eisen (1977); Tagiuri (1969); Tagiuri and Petrullo (1958)

FIGURE 14. An Overview of Social Cognition: Topics, Models, and Research.

am a serious worker); ideological and belief references (I am a conservative); and existential and individuating responses (me, I, myself).

In the same group a decrease in the following categories occurred as they grew older: territoriality (I am a New Yorker); possessions, resources (I own a motor scooter); physical self, body image (I am blond, slim, and tall).

The findings of the study suggest that with increasing age the self-conception of adolescents becomes more abstract and less concrete.

Adolescents perceive themselves in terms of more abstract and subjective attributes; they emphasize personal beliefs and motivational and interpersonal qualities more than children do. Implied in the findings is the idea that the more abstractly thinking older individuals may be more effective in differentiating between overt appearance and deeper underlying dispositional qualities in themselves and others.

SELMAN'S STAGE THEORY OF SOCIAL COGNITION

Selman (1971b; 1976a; 1976b; 1977; 1980) and Selman and Byrne (1974) have advanced a stage theory of social cognition based on the concept of an ontogenetic, invariant sequence of predictable stages in social perspective taking. Selman was greatly influenced by G. H. Mead's theory of self, by Piaget's theory of cognitive development (logical thought), and by Kohlberg's theory of moral judgment (moral thought). "Conceptually, role taking can be described as a form of social cognition intermediate between logical and moral thought" (Selman, 1976a: 307). The developmental changes in logical structure seem to manifest themselves first in the thinking related to physical events, later in the thinking concerned with social events, and still later in the thinking concerned with the moral domain.

Selman's model focuses on the child's ability to draw interpersonal inferences about somebody else's perceptual or conceptual social awareness. It is based on an investigation of the developmental changes that take place in social perception or role-taking skills. The assumption, well supported by empirical evidence (Selman, 1971b; 1977; 1980; Selman and Byrne, 1974), is that social role-taking skills (that is, skill in differentiating between the perspective of self and others and accurate perception of the thinking of others) increase with age, at least into adolescence. Social role taking is viewed by Selman (1971b) as a prototypical social cognitive skill. The basic theoretical issue rests on the assumption "that the unique aspect of social cognition and judgment that differentiates human from sub-human functioning is 'role-taking,' the ability to understand the self and the other as subjects, to react to others as like the self, and to react to the self's behavior from the other's point of view" (Selman and Byrne, 1974: 803).

The series of role-taking stages identified by Selman and Byrne are logically related and follow in a fixed developmental sequence. In that respect they meet the criteria for a structural developmental model. Selman makes an important distinction between the structure and the content of thought. What is being reasoned about is the content; in contrast, how the social reasoning is done is the structure. It is the structure of social reasoning that constitutes the basis for Selman's "Structural-Developmental Model of Social Cognition" (1977). Selman hypothesizes that "each level of social perspective taking provides the structural basis for a stage in the development of conceptions of interpersonal role relations" (1976b: 160).

Originally, Selman identified only four developmental levels of social perspective-taking skills between the ages of four and twelve. In his more recent work (Selman, 1976a; 1980; Selman, Jaquette, and Lavin, 1977), the model has been elaborated further and includes a fifth stage, corresponding to adolescence and reaching into adulthood. This theory has considerable empirical support, and since Selman places more emphasis on the developmental changes during adolescence than any of the previously mentioned social cognition models, his theory will be considered in greater detail.

Selman's model of interpersonal understanding is based on five distinct stages, although some further subdivision of these stages has been proposed. The names and the identifying characteristics of these stages are:

Stage 0.   The egocentric undifferentiated stage (approximately age three to six)

Stage 1.   The differentiated and subjective perspective-taking stage (age five to nine)

Stage 2.   Self-reflective thinking or reciprocal perspective-taking stage (age seven to twelve)

Stage 3.   The third-person or mutual perspective-taking stage (age ten to fifteen)

Stage 4.   The in-depth and societal perspective-taking stage (age twelve to adulthood)

These five stages constitute the developmental dimension in Selman's theory.

The progression through these stages is assessed, analyzed, and described in terms of four social domains that provide the content to understand the development in social cognition (see Figure 15). They are:

1. The individual concepts domain
2. The friendship concepts domain
3. The peer-group concepts domain
4. The parent-child concepts domain

These content domains of social cognition provide the conceptual frame of reference within which the specific developmental changes are investigated. The responses revealing the child's social awareness are elicited in the individual interview through various social dilemma situations. An illustration of such a dilemma from the domain "Concepts of Individuals" (self-awareness) is:

Individual	Friendship	Peer group	Parent-child relations
1. *Subjectivity*: covert properties of persons (thoughts), feelings, motives); conflicts between thoughts or feelings within the person	1. *Formation*: why (motives) and how (mechanisms) friendships are made; the ideal friend	1. *Formation*: why (motives) and how (mechanisms) groups are formed; the ideal member	1. *Formation*: motives for having children and why children need parents
2. *Self-awareness*: awareness of the self's ability to observe its own thoughts and actions	2. *Closeness*: types of friendship, ideal friendship, intimacy	2. *Cohesion–loyalty*: group unity	2. *Love and emotional ties*: between parents and children
3. *Personality*: stable or predictive character traits (a shy person, etc.)	3. *Trust*: doing things for friends; reciprocity	3. *Conformity*: range and rationale	3. *Obedience*: why children do as their parents tell them
4. *Personality change*: how and why people change (growing up, etc.)	4. *Jealousy*: feelings about intrusions into new or established friendships	4. *Rules–norms*: types of rules, and reasons for them	4. *Punishment*: the function of punishment from the parent's and the child's perspective
	5. *Conflict resolution*: how friends resolve problems	5. *Decision-making*: setting goals, resolving problems, working together	5. *Conflict resolution*: optimal ways for parents and children to resolve their differences
	6. *Termination*: how friendships break up	6. *Leadership*: qualities, and function to the group	
		7. *Termination*: why groups break up or members are excluded	

FIGURE 15. Issues of Interpersonal Understanding Related to Concepts of the Individual, Close Friendships, Peer-Group Organizations, and Parent-Child Relations (Selman, 1980).

Eight-year-old Tom is trying to decide what to buy his friend Mike for his birthday party. By chance, he meets Mike on the street and learns that Mike is extremely upset because his dog Pepper has been lost for two weeks. In fact, Mike is so upset that he tells Tom, "I miss Pepper so much I never want to look at another dog again." Tom goes off, only to pass a store with a sale on puppies; only two are left and those will soon be gone [Selman, 1980: 94].

The dilemma that Tom faces is whether or not to buy the puppy and he wonders how Mike would receive such a gift. After posing a dilemma, the interviewer follows up with standard questions, then with less structured questions to clarify the child's level of social reasoning. Sample questions from the interview are: "Mike said he never wanted to see another puppy again. Why did he say that?" Depending on the child's response level, the interviewer might pursue the issue through "stage-related" follow-up questions, such as these: "Can someone say something and not mean it?" "Is it possible that Mike does not know how he feels?" "Can you ever fool yourself into thinking you feel one way when you really feel another?" (Selman, 1980: 94).

This dilemma assesses the *issue* of self-awareness in the individual concepts domain. In each of the four social domains there are between four and seven issues (a total of twenty-two) that make up the practical concepts for assessing social cognition. Thus, for example, the six practical issues that are assessed in the friendship domain are:

1. The formation of friendships. How and why are friendships formed, and what might make an ideal friend?
2. The closeness of friendships. What are the different types of friendship? What constitutes the ideal kind of friendship? What is intimacy in friendship?
3. The role of trust in friendship. Under what circumstances does one do something for a friend and what is the role of reciprocity in friendship?
4. Jealousy in friendship. How does the person feel about the intrusion of others into an established friendship relationship?
5. Conflict resolution. How do friends resolve their conflicts when there is disagreement?
6. Termination of friendships. How and why are friendships terminated?

A similar group of issues are identified in the assessment of the other three social domains: individual, peer-group, and parent-child relations. In the following discussion of Selman's developmental stages of interpersonal understanding, at least one issue from each domain will serve as the focus of the presentation, in order to provide illustrations. The issue of *self-*

awareness will be the focus in the individual's concepts domain. *Conflict resolution* and *trust* will be used to illustrate the friendship concept domain. *Leadership* and *group loyalty* are the issues in the peer-group concepts domain, and *punishment* in the parent-child concepts domain. Having outlined the basic parameters of Selman's theory of social cognition, we will now turn to the five developmental stages of social perspective taking.

STAGE 0. EGOCENTRIC UNDIFFERENTIATED STAGE OF SOCIAL PERSPECTIVE TAKING (AGE THREE TO SIX)

At the egocentric undifferentiated stage of social perspective taking, children cannot make a clear distinction between their own interpretation of social situations and another's point of view. Nor can they understand that their own perception may not be the true or correct perspective. In social perspective-taking tasks, subject and object are not yet differentiated but are seen egocentrically from the subject's point of view. However, young children do seem to realize that the preferences and subjective experiences of others may be different from their own. Lacking still are the inferential skills to figure out what those subjective states of others could be. Children at this stage do not clearly distinguish between the physical and the psychological attributes of another individual. This confusion between subjective psychological and objective physical characteristics leads to difficulties in differentiating feeling from behavior, and it also interferes with the ability to distinguish intentional and unintentional behavior. While children understand that each person can have different feelings, they do not yet have the ability to determine how the thoughts and feelings of others might differ from their own (Forman and Sigel, 1979).

Characteristic of egocentric thinking is the cognitive inability to differentiate between different points of view. The differentiation between oneself and another is only accomplished in respect to physical qualities; the psychological characteristics remain undifferentiated. Since the subjective psychological perception remains undifferentiated, children are not aware that another person may interpret a social event quite differently (see Figure 16). Lacking is the awareness that another person possesses different perspectives; they cannot, so to speak, get "under the skin of another person," nor can they see the cause-effect relationship between

FIGURE 16. Figure and Other—Egocentric View. The other person is seen egocentrically, or undifferentiated from the self's own point of view.

thinking and behaving in other people. A girl may give her mother jelly beans for her birthday, not just because she herself likes jelly beans, or because she thinks her mother might like jelly beans, but because she views jelly beans as "things that are liked," without differentiating between her own point of view and those of others.

Self-Awareness in the Individual Concepts Domain. Stage 0 children are unable to differentiate an inner psychological experience from the more concrete nature of external experiences. They do possess an awareness of self; however, that self has quasi-physical attributes—for example, one part of the body tells another part what to do. When asked "When you think, where do you think?" the child may answer "In my mouth," or when asked "How do you think?" "My words tell me" (Selman, 1980: 95).

Conflict Resolution in the Friendship Concepts Domain. The child at this level uses two methods to resolve conflict. The first may be characterized as noninteraction; the child may say "Go play with another toy," or just "Go away." The going away is not thought of as a cooling off period but as an "out of sight, out of mind" approach to conflict resolution. The second approach is physical attack—"Go and hit him." No reflective consider-ations are given to such psychological variables as motives, feelings, or attitudes. Conflict is viewed not as a disagreement between two parties, but as a situation where one party does not get to do what he wants because of the behavior of the other party.

Leadership in the Peer-Group Concepts Domain. The young child views the leader as the one who has the physical power to tell group members what to do, and they must do it.

Punishment in the Parent-Child Concepts Domain. The Stage 0 child seems to be aware of the fact that punishment follows misbehavior but is unaware of the parents' motives for punishment. The child confuses punishment as a cause (I did something wrong because I was punished) and punishment as an effect (I was punished because I did something wrong).

The egocentric undifferentiated social perspective-taking stage seems to parallel closely the preoperational thinking structure in Piaget's theory of cognitive development and, in turn, seems to correspond to the premoral stage in Kohlberg's theory of moral judgment (see Figure 21).

STAGE 1. THE DIFFERENTIAL OR SUBJECTIVE PERSPECTIVE-TAKING STAGE OR THE SOCIAL-INFORMATIONAL ROLE-TAKING STAGE (AGE FIVE TO NINE)

Children at this stage realize that another person can have cognitive or social perspectives different from their own. One's subjective experiences are differentiated from the experiences of others; however, judgment of another person is still based on physical observations. The awareness dawns that others can interpret the same social situation differently.

Children understand that another person may feel or think differently because that person is in a different social situation or has access to different information. However, children are still unable to determine accurately what the other person's perspective looks like (Oppenheimer, 1978). In other words, they cannot maintain their own perspective and simultaneously assume the perspective of another. The interpersonal perspective of the other is conceived and conceptualized in one-way, unilateral terms (see Figure 17). Even though children realize that different perspectives of an event do exist, they still assume that there is only one correct point of view, either their own or that of the "authority."

There are three distinctive features of this level of social perspective taking. First, children become aware that they themselves and their own inner thoughts can be the object of another person's thinking, but they cannot accurately judge their own behavior as seen from the perspective of another person. There is no reciprocity between perspectives of self and others; perspective taking is a one-way affair. Only physical experiences can be understood as a two-way reciprocity—for example, the child who was hit, hits back. People react to the actions of other people with the same action.

Second, the Stage 1 child, in contrast to the Stage 0 child, distinguishes between the physical and the psychological dimensions of another person and between intentionality and unintentionality in behavior and thus begins to consider personal reasons as causes of actions. The child now realizes that others have their own unique psychological life, understands the concept of personal reasons, and recognizes that personal reasons are the causes of choices.

Third, Stage 1 children are capable of inferring the other person's intentions, feelings, and thoughts with some degree of accuracy. They also realize that other people have their own reasons for their thoughts and actions; however, the reasons themselves are not apparent to the outside observer, and since these children base their judgment of the feelings of others on physical observations, they are not always correct.

Self-Awareness. Since Stage 1 children are not yet able to distinguish between overt physical behavior and inward-looking psychological experiences, they do not yet understand that people may hide their true inner feelings. They know how to lie and know that others lie; however,

FIGURE 17. Self and Other—Interpersonal View. The other is seen as different from the self, but the other person's perception of the self is still undifferentiated.

they are not yet cognizant "that one can purposefully misrepresent one's inner experiences" (Selman, 1980: 96). Even though these children are aware that intention and behavior are two different things, they assume that the internal feelings eventually must manifest themselves in overt behavior. This is well illustrated by the child's responses to questions about the previously cited dilemma:

HOW DOES MIKE FEEL INSIDE? Sad.
HOW DO YOU KNOW? Because of the way he looks.
COULD HE LOOK SAD AND BE HAPPY INSIDE? He could but you would be able to tell if you watched him long enough; he'd show you he was happy [Selman, 1980: 97].

Finally, the distinction between awareness and unawareness is still quite vague and different from the more advanced levels that follow. "Fooling oneself" in the dilemma is seen more as changing one's feelings rather than as being unaware of them.

Conflict Resolution. The child begins to realize that the subjective or psychological effects in a conflict situation may be as important as the physical effects, the focus of attention of the Stage 0 child. However, awareness of the psychological effect is still a one-way proposition; that is, it can be applied to one of the two individuals involved in the situation. Thinking now expresses itself in two different approaches to the conflict situation:

1. to undo the actions that caused the conflict ("Give him back what you took from him.")
2. to perform a positive substitute action ("Give him something nice.")

The problem at this level is that the child assumes that a conflict is something started by one person, and reasons that the resolution of the conflict should come from that person; thus, conflict too is basically still a one-way proposition.

Friendship, Trust. Trust in a friendship relationship is also still a one-way proposition. The trust in a friendship is based, rather egotistically, on getting the other person to do what the child wants "his friend" to do. Selman quotes a child saying "You trust a friend if he does what you tell him" (Selman, Jaquette, and Lavin, 1977: 268).

Leadership. The child at Stage 1 of social perspective taking sees the leader as someone who (1) has the best skills and knowledge, and (2) helps the other members of the group to acquire skills ("He teaches them tricks"). Group leadership is still based on unilateral authority. Cooperation and coordination of activities are not yet evident.

Peer-Group Loyalty. Loyalty to the group becomes important at this stage, but the child defines loyalty as the "unilateral obedience to the dictates of a leader or other group members." One of Selman's eight-year-olds defines loyalty as "always doing what you are told, 'cause they kick you if you don't" (Selman, Jaquette, and Lavin, 1977: 269).

Punishment. In contrast to the earlier stage, the child now does consider the parents' motives for punishment; however, this too is seen as a one-way proposition, since the child does not yet consider the recipient's reactions toward punishment. Punishment serves three functions: (1) parents punish to teach their children a lesson; (2) punishment may be seen as a method parents use to protect their children from danger; and (3) punishment is viewed as a way of restoring the equilibrium—that is, "setting things straight" or "paying someone back."

The beginning of decentering in perspective taking characteristic of this stage of social cognition seems to find its counterpart in Piaget's transition from preoperational to operational thinking and is the developmental prerequisite for Kohlberg's stage one of moral judgment, "The Obedience and Punishment Orientation."

STAGE 2. SELF-REFLECTIVE THINKING OR RECIPROCAL PERSPECTIVE TAKING (AGE SEVEN TO TWELVE)

The preadolescent at Stage 2 realizes not only that other people have their own cognitive or social perspective because they think or feel differently, but the preadolescent also becomes aware that the other person thinks about his thinking and can take his, the subject's, role. Thus, the crucial developmental advance from Stage 1 to Stage 2 consists of the ability to leave oneself mentally and to take the perspective of another individual. The thought processes themselves can best be illustrated by the quote of a Stage 2 subject: "I know that she knows that I know she knows."

Individuals can now become capable of making inferences about the perspectives of other people; they can reflect about their own behavior and their own motivation as seen from the perspective of someone else. There is a self-reflecting anticipation of the other person's behavior toward the subject's own thought and purposes. However, such reflections about their own behavior and that of others are still limited since they do not occur simultaneously, but sequentially. Furthermore, they are aware that the other person can do the same thing (see Figure 18).

This new ability to reciprocate social perspectives introduces an awareness of relativity, since each person might have quite different goals, values, ideals, feelings, and thoughts. No single individual's social perspective is necessarily correct or valid in an absolute sense. Another person's point of view may be as correct as one's own.

In contrast to the mutual role-taking ability of Stage 3, which follows, perspective taking at Stage 2 is still based only on a two-way reciprocity; it is sequential but not yet simultaneous or mutual. The preadolescent thinks only within a two-person frame of reference—"I think; you think"—and cannot yet take a more general third-person perspective or understand a more general social relationship system.

Other people are now seen as operating on multimotivational levels rather than being motivated by one factor. The preadolescent becomes cognizant of the fact that one can experience two opposing emotions (such as repulsion and attraction) toward the same person or the same object simultaneously. Furthermore, the preadolescent can differentiate thoughts and feelings, and thus can understand that one might do some things that one did not intend to do. Preadolescents establish a hierarchy of motives and perceive the possibility that altruistic and instrumental motives may conflict with one another, both in their own mind and in the minds of others. They can take into account the hierarchy of motives in a situation where a person wants to do one thing but actually does another. A person's behavior may be the expression of different layers; outward clowning, for example, may be a cover-up for true hidden feelings of insecurity or unhappiness.

Self-Awareness. The Stage 2 preadolescent clearly distinguishes between outer (physical) and inner (psychological) reality and becomes aware that the two do not need to be congruent. Individuals may cover their true inner feelings to save face or avoid social embarrassment. Since preadolescents can take the perspective of another person, they can now monitor their own thoughts and actions from the perspective of another person. There emerges a new sense of priorities in that inner self-awareness matters more than outer appearances.

Conflict Resolution. The preadolescent in Stage 2 becomes aware that quite commonly both parties contribute to a conflict. Therefore, it becomes obvious that both parties must cooperate in seeking an effective solution. This is often done by appealing to the individual's sensitivity and good judgment. Lacking still is the notion of conflict resolution by mutual consensus. As in Stage 0, he may suggest a resolution of the conflict by getting away from each other; however, the idea in this suggestion is the establishment of a psychological space, or a cooling-off period.

Leadership. The preadolescent sees the issue of leadership as a reciprocal relationship. Leadership is based on bilateral equality and a reciprocity of

FIGURE 18.   Self and Other—Reciprocal View. The self can take the perspective of another person and becomes aware that the other person can also take the perspective of the self.

interest. The role of the leader is that of a mediator, organizer, and coordinator of group efforts. The leader encourages the efforts of group members through friendliness, recognition, support, and reward.

Friendship, Trust. Trust at Stage 2 is based much more on reciprocity between two friends than it was in Stage 1. However, self-interest still dominates the quality of trustworthiness in a friendship relationship, finding its clearest expression in the simple statement, "If you do something for me, I will do something for you."

Peer-Group Loyalty. Peer-group loyalty, like trust, is based on an even exchange of favors or mutual expression of affection, such as "I like you, if you like me," or "If he is loyal, the guys will be nice to one another."

Punishment. Punishment by parents may now be seen as an expression of the parents' concern for the child's well-being. He can conceptualize that parents punish to communicate with their children; thus, one purpose of punishment may be to make the child think about certain behavior. "Punishment is a message from one self-reflecting being to another" (Selman, 1980: 125). In addition, punishment is also seen as serving as a deterrent—it is likely to instill fear, which will become an internal agent of control in a similar situation.

The self-reflective perspective taking of Stage 2 finds its developmental parallel in Piaget's stage of operational thinking and sets the stage for the movement to stage two, "Instrumental Relativist Orientation," in Kohlberg's theory (see Figure 21).

STAGE 3. THE THIRD-PERSON OR MUTUAL PERSPECTIVE-TAKING STAGE (AGE TEN TO FIFTEEN)

The perspective-taking skills of early adolescence lead to a capacity for a more complex type of social cognition. The adolescent moves beyond simply taking the other person's perspective (in a back-and-forth kind of approach) and is able to see all parties from a more generalized third-person perspective. The third-person perspective "allows the adolescent to abstractly step outside an interpersonal interaction and simultaneously and mutually coordinate and consider the perspectives (and their interaction) of self and other(s)" (Selman, 1980: 39). In other words, the emerging concept of mutual role taking implies that adolescents can step outside of their own perspective and outside the partner's perspective and assume the perspective of a neutral third person. They thus can consider the mutual relationship involved, even as one of the participants (see Figure 19). As third-person observers they see themselves as both actor and object. Adolescents know that both they and their thoughts can also be the object of the other person's thought and vice versa (Oppenheimer, 1978).

Furthermore, there emerges the ability to distinguish between one's own point of view and a more generalized perspective that might be taken

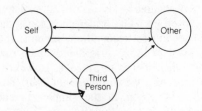

FIGURE 19. Self and Other—Objective View. The self can view the self–other interaction from the perspective of a neutral third person.

by an "average" member of the group. Adolescents can assume the role of such a disinterested average spectator and view the social interaction between themselves and somebody else from that spectator's position; they can see each party's perspective simultaneously and mutually. Furthermore, they reflect on their own self interacting with the self, an idea that Selman characterizes as "the observing ego."

Self-Awareness. The degree of self-awareness increases and the mind is seen as the observer of the self-aware self. Thus, the mind becomes the active psychological manipulator controlling the inner life. In other words, the mind is now viewed not as a storehouse of information but as an active participant deciding which ideas go where and which are kept out. Thus it becomes possible to fool the mind through an act of will. Thoughts and feelings may emerge even when opposed by will and mind. There is now a much more basic comprehension of the relationship between the self-as-subject and the self-as-object (Selman, 1980: 103).

Conflict Resolution. Friendship is now viewed not as a process of reciprocal back scratching but as a series of interactions over an extended period of time. They validate mutuality and involve emotional support and sharing of common feelings. Conflicts are seen as a natural, almost inevitable, part of a friendship relationship rather than as a problem of one individual. To resolve conflict in a friendship both sides must feel satisfied and both must be able to place themselves in the other person's shoes and be satisfied. Conflicts are seen as possibly emerging from different personality characteristics. Implied is the idea that a permanent conflict resolution might require some personality changes. In addition, there emerges the interesting notion that conflict resolution may actually contribute to strengthening a friendship—especially if there is a mutually satisfying way to work it out and find a harmonious compromise. Effectively working through a mutual problem seems to strengthen the commitment to the relationship. The adolescent can distinguish between the immediate or superficial reaction and the value of the long-term affectionate relationship. The bond that constitutes the friendship between the individuals becomes a factor contributing to conflict resolution. Mutual perspective taking, characteristic of early adolescence, implies an "active interpersonal communication and sharing" and relies on "verbal or mental rather than physical-action resolutions" (Selman, 1980: 112).

Trust. Friendship and trust during this stage are no longer defined as a fair exchange of favors. Friendship is built on a more basic and lasting mutual support system. More personal concerns and intimacies are shared; the relationship has more lasting consistency and one friend will stand up for the other "through thick and thin" even if there is no immediate benefit. "One thirteen-year-old said that trust in a friendship is when they get it off their chest if they talk to you; things that are going on in your life and in the other person's life" (Selman, Jaquette, and Lavin, 1977: 269).

Leadership. The group is viewed as a social system, and the role of the leader is to coordinate the efforts of the group, to hold the group together, to express the feelings of the group, and to encourage group solidarity. The leader encourages a sense of community and is seen as a catalyst in that process.

Loyalty. Loyalty to the group now requires a willingness to contribute to the welfare of the peer community, a kind of all-for-one loyalty. The underlying philosophy can be expressed by paraphrasing Kennedy's famous statement: "Ask not what the group can do for you, but what you can do for the group."

Punishment. Adolescents in this stage clearly distinguish between punishment as a general childrearing procedure and punishment that might be applied to themselves. They often feel that punishment is less applicable to them than to younger children. At this stage punishment is mutually perceived as serving a need for parents and a purpose for the child. Both parent and child have needs, characteristics, interests, and personalities that must be considered and, ideally, carefully weighed in a punishment decision. Adolescents now recognize that there may be methods other than punishment to achieve control or obedience and to ensure safety.

The mutual role-taking advances of adolescence seem to indicate the emergence (transition) of formal operations in the impersonal thinking domain and make possible the development of an "Interpersonal Concordance Orientation" in Kohlberg's moral judgment theory (see Figure 21).

STAGE 4. IN-DEPTH AND SOCIETAL PERSPECTIVE TAKING (ADOLESCENCE TO ADULT-HOOD)

During adolescence the individual may move to a still higher and more abstract level of interpersonal perspective taking, which now involves the "coordination of all possible third person perspectives—a societal perspective." The adolescent can conceptualize that the subjective perspectives of persons toward other persons not only operates on a level of common expectations and awareness but exists "simultaneously at multi-dimensional or deeper levels of communication" (Selman, 1980: 40). Thus, role taking is raised from the level of didactic relationships between people to the level of a general social system. "At this level the subject can compare and qualitatively contrast different sets and levels of perspectives" (Selman, 1976b: 160). Adolescents become aware of the relativity of perspectives held by themselves and by the social group. In other words, social facts are now understood as being interpreted by each individual according to that individual's own system of analysis (see Figure 20).

Stage 4 subjects understand that each person can consider the shared point of view of the "Generalized Other"—that is, the social system—which, in turn, makes possible accurate communication with and understanding of other people. Furthermore, the notion of law and morality as a social system depends on the idea of consensual group perspective, implied in Stage 4 role-taking ability. "At this level, the adolescent or young adult can abstract multiple mutual (generalized other) perspectives to a societal, legal or moral perspective in which all individuals can share" (Selman, 1980: 40).

There are two distinguishing features of the adolescents' conception of other people. First, they become aware that motives, actions, thoughts, and feelings are shaped by psychological factors. This notion of psychological determinants now includes the idea of the unconscious processes, although adolescents may not express this awareness in psychological terminology. Second, they begin to appreciate the fact that a personality is a system of traits, beliefs, values, and attitudes with its own developmental history.

Self-Awareness. Since adolescents are now discovering the idea of the unconscious mind, they become cognizant that there may be influences on thoughts, feelings, and motivations that they are not aware of and that, therefore, are not available for self-analysis. This means that beneath the inner reality of feelings and fantasies exists an even deeper reality that the individual is not aware of but that influences actions and behavior.

Friendship. The Stage 3 conception of friendship was characterized by an

FIGURE 20. Self and Other—Societal Perspective. The self can take a generalized societal perspective of the self–other interaction.

Piaget's Stages of Cognitive Development	Selman's Stages of Social Perspective Taking	Kohlberg's Stages of Moral Judgment
Stage 0	Sensorimotor and preoperational stages	The egocentric undifferentiated stage of social perspective taking	The premoral stage
Stage 1	Beginning of concrete operations	The differential or subjective perspective-taking stage or the social-informational role-taking stage	The obedience and punishment orientation
Stage 2	Well-developed concrete operations	Self-reflective thinking or mental perspective-taking stage	The instrumental relativist orientation
Stage 3	Beginning formal operations (Piaget's stage III-A)	The third-person or mutual perspective-taking stage	The interpersonal concordance orientation
Stage 4	Well-developed formal operations (Piaget's stage III-B)	The in-depth and societal perspective-taking stage	The orientation toward authority, law, and duty
Stage 5			The social contract orientation
Stage 6			The universal ethical principles orientation

FIGURE 21. Parallels Between Systems. The parallels between Piaget's stages of cognitive development, Selman's stages of social perspective taking, and Kohlberg's stages of moral judgment. According to Byrne (1974) at each stage, cognitive development appears to be a prerequisite for the corresponding stage of social perspective taking, which in turn precedes the emergence of the corresponding stage of moral judgment.

Adapted from Selman (1976a) and Papalia and Olds (1979).

awareness that friendships are based on close-knit mutuality. The adolescent in Stage 4 seems to reject that idea of mutuality partially, at least as long as it interferes with the autonomous growth and development of the individual. There is striving for independence, which may result in a rejection of overdependence and overbonding characteristic of Stage 3. However, friendship is based on an understanding that total independence is not the goal either, just as mutuality based on overdependence is not ideal. There is a striving for a balance between independence and dependence with a focus on the mutual relationships in the sense of "keeping the lines of communication open." The adolescent becomes aware that conflicts within one person may cause conflict between that person and his friend.

Trust. Adolescent and adult trust in friendship relationships becomes an ongoing process. "Trust means openness to change and growth, as well as stability in a relationship" (Selman, Jaquette, and Lavin, 1977: 269). The idea is well expressed by a college student who said, "Trust means that you've got to grow to let your friend grow. The more you hold on, the less you have. You have to have confidence in yourself as a good friend, then you'll have trust in your relationship" (Selman, Jaquette, and Lavin, 1977: 269).

Leadership. The leadership position is seen as being created by the group, and the leader's role, to enhance the collective good of the group. The leader is thus viewed as the embodiment of the group, and the function of the person is clearly separated from the leadership function. Leadership serves a fundamental social purpose that is abstracted from the members of the group. Furthermore, there now is a clearer understanding and differentiation of several different kinds of leadership.

Loyalty. Loyalty to the group takes on the quality of a contractual agreement. Loyalty presupposes that an individual member of the group is willing to relinquish personal goals for the benefit of the collective goals. "Loyalty is the unity of the group; that means that each member is willing to make a sacrifice for the good of the group—a sacrifice of himself" (Selman, Jaquette, and Lavin, 1977: 269).

Punishment. The one new idea that seems to emerge in the adolescent's conception of punishment is that punishment now may be seen as an unconscious effort to maintain psychological control over others.

The social perspective-taking ability identified as Stage 4, which constitutes the final and mature stage in social cognitive development, will not be reached by all adults. It corresponds to Piaget's ability to perform formal operations in logical reasoning and is the prerequisite for an orientation to the maintenance of social morality and social order as well as Kohlberg's postconventional level of moral judgment (see Figure 21).

Byrne (1974) investigated the relationship of these stages to Piaget's stages of logical development and Kohlberg's stages of moral judgment. He found that a relationship exists between Piaget's logical thinking stages and Selman's role-taking stages. However, the adolescent may reach a certain level of logical thinking without having reached the equivalent role-taking stage or moral judgment stage. On the other hand, rarely can an individual reach a given role-taking or moral judgment stage without having first attained the corresponding level of logical thinking. Furthermore, an individual may reach a certain social role-taking stage without evidence of an equivalent attainment in moral judgment, but it is unlikely that a specific moral judgment stage can be reached without the necessary role-taking stage. It thus appears that role taking is an intermediate step in social cognitive development that falls between the development of logical operations and the development of moral judgment during the years from ten to adulthood.

EDUCATIONAL IMPLICATIONS

Selman's theory supports an educational philosophy that emphasizes affective education, altruism, sympathy, social problem solving, and an increased social awareness. It implies a movement away from a limited concern with only the cognitive side of learning, toward an inclusion of interpersonal, social cognitive awareness.

The application of social cognition theory to education in general and curriculum in specific rests on the assumption that training in social reasoning will lead to more adequate forms of social functioning and produce an increase in the complexity and the effectiveness of social reasoning (Enright, 1976). Marsh, Serafica, and Barenboim (1980) were able to demonstrate that early adolescents could actually be trained in perspective-taking skills and that such training did indeed have a positive effect on the ability to solve interpersonal problems. Social problem solving was assessed by asking each subject to assume that one of his three close friends must be excluded from a rock concert and to develop an appropriate excuse. There were several interpersonal problems of this nature, and subjects had to decide: What is the problem? What factors must be considered? What are alternative ways of solving the problem? What are the consequences for each solution?

In another study it was shown that children who had developed better perspective-taking skills are more likely friendly, helpful, and show social problem-solving behavior when confronted with a child in need of assistance than are children with less social perspective-taking skills (Hudson, Peyton, and Brion-Maisels, 1976). Other researchers (Rosen, 1974; Shure and Spivack, 1978; Spivack and Shure, 1974) have reported similar positive effects of perspective-taking training on younger children. However, in these studies the perspective-taking part of the program was embedded in a more general social problem-solving context. The Shure and Spivack (1978) interpersonal problem-solving script is not designed only to help children in solving specific problems "now"; it is also intended to teach them to cope with new social problems, which inevitably will arise in the future. The two most important interpersonal problem-solving skills are *alternative-solution thinking* (the social skill to produce many different solutions to a problem), and *consequential thinking* (the social skill to predict what is most likely to happen with each alternative solution).

The movement from lower to higher levels of social cognition is a matter of interaction between nature and nurture. Growth in social cognition comes partly as a result of maturation, hence its strong association with age. However, social reasoning develops also as a result of experiences, stimulation, and education. The educational method that appears to be valuable in stimulating interpersonal growth is not a lecture or expository mode of teaching, but an exploratory mode of teaching, such as discussion and debate (Selman, 1976a).

A quite different educational issue suggests that methods of childrearing and the disciplinary methods of control used at home and in school may have an influence on social interpersonal development, and that certain kinds of childrearing practices help develop interpersonal skills, social cognition, and moral judgment.

Martin reviewed the literature investigating the influence of childrearing methods on moral development, and he reports that the following conditions foster moral development: "The parents of children with more mature conceptions of right and wrong favored high 'cognitive structuring,' including making clear statements of parental expectations, involving general moral principles to guide behavior, and emphasizing the consequences to others of the child's misbehavior" (Moore, 1979: 57). Other factors that were identified as making similar contributions to social cognitive development were a high degree of warmth toward children and low frequency in threat of punishment.

Spivack and Shure provide an entire training program or curriculum for teaching social problem-solving skills, and Elardo has developed a similar program to foster children's social awareness (Spivack and Shure, 1974; Elardo, 1974).

Recognizing the social cognitive stages of each child may help the teacher in several ways:

1. The teacher can better understand the behavior of the class by understanding how children view social relationships, rights, and obligations.
2. The teacher can better determine his/her own expectations for student's developmental goals, and

3. The teacher learns not to overestimate the affective, as well as the cognitive capacity of children [Selman, 1976a: 310].

Selman's work gives emphasis to an important, often neglected, educational goal: the development of understanding, sensitivity, and skills in social awareness, interpersonal relationships, and social problem-solving skills.

12: SOCIAL COGNITION. PART 2: DAVID ELKIND'S THEORY OF ADOLESCENT EGOCENTRISM

THE CONCEPT OF EGOCENTRISM

"Egocentrism" refers to the inability to clearly differentiate the nature of the subject-object interaction, or the subject-object relationship. Egocentric children cannot yet differentiate themselves from the rest of the world. The separation of the self from others and from objects is incomplete or difficult. Egocentric children consider their own *subjective point of view* as representing objective reality and even as the only possible point of view. They assume that others automatically share their pains and pleasures. The essential meaning of egocentrism has been defined as "an embeddedness in one's own point of view" (Looft, 1971: 485), and in that sense egocentrism is the opposite of role- or perspective-taking. Egocentric children thus are unable to put themselves phenomenologically into the situation or the position of someone else because they are not aware that other people have a different point of view. They think that everybody else thinks as they do. In its more primitive form, children believe that objects or landscapes do not look different from other perspectives, but that their own perspective is the "real," the only, perspective. In the early phases of development, egocentrism is so pervasive that it permeates virtually all spheres of functioning: cognition, perception, speech, emotions, and attitudes.

In the history of mankind, egocentrism is analogous to the earlier belief that the whole universe revolved around the earth. Copernicus, by discovering that the sun rather than the earth is the center of our planetary system, replaced the egocentric view of the world with a scientific view, contributing to the decentering process in man's view of himself in the larger scheme. Egocentric children view themselves as the center of the universe.

The concept "egocentrism" comes from Piaget's theory of cognitive development and is defined as the lack of differentiation between one's own point of view and those of others. Piaget is concerned with basic laws of development. Samples of such laws relevant to the decline in egocentrism as one moves from childhood to adolescence are:

1. All mental growth moves in a specific direction; that is, it moves from an egocentric toward a sociocentric orientation toward reality.
2. Mental growth is characterized by an increasing differentiation between subject and object, between thought and reality (Elkind, 1968: 143).
3. The child's language patterns change with increasing age from egocentric to sociocentric speech patterns.
4. Increasing cognitive maturation is characterized by the ability to decenter one's own thought processes. Abundant research evidence shows that egocentric thought processes decrease with age and the ability to decenter increases with age.
5. The entire process of cognitive development is an orientation process. Step by step, children realize that they are not the center of the world and that other persons and objects have their own independent existence. Children also slowly realize that the perceptions of other people are quite independent of their own.
6. The process of decentration of thinking is the essence of intellectual development. As intellectual maturity is developed, one's own limited egocentric point of view is replaced by the recognition of many possible different viewpoints.

According to Elkind (1967), as cognitive development progresses through the stages identified by Piaget (sensorimotor, preoperational, operational, and formal), the nature, quality, and characteristics of egocentrism change correspondingly, and each developmental stage has its own unique characteristics. The transition from one stage to another proceeds in a dialectic fashion: The emerging new and more sophisticated cognitive structures, which free the child from the entanglement in a lower-level egocentrism, lead to a higher-level egocentrism. In this sense egocentrism can be said to be a negative but necessary by-product of cognitive development, for it creates at each stage "a new set of unrealistic, non-object representations of the world" (Looft, 1971: 486), and thus the concept egocentrism enriches our understanding of the social and emotional domains that accompany cognitive development.

The major mechanism that contributes to the decline of egocentrism and to movement from lower to higher levels of egocentrism is the developmental process of decentering. The decentering process makes it possible to shift the focus of awareness from one limited aspect of reality or the self to several features and eventually to a whole array of different dimensions. Each of these steps produces a reorganization and expansion of earlier perceptions. The child decenters by becoming aware that he is not the center of the world and realizing that an object or another person has an existence of its own, quite independent of how it is perceived or who perceives it. Being able to assume the point of view of another person indicates a social decentration, that is, an increase in role-taking ability. The concepts of decentration and role-taking have been used in the literature as synonyms rather than as two different processes (Shantz, 1975). One can distinguish between social, emotional, and cognitive perspective-taking skills. Essentially, the development of decentration is facilitated by social interaction, because one-sided and one-dimensional perceptions are challenged and must be reexamined in view of the ideas expressed by others. In reconciling the dissonance between one's own one-sided perspective and the point of view of others, the individual progresses to see several dimensions of an issue and learns to take another person's point of view.

STAGES OF EGOCENTRISM

For each major stage of egocentrism, Elkind (1967) has identified a special problem of cognition that, although not the only problem, gives the egocentric thought at that stage its unique characteristics.

SENSORIMOTOR EGOCENTRISM (BIRTH TO AGE TWO)

The first stage can best be characterized as radical egocentrism, since infants lack the ability to differentiate between themselves and the larger world. The major cognitive task of the sensorimotor child is the conquest of the object.

Sensorimotor egocentrism implies a lack of ability to differentiate between the actual object and the sensory impressions that the object produces. Egocentrism at this stage is the belief that one's sensory impressions are essential for the existence of the object. "At the sensorimotor level, the infant does not at first know how to separate the effects of his own actions from the qualities of external objects or persons" (Inhelder and Piaget, 1958: 342). Egocentrism begins to decline when the infant realizes that the existence of an object is independent of his subjective perception of it; that is, as the concept of *object permanence* develops, sensorimotor egocentrism declines.

PREOPERATIONAL EGOCENTRISM (AGE TWO TO SIX)

The major cognitive task during the preschool period is the *conquest of the symbol,* and the most important symbolic system to be acquired is speech. Other areas where symbol confusion is common are self-created play symbols representing unavailable objects (e.g. the chair is imagined to be a train) and symbols that appear in dreams.

The preoperational egocentrism consists of the inability to differentiate between the symbol and its referent. The child does not yet understand the relationship between the signifier and what is signified (Elkind, 1968: 144). Initially, the symbols are viewed as *identical to their referents*. Furthermore, children believe that their personal perspective of the world is shared by others. The child has a particular understanding of the world and believes that everybody shares this particular view (and takes for granted that others think the same way). Egocentrism at the preoperational level takes the form of a ''relative lack of differentiation both between ego's and alter's point of view, between subjective and objective, but this time the lack of differentiation is representational rather than sensori-motor'' (Inhelder and Piaget, 1958: 343).

CONCRETE OPERATIONAL EGOCENTRISM (AGE SEVEN TO ELEVEN)

The major cognitive task of the operational child is the mastery of classes, relations, and quantities. Thinking has progressed to the point where elementary deductive and concrete logical thinking have become possible. In the concrete operational stage the process of decentering has gone so far that the child is ''able to structure relationships between classes, relations and numbers objectively. . . . He acquires skills in interindividual relations in a cooperative framework'' (Inhelder and Piaget, 1958: 343).

The school age child can nest classes, seriate relations, and conserve quantities; furthermore, he can now perform elementary syllogistic rea-soning and advance hypotheses as long as they concern concrete objects (Elkind, 1967). These operational skills of logical thinking lift children out of the egocentrism of the preoperational stage; however, at the same time they lower them into a new kind of egocentrism.

Children can advance concrete hypotheses about reality, but they do not realize that their hypotheses are their own mental constructs and must be tested against reality to be verified. Egocentric children too readily accept their own hypotheses as factually given and believe that the facts must adapt to fit their hypotheses. Concrete operational egocentrism consists of the inability to differentiate with some degree of accuracy between the products of one's own mental reasoning and what is perceptually given. To say it differently, it is the inability to differentiate between what one thinks and what one perceives. The inability to differentiate clearly between an assumption and a fact is what constitutes concrete operational egocentrism (Looft, 1971).

The failure to differentiate between hypothesis and fact means that the child may treat hypotheses as if they were facts and treat facts as if they were hypotheses. When these children produce a mental construct, they believe that the products of their thinking are real rather than the result of mental reasoning. When challenged, they do not change their mental constructions but reinterpret the data to fit the initial assumption. For example, when a child makes up an excuse or a story, he begins believing his own fabrications and defends them as if they were the truth. His own mental constructions "are experienced as imbued with a [logical] necessity" (Elkind, 1967: 1028).

Concrete egocentrism can best be illustrated by the findings of a research study by Weir (1964) entitled "Developmental Changes in Problem-Solving Strategies." The subjects, age four to seventeen, were exposed to a probability learning task involving a candy delivery machine with three knobs; one paid 66 percent of the time, one 33 percent, and one never. The child's task is to find a maximum pay-off strategy. Preoperational children maximized surprisingly early. They solved the problem without trying to figure it out cognitively. Their strategy was based primarily on trial and error. Adolescents developed various hypotheses, tested and rejected them, and eventually settled down to pressing the 66 percent knob all the time. They came to the right solution by reasoning it out. Operational children had considerable difficulties; they persisted rather stubbornly with wrong hypotheses, even though they had not found a strategy that paid off continuously. They tended to blame the machine ("It's rigged!") rather than attacking their own rigid adherence to incorrect hypotheses.

ADOLESCENT EGOCENTRISM (AGE ELEVEN TO ADULTHOOD)

The major cognitive task of adolescence is the *mastery of thought processes* that are logical and abstract. During adolescence, in the stage of formal operations, "the adolescent not only tries to adapt his ego to the social environment but, just as empathetically, tries to adjust the environment to his ego. . . . The result is a relative failure to distinguish between his own point of view . . . and the point of view of the group" (Inhelder and Piaget, 1958: 343). The adolescent learns to use formal operations in logic, to use combinatorial analysis, to construct contrary-to-fact propositions, and to form theories. This new mode of formal operational thinking is characterized by two abilities:

    a) the ability to think about one's own thinking, and
    b) the ability to recognize possibility as well as actualities [Looft, 1971: 487].

These abilities eliminate the egocentrism of the concrete operational stage, but contribute to the emergence of adolescent egocentrism.

Since adolescents in the formal operational stage acquire the ability to conceptualize their own thought processes, they now become able to submit their own thinking to introspection and to reflect on their own mental processes and personality traits (Elkind, 1967/68: 429). They also begin to conceptualize in their own minds the thought processes of others, especially their peers, and they are able to differentiate between their own thoughts and those of other people, but not between the objects that the thoughts of others are directed toward and objects that are the focus of their own concern. "It is this capacity to take account of other people's thought, however, which is the crux of adolescent egocentrism" (Elkind, 1967: 1029). Adolescents surmise that they become the object of the thoughts of others as if all others were personally concerned with them. "This egocentrism is one of the most enduring features of adolescence; it persists until the new and later decentering which makes possible the true beginnings of adult work" (Inhelder and Piaget, 1958: 343).

Actually, the thoughts of early adolescents are very much concerned with their own behavior, body changes, and physical appearance. There is a great deal of self-absorption, and psychoanalysts even speak of a resurgence of narcissism in adolescence (Blos, 1962). "It is this belief that others are preoccupied with his appearance and behavior that constitutes the egocentrism of the adolescent" (Elkind, 1967: 1030). The young child was unable to take another person's point of view; the adolescent, however, "takes the other person's point of view to an extreme degree. He is so concerned with the point of view of others and how they regard him that he often loses sight of his own point of view" (Elkind, 1968: 153). The concept of egocentrism thus can explain the power of the peer group over the individual during adolescence.

Egocentrism in thinking leads to a preoccupation with physical characteristics, so that each individual adolescent attaches much greater significance to his or her own physical attributes, especially shortcomings, than the peer group does. The egocentric dimension of the problem is that the adolescent does not yet recognize this. As soon as they realize that others are much less critical than they themselves are their egocentrism begins to disperse.

This kind of egocentrism is often exaggerated when individuals have a physical defect or an abnormality. They feel that the eyes of everyone are focused on them and that their defect is the topic of conversation when they are absent, or behind their backs. Surprisingly, this is even more true with minor defects or developmental deviations that are not immediately noticeable than with serious defects, the obvious reality of which cannot be denied by children and adults. For this reason those with physical deformities or deviations, though relatively happy and well adjusted as children, often experience their first real depression as they enter adolescence and begin to reflect on what others may think.

Another illustration of egocentric thinking is the not uncommon occurrence of an adolescent girl wearing a new dress or a new hair style and who cannot understand why others do not notice these new and carefully selected attributes. She egocentrically thinks that everybody is as concerned with her appearance as she is—and gets sulky if she does not receive the expected comments and compliments.

The idea of egocentrism can even be applied as an explanatory principle to several characteristics of youth in contemporary society:

> attention getting behavior may well express this egocentric need to be noticed, evaluated, visible, and "on stage.". . . shortlived romantic affairs, conformity to the influence of the peer group, and even friendships may serve an egocentric need for self-definition and self-respect [Elkind, 1968: 153, 154].

The egocentrically thinking adolescent feels that others (especially peers) are as critical and as concerned and admiring as he himself is. Consequently, he constructs and reacts and plays to what Elkind (1967) has characterized as an *imaginary audience*. The adolescent imagines that he is the center of attention of this audience of peers—a product of his own thinking rather than a real audience. This construct of the imaginary audience may help to account for the adolescent's common feeling of self-consciousness. Furthermore, since the audience is actually the product of the adolescent's own mental construction, each boy or girl knows precisely what this imaginary audience is looking for (or at) in terms of clothes, hair style, breast development, physical skills, improprieties, blemishes, being too fat or too thin, overall body configuration, and so on. In other words, the individual's own critical self-evaluations and preoccupations are superimposed or projected on this self-made audience. The adolescent boy believes that they are aware of the hardly noticeable spot on his trousers, or that he has been biting his fingernails again, or even that he has masturbated. The imaginary audience is assumed to be just as repulsed by these atrocities as he is. Adolescents will wear outlandish clothes to please this audience, sass the teacher to gain applause, or participate in other wild and risk taking behavior that may earn the audience's respect and admiration. Thus the adolescent is constantly on stage, and sees himself as the principal actor, and all peers are the audience. The adolescent's need for privacy and reluctance toward self-disclosure in other situations may well be a reaction against the egocentric feeling of being constantly evaluated, watched, and compared by peers.

Actually, most of the adolescent's peers are preoccupied with themselves and their own imaginary audience. Hence, in actuality they pay much less attention to each other than each assumes they do. For example, before a formal date the boy may spend a long time in front of the mirror making himself attractive, imagining his girl friend's reactions. The girl similarly changes her clothes repeatedly, rearranges her hair, and experiments with make-up in front of the mirror for hours, imagining the boy's reactions. When the two actually meet, they are much more concerned with being observed than with being the observer (Elkind, 1967).

A corollary concept that defines the nature of the adolescent's egocentrism is each individual's belief in his own *uniqueness*. Elkind uses the term "the personal fable" to identify this notion of uniqueness. The personal fable is seen in many adolescents' convictions that their beliefs, their feelings, their ideals are very special, even unique, and that others do not have and cannot even understand such feelings. The conviction that emerges is: I am a unique individual, nobody else has my experiences or my feelings. This idea of the uniqueness of feelings, thoughts, and experiences is a very common theme of many adolescent diaries. And puberty is the time when this kind of egocentric thinking is at its peak. The diaries of adolescents frequently illustrate a mixture of both acute egocentricity and an emotional and selfless devotion to humanity (Piaget, 1967). The diary becomes the only "confidante" to whom one can speak and who understands. At the same time parents are admonished by their offspring, "But, you don't know how it feels. . . ." Blos speaks of the vicarious relationship between outer reality and internal experiences during adolescence proper. However, in a more general sense—and here Blos writes about the same idea of *egocentric uniqueness* that Elkind developed from a cognitive point of view—"the fact remains that the adolescent does experience the outer world with a unique sensory quality which he thinks is not shared by others: 'Nobody ever felt the way I do.' 'Nobody sees the world the way I do.' Mother Nature becomes a personal respondent to the adolescent; the beauty of nature is discovered and exalted emotional states are experienced" (Blos, 1962: 93).

Part of the personal fable is the belief in one's own *indestructibility,* which impairs judgment in critical situations since it provides a false sense of power, often with catastrophic consequences (Blos, 1962). This attitude may find expression in the following convictions:

Death will never happen to me.
Pregnancy will never happen to me.
Accidents will never happen to me.
Drug addiction will never happen to me.
Alcohol addiction will never happen to me.
Marriage problems will never happen to us.

Egocentrism in the cognitive structure of the adolescent makes it difficult for the individual to differentiate between his own highly idealistic thought processes (how things ought to be) and the real world (how things are). "Adolescent egocentricity is manifested by belief in omnipotence of reflection, as though the world should submit itself to idealistic schemes rather than to systems of reality. It is the metaphysical age par excellence; the self is strong enough to reconstruct the universe and big enough to incorporate it" (Piaget, 1967: 64). Adolescents cannot and will not understand why the rest of the world does not accept their idealistic solutions to social, economic, or ecological problems, and they may get angry and express unwillingness to accept reality. The adolescent tries to adjust his ego to the real world. "In effect, the adolescent not only constructs ideal families, religions and societies, he also constructs ideal persons. The short-lived adolescent crush is a case in point" (Elkind, 1967/68: 432).

The results of this untested idealism are that adolescents dream "of a glorious future" which they hope to attain by transforming the world through ideas. They are idealistically critical of the way things are and unwilling to compromise between contending parties or ideas. Indeed, adolescents are often exceedingly effective in suggesting how to change the real world.

RESEARCH SUPPORT FOR AN ADOLESCENT EGOCENTRISM THEORY

The concept of egocentrism has been investigated extensively during the last decade. However, most studies have used younger children as subjects, and much of the methodology is based on Piaget's classical study of the child's perspective-taking skills, using a model landscape of the three different-sized mountains (see Chapter 8).

Research using adolescent subjects and focusing on adolescent egocentrism, in contrast, is sparse. However, those few research studies that do investigate the imaginary audience, the personal fable, adolescent self-consciousness, and adolescent role-taking skills contribute significantly to an understanding of adolescent social and emotional development.

Several generalizations emerge from egocentrism research with children, some of which cut across several developmental periods, and hence are relevant to our overall considerations:

1. Most widely supported is the theoretical assumption that egocentrism decreases with age and is replaced by a sociocentric point of view as the individual matures. With increasing age, the ability to decenter expands (Rubin, 1973; Stuart, 1967; Sullivan and Hunt, 1967). This fundamental theoretical assertion seems to hold true for several dimensions of egocentrism:

> spatial or cognitive egocentrism—visual perspective taking
> social egocentrism, or role-taking egocentrism
> communicative egocentrism
> egocentric speech
> affective or emotional egocentrism

2. Rubin (1973) has shown that a significant interrelationship exists among such social cognition concepts as spatial egocentrism, role-taking egocentrism, communicative egocentrism, and Piaget's concept of conservation. Rubin defines the commonality of these concepts as the "centration factor."

3. Piaget suggested in *Language and Thought of the Child* (1932a), that as the child moves from the preoperational stage to the operational stage of thinking, egocentric speech patterns decline and sociocentric speech patterns increase. Furthermore, he assumed as a correlate that the more egocentric children would be less popular (since they cannot take their peers' point of view) than children who are less egocentric. There is at least some evidence for this assertion, especially with younger children (Deutsch, 1974).

4. A negative relationship was found between egocentric speech patterns and the quality of peer interaction. Rubin calls this "communicative egocentrism" (Rubin, 1972; 1976).

5. More egocentric children have less adequate social schemata to understand such concepts as conformity and independence (Weinheimer, 1972) and are more likely to conform than less egocentric children (Tierney and Rubin, 1975).

6. The ability to decenter has been shown to be positively correlated with the ability to make mature moral and causal judgments (Stuart, 1967; Rubin and Schneider, 1973).

7. Institutionalized emotionally disturbed children are significantly more egocentric than noninstitutionalized children (Neale, 1966).

8. The idea of egocentric thought versus nonegocentric thought is not the same as Piaget's fundamental distinction between concrete and abstract thinking. Concrete evaluations can be egocentric or nonegocentric. Abstract evaluations, on the other hand, are most likely nonegocentric. In general, research has demonstrated that the basic developmental progression from concrete to abstract evaluation is paralleled by a corresponding transition from egocentric to nonegocentric thinking.

More recently, Elkind and Bowen (1979) have begun to examine the concept of adolescent egocentrism empirically, the focus of their investigation being the *imaginary audience* (defined as the belief that others are as concerned with our thoughts and behavior as we are). The researchers distinguished between (1) the *abiding self,* or long-lived permanent personality traits, such as mental ability, and (2) the *transient component of the self,* which is the momentary issue and transient behavior, such as the reaction of the adolescent to a bad haircut or a spot on an outfit or an unguarded inappropriate comment.

In agreement with the theoretical assumption of an imaginary audience created by the early adolescent, eighth-graders were significantly more self-conscious than both younger children and older adolescents. This finding was true for both subscales of the test, the abiding self and the transient self of the Imaginary Audience Scale. Elkind and Bowen also reported that females were more concerned about the imaginary audience at all age levels than males. This sex difference is consistent with previous research that has shown girls to be more self-conscious, more conforming, and more concerned about an imaginary audience than boys (Simmons, Rosenberg, and Rosenberg, 1973). Early adolescents are more self-conscious about imperfections and less willing to reveal their abiding self or transient self. Even if they were to go to a party with a grease spot on their clothes, they would be much more likely than either younger children or older adolescents to modify their behavior so that the spot would not be revealed to others. They say, for example, "I would stand in a dark corner," "I would hold my hand over the spot," or "I would spill something on the spot during the party."

Young adolescents, more than either the younger or the older age groups, think that they are able to conceal facts of the transient self (such as the spot) from peers. The desire to conceal imperfections in attire, appearance, and manners is interpreted as evidence of the awareness and the influence of the imaginary audience.

Enright and his colleagues (Enright, Lapsley, and Shukla, 1979; Enright and Sutterfield, 1980), in two methodologically similar studies using different population samples, investigated the relationship between adolescent egocentrism, sociocentrism, self-consciousness, and age, and thus contributed further to an understanding of egocentrism. These investigations focused on three components of egocentrism: the personal fable, the imaginary audience, and general self-focus. In addition, they included two additional subscales, identified as sociocentrism and nonsocial concerns, the assumption being that with increasing maturity, adolescents become more concerned with general social and political issues rather than with just their own world and their immediate social group.

The findings, even though based on a different methodology, are quite consistent both with Elkind's (1967) theoretical construct of adolescent egocentrism and with Elkind and Bowen's (1979) findings. Specifically, Enright et al. found support in their data for the following:

1. As adolescents move from early adolescence to late adolescence, there is a decline in the personal fable (that is, the belief that one is special and unique). Females are more inclined to believe the personal fable than are males.

2. Similarly, as a function of adolescent development, there is a decline in the importance of the imaginary audience (believing that others pay more attention to the individual than they actually do). Females, again, are more aware of an imaginary audience than are males.

3. Nonsocial concerns (such as watching TV) lose their importance as a function of adolescent development.
4. Political awareness or sociocentric focus (keeping up with the news) increases in importance with increasing age.
5. Self-consciousness is moderately correlated with egocentrism.
6. Egocentrism and sociocentrism are negatively correlated during adolescence, suggesting that as a function of development the former declines while the latter increases in importance.
7. Self-focus is high in early adolescence and declines during high school, but a surprising heightening of self-focus takes place in college. Females are reported as more self-focused than males.

Michael Chandler (1973) explored the role that a persistent social egocentrism might play in the development and maintenance of chronic antisocial behavior. Egocentrism was defined as the "relative inability to recognize or take into account the privileged character of one's own private thoughts and feelings." Social egocentrism, when it becomes a developmental deficit, interferes with the ability to assess the needs of others and to perform adequately in situations requiring empathy and social cooperation. As was shown in the studies cited above, in normal development, social egocentrism declines with age and makes space for a more sociocentric orientation that includes an understanding of other people's needs and the ability to take their perspective into account, to cooperate, and to empathize. Chandler hypothesized that a prolonged adherence to social egocentrism or a developmental delay of social perspective-taking skills during adolescence may be a crucial variable in the maintenance of antisocial behavior. Developmental delay in sociocentric thought has been shown to be related to a misunderstanding of social expectations, a misjudgment in the actions and intentions of others, and a disrespect for the rights and feelings of others. Social deviancy is therefore assumed to be associated with persistent egocentric thought if the latter is age-inappropriate. In accordance with these theoretical propositions, Chandler observed that a group of chronic delinquent adolescents did indeed have much greater difficulties in assuming the roles or perspectives of others than a nondelinquent control group. The assessment of social egocentrism was based on a series of ten cartoon sequences in which the behavior of a major character was shaped by a series of events. In the middle of such a sequence of events, a second character was introduced who did not know what had happened earlier. The question was, to what extent could subjects distinguish between their own complete, but partly privileged information and the more limited information of the late-arriving bystander.

Example: A boy had brought his father to the airport and was deeply saddened by his father's departure. Later he received a package with a toy airplane, which made the boy cry again as he remembered his father's departure. The mailman who witnessed the boy's distress on opening the package had, of course, no knowledge of the antecedent events [Chandler, 1973].

The subject who had all the information of the story was to assume the role of the mailman. The purpose was to determine whether the subject could set aside the privileged information known only to him and take the perspective of the late-arriving mailman, or whether he would intermingle the two perspectives, assigning to the mailman information that he, the mailman, could not possibly have.

Chandler did find that the group of chronic delinquent adolescents had much greater difficulty in correctly assuming the role or perspective of the late-arriving bystander. A nondelinquent control group had little difficulty in separating their own privileged information of the full story from the partial information of the late arriver.

The second contribution to egocentrism theory in Chandler's study dealt with the value of intervention, examining two issues: (1) Can social perspective-taking skills be taught? and (2) Does a reduction in social egocentrism have an effect on delinquent behavior? The training in social perspective-taking skills involved acting out dramas and making video films in which the subject takes the perspective, or the role, of a particular character.

When chronic delinquent adolescents were given systematic training in social perspective-taking skills, their level of egocentrism declined significantly. Since only half of the chronic delinquents received such training, Chandler was able to show, in a long-range follow-up study, that those chronic delinquents who had received special training in role-taking skills had a much lower recidivism rate than the delinquent control group. Apparently, social deviance is associated with egocentric thinking, and reducing social egocentrism through training in social perspective-taking skills tends to reduce the rate of delinquent behavior. Although one study may be insufficient evidence to start large-scale social action programs in an attempt to fight juvenile delinquency, nevertheless adolescent egocentrism theory does hold promise of having far-reaching implications.

EDUCATIONAL IMPLICATIONS

Assuming that the intriguing findings by Chandler (1973) are generalizable and replicable, it would appear most appropriate to provide children and adolescents with systematic learning opportunities that would require them to project themselves into the psychological situation of another human being. Some possibilities would be role playing, theatre productions, movie making, and verbal exercises similar to the mailman example discussed above and used as a method to assess egocentrism. Shantz, after an extensive review of the social cognition literature, concludes that role-taking skills "seem to be fostered by the opportunity to enact various roles" (1975: 310). Some role-taking activities are, of course, offered in schools, but usually only on the initiative of an especially interested teacher or for children and adolescents who are attracted to such activities and volunteer for such courses and/or programs. However, role playing and related "acting" activities are not generally and systematically offered as tools for aiding the social and personal development in a way that reaches all children.

Steinberg and his associates (1981) have suggested that early work experiences—including part-time and summer work—may enhance the development of social understanding during adolescence and thus serve as a partial antidote to adolescent egocentrism. Working experiences are assumed to have a potentially positive impact on the worker by advancing social as well as cognitive development. In the work setting, the adolescent must learn to shift between very diverse roles quickly and effectively. In a certain situation he must act authoritatively (e.g., in relationship to customers or to a junior worker), at other times he must behave deferentially (e.g., toward a supervisor or boss), at still other times he is expected to react to people on an egalitarian basis (e.g., toward coworkers). Furthermore, many jobs require frequent interaction with strangers who may be quite different in age, background, and attitude.

Social interaction patterns among the typical high school students frequently are limited to peers, teachers, and family members, and relationships with the latter two are often based on stereotyped attitudes and/or long established response patterns. In the economic marketplace, egocentrism, pseudostupidity, and social insensitivity (afflictions from which adolescents supposedly suffer and about which teachers frequently complain) are not rewarded but are quickly extinguished. Steinberg and his associates observed that egocentricity, pseudostupidity, and social insensitivity decline dramatically when the adolescent is paid in accordance with his willingness to behave in a nonegocentric fashion. It has been claimed that the kind of role-taking skills that the work setting requires will enhance the acquisition of skills that are not usually taught in school, and thus will contribute "to the development of responsibility and a sense of competency, lessen feelings of alienation and purposelessness and help to break down intergenerational barriers" (Steinberg et al., 1981: 142) and, more importantly, will show how to interact with various other people.

Teaching adolescents formally about the concept of egocentrism might better help them understand and deal with the problems that emerge from egocentric thoughts. Problems related to peer group conformity, preoccupation with physical development and physical appearance, excessive concern with what others think, and the egocentric need for risk-taking behavior with its social and health implications are fairly common during adolescence. And even if such understanding does not necessarily solve these problems, the individual would at least have a frame of reference within which to evaluate his own thinking. Furthermore, the idiosyncratic behavior of their peers would begin to be seen in a new light.

For the educator the most important insight to be gained from these considerations is the fact that adolescent egocentrism exists as a common, normal developmental phenomenon. Adolescents, even though they may have reached the operational stage of thinking—and partly because they are beginning to think operationally—still think in ways that are qualitatively different from those of the mature adult whose thought processes have become sociocentric. These differences need to be more fully recognized and appreciated in the daily interaction with adolescents in the classroom. Their comments and their behavior, which may appear silly or immature by adult standards, become meaningful when viewed as a manifestation of egocentric thought.

In order to avoid repetition, the reader is referred to the Educational Implications section at the end of Chapter 11, Social Cognition. Part I: Robert Selman's Theory of Role Taking.

13: SOCIAL LEARNING THEORY'S CONTRIBUTION TO AN UNDERSTANDING OF ADOLESCENCE

SOCIAL LEARNING THEORY

Social learning theory, with its unique implications for child and adolescent development, has emerged fairly recently. Baldwin (1967) described it as "a theory in the making," partly because its formalizations are not as rigidly stated as those of behavioristic learning theories or psychoanalytic theory and partly because, from its inception, social learning theorists have been firmly committed to verification of hypothetical relationships by way of empirical research. Since social learning theorists have objected to the use of theoretical constructs without empirical support, they have been thoroughly committed to a position in which theory and empirical research findings are viewed as closely interrelated and interdependent. However, since research findings in relatively complex forms of social behavior frequently do not systematically and unequivocally support theoretical hypotheses, continuous revisions of theoretical postulates have been an essential characteristic of social learning theory.

Social learning theory is eclectic in that it draws on concepts, hypotheses, and methodology from a variety of different psychological sources. Some research hypotheses are influenced by psychoanalytic constructs such as identification, frustration, aggression, regression, repression, rejection, dependency, ego strength, and transference, but they are investigated within the methodological approach of the experimentalist rather than the clinician. While social learning theory develops its own theoretical constructs, of which modeling and imitation are the most important, it freely draws on constructs of behavioristic learning theory, especially reinforcement. But even Skinner's concept of direct reinforcement is expanded to include social dimensions: vicarious reinforcement and self-reinforcement. Consequently, the nature of problems and concerns of social learning theorists go far beyond those of the narrow connection between a stimulus and a response and include the contribution of the mother-child relationship to personality development, the importance of models, and the imitation of models in the learning process. In addition, social learning theory has drawn freely on the findings of cultural anthropology. In short, the realm of investigation for the social learning theorist is the whole spectrum of the socialization process by which children learn, often through indirect teaching, to conform to the cultural expectations of acceptable behavior. The significance of the socializing agents as "a source of patterns of behavior" has been neglected in other theories, even though observational and empirical evidence indicates that this social aspect of the learning process is fundamental to socialization and personality development. Because of its eclectic orientation, social learning theory has contributed as much to an understanding of learning as to developmental and personality theory.

The advent of social learning theory cannot easily be credited to a single individual, since it constitutes a merger of thought that came not only from Clark Hull's drive reduction theory and from Skinner's reinforcement theory, but also from Freud's psychoanalytic theory. Social learning theory has been described as the translation of psychoanalytic constructs into behavioristic terminology. Men such as Miller and Dollard, as well as Mowrer, who have been concerned with the relationship between psychoanalytic theory and behavioristic theory and who have attempted to bridge the gap between these diverse points of view, seemed to give an early impetus to an approach to basic human, social, and developmental problems that coalesce into social learning theory. The concern with social aspects of learning is not new, but the systematic development of a theory of social learning begins with the publication of Miller and Dollard's *Social Learning and Imitation* (1941) and has been continued in the works of Mowrer and Sears. Miller and Dollard systematically integrated the concept of imitation into behavior theory. They referred to subjects imitating the behavior of their leader as "matched dependent behavior," because the subjects depended on their leader for cues in order to produce matching responses; but imitation was still viewed as a special case of instrumental conditioning.

However, within social learning theory, there is diversity rather than unanimity in point of view both in emphasis and in some rather basic conceptualizations. Some theorists tend to be closer to S-R (stimulus-response) explanations, whereas others are more oriented toward psychoanalytic constructs, and it is this cross-fertilization and open-mindedness that give social learning theory its vitality. Common to all appears to be the application of behavioristic constructs to basic social and developmental problems and a belief that environmental, situational, and social, rather than biological and maturational factors are primarily responsible for learning and development. They believe that the rewarding of imitative responses is the psychological explanation of the socialization process. Rotter and Crandall have placed particular emphasis on the efforts expended in obtaining goal satisfaction, the value of the goal, and the expectancy of obtaining it. For them the individual's subjective expectation is the central construct of social learning theory. Sears selected the parent-child relationship and especially the mother-child relationship as the focus of his research and theory. He suggested the study of dyadic units, rather than the monadic units of the stimulus-response type learning of an individual without social interaction, as in a Skinnerian program. The study of dyadic units illustrates his social emphasis and includes the combined actions and interactions of two or more people.

"Individual and group behavior are so inextricably intertwined both as to cause and effect, that an adequate behavior theory must combine both in a single internally congruent system" (Sears, 1951: 476). Sears has concentrated his efforts on the study of both the antecedents and the consequences of early child development, and while initially the parents' behavior is seen as the antecedent and the child's behavior as the consequent, both behaviors later become a matter of interaction. Antecedent-consequent statements are characteristic of social learning theory, since it is the relationship between social and environmental antecedents and their behavioral consequences that is the focus of investigations and theorizing. A well-known statement in this regard is Miller's (1941) hypothesis that frustration is the inevitable antecedent of aggressive behavior.

While Sears et al. (1957) contributed a considerable amount of information about patterns of childrearing, the focus of their work has been on childhood rather than adolescence. It is primarily through the work of Bandura (1925–) and Walters (1918–1967) that a number of studies emerge that express an explicit concern with the application of social learning theory, or, as they refer to it, a sociobehavioristic approach to adolescence. Bandura, a student of Sears, has remained closer to Sears, while Walters was closer to Skinner. Their major works relevant to theories of adolescence are *Adolescent Aggression* (Bandura and Walters, 1959) and, concentrating more specifically on child behavior, *Social Learning and Personality Development* (Bandura and Walters, 1963), as well as innumerable research studies. Since Bandura and Walters are more concerned than other social learning theorists with the period of adolescence, the major emphasis in this chapter will be on the work of these two men and their collaborators. However, it would be incorrect to identify Bandura and Walters' contribution as a "theory of adolescence," since they do not view adolescence as a separate stage, qualitatively different from either childhood or young adulthood, but are convinced of the continuity of human development from infancy to adulthood. Indeed, the contribution of social learning theory to an understanding of adolescence consists of seriously questioning the widely held assumption that adolescence is a distinct stage in human development that has its own unique characteristics and requires its own set of theoretical explanations. In that respect social learning theory has much in common with the idea of cultural relativism advanced by anthropology (see Chapter 6). A sociobehavioristic approach to adolescence implies that the principles of learning that help explain child development (Sears, 1951; Sears, et al., 1957) are equally applicable to adolescent development, since no fundamental qualitative differences exist among childhood, adolescence, and adulthood. What may differ at different age levels are sociocultural expectations, and adolescents frequently select models different from those of children. On many important social learning theory concepts, such as imitation, the frustration aggression hypothesis, and the nature of adolescence, Bandura and Walters are almost as critical of Miller and Dollard's earlier writing as they are of Freudian and Skinnerian theory.

MODELING, IMITATION, AND IDENTIFICATION

Bandura and his collaborators have shown that children watching the behavior of a model are quick in imitating the specific responses as well as the generalized response patterns of the model. This phenomenon of modeling has been observed repeatedly in a variety of experimental situations. Furthermore, personal observations of children and adolescents imitating mannerisms, language idiosyncrasies, and habits of their parents and teachers, often to the embarrassment of the model, are commonplace. Bandura, Ross, and Ross (1963b) demonstrated that watching unusual aggressive behavior heightened children's aggressive responses significantly when compared to controls who had observed a nonaggressive model. The first experimental group watched a real-life aggressive model; the second group saw the same model portraying aggressive behavior on film; the third group observed an aggressive cartoon character depicting the same behavior. Many of the children's responses in the test situation were rather accurate imitations of the unusual aggressive acts of the model, especially of the real-life and the film model. The overall increase in aggressive behavior was highly significant and about the same for all three experimental situations, but the cartoon aggressive model elicited less precise imitation. Walters and his associates have shown that the increase in aggressive behavior as a result of watching an aggressive model is not limited to children; they produced similar findings with high school students, young women, and male hospital attendants. These social learning theory studies on imitation of aggressive behavior have been influential in awakening social concern about the potential danger of children and adolescents repeatedly watching aggressive behavior on the television screen, since "exposure to filmed aggression heightens aggressive reactions in children" (Bandura, Ross, and Ross, 1963b: 9).

The potency of watching and imitating a model in altering response patterns has been demonstrated in such divergent areas as moral judgment

(Bandura and McDonald, 1963); self-imposed delay of reward pattern exhibited by the model (Bandura and Mischel, 1965); and self-reinforcement patterns closely following those of the model (Bandura and Kupers, 1964). And in contrast to popular belief, Bandura and Walters' (1959) findings suggest that adolescent boys may be more likely to engage in sexual intercourse when double and multiple dating, thereby imitating the sexual advances of each other. When behavior patterns are inhibited in the subject, observing a model perform that behavior seems to remove personal inhibitions. The factor that predicts drug use in an adolescent most accurately is whether or not friends use drugs (see Chapter 14). Apparently, an "if he can do it, I can do it" viewpoint prevails. According to Bandura, a great variety of social learning phenomena are acquired because a learner observes a model's behavior and imitates the behavior observed.

As children grow older they tend to imitate different models from their social environment. The young child usually identifies with parents and attempts to imitate their behavior, including language, gestures, and mannerisms as well as more basic attitudes and values. Identification with a teacher is not uncommon for the child entering school or for the preadolescent. The child does imitate speech patterns and mannerisms observed in the teacher. Ideas about social or community issues that the child expresses in dinner conversations and that are new to the family are often those of the teacher. With the onset of adolescence, parents and teachers frequently decline as important models, at least in regard to issues and choices that are of immediate consequence. During adolescence it is the peer group and selected entertainment heroes who become increasingly important as models, especially if communication between parents and adolescent breaks down. The adolescent peer group is particularly influential as a model in the use of verbal expressions, hair style, clothing, food, music, and entertainment preferences, as well as in regard to decisions related to rapidly changing social values (Brittain, 1963). Some of the problems that arise during adolescence may be the result of an individual modeling the behavior of peers who may be no more knowledgeable, intelligent, mature, and wise than the individual himself is.

Related to modeling and important in Bandura's social learning theory are the concepts of identification and imitation. In his earlier writing Bandura uses the concept of identification frequently, but later he rejects it as lacking specific content. Different definitions have been advanced for the concepts "identification" and "imitation." Although there is no complete agreement about the specific meaning of these concepts, identification is viewed as a more general way of modeling the behavior of another person even without the person's presence. Identification includes the incorporation of the model's values, beliefs, roles, and attitudes. Imitation, on the other hand, refers to the specific reproduction or matching of behavior sequences almost in the nature of mimicking behavior while the person whose behavior is imitated is or was personally present. Experimental psychologists speak of "imitation" whereas personality theorists speak of "identification." Bandura and Walters (1963) discuss the difference in existing definitions but prefer to use "imitation," which they define as referring to "the occurrence of matching responses."

The role of imitation has been recognized since antiquity as an important method of learning, and it is indeed surprising that behavioristic learning theory has shown so little concern for imitating and modeling. Imitation is particularly relevant for learning complex social behavior, such as language, self-control, altruism, aggression, sexual behavior, and so on. Imitation also plays an essential role in the learning of basic perceptual-motor skills such as handwriting, and much of the learning in the gymnasium and on the sports field is the result of observing and imitating a model who shows how to play correctly. In many languages the term "to teach" is synonymous with "to show" or, as in Hebrew, has the same root, revealing that modeling, or showing, is the basic method of teaching when the emphasis is on skills that can be acquired through observational learning (Bandura and Walters, 1963). The adolescent who wants to learn to drive a car does so first of all by observation and imitation. A youth totally naïve in the use of cars would endanger his own life and those of others if he were to attempt driving solely on the basis of trial and error or reinforcement. Bandura (1962) reports that natives in a Guatemalan subculture learn to operate a cotton textile machine by observing the correct operation of the machine for a number of days. During this training period the youthful trainee asks no questions and is given neither verbal instruction nor reinforcement. Yet, when she feels confident that she can master the process herself, she takes over the operation of the machine and usually succeeds on the very first trial in operating the machine without any difficulties and without further instruction. This kind of learning is based only on the apprentice observing an appropriate social model and imitating the behavior of the model.

SOCIAL LEARNING THEORY CONTRASTED WITH STAGE AND TRAIT THEORIES

Stage theorists of development, such as Freud, Erikson, Blos, and even Piaget, have postulated fairly specific age-related behavior dispositions that follow an invariant developmental sequence, possess cross-situational consistency, and are more or less universal and predetermined. Social learning theory, in contrast, assumes that behavior is primarily determined within a social situational context. Consequently, social learning theory focuses on the interrelationship between environmental and social changes as antecedents and the behavioral changes that occur in a given individual as consequences rather than as a function of age. Descriptions and statements about adolescence are not of such a general, all-encompassing nature, as is Erikson's theory, for example, which predicts that an adolescent will inevitably experience an identity crisis, or Piaget's prediction that adolescent thought processes will begin to follow formal logic and become increasingly more abstract. Rather, social learning theory statements are predictions of relationships between external factors and behavior. The strong emphasis in the sociobehavioristic approach on the influence of social conditions and cultural expectations, even on adolescent sexual behavior, becomes obvious in a statement such as: "In North American society, the marked increase in heterosexual behavior in middle and late adolescence is certainly due less to hormonal changes than to cultural expectations" (Bandura and Walters, 1963: 150). It appears as if they overstated their case, for hormonal changes during adolescence have been found to be related to sexual drive. Even Margaret Mead—who is certainly not an advocate of biological determination in adolescent development—recognizes that "the development of heterosexual interest and activity at puberty does serve to distinguish this period from the period preceding it and from maturity" (Mead, 1952: 537). The word "puberty" carries distinct connotations of physiological and hormonal changes. While Bandura admits that such changes in behavior do occur, he explains the phenomenon differently. In general, pronounced changes in behavior may occur during adolescence, not because of internal maturational forces but because of sudden changes in the social training situation, family structure, peer expectation, or other environmental factors.

Bandura, in "The Stormy Decade: Fact or Fiction?," has questioned the stage theory assumption that adolescence is a turbulent decade inevitably characterized by "storm and stress, tension, rebellion, dependency conflicts, peer-group conformity, black leather jackets and the like" (Bandura, 1964: 224). While he does not deny that some of these kinds of behavior occur in some individuals, such behaviors are due to cultural conditioning and social expectation rather than as inevitable developmental phenomena characteristic of the period of adolescence per se. Aggressive behavior in adolescence—when it does occur—is viewed as the consequence of specific antecedent conditions in the childrearing pattern and the parent-child relationship such as dependency training, socialization pressure, imitation, and modeling, rather than as the result of adolescent adjustment problems. Whenever such behaviors occur, they are viewed as being lawfully related to existing situations or to the preadolescent social situation—that is, the antecedent environmental conditions. The prototypical adolescent with turmoils and anxieties,* sexual tensions, compulsive conformity, and acute identity crisis so commonly described in the literature, according to Bandura (1964), fits only the actual behavior of perhaps "the deviant ten percent of the adolescent population." The "myth" that such behavior is believed to be a normal aspect of adolescent development is due more to cultural expectations and the representation of teen-agers in movies, literature, and the mass media than based on facts. Bandura (1964) does find, as does Offer in *The Psychological World of the Teenager* (1969), that responsible, happy, well-adjusted, parent-respecting youth are more common than had been assumed. Such positive findings are also interpreted not as characteristics of adolescence per se but in the light of antecedent home conditions such as having experienced a warm, supportive preadolescence in which firmness and socialization pressure in childhood slowly gave way to increasingly more freedom during adolescence.

As a general law of social and personal development, social learning theory assumes that there is continuity in human growth patterns and in the learning process and that no basic changes or clear-cut new stages in the mode of thinking appear at any one age level. Bandura and McDonald (1963) tested Piaget's (1932b) theory that objective moral judgment, which considers the material damage in an act, gives way at about the age of seven to subjective moral judgment, which considers the intent of the wrongdoers rather than the amount of damage. They did not find a distinct or abrupt change in the moral responses of their subjects, but there was a pronounced increase in subjective moral judgment and a decrease in objective moral judgment as a function of age. Bandura and McDonald consider changes in moral judgment to be primarily the result of changes in reinforcement contingencies in combination with the effects of modeling, rather than a function of maturation or a change from the preoperational to the operational stage in logical thinking. Bandura and McDonald (1963) demonstrated further that age-specific social responses such as moral judgment can be modified through the utilization of appropriate models and the application of social learning principles. Since the age-specific behavior postulated by Piaget's theory of two distinct stages of moral judgment can be modified through modeling and social reinforcement, some doubt is cast on the validity of the stage concept. It appears as if external social experiences have greater impact on behavior changes than the internal maturational forces postulated by stage theorists. Bandura and Mischel (1965) also

---

*Cattell and Scheier (1961) do find—in contrast to Bandura's claim—that during adolescence a noticeable increase in anxiety distinguishes that period from childhood and adulthood. "In the normal person, free anxiety is very high in adolescence, drops sharply as adulthood is reached. . . ."

show that delay of reward behavior can be modified through modeling techniques.

In contrast to stage theories, social learning theory is concerned with *interindividual* rather than with *intraindividual* differences. Some of the environmental variables in behavior are intelligence, sex, age, race, socioeconomic status, culture, home atmosphere, exposure to models, and different reinforcement schedules. "To the extent that children representing such diverse backgrounds experience differential contingencies and schedules of reinforcement, as well as exposure to social models who differ widely in the behavior they exhibit, considerable interindividual behavior variability would be expected" (Bandura and McDonald, 1963: 274).

Trait theorists, such as Raymond Cattell (Cattell and Scheier, 1961), have measured the basic components or traits of personality and postulated cross-situational consistency and developmental stability of behavior patterns, since they assumed that it was not so much the external situation but the internal trait that determined behavior. Since the primary cause of behavior is located within the person, trait theorists have searched for consistency in people's behavior across situational changes and ascribe consistency in behavior to such traits as ego strength, reality orientation, self-control, self-concept, maturity, and energy-binding ideation. Social learning theorists, in contrast, see situational changes in a lawful way related to behavior changes and, consequently, investigate the observable external causes of behavior. An adolescent may be rebellious, disobedient, insensitive, nonconforming, and tough, and yet the same person in a different situation may also be obedient, sensitive, conforming, and considerate. Social learning theory would not look at some of these traits as real and at the other group as defenses or compensations; nor would it view these diverse traits as inconsistent, arbitrary, or capricious. Social learning theory would consider all of these behaviors as lawfully related to specific social situations and antecedent factors. In other words, the issues then become when, how, where, and in interaction with whom did what behavior occur? Or what happened to the individual prior to the occurrence of a particular behavior?

Any consistency in behavior that can be observed is the result of similarity in the antecedent external social conditions rather than an internal trait. If antecedent conditions differ markedly or are expected to differ, behavior will differ and may appear quite inconsistent. A widely held assumption, especially among stage theorists, is that a consistent characteristic of middle adolescence is an antagonism toward adult authority. However, to illustrate the importance of antecedent social conditions, one might consider the common observation of an adolescent who has pronounced feelings of antagonism toward his father while, at the same time, expressing a great deal of admiration and respect for other adult authority figures such as his football coach, adult Boy Scout leader, or minister.

SOCIAL LEARNING THEORY CONTRASTED WITH BEHAVIORISTIC THEORY

Social learning theory also recognizes the very limited applicability of reinforcement theory to a wide variety of especially complex forms of social behavior such as language learning. Bandura (1962) considers the use of operant or instrumental conditioning as "tedious and ineffective" for most human learning. Skinner and others have assumed, without sufficient empirical verification, that reinforcement principles based on the findings of studies in highly structured laboratory situations apply equally to complex social situations. However, for a novel response to be reinforced, at least an approximation of that response must occur. Many complex forms of social learning would not easily emerge if they had to rely on reinforcement or drive reduction alone. A response that has never been made and observed has a zero probability of occurring and can hardly be acquired if there is no reliable eliciting stimulus. Reinforcement theory assumes that learning takes place only after a response has been made and is reinforced. However, reinforcement is not a precondition for the acquisition of a new response; it can only change the probability that an existing response will occur in the future. Bandura (1962) feels that people would not be socialized and many vocational and recreational skills would never be learned if they depended solely on reinforcement. A new behavior repertoire can only be learned from observing a model exhibiting that behavior and matching or imitating the behavior modeled. Operant conditioning effectively explains how the learned behavior is maintained and strengthened but not how it is initially acquired. The initial acquisition of a response pattern is more effectively explained by imitation, and this kind of observational learning can take place without direct reinforcement. Similarly, trial-and-error learning can be eliminated, or the number of trials reduced, by providing an opportunity to observe the necessary behavior performed by an appropriate model. This process of observing and imitating is referred to as modeling and constitutes the cornerstone of Bandura's sociobehavioristic approach. "What you know and how you behave depends on what you see and hear and not just on what you get" (Mischel, 1971: 71).

Social learning theory makes a clear and important distinction between the acquisition of potential response patterns and actual performance or responding. The acquisition of potential response patterns is a function of observing the behavior of others and depends on social variables, sensory input, and cognitive operations. Acquisition learning does take place before the subject responds, and many response patterns are acquired but not performed. Acquisition learning is particularly obvious in language learning. However, whether the acquired behavior will actually occur and the probability that it will occur are dependent on reinforcement (Mischel,

1971). In social learning theory, reinforcement takes the place of a secondary, supportive role in the learning process. Most complex learning is viewed primarily as social—namely, the imitation of social models, especially in the learning of novel response patterns. The difference between acquisition and performance may be illustrated by the fact that most adolescent boys may know how to use lipstick and cosmetics—the response patterns having been acquired through observation. However, because these responses have never been reinforced, their probability of occurring is very low and may actually be zero. Many response patterns are acquired through observing a model but are not expressed as long as the learned behavior is not functional. However, if the social situations change so that the acquired response patterns become functional, the previously acquired behavior may be performed without further observations, without trial and error, and without reinforcement. When social situations change, for example, children may surprise parents with language patterns or language skills that were acquired earlier but that had never before been used.

Some social behaviors may seem to be more dependent on the behavior of the model that is observed and imitated rather than upon the reinforcement or punishment. One persistent research finding is that parental punitiveness toward aggressive behavior appears to be associated with more rather than less aggressive behavior in the child.

> Parental modeling behavior may often counteract the effects of their direct training. When a parent punishes his child physically for having aggressed toward peers, for example, the intended outcome of this training is that the child should refrain from hitting others. The child, however, is also learning from parental demonstration how to aggress physically and this imitative learning may provide the direction for the child's behavior when he is similarly frustrated in subsequent social interactions [Bandura, 1967: 43].

"Do as I say, not as I do" is exactly the reverse of what social learning theory predicts will happen. The imitation of the model, the "as I do" part, apparently is more potent than the reinforcement or the punishment provided by the "as I say" part. And many adolescents complain about their parents' "hypocrisies," since their "model" behavior belies their verbal recommendations and admonitions. Many manuals on discipline emphasize that the modeling of desirable behavior is actually a much more potent influence than any verbalization or reward-punishment system. And the most valid general rule in regard to the training of children and adolescents is: "There is no sure way to guarantee that your child will grow up to be the kind of person you would like him to be. The most likely way is for you to be the kind of person you would like him to be."

In addition to its establishment, the maintenance of response patterns or learning in the behavioristic sense does not depend only on direct external reinforcement as in Skinner's theory. Bandura expands the traditional concept of reinforcement to include *vicarious reinforcement* and also *self-reinforcement*. Vicarious reinforcement depends on the positive or negative consequences that the subject observes in others—that is, in the model. Observing social models that are rewarded for aggressive behavior increases the likelihood of this behavior occurring in the observer, just as aggressive behavior punished in the model inhibits the same behavior in the subject.

Bandura, Ross, and Ross (1963c) showed two films of Rocky the Villain exhibiting almost identical aggressive behavior, except that in one instance his aggressive behavior was rewarded and in another it was punished. Children who watched the movie and saw that the aggressive behavior of Rocky was rewarded were quick in imitating both the physical violence and the verbal abuse that they had observed. Actually, they showed about two times as much aggressive behavior as a control group. However, in the situation in which the children observed that the villain was punished after his aggressive act they showed little imitation of the behavior they had watched. However, even though punishing the villain inhibited the overt learning effects that resulted from observing the "bad" model, it did not suppress the latent tendencies. Children did acquire these response patterns and could describe them with considerable accuracy, but they did not perform them unless such response patterns became functional under either the impact of provocation or the prospect of reward.

Self-reinforcement means that learners actually reward themselves for work that they consider of good quality. Verbal self-evaluations, which people administer frequently, are part of the self-reinforcing event. Bandura claims that "most human behavior is altered and maintained in the absence of immediate reinforcement" (Bandura, 1971: 248). In a variety of experiments children give themselves candy or tokens for attaining self-selected levels of performance on a miniature bowling game. The standards for their self-reinforcement are adopted from the comparison model (Bandura and Kupers, 1964; Bandura and Whalen, 1966); if the standards of the model are stringent, self-reinforcement is infrequent, but if the standards of the model are lenient, self-reinforcement is generous. Bandura and Perloff (1967) demonstrated that self-reinforcement and external reinforcement are equally effective, and both are significantly more effective than noncontingent reward or nonreward. Once the performance of a desirable response has acquired a positive value, such as an adolescent shooting baskets, the person can administer self-reinforcement by producing the desired basket and feeling good about the improving skills. Common observation illustrates that this kind of self-reinforcement can keep such behavior as basket shooting going for several hours on a Saturday afternoon. Adolescents are learning to set their own level of performance, and reaching that level makes them feel proud or satisfied and, therefore, carries its own reward. In other words, as we grow more mature, self-reinforcement patterns stabilize and become less and less dependent on parents, teachers, and bosses giving us our rewards. We increasingly judge the appropriateness and the quality of our own responses and reward them accordingly. Successful socialization requires that our own judgment of our work becomes a more important reinforcer than some outsider administering praise, candy, money, or other reinforcers. Mature adolescents may be able to make themselves feel good about work well done—that is, provide self-reinforcement—even though a critical teacher or an impatient father expresses dissatisfaction. In contrast to Skinner's emphasis on direct reinforcement often contingent on fairly specific types of responses, social learning theorists maintain that the more important reinforcers in terms of mature complex social behavior are self-administered.

THE ANTECEDENTS OF ADOLESCENT AGGRESSION

Bandura (1973b) rejects all hydraulic motivational theories of aggression—such as Freud's aggressive instinct theory and Lorenz's aggressive urge theory—since these theories view aggression as the natural response to frustration. Aristotle believed that emotional expression purges the emotions. Similarly, hydraulic models hold that as long as the cause of aggression is within the individual, the aggressive energy must find an outlet. Aggression is assumed to be reduced by aggressive behavior, and therapy provides safe and approved outlets for aggression.

Plato, in contrast, held that the overt expression of emotion arouses rather than reduces emotions. Bandura feels that Plato is the better psychologist. Social learning theory postulates that the causes of aggression are external, social, and environmental and can be found in the dependency training in childhood, imitation of aggressive models, and lack of internalization of social values. Studies (Bandura, Ross, and Ross, 1963b; 1963c) have shown that exposure to aggressive models increases aggressive behavior in the observer. As an alternative to the frustration-aggression hypothesis, Bandura assumes that, rather than frustration leading to aggression, it produces

> emotional arousal that can elicit a variety of behaviors depending on the types of reactions people have learned for coping with stressful conditions. When distressed, some people seek help and support; others display achievement behavior; others show withdrawal and resignation; some aggress; others exhibit heightened somatic activity; others anesthetize themselves with drugs or alcohol; and most intensify constructive efforts to overcome their problems [Bandura, 1973b: 204].

Bandura and Walters' interest in adolescence finds its most explicit expression in an extensive study entitled *Adolescent Aggression* (1959). The study is—as the subtitle, ''A Study of the Influence of Child Training Practices and Family Interrelationships,'' suggests—concerned with the antecedent variables in the parent-child relationship that contribute to the development of antisocial aggressive behavior. The specific antecedent home conditions investigated were derived from social learning theory hypotheses and involve such variables as dependency training, sex attitudes and behavior, the handling of discipline in the home, identification processes, and the socialization process. The socialization process is viewed as ''the development of habitual response patterns that are acceptable in the society in which the individual lives. The learning of such habits, or cue-response associations, requires the presence of some kind of drive or motivating process and the occurrence of a reward or reinforcement'' (1959: 23).

The conditions that contribute to effective socialization include the development of a dependency motive, so that the child desires approval and affection from others. In addition, since dependency alone is not sufficient, socialization pressure needs to be exerted by way of demands and limitations—in short, through discipline—so that the child learns to conform to the patterns of society. This socialization process is facilitated by the amount and quality of personal contact parents give their child and by withholding of secondary rewards such as approval and attention, while at the same time keeping the child in a dependent relationship. The socialization process is delayed or disrupted if dependency behavior is punished or discouraged, if parental discipline methods are inconsistent within the home, and if the parents' values are in conflict with the prevalent values of the community and society. One basic assumption of Bandura and Walters' study is that antisocial aggression develops from a disruption in the adolescent's earlier dependency training in relationship to parents. Dependency needs could be frustrated by lack of affectional nurturance, by parental rejection, or by lack of close dependency ties with one or both parents. An impairment in the development of healthy dependency relationships may directly contribute to feelings of hostility and to aggressive behavior. In addition, children without dependency motives experience less guilt and lack the capacity to control aggressive feelings sufficiently when aroused.

Bandura and Walters obtained their data from two groups of carefully selected boys aged fourteen to seventeen. Twenty-six pairs of boys were matched on a one-to-one basis in regard to age, intelligence, father's occupation, and area of residence. They differed in that the aggressive boys had a history of antisocial, aggressive patterns of behavior, and many of them were on probation. The nonaggressive control boys were neither markedly aggressive nor withdrawn. Both groups came from intact families, had average or above-average intelligence, did not live in a high-delinquency neighborhood, and were free from withdrawal tendencies, known organic involvement, or other psychiatric problems. Data were collected through extensive personal interviews of both groups of adolescents as well as their parents. In theoretical orientation and in methodology, the study may be considered an extension of Sears, Maccoby, and Levin's *Patterns of Child Rearing* (1957).

Sociological approaches relate incidence of delinquency to population density, poverty, broken homes, deteriorated houses and neighborhood, lack of recreational facilities, and social and personal discontent. These investigators, in contrast, looked at the nature of the parent-child relationship and related it to the absence or presence of aggressive behavior in the adolescent subjects, controlling most of the sociological factors by matching procedures. In contrast to the psychodynamic disease model of deviant behavior. Bandura and Walters assume that both deviant and prosocial behavior are governed by the same learning principles rather than by hidden, subconscious, internal dynamics or traits. It is the external stimulus condition that controls normal as well as deviant behavior, rather than underlying dispositions.

Furthermore, since social learning theorists believe in the continuity of human development, antisocial aggressive behavior in adolescent boys is seen not as a problem that emerges with puberty or as related to hormonal changes, but as a failure in the socialization process that begins very early in childhood and continues during development.

The first group of hypotheses developed from social learning theory compared the dependency behavior, dependency anxiety, feelings of rejection, and aggressive behavior in the aggressive adolescents with those of the nonaggressive adolescents. In general, there was no significant difference in mothers' warmth and affection with both groups of boys. However, the aggressive boys were, as social learning theory predicted, less dependent on their fathers, felt more rejected by their fathers, and spent less time with their fathers than the control boys.

The fathers of the two groups of boys did not report any difference in the amount of overt aggression directed toward them. Only a few of the mothers of aggressive boys reported physical aggression directed toward them, but they also admitted that they were more tolerant of aggressive behavior. The control mothers had firmer limits in the amount of aggression they would tolerate. In general, the differences in expression of aggression against parents and parents' tolerance of aggressive behavior between these two groups were not very pronounced. However, it became quite obvious that both the fathers and the mothers of the aggressive adolescents actively encouraged their sons to show aggression outside the home, to use their fists, to stand up for their rights; and the fathers seemed to get some vicarious enjoyment from the aggressive acts of their sons.

This difference, especially between the fathers of aggressive sons and the control fathers, was most pronounced. In a follow-up study of aggressive and inhibited preadolescent boys, Bandura (1960) found that the parents of the inhibited boys were nonpermissive and nonpunitive toward aggressive behavior, which means that they neither reinforced nor did they model aggressive behavior. The parents of aggressive boys, in contrast, were nonpermissive and punitive when the aggressive behavior was directed toward themselves, but they encouraged aggression toward other children and permitted sibling aggression.

Aggressive boys had more dependency anxiety—that is, they were less willing to express their dependency, seek help, talk about their problems, and show affection, even though they did have dependency needs. The dependency anxiety generalized from parents to peers and school. The control boys sought and appreciated help from their fathers more, and they also showed more help-seeking and approval-seeking behavior in relationship to their peers, while the feeling of being rejected in relationship to school and peers was more pronounced among the aggressive boys.

In relationship to sexual behavior, no difference was found in the handling of sexual behavior in both groups of parents, except that the fathers of the aggressive boys were more permissive concerning sexual behavior. However, it was found that the aggressive boys had had significantly more heterosexual experiences and expressed less anxiety about sex. Apparently, the permissive attitude in the fathers contributed to the greater sexual experience of the aggressive boys.

Several significant relationships were found in respect to the handling of rules, limitations, and the disciplining of these two groups of boys. The control parents used more reasoning as a disciplinary method and had higher achievement expectations for their sons. The control mothers were more consistent in enforcing rules and were more restrictive—that is, they used more socialization pressure, at least in the home. The methods used significantly more in disciplining the aggressive boys were physical and verbal punishment by their fathers, isolation, and more deprivation of privileges, although the latter method was common in both groups. The relationship between punitive parents and aggressive behavior in their children has been reported repeatedly in the literature. Apparently, the more children are punished at home for aggressive behavior, the more aggressively they act toward their peers (Eron, Walder, Toigo, and Lefkowitz, 1963; Sears, Maccoby, and Levin, 1957). The mothers of the aggressive boys reported that their sons resisted their demands, and the aggressive boys themselves admitted that they ignored parental requests and refused to do what they were told to do. The parent-child relationship of the aggressive adolescents may best be described as lacking in warmth and affection.

The crucial question from a social learning theory point of view relates to the identification of these two groups of boys with their parents and the internalization of controls. While there was no difference in terms of identification with the mother, control boys identified more strongly with their fathers. The control fathers were more demanding of masculine behavior in their boys. The aggressive boys experienced more disruption in affectional relationships between their fathers and their mothers and also more of a disruption in the emotional relationship between themselves and their parents, especially their fathers. In terms of internalization of controls, the nonaggressive group experienced more guilt when they transgressed, whereas the aggressive boys did not. The conscience of the aggressive boys differed from that of the control boys. The behavior of the control boys was governed by guilt, an internal avoidance, when confronted with temptation. The aggressive boys, in a situation involving transgression of rules, were not governed by guilt but, if they were inhibited at all, by fear of punishment. Since identification is not encouraged and rewarded in the aggressive boys, the internalization of values seems to suffer.

In summary, more important than the shortcomings in the dependency training of the aggressive boys—which were theoretically predicted but actually only weakly supported—was the imitation process. Aggressive boys seem to imitate their aggressive parents, who tend to use more physical punishment as a method of discipline and who encourage and reward the aggressive behavior of their sons, at least outside the home. By reinforcing aggressive behavior outside the home, by inhibiting aggressive behavior inside the home directed toward the parents, and by modeling aggressive behavior through physically punishing the boys, these parents "fostered displacement of aggression toward objects and situations eliciting much weaker inhibitory response" (Bandura, Ross, and Ross, 1961). These findings resulting from the study of aggressive behavior of adolescent boys in their natural environment are quite consistent with the results of laboratory studies of aggressive behavior of young children (Bandura, Ross, and Ross, 1961; 1963b; 1963c).

Antisocial aggressive behavior in adolescent boys is the consequence of identifiable socialization variables in the parent-child relationship.

EDUCATIONAL IMPLICATIONS

Social learning theory's basic assumption is that children and adolescents learn most complex skills more effectively by imitating the behavior of their parents, teachers, and peers rather than by reinforcement, trial and error, and, in certain situations, even better than by verbal instruction. Verbal instructions and verbal cues, if they represent the modeling behavior symbolically, can facilitate the learning process, at least for behavior already in the subject's response repertoire. An often neglected aspect of the role of the teacher is the effective model role, demonstrating correct response patterns to be imitated. Only secondarily is the teacher a good reinforcer who uses reinforcement to shape and maintain already learned response repertoires. A teacher serves the model function, and some pupils will imitate this behavior regardless of whether or not the teacher consciously chooses for them to do so. A teacher cannot limit her influence on students to academic competencies only but must be aware that some pupils will be influenced by her altruism or selfishness, cleanliness or slovenliness, organization or disorganization, and whether or not she is observed participating in political activities, religious activities, and so on.

Evidence indicates that there are at least three types of effects that observing the model's behavior has on the learner (Bandura, 1965; Bandura and Walters, 1963). First, there is the already discussed *modeling effect*. By imitating the model's behavior, children acquire response patterns that they did not have before, and the modeling responses closely match those of the model. Bandura provides strong evidence that modeling as a teaching-learning technique is more economical than the techniques of operant conditioning, at least in learning novel responses. Second, there is the *inhibitory or disinhibitory effect,* which is based on the consequence the model experiences. If the consequences of the model's behavior are pain or punishment, watching the model's reaction to pain or punishment has an inhibitory effect on the observer. On the other hand, if the model is rewarded for a certain behavior, this has a disinhibitory effect on the observer, and the probability that the observer will imitate that behavior is increased. Vicarious reinforcement contributes to the disinhibitory influence of modeling. Third, there is the *eliciting effect,* meaning that the model's behavior provides specific cues, or serves as an eliciting stimulus that facilitates the release of similar responses in the observer, thus aiding the learning process. In the case of the eliciting effect of the model the behavior that is imitated is not new, nor was it previously inhibited, but at least similar responses are already in the subject's response repertoire. For example, a study by White (1967) was concerned with the effects of instruction and modeling on the altruistic behavior of preadolescent children. It was shown that in eliciting altruistic responses in students, what the teacher *did* was more important than what the teacher *said.* Apparently, altruistic behavior can be elicited more effectively by modeling than by verbal instruction. Bandura and McDonald (1963) demonstrated that modeling procedures, especially when both the model and the observer are reinforced, are very powerful in changing preadolescents' moral judgments. Live and symbolic models have been found to have a significant influence on the learning of self-control (Bandura and Mischel, 1965).

LaFleur and Johnson (1972) were concerned with the application of social learning theory in influencing the behavior of adolescents in a counseling situation. The treatment condition consisted of having the subjects watch cartoon stick-figure models, who were similar to themselves in important characteristics, request information about educational and vocational goals. The cartoon characters in the modeling treatment group remained without reward. However, for the second experimental group, the cartoon characters not only served as models but were also reinforced for information-seeking behavior, thus providing modeling and vicarious reinforcement for subjects. A control group of adolescents received information about educational and vocational planning, but they were given no model to observe and imitate. Modeling in the first experimental group was as effective as modeling with vicarious reinforcement in the second experimental group; but both experimental groups were significantly more effective than the control situation, in which merely information was provided. The first two experimental groups imitated the modeled behavior; these adolescents became more interested in seeking information about planning their future, and they actually acquired more knowledge.

Teachers have an indirect but potent influence on children and adolescents in shaping the latter's values and attitudes by what they, the teachers themselves, are and what they do. This is in addition to the influence they exert through the cognitive, instructional curriculum that relates to their subject matter and teaching methods. Teachers can indirectly encourage altruism, moral values, social conscience, and human decency by exhibiting these virtues themselves. Even though adolescents as a group may reject teachers in general as identification models, it is not at all uncommon that an individual student may experience occasional infatuation, crushes, and adoration of an individual teacher. Furthermore, an adolescent may imitate the behavior of a teacher, even though a more general identification with the teacher as a person is lacking. Consequently, it is important to consider the conditions contributing to the imitation-identification process. First, the behavior to be imitated must be within the subject's perceptual and motor capacity. Furthermore, studies have shown that the identification process is facilitated if the model is warm, friendly, and supportive rather than cold and rejecting. However, each of the factors that generally contributes to imitation and learning must be evaluated in relationship to other factors and the overall context. For example, an overindulgent teacher or parent, providing too much warmth and giving the child too much nurturance, may inhibit rather than facilitate the learning or behavior that demands effort and self-denial.

Learning is more likely to occur if imitative or matching responses are directly rewarded, so that modeling and reinforcement jointly contribute to the acquisition of response patterns. Imitation, or matching of responses, can be further enhanced by vicarious reinforcement—that is, if the model who is being observed is also being rewarded.

Social power and the control of rewards make up another variable that influences imitation, and these factors are of importance in the school situation in which teachers do control the rewards and have social power. In an experiment, Bandura, Ross, and Ross (1963a) utilized an adult model who controlled the distribution of highly attractive toys. A second adult model received some of these toys, as did the children who served as subjects. Consequently, the children might have viewed the second model as a rival. Bandura observed that the children were much more likely to imitate the behavior of the first model who had the control (social power) over the toys rather than the behavior of the second model. Related to the findings of this study is the common observation that the higher-status model is much more likely to be imitated than the lower-status model. President Kennedy contributed to the popularity of rocking chairs and President Reagan to that of jellybeans.

In addition, it has been demonstrated (Bandura, 1962) that the effectiveness of the model in producing matching responses in the observer depends on a variety of factors, such as the model's attractiveness, prestige, competence, and willingness to dispense rewards and praise. If the model has some characteristics in common with the observing subject, the observer is more inclined to imitate the model's behavior. For children, adults often serve as more powerful models than peers, since they have status, prestige, competence, power, and are the dispensers of rewards. However, with adolescents, peer group members do serve as models and may actually have greater influence on imitative behavior than parents and teachers, partly because they share common characteristics, partly because the peer group has control over the rewards that matter.

The model's influence on imitative behavior of the subject also depends on the motivation and other characteristics of the subject. The person who has strong dependency needs, who is lacking in self-esteem or competence, and who, in the past, has been reinforced for producing matching responses, is more likely to imitate the model.

It appears crucial that adolescents have teachers with whom they can and want to identify. Since much learning occurs inadvertently due to the fact that the teacher serves as a socializing agent, it becomes more important that teachers be selected in the light of their qualities as models for youths and their potential for identification. The demand of radical groups that black students be taught by black teachers—since black children tend to identify better with black teachers—seems to receive some implicit support from social learning theory. Bandura (1962) has also pointed out that the sex of the model and the sex of the subject do influence the imitation of behavior. The power of imitating a model is so great that children will imitate sex-stereotypical play behavior of a same-sex model. Boys watching a male model play with a toy stove increase their stove-playing behavior when the model is gone, just as girls increase their truck-playing behavior after having observed a female model play with the truck (Wolf, 1973).

Social learning theory provides an explanation of why school integration does work and does produce results—although often only modest results—that are more effective than other compensatory reforms. As lower-class children move into academic settings in which peer models value learning, take school seriously, and aspire to academic success, their own attitudes and behavior will change to the extent that they accept and imitate the academic striving of their new peers.

14: FRIENDSHIP PATTERNS AND PEER GROUP INFLUENCES: AN ECOLOGICAL PERSPECTIVE BASED ON BRONFENBRENNER, KANDEL, AND DUNPHY

APPARENTLY there is no all encompassing macrotheory that focuses on the many diverse and interrelated aspects of friendship formation, peer group influences, and parent-peer cross pressures. This chapter will therefore draw on several different theoretical perspectives that are compatible and mutually supportive. The ecological perspective developed by Bronfenbrenner (1977) and applied to adolescence by Garbarino (1985) will serve to set the stage by providing the background for an ecological model. An ecological model goes far beyond what is presently known, opening up new perspectives and generating new hypotheses that are bound to move developmental research from the clearly defined, easily controllable research laboratory into the ecological field.

An application of Bronfenbrenner's ecological model finds expression in the more empirically based theory of friendship formation and parent-peer influences growing out of Kandel's work. Emphasis will be on her more recent work, which attempts to integrate theoretically her previous research findings on drug use, friendship formation, and adolescent-parent influences.

A final section focuses on Dunphy's model, which follows in the pattern of the traditional theories looking for age changes in adolescent social structure. Dunphy has presented us with a comprehensive and integrated view of the age changes in adolescent cliques and crowds, identifying clearly discernible patterns or stages. The combination of these perspectives offers a theoretical-empirical point of view about the influences of friends, peers, and parents on the social development of the adolescent.

BRONFENBRENNER'S ECOLOGICAL APPROACH TO HUMAN DEVELOPMENT

Ecology investigates the complex system of interlinked and interdependent relationships of our biological and social environment, interestingly illustrated by Darwin's story of the relationship between the cats and clover. This story has indelibly etched the concept of "ecology" in the author's mind.

Humblebees are apparently indispensable to the fertilization of red clover, since no other bee can reach the nectar in that particular variety.

> The inference is that if the humblebees became extinct or very rare in England . . . red clover would become very rare, or wholly disappear. However, the number of humblebees in any district depends in a great measure on the number of field mice, which destroy their combs and nests. It is estimated that more than two-thirds of them are thus destroyed all over England. Near villages and small towns the nests of humblebees are more numerous than elsewhere and this is attributed to the number of cats that destroy the mice. Thus next year's crop of purple clover in certain parts of England depends on the number of humblebees in the district, the number of humblebees depends upon the number of field mice, the number of field mice upon the number and enterprise of the cats [Park, 1936: 2].

To this ecological chain, probably with tongue in cheek, someone has added that the number of cats depends on the number of old maids who keep cats.

This amusing story can set the stage for Bronfenbrenner's (1977) ecological theory of human development. Social interactions, like biological interactions, are always part of a larger ecological system. For each individual adolescent, a continuously interacting set of complex social relationships exists (not simple one-to-one relationships). The problem has been in identifying and conceptualizing this multiplicity of sociocultural and environmental factors. The traditionally well-controlled research methodology in which an experimenter (E) manipulated specified variables and measured the changes in the subject's (S) behavior under various conditions led to the observation that "much of contemporary developmental psychology is the science of the strange behavior of children in strange situations with strange adults for the briefest period of time" (Bronfenbrenner, 1977: 513). The fact that the (S) might influence the (E) was not considered, and the relationship of the (S) to parents, siblings, friends, teachers, and neighbors usually did not become part of the research design. Yet all of these factors may be relevant. Various people exert influences on an individual; different ecological systems are in a continuous and complex interaction, which may be a more important process than S's measurable responses to specific stimuli. Bronfenbrenner argues that to understand human development, we need to go beyond directly observable or measurable behavior involving one or two people in a laboratory setting and expand our perspective to "the examinations of multiperson systems of interaction," taking "into account aspects of the environment beyond the immediate situation containing the subject" (Bronfenbrenner, 1977: 514). The question then becomes how adolescents adjust to an ever-changing, interrelated social and cultural environment. In response to these questions, Bronfenbrenner (1977) developed his theory of the "ecological model," which Garbarino (1985) applied to adolescent development. This ecological model contributes to an understanding of the sociocultural environment by identifying four major structural systems and describing the nature of their interactions: the microsystem, the mesosystem, the exosystem, and the macrosystem.

THE MICROSYSTEM

According to Bronfenbrenner, "a microsystem is the complex of relations between the developing person and environment in an immediate setting containing that person (e.g., home, school, workplace, etc.)" (1977: 514). The microsystem of an adolescent consists of a social network of interpersonal relationships involving direct face-to-face interactions with people with whom he or she has a lasting relationship, who are influential in his or her life, and who, in turn, are influenced by the adolescent. For most adolescents, the family is the primary microsystem, usually followed in importance by friends and school (see Figure 22). Other microsystems could include the siblings (as part of the family), teachers (as part of the school), neighbors, church members, and other social groups with whom the adolescent might have enduring personal and social relationships.

The microsystems change, since time and experience constantly change people. In addition, individuals may move in and out of important social settings; hence certain microsystems may become more or less significant for an adolescent as he joins a club, stops attending church, and so on. Furthermore, the adolescent himself is changing as a function of development. As development progresses, the complexity of the microsystem increases. The child's progression from a self-contained classroom in elementary school to a different social group in high school illustrates this phenomenon most clearly. In general, the peer microsystem during adolescence becomes more differentiated (Brown and Trujillo, in press) and more influential. The peer group provides powerful social rewards in terms of status, prestige, friendship, popularity, and acceptance. However, the peer microsystem can also assert a powerful negative influence by encouraging or rewarding such detrimental behavior as cheating, stealing, smoking, drinking, drug use, and irresponsible sex. A healthy microsystem is one that is based on reciprocity—in which, for example, parents concur with the reasonable requests of their adolescents and the adolescents reciprocate by honoring the reasonable requests of their parents. When reciprocity breaks down, as in the parent–adolescent communication pattern, the quality of the microsystem declines. A microsystem rich in information, with questions answered, exploration and experimentation encouraged, and guidance provided enhances learning and development and leads to

FIGURE 22. The Microsystem. An adolescent belongs to a number of different microsystems. Depicted are a family microsystem, a friends microsystem, and a sports-team microsystem. One person can play a role in more than one microsystem. For example, friend 3 is also player 3.

opportunities for success later in life. In these respects it is in marked contrast to an information-poor and exploration-inhibiting microsystem.

THE MESOSYSTEM

"A mesosystem comprises the interrelations among major settings containing the developing person at a particular point in his or her life. . . . A mesosystem is a system of microsystems" (Bronfenbrenner, 1977: 515). The mesosystem is composed of a network of relationships between the various microsystems in a person's life. The richness (or impoverishment) of the mesosystem is determined by the number and the quality of such interrelating links. For a twelve-year-old, these connecting links may consist of several microsystems, such as family, school, friends, church, and camp (see Figure 23).

A mesosystem analysis would look at the quality, frequency, and influ-

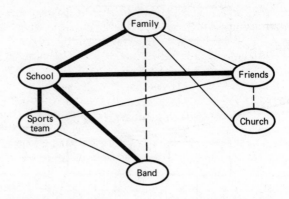

FIGURE 23. The Mesosystem. The interacting microsystems constitute the mesosystem. Some microsystems may be more heavily interrelated with others (e.g., family–school, school–band, school–team, etc.), while others may only show limited interaction (e.g., friends–church, family–band, etc.). Finally, there may be relatively little interaction, as, for example, between church and band or church and sports team.

ence of such interactions as family experiences are related to school adjustment, certain family characteristics and conformity to peer pressures, or the relationship between church attendance and early intimacy with the opposite sex. Like the microsystem, the mesosystem is concerned with actual interpersonal relationships, but the focus is on the linkage or the relationship between different microsystems. A microsystem and a mesosystem can operate in a congruent way to reinforce each other, or they may be quite divergent. For example, the values of parents and peers may be either in accordance or in opposition. Obviously, a congruent system of values exerts a more powerful and consistent influence.

An analysis of the relationships between microsystem and mesosystem reveals the potential for problems and risk:

1. In an impoverished mesosystem, there are no or only a few meaningful linkages between existing microsystems. Illustrations include parents who do not know their adolescent child's friends; parents who have no contact with the school and show no interest in their child's schoolwork; the adolescent's personal friends who do not attend the same school; and the adolescent whose church attendance is isolated from that of parents, friends, and neighbors.

2. A potential danger exists if different microsystems endorse divergent values. For example, the peer group may glamorize, encourage, and reward drinking (or smoking, drug use, early sexual behavior) while parents and church may view these behaviors negatively, disapproving or punishing them. In a more general sense, parents may disapprove of the values, attitudes, and behaviors of their child's friends and restrict his or

her opportunities to socialize with these friends. When basic values between different microsystems diverge, tensions arise in the mesosystem; as a result, the individual feels pulled in different directions, lives with stress, has to make a choice between the sets of values, or has "to pretend" that he or she follows both.

3. Problems will arise if the mesosystem, composed of interlinking microsystems, endorses or reinforces deviant or delinquent behavior that is in conflict with the exo- and macrosystems. For example, consider a situation in which both parents and peers encourage cheating to succeed, the selling of drugs to make money, or driving without a license.

Bronfenbrenner speaks of an "ecological transition" in which part of a mesosystem gets disrupted because old microsystems become defunct or new ones emerge. Such ecological transitions may involve a move from elementary to junior high school, from private to public school, or from one church affiliation to another; it may also take the form of a parental divorce or a family's move to a new community. All these changes would require—with the exception of the family—a whole new mesosystem. Children of army officers as well as those whose fathers' work calls for frequent relocation often experience this kind of "ecological transition." While some children quickly adapt and fit into new mesosystems, others suffer in the process. The well-being of the family microsystem seems to play a major role in determining whether such an ecological transition is smooth or difficult.

THE EXOSYSTEM

"An exosystem is an extension of the mesosystem embracing other specific social structures, both formal and informal, that do not themselves contain the developing person but impinge upon or encompass the immediate setting in which that person is found . . ." (Bronfenbrenner, 1977: 515). The exosystem is defined as the larger community in which the adolescent lives; although he or she does not directly participate in exosystem decision making, these decisions do have a direct and sometimes an indirect (via the parents or the school) influence on the adolescent. Examples of social settings and institutions that make up part of an exosystem include the school board, the local government, a parent's employer, the mass media, the transportation system, churches, civic groups, industry, and so on (see Figure 24).

The exosystem may impoverish or enrich the quality of the micro- and the mesosystems of an adolescent through exosystem decisions that affect what an adolescent can or cannot do. For example, the superiors in the parents' workplace determine the hours of work, the rate of pay, number of days and vacation schedules, and whether or not there will be flexible working hours. Employers may decide to move a parent from the East

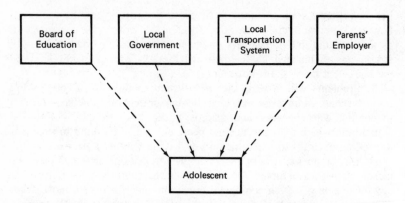

FIGURE 24. The Exosystem. The board of education, local government, local transportation system, and parents' employer exemplify the exosystem. Some exosystem decisions affect the individual adolescent. However, these influences are primarily impersonal, indirect, and one-way. The exosystem decision maker usually does not know the individual adolescent, and vice versa.

Coast to a new position on the West Coast, a decision that may have a profound influence on the micro- and the mesosystems of the adolescent and his relationship to other people and groups. The parents' working conditions, their roles in the workplace, their level of responsibility, and the degree of their participation in decision-making processes all have—as several studies have demonstrated—a direct influence on the parents' efforts to socialize their offspring.

The board of education decides what school the adolescent is to attend and what is to be offered in the curriculum. In order to save money, it might suspend the driver-education program or eliminate some extracurricular activity, even though these may be very important to the adolescent. The local government might open or close a youth center or the neighborhood community association might open or close the swimming pool, thus affecting available recreational resources. The adolescent in several of these examples can write a letter and complain about the actions taken, but in most instances he or she is relatively powerless vis-à-vis the exosystem. Later as adolescents grow older and participate more in community affairs, they do acquire more influence; at that point, part of the exosystem would become the mesosystem of these adolescents. Obviously, adults must question whether or not exosystem decisions are made with the adolescent's best interest in mind. Often they are not, because budgetary or political considerations carry more weight. Bronfenbrenner's theory encourages researchers to ask the question: How do those exosystem decisions that shape the lives of adolescents actually affect adolescent development?

THE MACROSYSTEM

The macrosystem consists of a broadly based "cultural blueprint that underlies the organization of institutions" (Garbarino, 1985: 60) in a given society. Although the macrosystem does not impinge directly on the life of the individual adolescent, it contains a societal ground plan for the ecology of human development. Of considerable importance, the macrosystem almost never receives systematic study except in anthropological research. The macrosystem includes a core of general cultural, social, legal, political, religious, economic, and educational values (see Figure 25).

When one refers to the Judeo-Christian culture, a communist country, Catholicism, capitalism, an industrial country, a constitutional democracy, the Protestant work ethic, a monarchy, and so on, one is referring to concepts that have a macrosystem quality. Historical, social, technological, cultural, and subcultural forces (wars, treaties, and legislation) shape and modify the macrosystem. Macrosystem values, in turn, find expression in what is considered fashionable and permissible. The macrosystem determines standards of physical attractiveness and what is appropriate (and inappropriate) behavior for each sex. It can influence health practices by, for example, increasing social and legislative restrictions on smoking or encouraging the advertisement and use of condoms to avoid AIDS and

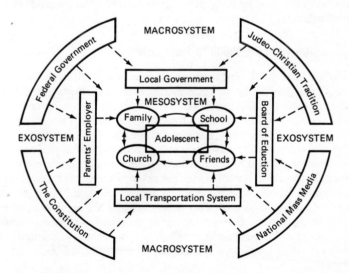

FIGURE 25. The Macrosystem. The individual is part of several microsystems, and several microsystems form the mesosystem. Interactions at the mesosystem level are personal and direct. The mesosystem is embedded in the exosystem and the more general social cultural macrosystem; effects at this level are impersonal and often indirect.

pregnancy. It can contribute to adolescent eating disorders such as anorexia and bulimia by equating thinness with beauty and sexual attractiveness (Muuss, 1985, 1986). Through legal and economic measures, the macrosystem determines who is an adolescent and distinguishes between adolescence and adulthood, although local subgroups (exosystems) may modify some of these criteria. Short of a violent revolution or military conquest, the macrosystem changes slowly. Nevertheless, industrialization, urbanization, democratization, equal-rights legislation, and women's liberation exemplify such fundamental though slow changes in the macrosystem. Through the concepts of postfigurative, cofigurative, and prefigurative cultures, Mead identified three qualitative leaps in the transformation of cultural macrosystems (see Chapter 6).

The remainder of this chapter will focus primarily on some aspects of the micro- and the mesosystems, since these areas have precipitated the most research and theorizing. The significance of the exo- and macrosystems should not be ignored, but at this point there is much less information about the influence of these.

Of great importance to almost any theory of adolescence is the intersection between the family microsystem and the peer group microsystem, which forms one of the most important adolescent mesosystems. Kandel has concentrated in her research on this aspect of the mesosystem. Hence her work will be highlighed, even though other researchers have also contributed.

The Transition from Childhood to Adolescence

A basic assumption of most theories of adolescence reflects the belief that the initial parent–child bond begins to loosen as the child grows older. This loosening of the symbolic emotional "umbilical cord" becomes especially noticeable as the child matures physically and grows into puberty and adolescence. Simultaneously, the cohort of age mates—especially the young adolescent's friends and peers—becomes increasingly influential and seems to contribute significantly to the process of development and socialization.

There are many explanations for the potency of peer influences during adolescence, but all of them depend on the fact that family ties inevitably loosen up during this period. This occurs because the helpless child must become self-sufficient and self-supporting in order to be accepted as an adult member of the larger society. The relevant constructs emphasized by different theorists all include this idea of a developmental push:

Autonomy (Blos, Erikson, Kohlberg)
Independence (Blos, Benedict, Gilligan)
Individuation or the development of individuality (Blos)
Identity formation (Erikson, Marcia)

Intimacy (Sullivan, Erikson, Marcia)

Abstract reasoning ability (Piaget, Kohlberg)

Decentering (Piaget, Elkind)

Responsibility (Benedict)

Parent microsystem supplanted by peer group microsystem

The "marginal man status" means that the adolescent stands on the boundaries between childhood and adulthood but belongs to neither. (Lewin)

The "loosening up of personality structure" (E. Douvan, 1983) as well as the "fluidity in personality boundaries" may explain the increased impulsivity that provokes parental complaints but which also provides youth with an increased motivation and the talent to form friendships.

"Sexual needs" must be added to this list, because it is a recognized fact that puberty awakens or accelerates sexual feelings; however, sexual gratification cannot be found in the family of orientation, only in the family of procreation (Freud, Blos, Erikson, Sullivan). Thus, the push from dependent childhood toward independent adulthood has both a societal and a biological component. The desire and need for friends at this stage in life may well be a particularly potent influence that contributes to these maturational processes and facilitates the transition into adulthood, as Sullivan (see Chapter 5) so cogently argues.

Theorizing about this movement from childhood dependence toward adolescence and adult independence has not stopped at simply recognizing the declining influences of the parents. Some psychologists have overemphasized the adolescent's efforts to immerse himself in new social relationships with his age mates, often creating an antagonistic or hostile stand vis-à-vis parents. This situation has been viewed as a choice between either one (peers) or the other (parents). Kandel (Kandel and Davies, 1982; Kandel and Lesser, 1972) refers to this either-or explanation as the *hydraulic model of interpersonal interaction,* in which the focal adolescent* can be close either to his parents or to his peers, but not both.

Since general social pressure and developmental patterns during adolescence constitute a movement away from parents and toward a new alignment with the peer group, much writing and research have gone into creating microtheories and gathering supportive evidence that emphasizes the importance of the peer group and the crises associated with this transition. Numerous studies have demonstrated the powerful and often

---

* The term "focal adolescent" will be used throughout this chapter to identify the adolescent who is the focus of the investigation—the person with whom the research is concerned.

opposite effects of peers and parents on the focal adolescent (Bronfenbrenner, 1986b: 727). The microtheories focus on the prevalence and the power of peer group influence and the associated, increasing antagonism and hostility toward parents and adults. Such an approach assumes that adolescents are caught in an almost inevitable struggle to free themselves from parental dependency and domination. Although these theories are too extensive to reference in this context, some important constructs and issues need to be identified: adolescent society (J. Coleman); adolescent subculture, adolescent contraculture, youth drug culture, hippie culture, generation gap, alienation, storm and stress (G. Stanley Hall); adolescent crisis (E. Erikson); and autonomous peer group, age segregation (J. Garbarino).

Because the nature of development propels adolescents toward their peers, the other side of the "hydraulic model" equation (maintaining identity with parents) has become less the focus of theoretical explanations. However, there are some highly adult-oriented adolescents who may prefer adult company or who may lack the social skills essential for peer group acceptance; they may become the butt of the peer group jokes, teasing, ostracism, and rejection.

Bronfenbrenner (Bronfenbrenner et al., 1965) and his collaborators have, in their research (especially cross-cultural research), distinguished between "adult-oriented" and "peer-oriented" subjects. Data based on cross-cultural comparison as well as research in the United States have demonstrated that puberty need not necessarily be a period of discontinuity and storm and stress. It can be a harmonious and continuous period of life if sufficient family, institutional, and interpersonal support and resources are directed toward facilitating adjustment (Bandura, 1964; Garbarino, 1977; Offer, 1975, 1981). Peer group influences can be congruent with parental and social influences; compatible parent–peer relationships are not only possible but much more common than the "adolescent subculture" and "generation gap" literature suggests. Bandura and Offer have reported, rather than storm and stress, much continuity in the developmental progression of their subjects. Piaget (1932b) had emphasized that peers can and do provide a constructive force in influencing moral and cognitive development.

As an alternative to the hydraulic model of interpersonal interaction, Kandel and Lesser (1972) and Kandel and Davies (1982) propose a more *generalized social-interaction model* and they present evidence in support of it. Their findings indicate that—in terms of mental health, school adjustment, and psychosocial development—the most beneficial pattern defining the individual's parent–peer relationships is one in which focal adolescents are actively involved with their friends and their peer group. They are effective in communicating with their parents, feel close to them, and do not reject them or feel rejected by them. Brown et al. (1986) also report moderate peer pressure toward preadult behavior, such as striving for good grades and getting along with parents. In other words, parent and peer relationships do not have to be mutually exclusive. Quite the contrary: positive parent–peer relationships—congruency between the micro- and mesosystems—are not only possible but appear ideal from a mental health perspective. This is a refreshing and insightful piece of information, since we know that heavy, one-sided involvement in the peer group without a positive relationship with parents is one of the strongest predictors of problem behavior not only for youths but even for young adults. Problem behaviors related to the peer group may cover a whole range of patterns: "poor school performance, aggressiveness or social withdrawal, school absenteeism or dropping out, smoking, drinking, early promiscuous sexual activity, teenage parenthood, drugs and juvenile delinquency" (Bronfenbrenner, 1986a: 433). Although Kandel does not provide specific information as to the percentage of adolescents who are able to maintain a constructive balance between peer involvement and parent relationship, Offer (1975), in a different context, suggests that about 23 percent may achieve continuity in their development without a major conflict with parents.

HOW ARE ADOLESCENT FRIENDSHIPS FORMED?

Kandel (1986) proposes two theoretical principles to explain the formation, stability, and dissolution of adolescent friendships: (1) the selection process and (2) the socialization process. The construct *selection process* implies that certain attributes (usually similar interests, personality traits, physical characteristics, attitudes, values, and behavior) exist prior to the onset of a friendship; these preexisting characteristics become the contributing factors for the interest of two people in each other. Because such attributes are of mutual importance, they eventually lead to the formation of a friendship. The adage "Birds of a feather flock together" identifies the underlying dynamics.

Another explanatory principle involves the *socialization process*. This implies that the similarity between a pair of friends increases as a result of their frequent, mutual interaction, irrespective of their prior similarities. Friends literally and symbolically influence, moderate, and socialize each other, so that they eventually tend to become more and more alike in important characteristics, attitudes, values, and behavior. Theories of interpersonal behavior assume that similarity contributes to liking but also that liking contributes to similarity.

According to Kandel (1978a, 1986), both selection efforts and socialization effects operate on a variety of attributes and contribute equally in the formation and the maintenance of a friendship, even though their respective potency may differ for different areas of an adolescent's life or for different phases in the life cycle of a friendship. Some characteristics may contribute more heavily to the initial attraction to another person—a feeling of mutuality that leads to the formation of a friendship. However, friends also tend to become mutually reinforcing—a tendency that strengthens their friendship.

Similarities in regard to these characteristics take on additional significance when viewed in relationship to *the phase or stage of the friendship-formation process.* Different attributes may be of greater importance in one rather than another phase of the life cycle of a friendship. Three basic stages are identified in the formation of a friendship: (1) the prospective friendship phase, the initial phase of people being attracted to and becoming interested in one another, or the beginning formation of a friendship; (2) the actual, ongoing, stable friendship phase; and (3) the phase of the beginning disintegration of an existing friendship.

Longitudinal data collected over the life span of a friendship have made it possible not only to identify similarities of friends in respect to relevant attributes at each of these three phases but also to compare the degree of similarity at one time in the relationship to the outcome of the friendship pattern at a later time. Specific characteristics that Kandel has investigated are listed in terms of their overall significance to the friendship: marijuana use, educational aspirations, participation in minor delinquent acts, and political attitudes.

The significance of these characteristics to the friendship pair was quite similar for all four. However, because friends agreed by far the most intensely about marijuana use, attitudes toward smoking marijuana illustrate clearly the patterns of the other characteristics. Results indicate that behavioral similarity between friends about the use of marijuana is strongest in the stable friendship phase—stronger than in either the initial stage of forming a new friendship or the resolution phase. However, agreement is stronger in a stable friendship pattern that will remain stable and weaker in a stable friendship pattern that will end within a few months. Behavioral similarity tends to be low in unstable friendship pairs and just prior to the termination of the relationship; it is especially low after the friendship has been discontinued.

THE INFLUENCE OF PARENTS VERSUS PEERS

How significant is the influence of parents relative to the influence of peers on the focal adolescent? Research findings have not conclusively answered this often raised question. Obviously, there are wide individual and situational variations. Human development never occurs in a "context-free situation" but always in a specific ecological setting—a unique family, a specific neighborhood, school, and community—a social context. However, data exist about some factors influential in the parents-versus-peers controversy. Actual consideration of these factors may place the question in a more specific context and make it more meaningful. One must ask: What type of parent or parents? What type of adolescent? What type of situation enhances parental or peer influence? Any theory or research project that simply reports parents or peers to be more influential without considering these and perhaps other factors must be one-sided or inadequate.

1. To answer the first question, the research must consider the characteristics of the parents and the quality of the parent–adolescent relationship. Bronfenbrenner et al. (1965) identified five types of family structure, depending on who has the relative power: patriarchal, patricentric, egalitarian, matricentric, and matriarchal. The most responsible and most self-reliant adolescents tended to come not from egalitarian families, as originally expected, but from patricentric or matricentric families. Egalitarian families were both the most affectionate and the most permissive. Current researchers express concern with what Bronfenbrenner and Crouter (1983) refer to as the "new demography," which includes fundamental changes in family structure and new ways of identifying families: the intact family, the one-parent family, the reconstituted family, the employed-mother family, the absent-father family, or the family with the father in the role of primary caregiver. Each of these new "family structure" factors has generated its own literature and its own theory. For a review of the complexity of the "ecology of the family" and an understanding of the multiplicity of factors that need to be considered, readers should consult Bronfenbrenner's (1986b) comprehensive and insightful review article, even though its primary focus is child development rather than adolescence. Obviously, there are many other appropriate models identifying parental characteristics or family structure.

2. The nature (structure, quality, orientation, and characteristics) of the peer group or adolescent subgroup obviously constitutes a second crucial variable in the influence of parents versus peers on the focal adolescent. Bronfenbrenner et al. (1965) distinguished peer-oriented versus adult-oriented adolescents. The essential difference involved the extent to which the individual was aligned with the values of peers as opposed to those of adults. Kandel, similarly, distinguishes a "high peer drug involvement group" from a "high peer involvement group" who does not use drugs. Brown and Trujillo (in press) have developed a very elaborate typology, including the typical groups that form the social structures among high school students. Brown identifies eleven distinct types of peer subgroups.

3. The third group of variables requiring consideration includes the issues, choices, values, and situational factors around which the potency of parent versus peer influences is being assessed. It is reasonable to assume—and past research (Brittain, 1963; Jennings and Niemi, 1974; Troll and Bengston, 1979) supports this assumption—that the influence of parents may be greater in respect to some values and behaviors, whereas

the influence of the peer group may prove stronger in other areas. Kandel has stated this general assumption more precisely: "For issues and concerns of immediate relevancy to the adolescent's life, such as drug involvement, peers play a crucial role. For issues relevant to basic values, such as religiosity, and to the adolescent's future, such as educational aspirations, parents are much more important than peers" (1986: 213).

Kandel (1986) tested these theoretical propositions empirically. She analyzed the drug use of the focal adolescent not only vis-à-vis the marijuana use of peers but also vis-à-vis the use of alcohol and medically prescribed psychoactive drugs used by parents. Kandel found that drug use among both friends and parents has independent effects on the drug use of the focal adolescent.

However, as suggested in the initial hypothesis, the drug use of peers appears to be a much stronger influence than that of the parents. These findings can be summarized briefly and very convincingly: If both parents (alcohol) and peers (marijuana) use drugs, 70 percent of the focal adolescents smoke marijuana. If the friends smoke marijuana but the parents do not drink, 58 percent of the focal adolescents use marijuana. If the friends do not use drugs and the parents drink, 22 percent of the focal adolescents smoke marijuana. Finally, if neither the friends nor the parents use drugs or alcohol, only 12 percent of the focal adolescents smoke marijuana. While the drug use of peers provides the more potent influence, the drinking behavior of the parents does have a strong modifying effect on the use of marijuana by their adolescent offspring. The same pattern of relative influence of peers versus parents emerges when the crucial behavior of the focal adolescent is not marijuana use but the drinking of hard liquor. The sequence described above remains the same, but with slightly modified percentages (61, 52, 39, and 31 percent).

The pattern of peer versus parent influence on the focal adolescent described above reverses itself in regard to the development of educational aspirations (e.g., "wanting to go to college"). On this issue, the effect of the parents' preferred choice proves much stronger than the college aspirations of friends. Again, the findings speak for themselves: If both parents and peers have college aspirations, 89 percent of the focal adolescents want to go to college. If parents want the focal adolescent to attend college but the peers do not plan to enter college, 68 percent of the focal adolescents have college aspirations. If the peers have college aspirations but the parents do not, 32 percent of the focal adolescents want to go to college. Finally, if neither parents nor peers have college aspirations, only 15 percent of the focal adolescents say they would like to go to college. These data strongly support the assumption that the parents' influence on the focal adolescent's college aspirations is stronger than that of peers. In relation to the peer group influence, the parents' impact on the educational aspirations is consistently higher for boys than for girls.

Among girls, the peer group influence is at a peak in ninth grade, but peer group influences decline during the remaining high school years.

Using a different methodology at a different time with different subjects, Brittain suggested in 1963 that the tendency to conform to parental or peer group expectations depended on the nature of the situation and the adolescent's perception of the relative competence of peers or parents as appropriate guides for behavior. Brittain's findings are quite compatible and supportive of the results of Kandel (1986) and others.

A TAXONOMY OF ADOLESCENCE OR A TYPOLOGY OF PEER GROUPS

Adolescents are not a homogeneous group of people but highly diversified and differentiated individuals. The concept "adolescence," which is complex and multidimensional, must be differentiated for clarity (Muuss, 1982b). Even the concept "peer group" does not imply a uniform and coherent collective of adolescents but a highly differentiated cluster of identifiable types or crowds who differ significantly in their orientation toward conventional, moral, social, parental, religious, school, sport, dating, drug, and other values. The number of different types of peer groups seems virtually endless, including all the contexts of the adolescent's life. Often, scholars have ignored even those most obvious subdivisions of the peer group by regarding all members of that group as the independent variable in developmental research. Some of the most obvious subdivisions include early, late, and middle adolescents; junior and senior high school students; freshmen, sophomores, juniors, seniors; same-sex and opposite-sex peer groups; students in academic, general, and vocational curriculums, and so on. Indeed, the possibilities seem limited only by the perceptions of the investigator.

Interests, attitudes, and behaviors hold each peer group together. Thus, a common value structure often draws together a particular group of individuals who share similar attributes; this then becomes the basis on which a social unit is formed. Peers who have much in common associate with each other freely. They share some common bond that undergirds the social structure of their group.

Brown and Trujillo (in press) developed a crowd or peer group typology based on adolescents' own perceptions of the clusters of values and behaviors that commonly bind group associations in contemporary high schools. The eleven types of peer groups that emerged from this investigation are quite familiar to the observer of the high school social scene, especially to the youth who finds it difficult to gain admission into a group that already exists. These types have found entry into the popular press and even into lay language as stereotypes, and they are built around such catchwords as "brains," "druggies," "jocks," "loners," "normals," "outcasts," "populars," "toughs," special-interest groups (e.g., "farmers," "band buddies"), and "hybrids" (e.g., "party jocks," "preppy brains") as well as unassignables and miscellaneous types (Brown and Trujillo, in press). Obviously, these categories are not clear-cut. They do overlap—as the idea of the "hybrid" implies—and an individual may belong to several groups or move from one group or group cluster to another. Furthermore, the nomenclature in vogue in any particular high school community to describe any of these categories may differ in other schools and reflect local flavor and lingo. For example, those identified as "brains" may, in different high school settings, become "academics," "eggheads," "intellectuals," "intelligentsia," "smarts," "smart groups," "straight-A's," "studious," and so on. High school students themselves seem to be aware of these peer group types, their unique characteristics, and what is required to become a member. On the other hand, the professional literature has often overused the peer group concept and depicted peer pressure as "a repressive, monolithic force (Brown et al., 1986) without examining subtle but highly relevant differences in value orientation.

Kandel (1978b) selected, for purposes of analysis, two such groups with contrasting values. Both exhibit a high degree of peer involvement. One showed a high level of drug use (most friends used marijuana) while the other group did not (friends did not smoke marijuana). She reported that these two groups were sharply distinct in respect to parent relationships, level of school adjustment, and interpersonal characteristics. The focal adolescents whose friends did not use marijuana had closer relationships with their parents, respected their parents more, and in general appeared to be more adult-oriented. They were less frequently absent from school, received better grades, had college aspirations, spent more time on homework, attended religious services more often, held more traditional values, and were less depressed than those focal adolescents whose friends used marijuana. Those whose friends used marijuana held the opposite values, were absent from school more often, received lower grades, did not attend religious services, and were less inclined to aspire to college.

In the literature—with some noticeable exceptions (Bronfenbrenner, Brown, Kandel, Muuss)—this kind of differential peer group value analysis has been conspicuously absent. The assumption seems to be, only too often, that the peer group has some general characteristics with one of the more prevalent being antagonism to adult values. From a theoretical and empirical point of view, readers must remember that different peer groups espouse different values—values that require identification whenever one refers to "the peer group." For example, in the typology listed above (Brown and Trujillo, in press), that the "brains" and "normals" tend to be more parent-oriented while the "druggies" and the "toughs" tend to be more peer-oriented might prove to be a reasonable expectation.

HOW DO ADOLESCENTS INFLUENCE EACH OTHER?

Kandel (1986) suggests two psychological constructs that help to explain how adolescents influence each other. These constructs, which come from social learning theory (see Chapter 13), include imitation and socialization.

Imitation or modeling implies that if an individual exhibits a certain behavior or attitude that the focal adolescent likes, accepts, and values, the latter eventually will imitate the observed or similar behavior.

Social reinforcement is different. In this situation the focal adolescent goes along with the behavioral suggestions of friends or peers for the sake of the social reinforcement (in terms of status, praise, recognition, or peer group admiration) received in return. In other words, the behavior or attitude exhibited brings about some social benefit.

Of these two constructs—at least in terms of smoking marijuana—modeling appears to have a more powerful effect than social reinforcement. However, there is insufficient evidence to support the claim that modeling in general is a more potent influence than social reinforcement.

The processes described for the formation of friendship patterns appear to be quite similar for both males and females. Girls in general—as Gilligan (see Chapter 10) has reported in a different context—appear to be quicker in picking up social cues, are more aware of social pressures (Brown et al., 1986), and are more in tune with interpersonal influences than boys, regardless whether these influences come from peers or parents. In general, girls seem to form intimate interpersonal relationships more easily than boys.

CROSS-CULTURAL DIFFERENCES IN FRIENDSHIP AND PEER RELATIONSHIPS

Wide social and cultural differences exist in respect to the influences of the peer group and that of friends versus parents during adolescence. Historically speaking, the construct "peer group" is of relatively recent origin. The significance of the peer group has increased with the increasing length of school attendance as well as the increasing number of adolescents who remain in high school until graduation. In the comprehensive high school, age cohorts spend most of their time together, not only during the regular school day but also in practices, rehearsals, and other after-school activities, both formal and informal.

In more traditional societies, especially if former schooling terminates at age fourteen or fifteen, the peer group never becomes as influential and relevant as when most adolescents attend school together.

In the more traditional societies the orientation becomes vertical in relation to one's elders, not horizontal, to one's peers. A comparison of second-, third-, and fourth-generation Chinese adolescents in Hawaii with a matched group of adolescents in Chicago revealed rather clearly that the former group was less troubled by adolescence, less rebellious, and more family-oriented, while the Chicago adolescents tended to be more peer-oriented (Hsu, Watrous, and Lord, 1961).

In societies where there is a single overriding national concern and commitment, as in the Soviet Union (or, for different reasons, in Israel), the social pressures from peers and from adults seem to act in the same direction. The more pluralistic the political and social structure of a society, the more likely the adolescent is to respond to social pressure from peers. Bronfenbrenner (1967) demonstrated that the divergence between peer group and adult values is much greater in the United States—as in other societies with a pluralistic political structure—than it is in the Soviet Union and other societies where peer group and adult values seem to converge around a politically endorsed core. The peer group advocates and reinforces a politically endorsed and socially approved set of values, so that the focal adolescent is exposed to fewer cross pressures between the expectations of peers and those of significant adults, as is frequently the case in the United States. Bronfenbrenner expresses concern that "the Russians have gone too far in subjecting the child and his peer group to conformity to a single set of values imposed by the adult society" (Bronfenbrenner, 1970: 165). However, he and others warn that we, in more pluralistic, egalitarian, and democratic societies, may have allowed the peer group excessive autonomy and have failed in utilizing the constructive and prosocial potential that the peer group can bring to bear on the individual in developing responsibility, considerations for others, social skills, and mental health.

FRIENDSHIP INFLUENCES AND PEER PATTERNS AS A FUNCTION OF AGE

Friendship relationships and peer patterns are influenced by age changes between preadolescence and adulthood. Garbarino et al. (1978), studying changes in the social network during the transition from childhood to adulthood, have reported that the social network in early adolescence includes significantly fewer adults than in the preceding period of late childhood. In addition, the stability of friendships over time increases with advancing age at least until age eighteen. Harry Stack Sullivan's stage theory emphasizes changing interpersonal quality as a function of age (see Chapter 5). Muuss (1982b) has distinguished the basic changes in social orientation that take place between early, middle, and late adolescence.

Dunphy (1980), in his often quoted and comprehensive study, has described adolescent social structure and identified common patterns of age change in social groups as a function of development. He does not consider the ecological interaction effect of other microsystems, and he fails to show

how different types of peer groups (of different socioeconomic status) affect this developmental progression. Nevertheless, Dunphy does clearly identify the age changes in adolescent social structure. Basically, he views the emerging new adolescent social structure as a function of modern urban life; he emphasizes that adolescent social groups are replacing the family in strength of influence and control. In particular, he focuses on the composition of and the change in cliques and crowds and the degree of heterosexual interaction. Cliques are defined as relatively small, socially cohesive groups (three to nine individuals) of buddies or close friends who are quite similar in terms of age, socioeconomic status, interests, attitudes, and preferences. Crowds are somewhat larger social groups (fifteen to thirty individuals), which often develop out of and are a combination of several cliques. Frequently, several—on an average three—cliques form a crowd. The crowd is not as cohesive a group as the clique, individuals are not necessarily buddies, and they share less of a common value structure than they would in a clique; nevertheless, they are compatible and have some common interests. Crowd members are of approximately the same age, and different crowds in the same community are differentiated from one another by age, typically within a range of about two years.

Beginning in early adolescence various isolated cliques form. Initially, these cliques are unisexual in structure, and interaction between the sexes is limited. Dunphy refers to these early cliques as stage 1, the precrowd stage. At a later point, several small cliques begin to interact with one another. Stage 2 defines the beginning of the crowd. Unisexual cliques begin to interact, including some interaction (teasing, bantering) with cliques of the opposite sex. Stage 3 finds the crowd in structural transition. Several unisexual cliques have joined each other to form the crowd, and the upper-status members begin to form heterosexual cliques. Stage 4 is the fully developed crowd, in which former unisexual cliques become heterosexual and crowd interaction becomes prevalent. Toward late adolescence, in stage 5, the crowd begins to disintegrate as individual members become preoccupied with dating and courtship. Heterosexual couples pair off because they are more interested in each other than in the crowd or clique. The couple now becomes the basic unit of social interaction.

Dunphy has contributed greatly to our understanding of age changes in the social structure of adolescent peer groups, especially cliques and crowds. However, he does emphasize the emergence of a ''youth subculture,'' a theme that became especially prevalent in the sixties and seventies. However, as Kandel (1986) has so poignantly emphasized, the adolescent subculture is a one-sided construct, and the interplay between the focal adolescent and his or her peers versus his or her parents is more subtle and complex than subculture theories have generally assumed.

REFERENCES

Aebli, H. *Über die geistige Entwicklung des Kindes.* Stuttgart: Klett, 1963.

Andrews, J. The relationship of values to identity achievement status. *Journal of Youth and Adolescence,* 1973, *2,* 133–138.

Aristotle. Magna moralia. In W. D. Ross, ed., *The works of Aristotle* (G. Stock, trans.), vol. 9. Oxford: Clarendon Press, 1925.

———. Ethica Nicomachea. In R. McKeon, ed., *The basic works of Aristotle* (W. D. Ross, trans.). New York: Random House, 1941(a).

———. Historia animalium. In R. McKeon, ed., *The basic works of Aristotle* (D. W. Thompson, trans.). New York: Random House, 1941(b).

———. Politica. In R. McKeon, ed., *The basic works of Aristotle* (B. Jowett, trans.). New York: Random House, 1941(c).

———. Rhetorica. In R. McKeon, ed., *The basic works of Aristotle* (W. R. Roberts, trans.). New York: Random House, 1941(d).

Arlin, P. K. Cognitive development in adulthood: A fifth stage? *Developmental Psychology,* 1975, *11,* 602–606.

Ausubel, D. P. *Theory and problems of child development.* New York: Grune & Stratton, 1958.

Bacon, M. K., Child, I. L., and Barry, H. A cross-cultural study of correlates of crime. *Journal of Abnormal and Social Psychology,* 1963, *66,* 291–300.

Baldwin, A. L. *Theories of child development.* New York: Wiley, 1967.

Baldwin, C. P., and Baldwin, A. L. Children's judgments of kindness. *Child Development,* 1970, *41,* 29–47.

Ball, W. B. Religion and public education: The Post-Schempp years. In T. R. Sizer, ed., *Religion and public education.* Boston: Houghton Mifflin, 1967.

Bandura, A. Relationship of family patterns to child behavior disorders. Progress Report, U.S.P.H. Research Grant M–1734. Stanford, Calif.: Stanford University, 1960.

———. Social learning theory through imitation. In M. R. Jones, ed., *Nebraska symposium on motivation,* vol. 10. Lincoln: University of Nebraska Press, 1962.

———. The stormy decade: Fact or fiction? *Psychology in the Schools,* 1964, *1,* 224–231.

―――. Behavioral modifications through modeling procedures. In L. Krasner and L. P. Ullmann, eds., *Research in behavior modification*. New York: Holt, Rinehart & Winston, 1965.

―――. The role of modeling processes in personality development. In W. W. Hartup and N. L. Smothergill, eds., *The young child: Reviews of research*. Washington, D.C.: National Association for the Education of Young Children, 1967.

―――. *Principles of behavior modification*. New York: Holt, Rinehart & Winston, 1969.

―――. Vicarious and self-reinforcement processes. In R. Glaser, ed., *The nature of reinforcement*. New York: Academic Press, 1971.

―――. *Aggression: A social learning analysis*. Englewood Cliffs, N.J.: Prentice-Hall, 1973(a).

―――. Social learning theory of aggression. In J. F. Knutson, ed., *The control of aggression: Implications from basic research*. Chicago: Aldine Publishing Company, 1973(b).

Bandura, A., and Kupers, C. J. Transmission of patterns of self-reinforcement through modeling. *Journal of Abnormal and Social Psychology*, 1964, *69*, 1–9.

Bandura, A., and McDonald, F. J. Influence of social reinforcement and the behavior of models in shaping children's moral judgments. *Journal of Abnormal and Social Psychology*, 1963, *67*, 274–281.

Bandura, A., and Mischel, W. Modification of self-imposed delay of reward through exposure to live and symbolic models. *Journal of Personality and Social Psychology*, 1965, *2*, 698–705.

Bandura, A., and Perloff, B. Relative efficacy of self-monitored and externally imposed reinforcement systems. *Journal of Personality and Social Psychology*, 1967, *7*, 111–116.

Bandura, A., Ross, D., and Ross, S. A. Transmission of aggression through imitation of aggressive models. *Journal of Abnormal and Social Psychology*, 1961, *63*, 575–582.

―――. A comparative test of the status envy, social power, and secondary reinforcement theories of identificatory learning. *Journal of Abnormal and Social Psychology*, 1963, *67*, 527–534(a).

―――. Imitation of film-mediated aggressive models. *Journal of Abnormal and Social Psychology*, 1963, *66*, 3–11(b).

―――. Vicarious reinforcement and imitative learning. *Journal of Abnormal and Social Psychology*, 1963, *67*, 601–607(c).

Bandura, A., and Walters, R. H. *Adolescent aggression*. New York: Ronald Press, 1959.

―――. *Social learning and personality development*. New York: Holt, Rinehart & Winston, 1963.

Bandura, A., and Whalen, C. K. The influence of antecedent reinforcement and divergent modeling cues on patterns of self-reward. *Journal of Personality and Social Psychology*, 1966, *3*, 373–382.

Bart, W. M. Issues in measuring formal operational reasoning. *The Genetic Epistemologist*, 1978, 7, 3–4.

Baumrind, D. Sex differences in moral reasoning: Response to Walker's (1984) conclusion that there are none. *Child Development*, 1986, 57, 511–521.

Bell, N. D. The relationship of occupational choice to ego identity and self-concept. Unpublished doctoral dissertation, Utah University, 1969.

Benedict, R. *Patterns of culture*. New York: New American Library, 1950. (Originally published 1934.)

———. Continuities and discontinuities in cultural conditioning. In R. E. Muuss, ed., *Adolescent behavior and society: A book of readings*, 3rd ed. New York: Random House, 1980. (Originally published 1938.)

Berndt, T. J., and Berndt, E. G. Children's use of motives and intentionality in person perception and moral judgment. *Child Development*, 1975, 46, 904–912.

Blatt, M. Experimental studies in moral education using a developmental approach. Unpublished doctoral dissertation, University of Chicago, 1959.

Block, J. Ego identity, role variability, and adjustment. *Journal of Consulting Psychology*, 1961, 25, 392–397.

———. Conceptions of sex role: Some cross-cultural and longitudinal perspectives. *American Psychologist*, 1973, 28, 512–526.

Blos, P. *The adolescent personality: A study of individual behavior*. New York: D. Appleton-Century, 1941.

———. *On adolescence: A psychoanalytic interpretation*. New York: Free Press, 1962.

———. The initial stage of male adolescence. *The psychoanalytic study of the child*, vol. 20. New York: International Universities Press, 1965.

———. The second individuation process of adolescence. *The psychoanalytic study of the child*, vol. 22. New York: International Universities Press, 1967.

———. *The young adolescent: Clinical studies*. New York: Free Press, 1970.

———. The child analyst looks at the young adolescent. *Daedalus*, 1971, 100, 961–978.

———. *The adolescent passage: Developmental issues*. New York: International Universities Press, 1979.

———. Modifications in the traditional psychoanalytic theory of female adolescent development. In S. C. Feinstein, P. L. Giovacchini, J. G. Looney, A. Z. Schwartzberg, and A. D. Sorosky, *Adolescent psychiatry*, vol. 8. Chicago: University of Chicago Press, 1981.

Boas, F. Foreword to *Coming of age in Samoa*. New York: New American Library, 1950. (Originally published 1928.)

Bob, S. An investigation of the relationship between identity status, cognitive style, and stress. Unpublished doctoral dissertation, State University of New York at Buffalo, 1968.

Bourne, E. The state of research on ego identity: A review and appraisal. Part I. *Journal of Youth and Adolescence*, 1978, 7, 223–251.

Boyd, W. *The history of Western education.* New York: Barnes & Noble, 1965.

Brabeck, M. Moral judgment: Theory and research on differences between males and females. *Developmental Review,* 1983, *3,* 274–291.

Breuer, H. Ego identity status in late-adolescent college males, as measured by a group-administered incomplete sentence blank and related to inferred stance toward authority. Unpublished doctoral dissertation, New York University, 1973.

Brittain, C. V. Adolescent choices and parent-peer cross-pressures. *American Sociological Review,* 1963, *28,* 385–391.

————. Age and sex of siblings and conformity toward parents versus peers in adolescence. *Child Development,* 1966, *37,* 709–714.

Bronfenbrenner, U. Response to pressure from peers versus adults among Soviet and American school children. *International Journal of Psychology,* 1967, *2,* 199–207.

————. *Two worlds of childhood: U.S. and U.S.S.R.* New York: Simon and Schuster, 1970.

————. Toward an experimental ecology of human development. *American Psychologist,* 1977, *32,* 513–531.

————. Alienation and the four worlds of childhood. *Phi Delta Kappan,* 1986, *67,* 430–436(a).

————. Ecology of the family as a context for human development: Research perspectives. *Developmental Psychology,* 1986, *22,* 723–742(b).

————, and Crouter, A. C. The evolution of environmental models in developmental research. In P. H. Mussen, ed., *Handbook of child psychology,* 4th ed. New York: Wiley, 1983, vol. 1, pp. 357–414.

————, Devereux, E. C. Jr., Suci, G. J., and Rodgers, R. R. Adults and peers as sources of conformity and autonomy. Paper presented at the Conference on Socialization for Competence, sponsored by the Social Science Research Council, Puerto Rico, 1965.

Bronson, G. W. Identity diffusion in late adolescents. *Journal of Abnormal and Social Psychology,* 1959, *59,* 414–417.

————. Fear of visual novelty: Developmental patterns in males and females. In L. J. Stone, H. T. Smith, and L. B. Murphy, eds., *The competent infant.* New York: Basic Books, 1973.

Brown, B. B., Lohr, M. J., and McClenahan, E. L. Early adolescents' perceptions of peer pressure. *Journal of Early Adolescence,* 1986, *6,* 139–154.

Brown, B. B., and Trujillo, C. M. Adolescents' perceptions of peer group stereotypes. (Manuscript submitted.)

Brownstone, J. E., and Willis, R. H. Conformity in early and late adolescence. *Developmental Psychology,* 1971, *4,* 334–337.

Bruner, J. S. *The process of education.* New York: Vintage Books, 1960.

Bunt, M. E. Ego identity: Its relationship to the discrepancy between how an adolescent views himself and how he perceives that others view him. *Psychology,* 1968, *5,* 14–25.

Burk, D. *Piagetian attainment kit.* Monterey, Calif.: Publishers Test Service, 1973.

Byrne, D. F. The development of role taking in adolescence. *Dissertation Abstract,* 1974, *34,* No. 11, 5647B.

Calhoun, J. F. *Abnormal psychology: Current perspectives,* 2nd ed. New York: CRM/Random House, 1977.

Cattell, R. B., and Scheier, I. H. *The meaning and measurement of neuroticism and anxiety.* New York: Ronald Press, 1961.

Cauble, M. A. Formal operations, ego identity, and principled morality: Are they related? *Developmental Psychology,* 1976, *12,* 363–364.

Chandler, M. J. Egocentrism and antisocial behavior: The assessment and training of social perspective-taking skills. *Developmental Psychology,* 1973, *9,* 326–332.

Coady, H. Behavioral correlates of moral judgment. *Journal of Psychology,* 1986, *120,* 191–198.

Comenius, J. A. *The great didactic* (M. W. Keatinge, ed. and trans.). London: A. & C. Black, 1923. (Originally published 1657.)

Conger, J. J. *Adolescence and youth,* 2nd ed. New York: Harper & Row, 1977.

Constantinople, A. An Eriksonian measure of personality development in college students. *Developmental Psychology,* 1969, *1,* 357–372.

Corsini, R. J. *Current personality theories.* Itasca, Ill.: F. E. Peacock, 1977.

Costanzo, P. R. Conformity and development as a function of self-blame. *Journal of Personality and Social Psychology,* 1970, *14,* 366–374.

Costanzo, P. R., and Shaw, M. E. Conformity as a function of age level. *Child Development,* 1966, *37,* 967–975.

Cross, H. J., and Allen, J. G. Paternal antecedents of identity status in college males. Paper presented at the Eastern Psychological Association Convention, Philadelphia, 1969.

———. Ego identity status, adjustment, and academic achievement. *Journal of Consulting and Clinical Psychology,* 1970, *34,* 288.

———. Antecedents of identity status: Differences between males and females. Paper presented at the Eastern Psychological Association Convention, New York, 1971.

Damon, W. *The social world of the child.* San Francisco: Jossey-Bass, 1977.

———. Patterns of change in children's social reasoning: A two-year longitudinal study. *Child Development,* 1980, *51,* 1010–1017.

Darwin, C. R. *The origin of species by means of natural selection.* London: J. Murray, 1859.

Davies, M., and Kandel, D. B. Parental and peer influences on adolescents' educational plans: Some further evidence. *American Journal of Sociology,* 1981, *87,* 363–387.

Deutsch, F. Observational and sociometric measures of peer popularity and their relationship to egocentric communication in female preschoolers. *Developmental Psychology,* 1974, *10,* 745–747.

Donovan, J. M. A study of ego identity formation. *Dissertation Abstract,* 1971, *B31,* 4986–4987.

————. Identity status and interpersonal style. *Journal of Youth and Adolescence,* 1975, *4,* 37–55.

Douvan, E. Commentary: Theoretical perspectives on peer association. In J. L. Epstein and N. Karweit, eds., *Friends in school: Patterns of selection and influence in secondary schools.* New York: Academic Press, 1983.

Douvan, E., and Adelson, J. *The adolescent experience.* New York: Wiley, 1966.

Dufresne, J., and Cross, J. H. Personality variables in student drug use. Unpublished master's thesis, University of Connecticut, 1972.

Dulit, E. Adolescent thinking à la Piaget: The formal stage. *Journal of Youth and Adolescence,* 1972, *1,* 281–301.

Dunphy, D. C. Peer group socialisation. In R. E. Muuss, ed., *Adolescent behavior and society: A book of readings.* New York: Random House, 1980.

Dye, P., Marquiss, J., and LaVoie, J. C. Ego identity in normal and socially maladjusted adolescent females. Unpublished manuscript, University of Nebraska at Omaha, 1975.

Eisenberg-Berg, N., and Mussen, P. Empathy and moral development in adolescence. *Developmental Psychology,* 1978, *14,* 185–186.

Elardo, P. Project AWARE: A school program to facilitate social development of children. Paper presented at the Fourth H. Blumberg Symposium, Chapel Hill, N.C., 1974.

Elkind, D. Children's discovery of the conservation of mass, weight, and volume: Piaget replication study II. *Journal of Genetic Psychology,* 1961, *98,* 219–227(a).

————. Quantity conceptions in junior and senior high school students. *Child Development,* 1961, *32,* 551–560(b).

————. Egocentrism in adolescence. *Child Development,* 1967, *38,* 1025–1034.

————. Cognitive structure and adolescent experience. *Adolescence,* 1967/68, *2,* 427–434.

————. Cognitive development in adolescence. In J. F. Adams, ed., *Understanding adolescence.* Boston: Allyn & Bacon, 1968.

————. Is Piaget passé in elementary education? *Genetic Epistemologist,* 1978, *7,* 1–2.

Elkind, D., and Bowen, R. Imaginary audience behavior in children and adolescents. *Developmental Psychology,* 1979, *15,* 38–44.

Enright, R. D. Social cognition in children: A model for intervention. *Counseling Psychologist,* 1976, *6,* 65–70.

Enright, R. D., Lapsley, D. K., and Shukla, D. G. Adolescent egocentrism in early and late adolescence. *Adolescence,* 1979, *14,* 687–695.

Enright, R. D., Shukla, D. G., and Lapsley, D. K. Adolescent egocentrism-sociocentrism and self-consciousness. *Journal of Youth and Adolescence,* 1980, *9,* 101–116.

Enright, R. D., and Sutterfield, S. J. An ecological validation of social cognition development. *Child Development*, 1980, *51*, 156–161.

Erikson, E. H. *Childhood and society*. New York: Norton, 1950.

————. *Young man Luther*. New York: Norton, 1958.

————. Identity and the life cycle: Selected papers. *Psychological Issues Monographic Series I.*, no. 1. New York: International Universities Press, 1959.

————, ed. *The challenge of youth*. Garden City, N.Y.: Doubleday/Anchor Books, 1965.

————. *Identity: Youth and crisis*. New York: Norton, 1968.

————. *Gandhi's truth*. New York: Norton, 1969.

————. Autobiographic notes on the identity crisis. *Daedalus*, 1970, *99*, 730–759.

Eron, L. D., Walder, L. O., Toigo, R., and Lefkowitz, M. M. Social class, parental punishment for aggression, and child aggression. *Child Development*, 1963, *34*, 849–867.

Feshbach, N. D. Empathy: An interpersonal process. Paper presented at the American Psychological Association Convention, Montreal, 1973.

————. Empathy in children: Some theoretical and empirical considerations. *Counseling Psychologist*, 1975, *5*, 25–30.

Fisher, S., and Greenberg, R. P. *The scientific credibility of Freud's theories and therapy*. New York: Basic Books, 1977.

Flanagan, J. C. Findings from Project TALENT. *Educational Forum*, 1979, *43*, 489–490.

Flavell, J. H. *The developmental psychology of Jean Piaget*. New York: Van Nostrand, 1963(a).

————. Piaget's contributions to the study of cognitive development. *Merrill-Palmer Quarterly*, 1963, *9*, 245–252(b).

————. *The development of role-taking and communications skills in children*. New York: Wiley, 1968.

————. The development of inferences about others. In T. Mischel, ed., *Understanding other persons*. Oxford: Blackwell, 1974.

————. *Cognitive development*. Englewood Cliffs, N.J.: Prentice-Hall, 1977.

————. Metacognition. In E. Langer (Chair), *Current perspectives on awareness and cognitive processes*. Symposium presented at the American Psychological Association Convention, Toronto, 1978.

Flynn, W. R. The pursuit of purity: A defensive use of drug abuse in adolescence. *Adolescence*, 1970, *5*, 141–150.

Fodor, E. M. Delinquency and susceptibility to social influence among adolescents as a function of level of moral development. *Journal of Social Psychology*, 1972, *86*, 257–260.

Forman, G. E., and Sigel, I. E. *Cognitive development: A life-span view*. Monterey, Calif.: Brooks/Cole, 1979.

Freeman, D. *Margaret Mead and Samoa: The making and unmaking of an anthropological myth*. Cambridge, Mass.: Harvard University Press, 1983.

Freud, A. *Introduction to psychoanalysis for teachers*. London: Allen & Unwin, 1931.

————. *The ego and the mechanisms of defence* (C. Baines, trans.). New York: International Universities Press, 1948.

Freud, S. *Further remarks on the neuro-psychoses of defense*. Standard edition, vol. 3. London: Hogarth, 1962. (Originally published 1896.)

————. *The interpretation of dreams*. Standard edition, vols. 4 & 5. London: Hogarth, 1953. (Originally published 1900.)

————. *The unconscious*. Standard edition, vol. 14. London: Hogarth, 1957. (Originally published 1915.)

————. *The ego and the id*. Standard edition, vol. 19. London: Hogarth, 1961. (Originally published 1923a.)

————. *The infantile genital organization of the libido*. Collected Papers, vol. 2. London: Hogarth, 1949. (Originally published 1923b.)

————. Three contributions to the sexual theory. *Nervous and Mental Disease Monograph Series*, no. 7. New York: Nervous and Mental Disease Publishing Co., 1925.

————. Some psychical consequences of the anatomical distinction between the sexes. In J. Strachey, ed., Standard edition, vol. 19. London: Hogarth Press, 1961. (Originally published 1925.)

————. *New introductory lectures on psycho-analysis*. Standard Edition, vol. 22. London: Hogarth, 1964. (Originally published 1933.)

————. *Analysis, terminable and interminable*. Collected Papers, vol. 5. London: Hogarth, 1950. (Originally published 1937.)

————. *A general introduction to psychoanalysis* (J. Riviere, trans.). New York: Permabooks, 1953.

Furth, H. G. *An inventory of Piaget's developmental tasks*. Washington, D.C.: Catholic University Center for Research in Thinking and Language, 1970.

————. Children's societal understanding and the process of equilibration. In W. Damon, ed., *New directions for child development*, vol. 1. San Francisco: Jossey-Bass, 1978.

Furth, H. G., Baur, M., and Smith, J. W. Children's conceptions of social institutions: A Piagetian framework. *Human Development*, 1976, *19*, 351–374.

Furth, H. G., and Wachs, H. *Thinking goes to school: Piaget's theory in practice*. New York: Oxford University Press, 1975.

Gallagher, J. M. The future of formal thought research: The study of analogy and metaphor. In B. Z. Presseisen, D. Goldstein, and M. Appel, eds., *Topics in cognitive development: Language and operational thought*, vol. 2. New York: Plenum Press, 1978.

Garbarino, J. Adolescent development: An ecological perspective. Paper presented at the International Seminar on Developmental Psychology. Trier, West Germany, July 31–August 20, 1977.

————. *Adolescent development: An ecological perspective*. Columbus, Ohio: Charles E. Merrill, 1985.

Garbarino, J., Burston, N., Raber, S., Russel, R., and Crouter, A. The social maps of children approaching adolescence: Studying the ecology of youth development. *Journal of Youth and Adolescence,* 1978, *7,* 417–428.

Gardner, H. *The arts and human development.* New York: Wiley, 1973.

Gilligan, C. In a different voice: Women's conceptions of self and of morality. *Harvard Educational Review,* 1977, *47,* 481–517.

————. Moral development. In A. W. Chickering, ed., *The modern American college.* San Francisco: Jossey-Bass, 1981.

————. *In a different voice: Psychological theory and women's development.* Cambridge, Mass.: Harvard University Press, 1982.

————. Remapping the moral domain in personality research and assessment. Invited address presented at the American Psychological Association Convention, Toronto, 1984.

————, and Belenky, M. F. A naturalistic study of abortion decisions. In R. Selman and R. Yando, eds., *Clinical-developmental psychology.* San Francisco: Jossey-Bass, 1980.

Gilligan, C., Kohlberg, L., Lerner, J., and Belenky, M. Moral reasoning about sexual dilemmas. *Technical Report of the Commission on Obscenity and Pornography,* vol. I. Washington, D.C.: U.S. Government Printing Office, 1971.

Glucksberg, S., Krauss, R. M., and Higgens, T. The development of referential communication skills. In F. D. Horowitz, ed., *Review of child development research,* vol. 4. Chicago: University of Chicago Press, 1975.

Goddard, H. H., *The Kallikak Family.* New York: Macmillan, 1914.

Gordon, C. Self-conceptions: Configurations of content. In C. Gordon and K. J. Gergen, eds., *The self in social interaction,* vol. 1. New York: Wiley, 1968.

Green, R. Human sexuality: Research and treatment frontiers. In S. Arieti, ed., *American handbook of psychiatry,* 2nd ed., vol. 6. New York: Basic Books, 1975.

Gruen, W. Rejection of false information about oneself as an indication of ego identity. *Journal of Consulting Psychology,* 1960, *24,* 231–233.

Haan, N., Smith, M. B., and Block, J. Moral reasoning of young adults: Political-social behavior, family background, and personality correlates. *Journal of Personality and Social Psychology,* 1968, *10,* 183–201.

Hains, A. A., and Miller, D. J. Moral and cognitive development in delinquent and nondelinquent children and adolescents. *Journal of Genetic Psychology,* 1980, *137,* 21–35.

Hall, C. S. *A primer of Freudian psychology.* New York: World, 1954.

Hall, G. S. *Adolescence.* 2 vols. New York: Appleton, 1916.

Hamburg, D. A., and Lunde, D. T. Sex hormones in the development of sex differences in human behavior. In E. E. Maccoby, ed., *The development of sex differences.* Stanford, Calif.: Stanford University Press, 1966, pp. 1–24.

Hampden-Turner, C., and Whitten, P. Morals left and right. *Psychology Today,* 1971, *4,* no. 11, 39–43, 74–76.

Harris, D. B. The climate of achievement. *Child Study,* 1958, *34,* 8–14.

Hartshorne, H., and May, M. A. *Studies in the nature of character.* 3 vols. New York: Macmillan, 1928–1930.

Hartsoeker, N. *Essai de Dioptrique.* Sect. 88, Paris, 1694.

Havighurst, R. J., and MacDonald, D. V. Development of the ideal self in New Zealand and American children. *Journal of Educational Research,* 1955, *49,* 263–273.

Hayes, J. M. Ego identity and moral character development in male college students. Unpublished doctoral dissertation, The Catholic University of America, 1977.

Healy, W., Bronner, A. F., and Bowers, A. M. *The structure and meaning of psychoanalysis.* New York: Knopf, 1930.

Hickey, J. E. The effects of guided moral discussion upon youthful offenders' level of moral judgment. *Dissertation Abstracts International,* 1972, *33* (4-A), 1551.

Hill, S. D., and Tomlin, C. Self-recognition in retarded children. *Child Development,* 1981, *52,* 145–150.

Hobbes, T. *Leviathan.* London: 1651.

Hoffman, M. L. Empathy, role-taking, guilt, and development of altruistic motives. In T. Lickona, ed., *Moral development and behavior: Theory, research and social issues.* New York: Holt, Rinehart & Winston, 1976.

Holstein, C. B. Irreversible, stepwise sequence in the development of moral judgment: A longitudinal study of males and females. *Child Development,* 1976, *47,* 51–61.

Horner, M. S. Toward an understanding of achievement-related conflicts in women. *Journal of Social Issues,* 1972, *28,* 157–175.

Howard, M. R. Ego identity status in women, fear of success, and performance in a competitive situation. Unpublished doctoral dissertation, State University of New York at Buffalo, 1975.

Hsu, F. L. K., Watrous, B. G., and Lord, E. M. Culture pattern and adolescent behaviour. *International Journal of Social Psychiatry,* 1961, *7,* 33–53.

Hudson, L. M., Peyton, E. F., and Brion-Maisels, S. Social reasoning and relating: An analysis of videotaped social interactions. In H. Furth (Chair), *Integrations of development in social cognition and social behavior.* Symposium presented at the American Psychological Association Convention, Washington, D.C., 1976.

Hughes, R. Jr., Tingle, B. A., and Sawin, D. B. Development of empathic understanding in children. *Child Development,* 1981, *52,* 122–128.

Hunt, J. McV. *Intelligence and experience.* New York: Ronald Press, 1961.

Inhelder, B. Cognitive development and its contribution to the diagnosis of some phenomena of mental deficiency. *Merrill-Palmer Quarterly,* 1966, *12,* 299–319.

Inhelder, B., and Piaget, J. *The growth of logical thinking* (A. Parsons and S. Milgram, trans.). New York: Basic Books, 1958.

Iscoe, I., Williams, M., and Harvey, J. Modification of children's judgments by a simulated group technique: A normative developmental study. *Child Development,* 1963, *34,* 963–978.

Jamison, W., and Signorella, M. L. Sex-typing and spatial ability: The association between masculinity and success on Piaget's water-level task. *Sex Roles,* 1980, *6,* 345–353.

Jennings, M. K., and Niemi, R. G. *The political character of adolescence: The influence of families and schools.* Princeton, N.J.: Princeton University Press, 1974.

Jessor, S. L., and Jessor, R. Transition from virginity to nonvirginity among youth: A social-psychological study over time. *Developmental Psychology,* 1975, *11,* 473–484.

Jones, R. M. *An application of psychoanalysis to education.* Springfield, Ill.: Charles C Thomas, 1960.

Jordan, D. Parental antecedents of ego identity formation. Unpublished master's thesis, State University of New York at Buffalo, 1970.

————. Parental antecedents and personality characteristics of ego identity statuses. Unpublished doctoral dissertation, State University of New York at Buffalo, 1971.

Josselson, R. L. Psychodynamic aspects of identity formation in college women. *Journal of Youth and Adolescence,* 1973, *2,* 3–52.

Josselson, R., Greenberger, E., and McConochie, D. Phenomenological aspects of psychosocial maturity in adolescence. *Journal of Youth and Adolescence,* 1977, *6,* 25–55, 145–167.

Kandel, D. B. Similarity in real-life adolescent friendship pairs. *Journal of Personality and Social Psychology,* 1978, *36,* 306–312(a).

————. Homophily, selection and socialization in adolescent friendships. *American Journal of Sociology,* 1978, *84,* 427–436(b).

————. Processes of peer influences in adolescence. In R. K. Silbereisen et al., eds., *Development as action in context.* Berlin: Springer-Verlag, 1986.

————, and Davies, M. Epidemiology of depressive mood in adolescents. *Archives of General Psychiatry,* 1982, *39,* 1205–1212.

Kandel, D. B., and Lesser, G. S. Parental and peer influence on educational plans of adolescents. *American Sociological Review,* 1969, *34,* 212–223.

————. *Youth in two worlds.* San Francisco: Jossey-Bass, 1972.

Kaplan, L., and Baron, D. *Mental hygiene and life.* New York: Harper & Brothers, 1952.

Keasey, C. B. Social participation as a factor in the moral development of preadolescents. *Developmental Psychology,* 1971, *5,* 216–220.

Keating, D. P. A search for social intelligence. *Journal of Educational Psychology,* 1978, *70,* 218–223.

Keating, D. P., and Clark, L. V. Development of physical and social reasoning in adolescence. *Developmental Psychology,* 1980, *16,* 23–30.

Keating, D. P., and Schaefer, R. A. Ability and sex differences in the acquisition of formal operations. *Developmental Psychology,* 1975, *11,* 531–532.

Kelley, H. H. The processes of causal attribution. *American Psychologist,* 1973, *28,* 107–128.

Keniston, K. Social change and youth in America. In E. H. Erikson, ed., *The challenge of youth.* Garden City, N.Y.: Doubleday/Anchor, 1965.

———. The tasks of adolescence. In *Developmental psychology today.* Del Mar, Calif.: CRM Books, 1971, chap. 20.

King, M. L. *Why we can't wait.* New York: Harper & Row, 1964.

Kohlberg, L. The development of children's orientations toward a moral order. *Vita Humana,* 1963, *6,* 11–33.

———. Development of moral character and moral ideology. In M. L. Hoffman and L. W. Hoffman, eds., *Review of child development research,* vol. 1. New York: Russell Sage Foundation, 1964.

———. Moral and religious education and the public schools: A developmental view. In T. R. Sizer, ed., *Religion and public education.* Boston: Houghton Mifflin, 1967.

———. Stage and sequence: The cognitive-developmental approach to socialization. In D. A. Goslin, ed., *Handbook of socialization theory and research.* Chicago: Rand McNally, 1969.

———. Moral development and the education of adolescents. In R. F. Purnell, ed., *Adolescents and the American high school.* New York: Holt, Rinehart & Winston, 1970.

Kohlberg, L., and Blatt. M. The effects of classroom discussion on level of moral development. In L. Kohlberg and E. Turiel, eds., *Recent research in moral development.* New York: Holt, Rinehart & Winston, 1972.

Kohlberg, L., Colby, A., Gibbs, J., Speicher-Dubin, B., and Powers, C. *Assessing moral development stages: A manual.* Cambridge, Mass.: Center for Moral Education, 1978.

Kohlberg, L., and Gilligan, C. The adolescent as a philosopher. In J. Kagan and R. Coles, eds., *Twelve to sixteen: Early adolescence.* New York: Norton, 1972.

Kohlberg, L., and Kramer, R. Continuities and discontinuities in childhood and adult moral development. *Human Development,* 1969, *12,* 93–120.

Krebs, D. L. Altruism—An examination of the concept and a review of the literature. *Psychological Bulletin,* 1970, *73,* 258–302.

Kubie, L. S. *Neurotic distortion of the creative process.* Lawrence, Kans.: University of Kansas Press, 1958.

———. Introduction. In R. M. Jones, *An application of psychoanalysis to education.* Springfield, Ill.: Charles C Thomas, 1960.

Kuhn, D. The significance of Piaget's formal operations stage in education. *Journal of Education,* 1979, *161,* 34–50.

Kuhn, M. H., and McPartland, T. S. An empirical investigation of self-attitudes. *American Sociological Review,* 1954, *19,* 68–76.

Kurdek, L. A. Perspective taking as a cognitive basis of children's moral development: A review of the literature. *Merrill-Palmer Quarterly,* 1978, *24,* 3–28.

LaFleur, N. K., and Johnson, R. G. Separate effects of social modeling and reinforcement in counseling adolescents. *Journal of Counseling Psychology,* 1972, *19,* 292–295.

Lambert, G. B., Rothschild, B. F., Atland, R., and Green, L. B. *Adolescence: Transition from childhood to maturity,* 2nd ed. Monterey, Calif.: Brooks/Cole, 1978.

Lavatelli, C. *Early childhood curriculum: A Piaget program.* Boston: American Science and Engineering, 1970.

LaVoie, J. C. Ego identity formation in middle adolescence. *Journal of Youth and Adolescence,* 1976, *5,* 371–385.

Lewin, K. Environmental forces in child behavior and development. In C. Murchison, ed., *Handbook of child psychology.* Worchester, Mass.: Clark University Press, 1931.

————. *A dynamic theory of personality.* New York: McGraw-Hill, 1935.

————. *Principles of topological psychology.* New York: McGraw-Hill, 1936.

————. The conceptual representation and the measurement of psychological forces. Duke University Series, *Contributions to Psychological Theory,* 1938, *1*(4).

————. Field theory and experiment in social psychology: Concepts and methods. *American Journal of Sociology,* 1939, *44,* 868–896.

————. Field theory and learning. In *The Psychology of Learning, the Yearbook of the National Society for the Study of Education,* 1942, *41,* part II.

————. Behavior and development as a function of the total situation. In L. Carmichael, ed., *Manual of child psychology.* New York: Wiley, 1946.

————. *Resolving social conflicts.* New York: Harper and Brothers, 1948.

————. *Field theory in social science.* New York: Harper & Row, 1951.

Liben, L. S. Operative understanding of horizontality and its relation to long-term memory. *Child Development,* 1974, *45,* 416–424.

————. Long-term memory for pictures related to seriation, horizontality, and verticality concepts. *Developmental Psychology,* 1975, *11,* 795–806.

————. Performance on Piagetian spatial tasks as a function of sex, field dependence, and training. *Merrill-Palmer Quarterly,* 1978, *24,* 97–110.

Liben, L. S., and Golbeck, S. L. Sex differences in performance on Piagetian spatial tasks: Differences in competence or performance? *Child Development,* 1980, *51,* 594–597.

Livesley, W. J., and Bromley, D. B. *Person perception in childhood and adolescence.* New York: Wiley, 1973.

Locke, J. *An essay concerning human understanding.* London: 1753.

————. Treatise on civil government. In *The work of John Locke.* London: 1768.

Loevinger, J. *Ego development.* San Francisco: Jossey-Bass, 1976.

Looft, W. R. Egocentrism and social interaction in adolescence. *Adolescence,* 1971, *6,* 485–494.

Lovell, K. A follow-up study of Inhelder and Piaget's *The growth of logical thinking.* British Journal of Psychology, 1961, *52,* 143–153.

Mahler, C. The assessment and the evaluation of the coping styles of two ego identity status groups: Moratorium and foreclosure, to identity conflict-arousing stimuli. Unpublished master's thesis, State University of New York at Buffalo, 1969.

Mahler, M. S. Thoughts about development and individuation. *The psychoanalytic study of the child,* vol. 18. New York: International Universities Press, 1963.

Marcia, J. E. Development and validation of ego-identity status. *Journal of Personality and Social Psychology,* 1966, *3,* 551–558.

————. Ego identity status: Relationship to change in self-esteem, "general maladjustment," and authoritarianism. *Journal of Personality,* 1967, *35,* 118–133.

————. The case history of a construct: Ego identity status. In E. Vinacke, ed., *Readings in general psychology.* New York: Van Nostrand Reinhold, 1968.

————. Identity six years after: A follow-up study. *Journal of Youth and Adolescence,* 1976, *5,* 145–160(a).

————. Studies in ego identity. Unpublished research monograph, Simon Fraser University, 1976(b).

————. Identity in adolescence. In J. Adelson, ed., *Handbook of adolescent psychology.* New York: Wiley, 1980.

Marcia, J. E., and Friedman, M. L. Ego identity status in college women. *Journal of Personality,* 1970, *38,* 249–263.

Marsh, D. T., Serafica, F. C., and Barenboim, C. Effect of perspective-taking training on interpersonal problem solving. *Child Development,* 1980, *51,* 140–145.

Martin, B. Parent-child relations. In F. D. Horowitz, ed., *Review of child development research,* vol. 4. Chicago: University of Chicago Press, 1975.

Matteson, D. R. Alienation vs. exploration and commitment: Personality and family corollaries of adolescent identity statuses. *Report from the Project for Youth Research.* Copenhagen: Royal Danish School of Educational Studies, 1974.

Mead, G. H. *Mind, self and society.* Chicago: University of Chicago Press, 1934.

Mead, M. *Male and female.* New York: Morrow, 1949.

————. *Coming of age in Samoa.* New York: New American Library, 1950. (Originally published 1928.)

————. *Sex and temperament in three primitive societies.* New York: New American Library, 1950. (Originally published 1935.)

————. Adolescence in primitive and in modern society. In G. E. Swanson, T. M. Newcomb, and E. L. Hartley, eds., *Readings in social psychology,* rev. ed. New York: Henry Holt, 1952.

————. *Growing up in New Guinea.* New York: New American Library, 1953.

————. The young adult. In E. Ginzberg, ed., *Values and ideals of American youth.* New York: Columbia University Press, 1961.

————. *Culture and commitment.* New York: American Museum of Natural History, 1970.

Meilman, P. W. Cross-sectional age changes in ego identity status during adolescence. *Developmental Psychology,* 1979, *15,* 230–231.

Miller, N. E. The frustration-aggression hypothesis. *Psychological Review,* 1941, *48,* 337–342.

Miller, N. E., and Dollard, J. *Social learning and imitation.* New Haven, Conn.: Yale University Press, 1941.

Mischel, W. *Introduction to personality.* New York: Holt, Rinehart & Winston, 1971.

Montemayor, R., and Eisen, M. The development of self-conceptions from childhood to adolescence. *Developmental Psychology,* 1977, *13,* 314–319.

Moore, S. G. Social cognition: Knowing about others. *Young Children,* 1979, *34,* 54–61.

Mullahy, P. *Psychoanalysis and interpersonal psychiatry: The contributions of Harry Stack Sullivan.* New York: Science House, 1970.

Murphy, J. M., and Gilligan, C. Moral development in late adolescence and adulthood: A critique and reconstruction of Kohlberg's theory. *Human Development,* 1980, *23,* 77–104.

Muuss, R. E. *First-aid for classroom discipline problems.* New York: Holt, Rinehart & Winston, 1962.

————. Adolescent development and the secular trend. *Adolescence,* 1970, *5,* 267–284(a).

————. Puberty rites in primitive and modern societies. *Adolescence,* 1970, *5,* 109–128(b).

————. Die Entwicklung der Egozentrizität in der Kindheit und der Adoleszenz. *Der Kinderarzt,* 1981, vol. 12, #2, 189–193; #3, 339–343; #4, 519–531.

————. Psychosoziale Probleme der Sexualität in der Adoleszenz. In T. Hellbrügge, ed., *Die Entwicklung der kindlichen Sexualität.* München: Urban & Schwarzberg 1982(a).

————. *Grundlagen der Adoleszentenpsychologie.* Lübeck, Germany: Hansisches Verlagskontor, 1982(b).

————. Adolescent eating disorders: Anorexia nervosa. *Adolescence,* 1985, *20,* 525–536.

————. Adolescent eating disorders: Bulimia. *Adolescence,* 1986, *21,* 257–267.

Neale, J. M. Egocentrism in institutionalized and noninstitutionalized children. *Child Development,* 1966, *37,* 97–101.

Neuber, K. A., and Genthner, R. W. The relationship between ego identity, personal responsibility, and facilitative communication. *Journal of Psychology,* 1977, *95,* 45–49.

Nisan, M., and Kohlberg, L. Universality and variation in moral judgment: A longitudinal and cross-sectional study in Turkey. *Child Development,* 1982, *53,* 865–876.

Offer, D. *The psychological world of the teenager.* New York: Basic Books, 1969.

————, and Offer, J. B. *From teenage to young manhood.* New York: Basic Books, 1975.

Offer, D., Ostrov, E., and Howard, K. I. *The adolescent: A psychological self-portrait.* New York: Basic Books, 1981.

Ojemann, R. H., and Pritchett, K. Piaget and the role of guided experiences in development. *Perceptual and Motor Skills,* 1963, *17,* 927–940.

Oppenheimer, L. The development of the processing of social perspectives: A cognitive model. *International Journal of Behavioral Development,* 1978, *1,* 149–171.

Orlofsky, J. L. Identity formation, nAchievement, and fear of success in college men and women. *Journal of Youth and Adolescence,* 1978, *7,* 49–62.

Orlofsky, J. L., Marcia, J. E., and Lesser, I. M. Ego identity status and the intimacy versus isolation crisis of young adulthood. *Journal of Personality and Social Psychology,* 1973, *27,* 211–219.

Oshman, H., and Manosevitz, M. The impact of the identity crisis on the adjustment of late adolescent males. *Journal of Youth and Adolescence,* 1974, *3,* 207–216.

Papalia, D. E., and Olds, S. W. *A child's world,* 2nd ed. New York: McGraw-Hill, 1979.

Park, R. E. Human ecology. *American Journal of Sociology,* 1936, *42,* 1–15.

Patel, A. S., and Gordon, J. E. Some personal and situational determinants of yielding to influence. *Journal of Abnormal and Social Psychology,* 1960, *61,* 411–418.

Patterson, H. O., and Milakofsky, L. A paper-and-pencil inventory for the assessment of Piaget's tasks. *Applied Psychological Measurement,* 1980, *4,* 341–353.

Perry, H. S. *Psychiatrist of America: The life of Harry Stack Sullivan.* Cambridge, Mass.: Belknap Press, 1982.

Petrone, F. R. *The developmental kindergarten.* Springfield, Ill.: Charles C Thomas, 1976.

Piaget, J. *The child's conception of the world.* New York: Harcourt, Brace, 1929.

————. *The child's conception of physical causality.* London: Routledge & Kegan Paul, 1930.

————. *The language and thought of the child,* 2nd ed. New York: Harcourt, Brace, 1932(a).

————. *The moral judgment of the child.* London: Kegan Paul, 1932(b).

————. The moral development of the adolescent in two types of society, primitive and "modern." Lecture given to the United Nations Educational, Scientific and Cultural Organization, Paris, 1947(a).

————. *The psychology of intelligence* (M. Piercy and D. E. Berlyne, trans.). New York: Harcourt, Brace, 1947(b).

————. *The child's conception of number.* New York: Humanities Press, 1952(a).

————. *The origins of intelligence in children* (M. Cook, trans.). New York: Norton, 1952(b).

————. Three lectures. *Bulletin of the Menninger Clinic,* 1962, *26,* 120–145.

————. The attainment of invariants and reversible operations in the development of thinking. *Social Research,* 1963, *30,* 283–299.

————. *Six psychological studies.* New York: Random House, 1967.

————. Intellectual evolution from adolescence to adulthood. In R. E. Muuss, ed., *Adolescent behavior and society: A book of readings,* 3rd ed. New York: Random House, 1980.

Piaget, J., and Inhelder, B. *The child's conception of space.* London: Routledge & Kegan Paul, 1967.

————. *The psychology of the child.* New York: Basic Books, 1969.

Pinard, A., and Laurendeau, M. A scale of mental development based on the theory of Piaget: A description of a project. *Journal of Research in Science Teaching,* 1964, *2,* 253–260.

Plato. *The republic* (B. Jowett, trans.). Oxford: Clarendon Press, 1921.

————. Phaedo. In *The dialogues of Plato* (B. Jowett, trans.), vol. 1, 3rd ed. New York: Random House, 1937.

————. Laws. In *The dialogues of Plato* (B. Jowett, trans.), vol. 4, 4th ed. Oxford: Clarendon Press, 1953.

Podd, M. H. Ego identity status and morality: The relationship between two developmental constructs. *Developmental Psychology,* 1972, *6,* 497–507.

Podd, M. H., Marcia, J. E., and Rubin, B. M. The effects of ego identity and partner perception on a prisoner's dilemma game. *Journal of Social Psychology,* 1970, *82,* 117–126.

Pollak, S., and Gilligan, C. Images of violence in thematic apperception test stories. *Journal of Personality and Social Psychology,* 1982, *42,* 159–167.

Poppen, P. J. The development of sex differences in moral judgment for college males and females. Unpublished doctoral dissertation, Cornell University, 1974.

Rank, O. *Will therapy and truth and reality.* New York: Knopf, 1945.

Rasmussen, J. E. Relationship of ego identity to psychosocial effectiveness. *Psychological Reports,* 1964, *15,* 815–825.

Ray, W. J., Georgiou, S., and Ravizza, R. Spatial abilities, sex differences, and lateral eye movements. *Developmental Psychology,* 1979, *15,* 455–457.

Reid, B. V. An anthropological reinterpretation of Kohlberg's stages of moral development. *Human Development,* 1984, *27,* 57–64.

Rest, J. The hierarchical nature of moral judgment: A study of patterns of preference of comprehension and preference of stages. *Journal of Personality,* 1973, *41,* 86–109.

————. The cognitive developmental approach to morality: The state of the art. *Counseling and Values,* 1974, *18,* 64–78.

————. *Development in judging moral issues.* Minneapolis: University of Minnesota Press, 1979.

Rosen, C. E. The effects of sociodramatic play on problem-solving behavior among culturally disadvantaged preschool children. *Child Development,* 1974, *45,* 920–927.

Rousseau, J. J. *Émile* (W. H. Payne, trans.). New York: Appleton, 1911. (Originally published 1780.)

Rowe, I., & Marcia, J. E. Ego identity status, formal operations, and moral development. *Journal of Youth and Adolescence*, 1980, *9*, 87–99.

Rubin, K. H. Relationship between egocentric communication and popularity among peers. *Developmental Psychology*, 1972, *7*, 364.

———. Egocentrism in childhood: A unitary construct? *Child Development*, 1973, *44*, 102–110.

———. Social interaction and communicative egocentrism in preschoolers. *Journal of Genetic Psychology*, 1976, *129*, 121–124.

Rubin, K. H., and Schneider, F. W. The relationship between moral judgment, egocentrism, and altruistic behavior. *Child Development*, 1973, *44*, 661–665.

Saltzstein, H. D., Diamond, R. M., and Belenky, M. Moral judgment level and conformity behavior. *Developmental Psychology*, 1972, *7*, 327–336.

Schenkel, S. Relationship among ego identity status, field-independence, and traditional femininity. *Journal of Youth and Adolescence*, 1975, *4*, 73–82.

Schenkel, S., and Marcia, J. E. Attitudes toward premarital intercourse in determining ego identity status in college women. *Journal of Personality*, 1972, *40*, 472–482.

Schmuck, R. Sex of sibling, birth order position, and female dispositions to conform in two-child families. *Child Development*, 1963, *34*, 913–918.

Sears, R. R. A theoretical framework for personality and social behavior. *American Psychologist*, 1951, *6*, 476–483.

Sears, R. R., Maccoby, E. E., and Levin, H. *Patterns of child rearing*. Evanston, Ill.: Row, Peterson, 1957.

Selman, R. L. The relation of role taking to the development of moral judgment in children. *Child Development*, 1971, *42*, 79–91(a).

———. Taking another's perspective: Role-taking development in early childhood. *Child Development*, 1971, *42*, 1721–1734(b).

———. Social-cognitive understanding: A guide to educational and clinical practice. In T. Lickona, ed., *Moral development and behavior: Theory, research and social issues*. New York: Holt, Rinehart & Winston, 1976(a).

———. Toward a structural analysis of developing interpersonal relations concepts: Research with normal and disturbed preadolescent boys. In A. D. Pick, ed., *Minnesota symposia on child psychology*, vol. 10. Minneapolis: University of Minnesota Press, 1976(b).

———. A structural-developmental model of social cognition: Implications for intervention research. *Counseling Psychologist*, 1977, *6*, 3–6.

———. *The growth of interpersonal understanding: Developmental and clinical analyses*. New York: Academic Press, 1980.

Selman, R. L., and Byrne, D. F. A structural-developmental analysis of levels of role taking in middle childhood. *Child Development*, 1974, *45*, 803–806.

Selman, R. L., Jaquette, D., and Lavin, D. R. Interpersonal awareness in children:

Toward an integration of developmental and clinical child psychology. *American Journal of Orthopsychiatry*, 1977, *47*, 264–274.

Shantz, C. U. The development of social cognition. In E. M. Hetherington, ed., *Review of child development research*, vol. 5. Chicago: University of Chicago Press, 1975.

Shure, M. B., and Spivack, G. *Problem-solving techniques in childrearing*. San Francisco: Jossey-Bass, 1978.

———. Interpersonal problem solving as a mediator of behavioral adjustment in preschool and kindergarten children. *Journal of Applied Developmental Psychology*, 1980, *1*, 29–44.

Simmons, R. G., Rosenberg, F., and Rosenberg, M. Disturbance in the self-image at adolescence. *American Sociological Review*, 1973, *38*, 553–568.

Spiegel, L. A. A review of contributions to a psychoanalytic theory of adolescence: Individual aspects. In R. S. Eissler, A. Freud, H. Hartman, and E. Kris, eds., *The psychoanalytic study of the child*, vol. 6. New York: International Universities Press, 1951.

Spivack, G., and Shure, M. B. *Social adjustment of young children*. San Francisco: Jossey-Bass, 1974.

Spivack, G., Platt, J. J., and Shure, M. B. *The problem-solving approach to adjustment*. San Francisco: Jossey-Bass, 1976.

Steinberg, L. D., Greenberger, E., Jacobi, M., and Garduque, L. Early work experience: A partial antidote for adolescent egocentrism. *Journal of Youth and Adolescence*, 1981, *10*, 141–157.

Stuart, R. B. Decentration in the development of children's concepts of moral and causal judgment. *Journal of Genetic Psychology*, 1967, *111*, 59–68.

Sullivan, E. V., and Hunt, D. E. Interpersonal and objective decentering as a function of age and social class. *Journal of Genetic Psychology*, 1967, *110*, 199–210.

Sullivan, H. S. *Conceptions of modern psychiatry*. New York: Norton, 1947.

———. The illusion of personal individuality. *Psychiatry*, 1950, *13*, 317–332.

———. *The interpersonal theory of psychiatry*. New York: Norton, 1953.

———. *The fusion of psychiatry and social science*. New York: Norton, 1964.

———. *Personal psychopathology*. New York: Norton, 1972.

Sund, R. B. *Piaget for educators: A multimedia program*. Columbus, Ohio: Charles E. Merrill, 1976.

Tagiuri, R. Person perception. In G. Lindzey and E. Aronson, eds., *The handbook of social-psychology*, vol. 3, 2nd ed. Reading, Mass.: Addison-Wesley, 1969.

Tagiuri, R., and Petrullo, L., eds., *Person perception and interpersonal behavior*. Stanford, Calif.: Stanford University Press, 1958.

Tanner, J. M. *Growth at adolescence*, 2nd ed. Oxford: Blackwell, 1962.

———. Earlier maturation in man. *Scientific American*, 1968, *218*, 21–27.

Thomas, H., and Jamison, W. On the acquisition of understanding that still water is horizontal. *Merrill-Palmer Quarterly*, 1975, *21*, 31–44.

Thomas, H., Jamison, W., and Hummel, D. Observation is insufficient for discovering that the surface of still water is invariantly horizontal. *Science,* 1973, *181,* 173–174.

Tierney, M. C., and Rubin, K. H. Egocentrism and conformity in childhood. *Journal of Genetic Psychology,* 1975, *126,* 209–215.

Toder, N. L., and Marcia, J. E. Ego identity status and response to conformity pressure in college women. *Journal of Personality and Social Psychology,* 1973, *26,* 287–294.

Troll, L., and Bengston, V. Generations in the family. In Burr, W. R., Hill, R., Nye, F. I., and Reiss, I. L., eds., *Contemporary theories about the family,* vol. 1. New York: Free Press, 1979, pp. 127–161.

Turiel, E. An experimental test of the sequentiality of developmental stages in the child's moral judgments. *Journal of Personality and Social Psychology,* 1966, *3,* 611–618.

—————. Developmental processes in the child's moral thinking. In P. Mussen, J. Langer, and M. Covington, eds., *Trends and issues in developmental psychology.* New York: Holt, Rinehart & Winston, 1969.

—————. Conflict and transition in adolescent moral development. *Child Development,* 1974, *45,* 14–29.

—————. The development of social concepts: Mores, customs, and conventions. In D. J. DePalma and J. M. Foley, eds., *Moral development: Current theory and research.* Hillsdale, N.J.: Erlbaum, 1975.

—————. Social regulations and the domains of social concepts. In W. Damon, ed., *New directions for child development,* vol. 1. San Francisco: Jossey-Bass, 1978.

Urberg, K. A. Sex role conceptualizations in adolescents and adults. *Developmental Psychology,* 1979, *15,* 90–92.

Uzgiris, I. C., and Hunt, J. McV. *Assessment in infancy: Ordinal scale of psychological development.* Urbana: University of Illinois Press, 1976.

Wachtel, P. L. *Psychoanalysis and behavior therapy.* New York: Basic Books, 1977.

Wagner, J. A study of the relationship between formal operations and ego identity in adolescence. Unpublished doctoral dissertation, State University of New York at Buffalo, 1976.

Walker, L. J. Sex differences in the development of moral reasoning: A critical review. *Child Development,* 1984, *55,* 677–691.

—————. Sex differences in the development of moral reasoning: A rejoinder to Baumrind. *Child Development,* 1986, *57,* 522–526.

Waterman, A. S., and Goldman, J. A. A longitudinal study of ego identity development at a liberal arts college. *Journal of Youth and Adolescence,* 1976, *5,* 361–369.

Waterman, A. S., and Waterman, C. K. The relationship between ego identity status and satisfaction with college. *Journal of Educational Research,* 1970, *64,* 165–168.

—————. Relationship between freshman ego identity status and subsequent academic behavior: A test of the predictive validity of Marcia's categorization system for identity status. *Developmental Psychology,* 1972, *6,* 179.

Waterman, C. K., Beubel, M. E., and Waterman, A. S. Relationship between resolution of the identity crisis and outcomes of previous psychosocial crises. *Proceedings 78th Annual Convention American Psychological Association,* 1970, 467–468.

Waterman, C. K., and Nevid, J. S. Sex differences in the resolution of the identity crises. *Journal of Youth and Adolescence,* 1977, *6,* 337–342.

Waterman, C. K., and Waterman, A. S. Ego identity status and decision styles. *Journal of Youth and Adolescence,* 1974, *3,* 1–6.

Weikart, D. P., Roger, L., and Adcock, C. *The cognitively oriented curriculum.* Washington, D.C.: National Association for the Education of Young Children, 1971.

Weiner, B., ed., *Achievement motivation and attribution theory.* Morristown, N.J.: General Learning Press, 1974.

Weinheimer, S. Egocentrism and social influence in children. *Child Development,* 1972, *43,* 567–578.

Weir, M. W. Developmental changes in problem-solving strategies. *Psychological Review,* 1964, *71,* 473–490.

White, G. M. The elicitation and durability of altruistic behavior in children. *Research Bulletin* No. 67–27. Princeton N.J.: Educational Testing Service, 1967.

White, R. W. Competence and the psychosexual stages of development. *Nebraska symposium on motivation,* vol. 8. Lincoln: University of Nebraska Press, 1960.

Wolf, T. M. Effects of live modeled sex-inappropriate play behavior in a naturalistic setting. *Developmental Psychology,* 1973, *9,* 120–123.

Youniss, J. Another perspective on social cognition. In A. D. Pick, ed., *Minnesota symposia on child psychology,* vol. 9. Minneapolis: University of Minnesota Press, 1975.

———. *Parents and peers in social development: A Sullivan-Piaget perspective.* Chicago: University of Chicago Press, 1980.

INDEX

ABOUT THE AUTHOR

ROLF E. MUUSS received his Teaching Diploma from the Pädagogische Hochschule Flensburg, Germany, his M.Ed. from Western Maryland College, and his Ph.D. from the University of Illinois. He was Research Assistant Professor at the State University of Iowa, and has been Professor, Chairman of Education, and Chairman of Sociology and Anthropology at Goucher College, where he held the Elizabeth C. Todd Distinguished Professorship (1980–1985). He currently serves as the Director of Special Education at Goucher College. Professor Muuss has been a frequent speaker at both the International Congress of Pediatrics and the Congress of Socialpediatrics in Western Europe. He has edited three editions of *Adolescent Behavior and Society: A Book of Readings* (1971, 1975, 1980). The author of *First-Aid for Classroom Discipline Problems* (1962) and *Grundlagen der Adoleszentenpsychologie* (1982), he has also published over sixty articles in American, German, Swiss, English, and Swedish journals.